DEFENSE, SECURITY AND STRATEGIES

THE MILITARY COMMISSIONS ACT AND DETAINEE TRIALS

DEFENSE, SECURITY AND STRATEGIES

Additional books in this series can be found on Nova's website under the Series tab.

Additional E-books in this series can be found on Nova's website under the E-books tab.

DEFENSE, SECURITY AND STRATEGIES

THE MILITARY COMMISSIONS ACT AND DETAINEE TRIALS

JOSHUA SEGEL
AND
SOTO KIMURA
EDITORS

Nova Science Publishers, Inc.
New York

Library of Congress Cataloging-in-Publication Data

The Military Commissions Act and detainee trials / editors, Joshua Segel and Soto Kimura.
p. cm.
Includes index.
ISBN 978-1-61470-072-2 (hardcover)
1. Military courts--United States. 2. United States. Military Commissions Act of 2009. I. Segel, Joshua. II. Kimura, Soto.
KF7661.A25 2011
343.73'0143--dc23

2011020037

Published by Nova Science Publishers, Inc. † New York

CONTENTS

PREFACE

The use of military commissions to try suspected terrorists has been the focus of intense debate since President Bush issued his original Military Order authorizing such trials in November, 2001. The Military Order specified that persons subject to it would have no recourse in the U.S. court system to appeal a verdict or obtain any other sort of relief, but the Supreme Court essentially invalidated that provision in its 2004 opinion, Rasul v. Bush. In response, Congress enacted the Detainee Treatment Act of 2005 (DTA). This book provides a background and analysis comparing military commissions as envisioned under the revised Military Commissions Act (MCA) to those established by the MCA 2006. After reviewing the history of the implementation of military commissions in the "global war on terrorism," this book provides an overview of the procedural safeguards provided in the MCA.

Chapter 1- On November 13, 2001, President Bush issued a Military Order (M.O.) pertaining to the detention, treatment, and trial of certain non-citizens in the war against terrorism. Military commissions pursuant to the M.O. began in November 2004 against four persons declared eligible for trial, but the Supreme Court in Hamdan v. Rumsfeld invalidated the military commissions as improper under the Uniform Code of Military Justice (UCMJ). To permit military commissions to go forward, Congress approved the Military Commissions Act of 2006 (MCA), conferring authority to promulgate rules that depart from the strictures of the UCMJ and possibly U.S. international obligations. Military commissions proceedings were reinstated and resulted in three convictions.

Chapter 2- The Obama Administration's decision to try certain detainees and other terrorist suspects in federal criminal court, including those accused of conspiring to commit the 9/11 terrorist attacks and the man arrested after a failed aircraft bombing on Christmas day, and to try other detainees by military commission, has focused attention on the procedural differences between trials in federal court and those conducted under the Military Commissions Act, as recently amended. Some who are opposed to the decision argue that bringing detainees to the United States for trial poses a security threat and risks disclosing classified information, or could result in the acquittal of persons who are guilty. Others have praised the decision as recognizing the efficacy and fairness of the federal court system and have voiced confidence in the courts' ability to protect national security while achieving justice that will be perceived as such among U.S. allies abroad. Some continue to object to the planned trials of detainees by military commission, despite the amendments Congress enacted as Title XVIII of the National Defense Authorization Act for Fiscal Year 2010, P.L. 111-84, because they say it demonstrates a less than full commitment to justice or that it casts doubt on the strength of the government's case against those detainees. Seven bills have been introduced to prohibit federal trial or to require military commission trials for certain classes of suspected terrorists, or to authorize their detention, H.R. 4111, H.R. 4463, H.R. 4127, H.R. 4738, S. 2977, H.R. 4588, and H.R. 4556. One bill, H.R. 4415, would authorize the President to determine which persons are subject to detention or military commission trial as unlawful enemy combatants. One bill in the Senate, S. 2943, would require the Attorney General to consult with the Director of National Intelligence as well as the Secretaries of Defense and Homeland Security prior to proceeding against a terrorism suspect in the criminal justice system.

Chapter 3- This is an edited, reformatted and augmented version of testimony given by Peter R. Masciola, Colonel, United States Air Force – ANGUS Chief Defense Counsel, before Subcommittee on the Constitution, Civil Rights, and Civil Liberties publication, on July 30, 2009.

Chapter 4- This is an edited, reformatted and augmented version of testimony given by Peter R. Masciola, Colonel, United States Air Force – ANGUS Chief Defense Counsel, before Subcommittee on the Constitution, Civil Rights, and Civil Liberties publication, on July 30, 2009.

Chapter 5- This is an edited, reformatted and augmented version of testimony given by Eugene R. Fidell President, National Institute of Military Justice and Senior Research Scholar in Law and Florence Rogatz Lecturer in Law, Yale Law School before the United States House of Representatives on Hearing Before the Subcommittee on the Constitution, Civil Rights and Civil Liberties Committee on the Judiciary, on July 30, 2009.

In: The Military Commissions Act…
Editors: J. Segel, Soto Kimura ISBN: 978-1-61470-072-2

Chapter 1

THE MILITARY COMMISSIONS ACT OF 2009: OVERVIEW AND LEGAL ISSUES*

Jennifer K. Elsea

SUMMARY

On November 13, 2001, President Bush issued a Military Order (M.O.) pertaining to the detention, treatment, and trial of certain non-citizens in the war against terrorism. Military commissions pursuant to the M.O. began in November 2004 against four persons declared eligible for trial, but the Supreme Court in Hamdan v. Rumsfeld invalidated the military commissions as improper under the Uniform Code of Military Justice (UCMJ). To permit military commissions to go forward, Congress approved the Military Commissions Act of 2006 (MCA), conferring authority to promulgate rules that depart from the strictures of the UCMJ and possibly U.S. international obligations. Military commissions proceedings were reinstated and resulted in three convictions.

Upon taking office in 2009, President Obama temporarily halted military commissions to review their procedures as well as the detention program at Guantánamo Bay in general, pledging to close the prison facilities there by January 2010, a deadline that passed unmet. The Secretary of Defense was also required to take steps to ensure that all

* This is an edited, reformatted and augmented version of a Congressional Research Service 7-5700, R41163 publication, dated April 6, 2010.

proceedings before military commissions and the United States Court of Military Commission Review were halted, although some pretrial proceedings continued to take place. One case was moved to a federal district court.

In May, 2009, the Obama Administration announced that it was considering restarting the military commission system with some changes to the procedural rules. Congress enacted the Military Commissions Act of 2009 (MCA 2009) as part of the Department of Defense Authorization Act (NDAA) for FY2010, P.L. 111-84, to provide some reforms the Administration supported and to make other amendments to the Military Commissions Act, as described in this report. The plan to transfer five "high value detainees" to New York for trial in federal court, announced in November, 2009, has been placed on hold due to resistance from Congress and some New York officials. (See H.R. 4738, S. 2977, H.R. 4588, H.R. 4556, H.R. 4463, and H.R. 4127).

This report provides a background and analysis comparing military commissions as envisioned under the revised MCA to those established by the MCA 2006. After reviewing the history of the implementation of military commissions in the "global war on terrorism," the report provides an overview of the procedural safeguards provided in the MCA. Finally, the report provides two tables comparing the MCA as amended by the MCA 2009 to the original MCA enacted in 2006 and to general courts-martial. The first table describes the composition and powers of the military tribunals, as well as their jurisdiction. The second table, compares procedural safeguards in courts-martial to the MCA as enacted and as amended, to facilitate comparison with safeguards provided in federal court and international criminal tribunals.

INTRODUCTION

The use of military commissions to try suspected terrorists has been the focus of intense debate (as well as significant litigation) since President Bush in November, 2001 issued his original Military Order authorizing such trials.[1] The M.O. specified that persons subject to it would have no recourse to the U.S. court system to appeal a verdict or obtain any other sort of relief, but the Supreme Court essentially invalidated that provision in its 2004 opinion, *Rasul v. Bush*.[2] In response, Congress enacted the Detainee Treatment Act of 2005 (DTA).[3] The DTA did not authorize military commissions, but amended title 28, U.S. Code to revoke all judicial jurisdiction over habeas claims by persons detained as "enemy combatants," and it created jurisdiction in the Court of

Appeals for the District of Columbia Circuit to hear appeals of final decisions of military commissions.

The Supreme Court, after finding that Congress's efforts to strip it of jurisdiction did not apply to a case already pending before the Court, *Hamdan v. Rumsfeld*,[4] invalidated the military commission system established by presidential order. The Court held that although Congress had in general authorized the use of military commissions, such commissions were required to follow procedural rules as similar as possible to courts-martial proceedings, as required by the Uniform Code of Military Justice (UCMJ).[5] In response, Congress promptly passed the Military Commissions Act of 2006 (MCA 2006)[6] to authorize military commissions and establish procedural rules that are modeled after, but depart from in some significant ways, the UCMJ. The MCA 2006 also amended the Detainee Treatment Act in order to strip the judiciary of habeas jurisdiction in all cases brought by detainees, including pending cases,[7] but the Supreme Court held that provision to be an unconstitutional suspension of the Writ of Habeas Corpus.[8]

The Department of Defense issued regulations for the conduct of military commissions pursuant to the MCA 2006[9] and restarted the military commission proceedings, which have resulted in three convictions to date. One detainee, David Matthew Hicks of Australia, was convicted of material support to terrorism pursuant to a plea agreement in 2007.[10] In 2008, Salim Hamdan was found guilty of one count of providing material support for terrorism and sentenced to 66 months' imprisonment, but credited with five years' time served.[11] Both men are now free from detention. Ali Hamza Ahmad Suliman al Bahlul of Yemen was found guilty of multiple counts of conspiracy and solicitation to commit certain war crimes and of providing material support for terrorism in connection with his role as Al Qaeda's "propaganda chief."[12] He refused representation and boycotted most of his trial, and was subsequently sentenced to life imprisonment. His case is on review.

No challenge to military commissions under the MCA 2006 has reached the Supreme Court. President Obama halted the proceedings upon taking office in January, 2009 in order to review whether to continue their use. The President issued an Executive Order requiring that the Guantánamo detention facility be closed no later than a year from the date of the Order.[13] The Order requires specified officials to review all Guantánamo detentions to assess whether the detainee should continue to be held by the United States, transferred or released to another country, or be prosecuted by the United States for criminal offenses.[14] The Secretary of Defense was also required to take steps to ensure that all proceedings before military commissions and the United States Court of Military Commission Review were halted, although some pretrial proceedings continued to take place. One case was moved to a federal district court.[15]

In May, 2009, the Obama Administration announced that it was considering restarting the military commission system with some changes to the procedural rules.[16] The Department of Defense informed Congress about modifications to the Manual for Military Commissions, to take effect July 14, 2009.[17] The Senate passed the Military Commissions Act of 2009 (MCA 2009) as part of the Department of Defense Authorization Act (NDAA) for FY2010, S. 1391, to provide some reforms the Administration supported and to make other amendments to the Military Commissions Act, as described below. The bill that emerged from conference (H.R. 2647) contained some, but not all, of the proposals submitted by the Obama Administration, and was enacted October 28, 2009, P.L. 111-84.

President Obama's Detention Policy Task Force issued a preliminary report July 20, 2009, reaffirming that the White House considers military commissions to be an appropriate forum for trying some cases involving suspected violations of the laws of the war, although federal criminal court would be the preferred forum for trials of detainees.[18] The disposition of each case is to be assigned to a team comprised of Department of Justice (DOJ) and Department of Defense (DOD) personnel, including prosecutors from the Office of Military Commissions. Appended to the report was a set of criteria to govern the disposition of cases involving Guantánamo detainees. This protocol identifies three broad categories of factors to be taken into consideration:

- Strength of interest, namely, the nature and gravity of offenses or underlying conduct; identity of victims; location of offense; location and context in which the individual was apprehended; and the conduct of the investigation.
- Efficiency, namely, protection of intelligence source and methods; venue; number of defendants; foreign policy concerns; legal or evidentiary problems; efficiency and resource concerns.
- Other prosecution considerations, namely, the extent to which the forum and offenses that can be tried there permit a full presentation of the wrongful conduct, and the available sentence upon conviction.

Federal prosecutors are to evaluate their cases under "traditional principles of federal prosecution."

On November 13, 2009, Attorney General Holder announced his decision to transfer the five "9/11 conspirators," who include Khalid Sheikh Mohammed, Walid Muhammed Salih Mubarak Bin Attash, Ramzi Bin Al Shibh, Ali Abdul-Aziz Ali, and Mustafa Ahmed Al Hawsawi, to the Southern District of New York to stand trial.[19] Five other detainees are to be tried by military commission. These include Omar Khadr, a Canadian citizen captured as a teenager and charged before a military commission for allegedly throwing a hand grenade that killed a U.S. medic in Afghanistan; Abd al-Rahim al-Nashiri, whose military commission charges related to the October 2000 attack on the USS Cole were previously withdrawn in February, 2009; Ahmed Mohammed Ahmed Haza al Darbi, who is accused of participating in an al-Qaeda plot to blow up oil tankers in the Straits of Hormuz, and two other detainees about whom no further information was given.

As the deadline for closing the detention facility at Guantánamo passed unmet, the Obama Administration reportedly completed its assessment, determining that about 50 of the detainees held there will continue to be held without trial, that around 40 detainees will be prosecuted in military commission or federal court, and that the remaining 110 detainees will be released once a suitable country has agreed to take each of them.[20] However, the transfer of 30 detainees of Yemeni nationality was stymied because an Al Qaeda affiliate in Yemen is suspected to have been behind attempt to blow up a civilian airliner on Christmas Day, 2009.[21]

MILITARY COMMISSIONS

Military commissions are courts usually set up by military commanders in the field to try persons accused of certain offenses during war.[22] They may also try persons for ordinary crimes during periods of martial law or military occupation, where regular civil courts are not able to function.[23] Past military commissions trying enemy belligerents for war crimes directly applied the international law of war, without recourse to domestic criminal statutes, unless such statutes were declaratory of international law.[24] Historically, military commissions have applied the same set of procedural rules that applied in courts-martial.[25] By statute, military commissions have long been available to try "offenders or offenses designated by statute or the law of war."[26] For the most part, military commissions have been employed where U.S. armed forces have established a military government or martial law, as in the war with

Mexico, 1846 - 1848, the Civil War, the Philippine Insurrection of 1899 - 1902, and in occupied Germany and Japan after World War II.[27]

President Bush's Military Order setting up military commissions appeared to have been designed to replicate a pair of military commission orders issued during World War II by President Roosevelt for the trial of German saboteurs caught within the territory of the United States after having evaded U.S. coastal defenses. These tribunals were historically a bit anomalous in that they took place in Washington, D.C. during a period when the civilian courts were open. A similar practice during the Civil War, which accounted for a small number of the military commission cases, was held unconstitutional. The Supreme Court held essentially in *Ex parte Milligan*[28] that military trials of persons who had never been members of the armed forces of the United States could never be valid on friendly territory where martial law has not been declared and civilian courts are functioning. However, the Supreme Court upheld the F.D.R. tribunals by explaining that the holding in *Milligan* was limited to cases in which civilians – persons who are not members of the armed forces of an enemy government – were tried by military commission, and did not preclude the government from trying enemy belligerents for violations of the law of war, regardless of the operational status of the civilian courts.

The Bush Administration established rules prescribing detailed procedural safeguards for the tribunals.[29] These rules were praised as a significant improvement over what might have been permitted under the language of the M.O., but some continued to argue that the enhancements did not go far enough.[30] Critics also noted that the rules did not address the issue of indefinite detention without charge, as appeared to be possible under the original M.O.,[31] or that the Department of Defense may continue to detain persons who have been cleared by a military commission.[32] The Pentagon reportedly stated that its Inspector General (IG) looked into allegations, made by military lawyers assigned as prosecutors to the military commissions, that the proceedings were rigged to obtain convictions, but the IG did not substantiate the charges.[33]

The Military Commissions Act ("MCA")[34] grants the Secretary of Defense express authority to convene military commissions to prosecute those fitting the definition under the MCA of "alien unlawful enemy combatants."[35] The Secretary delegated the authority to a specially appointed "convening authority," who has responsibility for accepting or rejecting charges referred by the prosecution team, convening military commissions for trials, detailing military commission members and other personnel, approving requests from trial counsel to communicate with the media, approving requests for expert witnesses, approving plea agreements, carrying out post-trial reviews and forwarding cases for review, along with other duties spelled out in the MCA or in DOD's Regulation for Trial by Military Commission.[36]

The MCA eliminates the requirement for military commissions to conform to either of the two uniformity requirements in article 36, UCMJ, which President Bush's military commissions were held in *Hamdan* to violate. Instead, it establishes chapter 47A in title 10, U.S. Code and excepts military commissions under this chapter from the requirements in article 36.[37] It provides that the UCMJ "does not, by its terms, apply to trial by military commissions except as specifically provided in this chapter." While declaring that the enacted chapter is "based upon the procedures for trial by general courts-martial under [the UCMJ]," it establishes that "[t]he judicial construction and application of [the UCMJ] are not binding on military commissions established under this chapter."[38] It expressly exempts these military commissions from UCMJ articles 10 (speedy trial), 31 (self-incrimination warnings) and 32 (pretrial investigations), and amends articles 21, 28, 48, 50(a), 104, and 106 of the UCMJ to except military commissions under chapter 47A.[39] Other provisions of the UCMJ are to apply to trial by military commissions under chapter 47A only to the extent provided therein.[40]

Jurisdiction

The MCA establishes jurisdiction for military commissions somewhat more narrowly than that asserted in President Bush's M.O. The M.O. was initially criticized by some as overly broad in its assertion of jurisdiction, because it could be interpreted to cover non-citizens who had no connection with Al Qaeda or the terrorist attacks of September 11, 2001, as well as offenders or offenses not triable by military commission pursuant to statute or the law of war.[41] A person designated by President Bush as subject to his M.O. was amenable to detention and possible trial by military tribunal for violations of the law of war and "other applicable law."[42] The MCA 2006 largely validated President Bush's jurisdictional scheme for military commissions.

Personal Jurisdiction

The MCA, as amended, authorizes military commissions to try any "alien unprivileged enemy belligerent," which includes an individual (other than a privileged belligerent)[43] who:

(A) has engaged in hostilities against the United States or its coalition partners;
(B) has purposefully and materially supported hostilities against the United States or its coalition partners; or
(C) was a part of Al Qaeda at the time of the alleged offense under [chapter 47A of title 10, U.S. Code].[44]

Thus, persons who do not directly participate in hostilities, but "purposefully and materially" support hostilities, are subject to trial under the MCA.[45] Citizens who fit the definition of "unprivileged enemy belligerent" are not amenable to trial by military commission under the MCA, but their detention is not expressly precluded.[46]

The MCA, as amended, defines "hostilities" to mean any conflict "subject to the laws of war."[47] It does not explain what conduct amounts to "supporting hostilities." To the extent that the jurisdiction is interpreted to include conduct that falls outside the accepted definition of participation in an armed conflict, the MCA might run afoul of the courts' historical aversion to trying civilians before military tribunals when other courts are available.[48] It is unclear whether this principle would apply to aliens captured and detained overseas, but the MCA does not appear to exempt from military jurisdiction permanent resident aliens captured in the United States who might otherwise meet the definition of "unprivileged enemy belligerent." It is generally accepted that aliens within the United States are entitled to the same protections in criminal trials that apply to U.S. citizens. Therefore, to subject persons to trial by military commission who do not meet the exception carved out by the Supreme Court in *ex parte Quirin*[49] for unlawful belligerents, to the extent such persons enjoy constitutional protections, would likely raise significant constitutional questions. To date, no resident aliens have been charged for trial before a military commission under the MCA.

As originally enacted, the MCA did not specifically identify who was to make the determination that defendants met the definition of "unlawful enemy combatant." The government sought to establish jurisdiction based on the determinations of Combatant Status Review Tribunals (CSRTs), set up by the Pentagon to determine the status of detainees using procedures similar to those the Army uses to determine POW status during traditional wars.[50] The CSRTs, however, are not empowered to determine whether the enemy combatants are unlawful or lawful, which led two military commission judges to hold that CSRT determinations are inadequate to form the basis for the jurisdiction of military commissions.[51] The Court of Military Commission Review (CMCR) reversed.[52] While it agreed that the CSRT determinations are insufficient by themselves to establish jurisdiction, it found the military judge erred in declaring that the status determination had to be made by a competent tribunal other than the military commission itself.

In denying the government's request to find that CSRT determinations are sufficient to establish jurisdiction over the accused, the CMCR interpreted the MCA to require more than establishing membership in Al Qaeda or the Taliban. The CMCR found:

> no support for [the government's] claim that Congress, through the M.C.A., created a "comprehensive system" which sought to embrace and adopt all prior C.S.R.T. determinations that resulted in "enemy combatant" status assignments, and summarily turn those designations into findings that persons so labeled could also properly be considered " unlawful enemy combatants." Similarly, we find no support for [the government's] position regarding the parenthetical language contained in § 948a(1)(A)(i) of the M.C.A.—"including a person who is part of the Taliban, Al Qaeda, or associated forces." We do not read this language as declaring that a member of the Taliban, Al Qaeda, or associated forces is per se an "unlawful enemy combatant" for purposes of exercising criminal jurisdiction before a military commission. We read the parenthetical comment as simply elaborating upon the sentence immediately preceding it. That is, that a member of the Taliban, Al Qaeda, or associated forces who has engaged in hostilities or who has purposefully and materially supported hostilities against the United States or its co-belligerents will also qualify as an " unlawful enemy combatant" under the M.C.A. (emphasis added [by the court]).[53]

As a consequence of the decision, the prosecution has the burden of proving jurisdiction over each person charged for trial by a military commission. The Manual for Military Commissions was amended in May 2009 to reflect this practice,[54] and the 2009 MCA amended 10 U.S.C. § 948d to task the military commission with establishing its own jurisdiction. Under the amended language, membership in Al Qaeda (but not the Taliban) appears sufficient to establish jurisdiction, regardless of whether the defendant participated in or even supported hostilities, although the defendant must generally be alleged to have committed one of the listed crimes "in the context of and associated with hostilities."[55]

Subject Matter Jurisdiction

The MCA provides jurisdiction to military commissions to try alien unprivileged belligerents for listed offenses as well as sections 904 and 906 of title 10 (aiding the enemy and spying), or the law of war, "whether such offense was committed before, on, or after September 11, 2001."[56] Crimes to be triable by military commission are defined in subchapter VIII (10 U.S.C. §§ 950p – 950t). The MCA defines the following offenses: murder of protected persons; attacking civilians, civilian objects, or protected property; pillaging; denying quarter; taking hostages; employing poison or similar weapons; using protected persons or property as shields; torture, cruel or inhuman treatment; intentionally causing serious bodily injury; mutilating or maiming; murder in violation of the law of war; destruction of property in violation of the law of war; using treachery or perfidy; improperly using a flag of truce or distinctive emblem; intentionally mistreating a dead body; rape; sexual assault or abuse; hijacking or hazarding a vessel or aircraft; terrorism; providing material support for terrorism; wrongfully aiding the enemy; spying; attempts; conspiracy; solicitation; contempt; perjury and obstruction of justice.

The MCA largely adopted the list of offenses DOD had authorized for trial by military commission under the presidential order.[57] That list was not meant to be exhaustive. Rather, it was intended as an illustration of acts punishable under the law of war[58] or triable by military commissions.[59] The regulations contained an express prohibition of trials for *ex post facto* crimes.[60]

Although many of the crimes defined in the MCA seem to be well established offenses against the law of war, at least in the context of an international armed conflict,[61] a court might conclude that some of the listed crimes are new. For example, a plurality of the Supreme Court in *Hamdan* agreed that conspiracy is not a war crime under the traditional law of war.[62] The crime of "murder in violation of the law of war," which punishes persons who commit hostile acts that result in the death of any persons, including lawful combatants, may also be new, depending on how it is interpreted. The Department of Defense argued that the element "in violation of the law of war" is established by showing that the perpetrator is an unprivileged belligerent.[63] While it appears to be well established that a civilian who kills a lawful combatant is triable for murder and cannot invoke the defense of combatant immunity, [64] it is not clear that the murder constitutes a violation of the law of war (rather than domestic or martial law), or that the same principle applies in armed conflicts of a non-international nature, where combatant immunity does not apply. [65] The International Criminal Tribunal for the former Yugoslavia (ICTY) has found that war crimes in the context of non-international armed conflict include murder of protected persons, but have found that the killing of a combatant is not necessarily a war crime.[66] Thus, prison guards at Omarska and other detention camps were found guilty, among other crimes, of "murder, as a violation of the laws or customs of war" for causing the deaths of prisoners.[67] Similarly, the International Criminal Court applies a definition of murder in the context of a non-international armed conflict to require that the victim is a protected person,[68] while the killing (or wounding) of a "combatant adversary" is defined as a war crime only if it is done "treacherously."[69]

While one of the Guantánamo military commission judges found, without elaborating on what "murder in violation of the law of war" entails, that Congress could reasonably conclude that it constitutes a common law violation of the law of war,[70] another read the crime to consist of two elements: "the [attempted] killings ...were committed by an unlawful enemy combatant AND (2) that the method, manner or circumstances used violated the law of war."[71] There is historical support for the view that the offense pertains to means and methods of killing, but the requirement that the offender be an "unlawful combatant" is not well supported. Military commissions were used during the U.S. Civil War to try the charge of "murder in violation of the law of war," but this charge apparently applied to *privileged belligerents* who committed murder perfidiously or who killed prisoners of war,[72] while unprivileged belligerents were charged simply with murder.[73] The charge of "murder, in violation of the laws of war" was occasionally brought against Filipino natives during the Philippine Insurrection, generally involving the killing of unarmed civilians or prisoners.[74] However, it is not easy to discern why some cases were charged as "murder" while others had added the phrase "in violation of the laws of war."[75] Sometimes the distinction appears to turn on the status of the victim, other times the determining factor seems to be the status of the perpetrator or more precisely, the authority under which the hostile act was carried out. Murder qualified by reference to the law of war was charged most frequently against those whose legitimacy as combatants was not challenged. In one case in which insurgents killed U.S. soldiers during a firefight, the conviction for murder in the violation of the laws of war was overturned in part on the basis that "[t]he killing of the deceased soldiers in an engagement with a regular detachment of the public enemy is not murder but a natural consequence incidental to a state of war."[76]

Similarly, defining as a war crime the "material support for terrorism"[77] does not appear to be supported by historical precedent. The military judge in the *Hamdan* military commission case deferred to Congress's determination in the MCA that "material support for terrorism" describes a traditional offense against the law of war, citing Civil War precedents for trying crimes such as cooperating with guerrillas or "guerrilla-marauders."[78] Yet the Supreme Court's decision in *Ex parte Milligan*[79] may have limited the extent to which such crimes may be tried by military commissions where martial law has not been established, and may also call into question whether such crimes are properly considered war crimes or should be treated as ordinary crimes triable by military commissions when necessity demands it.[80] Charges related to aiding guerrillas were typically accompanied by a specification stating that the accused was a citizen and owed allegiance to the United States, but not ordinarily stating that the activity violated the law of war,[81] suggesting that the offense was a violation of martial law rather than the international law of war applicable to belligerents.

Many persons were tried by military commissions during the Philippine Insurrection for consorting with insurgents or other armed outlaws, but only after the commanding general issued a proclamation to the public explaining its obligation under the law of military occupation (a subset of the law of war analogous to martial law) to refrain from such activity.[82] In any event, the Obama Administration has expressed misgivings as to whether the crime of "material support for terrorism" amounts to an *ex post facto* law, and recommended the offense be eliminated from the MCA.[83] All but one of the detainees against whom charges have been filed so far have had at least one count of "material support for terrorism" among them,[84] although in most cases the allegations underlying the charge appear under other charges as well. Congress chose not to eliminate the material support charge when it amended the MCA in 2009.

Temporal and Spatial Jurisdiction

The law of war has traditionally applied within the territorial and temporal boundaries of an armed conflict between at least two belligerents.[85] It traditionally has not been applied to conduct occurring on the territory of neutral states or on territory not under the control of a belligerent, to conduct that preceded the outbreak of hostilities, or to conduct during hostilities that do not amount to an armed conflict. Unlike the conflict in Afghanistan, the conflict related to the September 11 attacks does not have clear boundaries in time or space,[86] nor is it entirely clear in all cases who the belligerents are.

The broad reach of President Bush's M.O. to encompass conduct and persons customarily subject to ordinary criminal law evoked criticism that the claimed jurisdiction of the military commissions exceeded the customary law of armed conflict, although DOD regulation purported to restate customary law.[87] The MCA provides jurisdiction to military commissions over covered offenses "when committed by an alien unprivileged enemy belligerent before, on, or after September 11, 2001."[88] Further, the MCA states that it codifies offenses "that have traditionally been triable by military commission" and establishes no "new crimes that did not exist before the its enactment"; and that therefore it "does not preclude trial for offenses that occurred before the date of the enactment of this subchapter, as so amended."[89] Whether, in fact, the offenses were established under the law of war prior to the enactment of the MCA will likely be the subject of many challenges by defendants.

In enacting the MCA, Congress seems to have provided the necessary statutory definitions of criminal offenses to overcome previous objections with respect to subject matter jurisdiction of military commissions. However, questions may still arise with respect to the necessity for conduct to occur in the context of hostilities in order to be triable by military commission. In 2008, the military judge in the *Hamdan* case concluded that a nexus with hostilities was required, holding that a charge of "[m]embership in a conspiracy that planned and carried out the attacks of September 11th, 2001 will be deemed to be in violation of the law of war; membership in a conspiracy that planned or carried out other attacks long before that date and unrelated to hostilities will not."[90]

Composition and Powers

The MCA provides for a qualified military judge to preside over panels of at least five military officers, except in the cases in which the death penalty is sought, in which case panels are to consist of twelve members unless that number are not reasonably available, in which case the minimum is nine panel members.[91] Procedures for assigning military judges as well as the particulars regarding the duties they are to perform are left to the Secretary of Defense to prescribe, except that the military judge may not be permitted to consult with members of the panel outside of the presence of the accused and counsel except as prescribed in 10 U.S.C. § 949d.[92] The military judge has the authority to decide matters related to the admissibility of evidence, including the treatment of classified information, but has no authority to compel the government to produce classified information.

The MCA empowers military commissions to maintain decorum during proceedings. Previously, under the DoD rules prior to enactment of the 2006

MCA, the presiding officer was authorized "to act upon any contempt or breach of Commission rules and procedures," including disciplining any individual who violates any "laws, rules, regulations, or other orders" applicable to the commission, as the presiding officer saw fit. Presumably this power was to include not only military and civilian attorneys but also any witnesses who had been summoned under order of the Secretary of Defense.[93] The MCA, 10 U.S.C. § 950t authorizes the military commissions to "punish for contempt any person who uses any menacing word, sign, or gesture in its presence, or who disturbs its proceedings by any riot or disorder." It is unclear whether this section is meant to expand the jurisdiction of military commissions to cover non-enemy combatant witnesses or civilian observers, but the M.M.C. expressly provides for jurisdiction over all persons, including civilians, and permits military judges to sentence those convicted with both fines and terms of confinement.[94] In the case of military commissions established under the UCMJ, there is statutory authority for military commissions to punish contempt with a fine of $100, confinement for up to 30 days, or both.[95] Neither the MCA nor the M.M.C. sets any limit on punishment for contempt.

The MCA provides that military commissions have the same power as a general court-martial to compel witnesses to appear in a manner "similar to that which courts of the United States having criminal jurisdiction may lawfully issue."[96] However, rather than providing that the trial counsel and the defense are to have equal opportunity to obtain witnesses and evidence, as is the case in general courts-martial, the MCA provides the defense a "reasonable opportunity" to obtain witnesses and evidence, in a manner comparable "to the opportunity available to a criminal defendant" in an article III court.[97] The M.M.C. provides the trial counsel with responsibility for producing witnesses requested by the defense, unless trial counsel determines the witness's testimony is not required, but the defense counsel may appeal the determination to the convening authority or, after referral, the military judge.[98]

Under article 47 of the UCMJ, a duly subpoenaed witness who is not subject to the UCMJ and who refuses to appear before a military commission may be prosecuted in federal court.[99] Presumably, this article could be used to prosecute civilians residing in U.S. territory who refuse to comply with a subpoena issued under the MCA. The M.M.C. provides the military judge or any person designated to take evidence authority to issue a subpoena to compel the presence of a witness or the production of documents. As is the case with general courts-martial, the military judge may issue a warrant of attachment to compel the presence of a witness who refuses to comply with a subpoena.[100] Subpoena authority under the UCMJ may not be used to compel a civilian witness to travel abroad in order to provide testimony,[101] so the corresponding authority under the MCA may be insufficient to compel civilian witnesses to travel to Cuba. Testimony by video transmission may be permitted in such cases.[102]

One of the perceived shortcomings of the M.O. had to do with the problem of command influence over commission personnel. M.C.O. No. 1 provided for a "full and fair trial," but contained few specific safeguards to address the issue of impartiality. The President or his designee were empowered to decide which charges to press; to select the members of the panel, the prosecution and the defense counsel, and the members of the review panel; and to approve and implement the final outcome. The President or his designees had the authority to write procedural rules, interpret them, enforce them, and amend them. Justice Kennedy remarked in his concurring opinion in *Hamdan v. Rumsfed* that the concentration of authority in the Appointing Authority was a significant departure from the structural safeguards Congress has built into the military justice system.[103]

The MCA, by providing requirements for the procedural rules to guard against command influence, may alleviate some of these concerns. In particular, the MCA prohibits the unlawful influence of military commissions and provides that neither the military commission members nor military counsel may have adverse actions taken against them in performance reviews. Many of the procedural rules are left to the discretion of the Secretary of Defense or his designee, more so than is the case under the UCMJ. Rule 104 of the Rules for Military Commissions (R.M.C.) prohibits command influence in terms similar to those in the Manual for Courts-Martial, except that they apply more broadly to "all persons" rather than only to "all persons subject to the [UCMJ]."

On the other hand, it has been argued that the multiple roles assigned to the convening authority, i.e., the DOD official who decides which charges to bring, allocates resources among the parties, and then approves or disapproves the findings of the military commission, create an inherent risk of unfairness (or the perception of unfairness).[104] While the convening authority for courts-martial also plays multiple roles, these functions serve as commanders' tools for enforcing discipline among subordinates, a context that arguably differs in important ways from bringing criminal cases against alleged enemies.[105] Improper influence by the legal advisor to the convening authority has been alleged at a few military commission proceedings, prompting military judges to issue orders in some cases granting relief.[106] Executive branch control over who serves as military judges has also led to charges of unfairness.[107]

Procedures Accorded the Accused

The MCA lists a minimum set of rights to be afforded the accused in any trial, and provides the accused an opportunity to appeal adverse verdicts to the United States Court of Appeals for the District of Columbia Circuit, but only "with respect to the findings and sentence as approved by the convening authority and as affirmed or set aside as incorrect in law by the United States Court of Military Commission Review." The circuit court is empowered to take action "only with respect to matters of law, including the sufficiency of the evidence to support the verdict."[108] The MCA provides that the accused is to be informed of the charges as soon as practicable after the charges and specifications are referred for trial.[109] The accused is to be presumed innocent until determined to be guilty. The presumption of innocence and the right against self-incrimination are to result in an entered plea of "Not Guilty" if the accused refuses to enter a plea or enters a "Guilty" plea that is determined to be involuntary or ill informed.[110] The accused has the right not to testify at trial and to have the opportunity to present evidence and cross-examine witnesses for the prosecution.[111]

Open Hearing

Because the public, and not just the accused, has a constitutionally protected interest in public trials, the extent to which trials by military commission are open to the press and public may be subject to challenge by media representatives.[112] The First Amendment right of public access extends to trials by court-martial,[113] but is not absolute. It does not impose on the government a duty "to accord the press special access to information not shared by members of the public generally."[114] The reporters' right to gather information does not include an absolute right to gain access to areas not open to the public.[115] In general, trials may be closed only where the following test is met: the party seeking closure demonstrates an overriding interest that is likely to be prejudiced; the closure is narrowly tailored to protect that interest; the trial court has considered reasonable alternatives to closure; and the trial court makes adequate findings to support the closure.[116]

The MCA provides that the military commission judge may close portions of a trial only to protect information from disclosure where such disclosure could reasonably be expected to cause damage to the national security, such as information about intelligence or law enforcement sources, methods, or activities; or to ensure the physical safety of individuals.[117] The information to be protected from disclosure does not necessarily have to be classified. To the extent that the exclusion of the press and public is based on the discretion of the military judge without consideration of the constitutional requirements relative to the specific exigencies of the case at trial, the procedures may implicate the First Amendment rights of the press and public. The M.M.C. provides, in Rule 806, that the military judge may close proceedings only to protect information designated for such protection by a government agency or to secure the physical safety of individuals. However, the rule also provides that "in order to maintain the dignity and decorum of the proceedings or for other good cause, the military judge may reasonably limit the number of spectators in, and the means of access to, the courtroom, and exclude specific persons from the courtroom." Such limitations must be supported by written findings.

One method military judges have adopted to protect classified information without closing a hearing to the public is to employ a time-delay on the audio feed of the proceedings to the public in the gallery in order to permit the judge or other authorized person to turn off the audio in the event classified information has been or is about to be disclosed.[118] The measure was said to be necessary because the statements of the accused are presumptively classified. If the switch is activated, the judge was to order a halt to the proceedings to evaluate the nature of the information or to permit the prosecution to assert a national security privilege.

The MCA of 2009 inserted a new subtitle V to provide procedures for handling classified or sensitive information, including the closure of evidentiary hearings when such information is to be discussed, the sealing of records, and the issuance of protective orders. It states that the trial counsel may "object to any question or line of inquiry that may require the witness to disclose classified information not previously found to be admissible" during testimony.[119] In such circumstances, the military judge is to "take such suitable action to determine whether the response is admissible as will safeguard against the compromise of any classified information," which may leave room for the use of time delay devices as described above, though the measure isn't expressly authorized.

Right to Be Present

Under UCMJ art. 39,[120] the accused at a court-martial has the right to be present at all proceedings other than the deliberation of the members. Under the DOD rules for military commissions prior to the MCA, the accused or the accused's civilian attorney could be precluded from attending portions of the trial for reasons involving national security, but a detailed (assigned) defense counsel was to be present for all hearings.[121] The MCA does not provide for the exclusion of the accused from portions of his trial, and does not allow classified information to be presented to panel members that is not disclosed to the accused. The accused may be excluded from trial proceedings (other than panel deliberations) by the military judge only upon a determination that the accused persists in disruptive or dangerous conduct.[122] However, the accused may be excluded from *in camera* considerations regarding the treatment of classified information.[123] The accused may not waive the right to be present at his trial, but may forfeit it through disruptive behavior or refusal to attend proceedings.[124]

Right to Counsel

As is the case in military courts-martial, an accused before a military commission under the MCA has the right to have military counsel assigned free of charge. The right to counsel attaches much earlier in the regular military justice system, where the accused has a right to request an attorney prior to being interrogated about conduct relating to the charges contemplated, than under the MCA. Under the MCA, at least one qualifying military defense counsel is to be detailed "as soon as practicable after the swearing of charges...."[125] The accused may also hire a civilian attorney who is a U.S. citizen, is admitted to the bar in any state, district, or possession, has never been disciplined, has a SECRET clearance (or higher, if necessary for a particular case), and agrees to comply with all applicable rules. If civilian counsel is hired, the detailed military counsel serves as associate counsel.[126] Unlike the previous DOD rules, the MCA provides that the accused has the right to self-representation.[127]

Previous DOD rules provided that defense counsel was to be assigned free of cost once charges were referred, but permitted the accused to request another JAG officer to be assigned as a replacement if available in accordance with any applicable instructions or supplementary regulations that might later be issued.[128] The MCA, as amended, incorporates this measure, providing the accused an opportunity to request a specific JAG officer to act as counsel, if the requested officer is reasonably available.[129] DOD regulations provide that the accused may request a specific military attorney from the defense team at the beginning of the proceedings, and may request a replacement counsel from the Chief Defense Counsel if he believes his detailed counsel has been ineffective or if he is otherwise materially dissatisfied with his assigned counsel.[130] If the accused retains the services of a civilian attorney, the MCA provides that military defense counsel is to act as associate counsel.[131] The M.M.C. provides that, in the event the accused elects to represent himself, the detailed counsel shall serve as "standby counsel,"[132] and the military judge may require that such defense counsel remain present during proceedings.[133]

The MCA requires civilian attorneys defending an accused before military commission to meet the same strict qualifications that applied under DOD rules.[134] A civilian attorney must be a U.S. citizen with at least a SECRET clearance with membership in any state or territorial bar and no disciplinary record.[135] The MCA does not set forth in any detail what rules might be established to govern the conduct of civilian counsel. Under the last-issued regulation, the Chief Defense Counsel has the responsibility of determining the eligibility of civilian defense counsel, and may reconsider the determination based on "subsequently discovered information indicating material nondisclosure or misrepresentation in the application, or material violation of obligations of the civilian defense counsel, or other good cause."[136] Alternatively, the Chief Defense Counsel may refer the matter to either the convening authority or the DOD Deputy General Counsel (Personnel and Health Policy), who may revoke or suspend the qualification of any member of the civilian defense counsel pool.

The MCA does not address the monitoring of communications between the accused and his attorney, and does not provide for an attorney-client privilege. Rule 502 of the Military Commission Rules of Evidence (Mil. Comm. R. Evid.) provides for substantially the same lawyer-client privilege that applies in courts-martial.[137] With respect to the monitoring of attorney-client communications, the previous DOD rules for military commissions initially provided that civilian counsel were required to agree that communications with the client were subject to monitoring. That requirement was later modified to require prior notification and to permit the attorney to notify the client when monitoring is to occur.[138] Although the government was not permitted to use information against the accused at trial, some argued that the absence of the normal attorney-client privilege could impede communications between them, possibly decreasing the effectiveness of counsel. Civilian attorneys were bound to inform the military counsel upon learning of information about a pending crime that could lead to "death, substantial bodily harm, or a significant impairment of national security."[139] The required agreement under the current regulations imposes a similar duty to inform, but does not mention monitoring of communications.[140]

Evidentiary Matters

The Sixth Amendment to the U.S. Constitution guarantees that those accused in criminal prosecutions have the right to be "confronted with the witnesses against [them]" and to have "compulsory process for obtaining witnesses in [their] favor."[141] The Supreme Court has held that "[t]he central concern of the Confrontation Clause is to ensure the reliability of the evidence against a criminal defendant by subjecting it to rigorous testing in the context of an adversary proceeding before the trier of fact."[142] In courts-martial, the Military Rules of Evidence (Mil. R. Evid.)[143] provide that "[a]ll relevant evidence is admissible, except as otherwise provided by the Constitution of the United States [and other applicable statutes, regulations and rules]."[144] Relevant evidence is excluded if its probative value is outweighed by other factors.[145] The accused has the right to view any documents in the possession of the prosecution related to the charges, and evidence that reasonably tends to negate the guilt of the accused, reduce the degree of guilt or reduce the punishment,[146] with some allowance for protecting non-relevant classified information.[147]

Supporters of the use of military commissions to try suspected terrorists have viewed the possibility of employing evidentiary standards that vary from those used in federal courts or in military courts-martial as a significant advantage over those courts. The Supreme Court seemed to indicate that the previous DOD rules were inadequate under international law, remarking that "various provisions of Commission Order No. 1 dispense with the principles, articulated in Article 75 [of Protocol I to the Geneva Conventions] and indisputably part of the customary international law, that an accused must, absent disruptive conduct or consent, be present for his trial and must be privy to the evidence against him."[148]

The MCA provides that the "accused shall be permitted to present evidence in his defense, to cross-examine the witnesses who testify against him, and to examine and respond to evidence admitted against him on the issue of guilt or innocence and for sentencing."[149] It is not clear what evidence might be excluded from this requirement as irrelevant to the issues of guilt, innocence, or appropriate punishment. It is possible that this provision could be interpreted not to apply to evidence relevant to the credibility of a witness or the authenticity of a document, so that the accused would have no right to examine and respond to such evidence, unless expressly provided elsewhere in the MCA.

Discovery

The MCA provides that defense counsel is to be afforded a reasonable opportunity to obtain witnesses and other evidence, including evidence in the possession of the United States, as specified in regulations prescribed by the Secretary of Defense.[150] It does not guarantee the defense equal opportunity with the prosecution to obtain such evidence, as is the case at general courts-martial.[151] The MCA provides that all of the information admitted into evidence at trial under any rule must be provided to the accused.[152] The accused is also entitled to exculpatory and mitigating information known to the prosecution or investigators, [153] with procedures permitting some variance for security concerns.[154]

The MCA provides for the protection of national security information during the discovery phase of a trial under procedures similar to the Classified Information Procedures Act and the Manual for Courts-Martial.[155] Classified information is privileged and need not be disclosed.[156] Where M.C.O. No. 1 permitted the withholding of any "Protected Information,"[157] the MCA permits the government to withhold only information determined by the United States Government pursuant to statute, Executive order, or regulation to require protection against unauthorized disclosure for reasons of national security.[158] Further, if the government wishes to withhold any classified information, the trial counsel must submit a declaration, signed by a knowledgeable official with classification authority, invoking the United States' classified information privilege and setting forth the damage to the national security that the discovery of or access to such information reasonably could be expected to cause.[159] The military judge may authorize production of the classified information if she determines that it would be "noncumulative, relevant, and helpful to a legally cognizable defense, rebuttal of the prosecution's case, or to sentencing," in accordance with standards generally applicable in federal criminal cases.[160] Specifically, the military judge may authorize the government to delete specified portions of evidence to be made available to the accused, or may allow an unclassified summary or statement setting forth the facts the evidence would tend to prove, to the extent practicable in accordance with the rules used at general courtsmartial.[161] Trial counsel may submit applications for protective measures on an ex parte basis, and the MCA does not provide defense counsel with access to the classified information that serves as the basis for substitute or redacted proffers. The decision to permit a substitution or grant other relief, which is required so long as the military judge determines such relief would "provide the accused with substantially the same ability to make a defense" as would access to the classified information itself, is not subject to a motion for reconsideration, but all of the submitted information and hearing transcripts are sealed and preserved for submission in case of appeal.

Admissibility of Evidence

The Secretary of Defense may prescribe in the rules of evidence that evidence is admissible as authentic if the military judge determines that "there is sufficient evidence that the evidence is what it is claimed to be," and instructs the members that they may consider any issue as to authentication or identification of evidence in determining the weight, if any, to be given to the evidence.[162] The accused is entitled to the exclusion of evidence that is not probative or reliable, or of evidence the probative value of which is substantially outweighed by the "danger of unfair prejudice, confusion of the issues, or misleading the members"; or by "considerations of undue delay, waste of time, or needless presentation of cumulative evidence."[163]

Coerced Statements

The MCA prohibits the use of statements obtained through torture as evidence in a trial, except to prove torture where the defendant is accused of committing torture. For information obtained through coercion that does not amount to torture, the 2006 MCA provided a different standard for admissibility depending on whether the statement was obtained prior to or after the enactment of the DTA. Statements elicited through such methods prior to the DTA were admissible if the military judge were to find that the "totality of circumstances under which the statement was made renders it reliable and possessing sufficient probative value" and "the interests of justice would best be served" by admission of the statement. Statements taken after passage of the DTA were admissible if, in addition to the two criteria above, the military judge were to find that "the interrogation methods used to obtain the statement do not violate the cruel, unusual, or inhumane treatment or punishment prohibited by the Fifth, Eighth, and Fourteenth Amendments to the U.S. Constitution."

The 2009 MCA eliminates the distinction above, making statements obtained through cruel, inhuman or degrading methods inadmissible regardless of when they were made. The Obama Administration had already amended the military commission regulations in May, 2009 to remove the discrepancy.[164] Otherwise, out-of-court statements by the accused may be admitted if the military judge finds that the totality of the circumstances renders the statement reliable and possessing sufficient probative value; and either that the statement was voluntarily given or that the statement was made "incident to lawful conduct during military operations at the point of capture or during closely related active combat engagement, and the interests of justice would best be served by admission of the statement into evidence."[165] Voluntariness is to be determined considering the totality of the circumstances, including:

1) The details of the taking of the statement, accounting for the circumstances of the conduct of military and intelligence operations during hostilities.
2) The characteristics of the accused, such as military training, age, and education level.
3) The lapse of time, change of place, or change in identity of the questioners between the statement sought to be admitted and any prior questioning of the accused.[166]

The defense is required to make any objections to the proposed use of any statements by the accused prior to entering a plea, if the trial counsel has disclosed the intent to use the statement, otherwise the objection will be deemed to have been waived.[167] The military judge may require the defense to establish the grounds for excluding the statement. However, the government has the burden of establishing the admissibility of the evidence. If the statement is ruled admissible, the defense is permitted to present evidence with respect to the voluntariness of the statement, and the military judge must instruct the members to consider that factor in according weight to the evidence. Testimony given by the accused for the purpose of denying having made a statement or for disputing the admissibility of a statement is not to be used against him for any purpose other than in prosecution for perjury or false statements.[168]

Mil. Comm. R. Evid. 304 is modeled on Mil. R. Evid. 304, which prescribes rules for courts-martial to provide for the admission into evidence of confessions and admissions (self-incriminating statements not amounting to an admission of guilt). Under court-martial rules, such a statement and any evidence derived as a result of such a statement are admissible only if the statement was made voluntarily. Involuntary statements are those elicited through coercion or other means in violation of constitutional due process. To be used as evidence of guilt against the accused at court martial, a confession or admission must be corroborated by independent evidence. There is no requirement for corroboration of such statements at military commissions; however, the military judge may take the existence of corroborating evidence into consideration in determining the probative value and reliability of the statement.

In one case before a military commission, the military judge ordered a detainee's statements to Afghan officials at the time of his capture suppressed on the basis of death threats against the detainee as well as his family.[169] Such treatment is regarded as torture under the Military Commission Rules of Evidence.[170] Further, the military judge ruled that statements subsequently made by the accused to U.S. interrogators likewise were required to be suppressed because they were taken under circumstances that did not sufficiently dissipate the coercive effect of the earlier threats.[171] The government sought to appeal the latter ruling, but has since dropped the charges against the detainee after he prevailed in his habeas petition.[172]

Hearsay

Hearsay evidence is an out-of-court statement, whether oral, written, or conveyed through nonverbal conduct, introduced into evidence to prove the truth of the matter asserted. M.C.O. No. 1 did not exclude hearsay evidence. The MCA allows for the admission of hearsay evidence that would not be permitted under the Manual for Courts-Martial[173] only if the proponent of the evidence notifies the adverse party sufficiently in advance of trial of the intention to offer the evidence, as well as the "particulars of the evidence (including [unclassified] information on the general circumstances under which the evidence was obtained)."[174] Originally, the evidence was to be inadmissible only if the party opposing its admission "clearly demonstrates that the evidence is unreliable or lacking in probative value."[175] The May, 2009 changes to the regulations reverse the burden of demonstrating reliability to the proponent of the evidence,[176] and the MCA 2009 reflects the change.

The rule regarding hearsay is provided in Mil. Comm. R. Evid. 801 to 807. In contrast to the relatively restrictive rule applied in courts-martial, where hearsay is not admissible except as permitted by a lengthy set of exceptions,[177] the military commission rules provide that hearsay *is* admissible on the same basis as any other form of evidence except as provided by these rules or an act of Congress, perhaps creating a presumption of admissibility for hearsay evidence in military commissions. The rules as they currently stand do not set forth any prohibitions with respect to hearsay evidence. Mil. Comm. R. Evid. 803 provides that hearsay may be admitted if it would be admissible at courts-martial. Alternatively, hearsay is admissible if the party proffering it notifies the adverse party thirty days in advance of trial or hearing of its intent to offer such evidence and provides any materials in its possession regarding the time, place, and conditions under which the statement was procured. Absent such notice, the military judge is responsible for determining whether the opposing party has been provided a "fair opportunity under the totality of the circumstances."[178] Hearsay evidence is admissible only if the proponent demonstrates by a preponderance of the evidence that such hearsay is reliable under the totality of the circumstances.[179]

Classified Evidence

At military commissions convened pursuant to the MCA, classified information is to be protected during all stages of proceedings and is privileged from disclosure for national security purposes.[180] Whenever the original classification authority or head of the agency concerned determines that information is properly classified and its release would be detrimental to the national security, the military judge "shall authorize, to the extent practicable," the "deletion of specified items of classified information from documents made available to the accused"; the substitution of a "portion or summary of the information"; or "the substitution of a statement admitting relevant facts that the classified information would tend to prove." The military judge must consider a claim of privilege and review any supporting materials in camera, and is not permitted to disclose the privileged information to the accused.[181]

With respect to the protection of intelligence sources and methods relevant to specific evidence, the military judge is required to permit trial counsel to introduce otherwise admissible evidence before the military commission without disclosing the "sources, methods, or activities by which the United States acquired the evidence" if the military judge finds that such information is classified and that the evidence is reliable.[182] The military judge may (but need not) require trial counsel to present an unclassified summary of such information to the military commission and the defense, "to the extent practicable and consistent with national security."[183]

The MCA does not explicitly provide an opportunity for the accused to contest the admissibility of substitute evidence proffered under the above procedures. It does not appear to permit the accused or his counsel to examine the evidence or a proffered substitute prior to its presentation to the military commission. If constitutional standards required in the Sixth Amendment are held to apply to military commissions, the MCA may be open to challenge for affording the accused an insufficient opportunity to contest evidence. An issue may arise as to whether, where the military judge is permitted to assess the reliability of evidence based on ex parte communication with the prosecution, adversarial testing of the reliability of evidence before the panel members meets constitutional requirements. If the military judge's determination as to reliability is conclusive, precluding entirely the opportunity of the accused to contest its reliability, the use of such evidence may serve as grounds to challenge the verdict.[184] On the other hand, if evidence resulting from classified intelligence sources and methods contains "'particularized guarantees of trustworthiness' such that adversarial testing would be expected to add little, if anything, to [its] reliability,"[185] it may be admissible and survive challenge.

Classified evidence is privileged under Mil. Comm. R. Evid. 505. Commentary to the rule notes that, because the defense has had no opportunity to evaluate the evidence to formulate any objections, "the military judge's consideration must encompass a broad range of potential objections."[186] During the examination of witnesses at trial, the trial counsel may make an objection to any question or motion that might lead to the disclosure of classified information. The military judge is required to take appropriate action, such as reviewing the matter in camera or granting a delay to allow the trial counsel to confer with the relevant agency officer to determine whether the privilege should be asserted. The judge may order that only parts of documents or other materials be entered into evidence, or permit proof of the contents of such materials without requiring introduction into evidence of the original or a duplicate.[187] In the event the defense reasonably expects to disclose classified information at trial, defense counsel must notify the trial counsel and the judge, and is precluded from disclosing information known or believed to be classified until the government has had a reasonable opportunity to move for an in camera determination as to protective measures.[188] Mil. Comm. R. Evid. 505 is modeled after the corresponding rule that applies in general courts-martial,[189] which in turn are modeled after the procedures that apply in federal criminal court, the Classified Information Procedures Act.[190]

Sentencing

The MCA provides that military commissions may adjudge "any punishment not forbidden by [it or the UCMJ], including the penalty of death...."[191] It specifically proscribes punishment "by flogging, or by branding, marking, or tattooing on the body, or any other cruel or unusual punishment, ... or [by the] use of irons, single or double."[192] A vote of two-thirds of the members present is required for sentences of up to 10 years. Longer sentences require the concurrence of three-fourths of the members present. The death penalty must be approved unanimously, both as to guilt and to the sentence, by all members present for the vote. The necessity for unanimity as to guilt has reportedly been interpreted to preclude the death penalty in cases where a plea of guilty is entered.[193]

In cases where the death penalty is sought, a panel of 12 members is required (unless the convening authority certifies that 12 members are not "reasonably available" because of physical conditions or military exigencies, in which case no fewer than nine are required), with all members present for the vote agreeing on the sentence. The death penalty must be expressly authorized for the offense,[194] and the charges referred to the commission must have expressly sought the penalty of death.[195] The death sentence may not be executed until the commission proceedings have been finally adjudged lawful and all appeals are exhausted,[196] and after the President approves the sentence.[197] The President is permitted to "commute, remit, or suspend [a death] sentence, or any part thereof, as he sees fit."[198] For sentences other than death, the Secretary of the Defense or the convening authority is permitted to adjust the sentence downward.[199]

Chapter X of the Rules for Military Commissions covers sentencing. "Aggravating factors" that may be presented by the trial counsel include evidence that "any offense of which the accused has been convicted comprises a violation of the law of war."[200] Unlike the rules for courts-martial, there is no express opportunity for the trial counsel to present evidence regarding rehabilitative potential of the accused. However, the rules provide that the accused may make a sworn or unsworn statement to present mitigating or extenuating circumstances or to rebut evidence of aggravation submitted by the trial counsel. In the case of an unsworn statement, which may be written or oral, the accused is not subject to cross-examination by the trial counsel.[201]

The death penalty may only be adjudged if expressly authorized for the offense listed or if it is authorized under the law of war; and all twelve members of the commission voted to convict the accused; and found that at least one of the listed aggravating factors exists, agreed that such factors outweigh any extenuating or mitigating circumstances, and voted to impose the death penalty. Aggravating factors include that "the accused was convicted of an offense, referred as capital, that is a violation of the law of war," that the offense resulted in the death of or substantially endangered the life of one or more other persons, the offense was committed for the purpose of receiving money or a thing of value, the offense involved torture or certain other mistreatment, the accused was also found guilty of another capital crime, the victim was below the age of fifteen, or that the victim was a protected person.[202] Other aggravating circumstances include specific law-of-war violations, which, except for spying, are not to be applied to offenses of which they are already an element.

Post-Trial Procedure

Subchapter VI of the MCA prescribes post-trial procedure and appeals, similar to procedures DOD had implemented. It provides for an administrative review of the trial record by the convening authority followed by a review panel.

Review and Appeal

The MCA codified the establishment of the review body set up under the previous DOD rules for military commissions.[203] The Court of Military Commission Review (CMCR) is comprised of appellate military judges who meet the same qualifications as military judges or comparable qualifications for civilian judges.[204] The accused may appeal a final decision of the military commission with respect to issues of law to the CMCR. Like the UCMJ, the MCA prohibits the invalidation of a verdict or sentence due to an error of law unless the error materially prejudices the substantial rights of the accused.[205] If the CMCR approves the verdict, the accused may appeal the final decision to the United States Court of Appeals for the District of Columbia Circuit.[206] Appellate court decisions may be reviewed by the Supreme Court under writ of certiorari.[207]

Post-trial procedures for military commissions are set forth in Chapter XI of the Rules for Military Commissions. Post-trial proceedings may be conducted to correct errors, omissions, or inconsistencies, where the revision can be accomplished without material prejudice to the accused.[208] Sessions without members may be ordered to reconsider any trial ruling that substantially affects the legal sufficiency of any findings of guilt or the sentence.

Once the record is authenticated and forwarded to the convening authority, the accused is permitted, within 20 days unless additional time is approved, to submit matters relevant to whether to approve the sentence or disapprove findings of guilt.[209] The convening authority is required to consider written submissions. If the military commission has made a finding of guilty, the legal advisor also reviews the record and provides recommendations to the convening authority.[210] The convening authority may not take an action disapproving a finding of not guilty or a ruling that amounts to a finding of not guilty.[211] However, in the case of a finding of not guilty by reason of lack of mental responsibility, the convening authority may commit the accused to a suitable facility for treatment pending a hearing to determine whether the accused may be released or detained under less than the most stringent circumstances without posing a danger to others.[212]

Rehearings of guilty findings may be ordered at the discretion of the convening authority, except where there is a lack of sufficient evidence to support the charge or lesser included offense. Rehearings are permitted if evidence that should not have been admitted can be replaced by an admissible substitute.[213] Any part of a sentence served pursuant to the military commission's original holding counts toward any sentence that results from a hearing for resentencing.[214]

In all cases in which the convening authority approves a finding of guilty, the record is forwarded to the CMCR, unless the accused (where the sentence does not include death) waives review.[215]

No relief may be granted by the CMCR unless an error of law prejudiced a substantial trial right of the accused.[216] The accused has 20 days after receiving notification of the CMCR decision to submit a petition for review with the U.S. Court of Appeals for the District of Columbia Circuit. Within two years after a military commission conviction becomes final, an accused may petition the convening authority for a new trial on the ground of newly discovered evidence or fraud on the military commission.[217]

Protection against Double Jeopardy

Prior to the MCA, DOD regulations for military commissions provided that the accused could not be tried for the same charge twice by any military commission once the commission's finding on that charge became final (meaning once the verdict and sentence had been approved).[218]

However, the regulations appeared to permit revisions of a verdict prior to its becoming final in ways that might have resulted in double jeopardy.[219]

The MCA provides that "[n]o person may, without his consent, be tried by a military commission under this chapter a second time for the same offense."[220] Jeopardy attaches when a guilty finding becomes final after review of the case has been fully completed. The MCA prevents double jeopardy by expressly eliminating the possibility that a finding that amounts to a verdict of not guilty is subject to reversal by the convening authority or to review by the CMCR or the D.C. Circuit. The severity of a sentence adjudged by the military commission cannot be increased on rehearing unless the sentence prescribed for the offense is mandatory.[221] These protections are covered in Chapter XI of the Rules for Military Commission. Proceedings are not authorized to reconsider any ruling that amounts to a finding of not guilty as to any charge or specification, except with respect to a charge where the record indicates guilt as to a specification that may be charged as a separate offense under the MCA.[222] Proceedings for increasing the severity of a sentence are not permitted unless the commission failed to adjudge a proper sentence under the MCA or the sentence was less than that agreed to in a plea agreement.[223]

The inadequacy of an indictment in specifying charges could raise double jeopardy concerns. If the charge does not adequately describe the offense, another trial for the same offense under a new description is not as easily prevented. The MCA requires that charges and specifications be signed under oath by a person with personal knowledge or reason to believe that matters set forth therein are true,[224] and requires that they be served on the accused written in a language he understands.[225] There is no express requirement regarding the specificity of the charges in the MCA, but the Rules for Military Commission provide that the charge must state the punitive article of the act, law of war, or offense as defined in the Manual for Military Commissions that the accused is alleged to have violated.[226] A specification must allege every element of the charged offense expressly or by necessary implication.[227] The Rules for Military Commissions make the trial counsel responsible for causing the accused to be served a copy of the charges in English and another language that the accused understands, where appropriate.[228] After the accused is arraigned, the military judge may permit minor changes in the charges and specifications before findings are announced if no substantial right of the accused is prejudiced, but no major changes may be made over the objection of the accused without a new referral.[229]

President Bush's 2001 Military Order also left open the possibility that a person subject to the order might be transferred at any time to some other governmental authority for trial, or that a person already charged for crimes in federal courts could be made subject to the Order and transferred for trial by military commission.[230] Double jeopardy might have arisen in either event, depending on whether jeopardy had attached prior to transfer, even if the trial did not result in a final verdict. The MCA does not expressly address such transfers or prohibit trial in another forum. The Rules for Military Commissions, however, provide the accused a waivable right to move to dismiss charges on the basis that he has previously been tried by a federal civilian court for the same offense.[231]

The following tables provide a comparison of general courts-martial to the military tribunals under the Military Commissions Act of 2006 as initially enacted and as amended by the Military Commissions Act of 2009. *Table 1* compares the legal authorities for establishing military tribunals (including courts-martial), the jurisdiction over persons and offenses, and the structures of the tribunals. *Table 2,* which compares procedural safeguards, follows the same order and format used in CRS Report RL31262, *Selected Procedural Safeguards in Federal, Military, and International Courts*, by Jennifer K. Elsea, in order to facilitate comparison of the proposed legislation to safeguards provided in federal court,[232] the international military tribunals that tried World War II crimes at Nuremberg and Tokyo, and contemporary ad hoc tribunals set up by the UN Security Council to try crimes associated with hostilities in the former Yugoslavia and Rwanda.

CHART 1. COMPARISON OF MILITARY COMMISSION RULES

Authority

General Courts Martial	Military Commissions Act of 2006	Military Commissions Act of 2009
U.S. Constitution, Article I, § 8, in particular cl. 14 "To make Rules for the Government and Regulation of the land and naval Forces."	U.S. Constitution, Article I, § 8, in particular, cl. 10, "To define and punish Piracies and Felonies committed on the high Seas, and Offences against the Law of Nations"; cl. 11, "To declare War, grant Letters of Marque and Reprisal, and make Rules concerning Captures on Land and Water"; and cl. 14 (Necessary and Proper Clause).	Same as for MCA 2006.

Procedure

General Courts Martial	Military Commissions Act of 2006	Military Commissions Act of 2009
Rules are provided by the Uniform Code of Military Justice (UCMJ), chapter 47, title 10, and the Rules for Courts-Martial (R.C.M.) and the Military Rules of Evidence (Mil. R. Evid.), issued by the President pursuant to art. 36, UCMJ, 10 U.S.C. § 836.	The Secretary of Defense may prescribe rules of evidence and procedure for military commissions not inconsistent with the MCA. Rules applicable to courts-martial under the UCMJ are to apply except as otherwise specified. 10 U.S.C. § 949a(a). The Secretary of Defense, in consultation with the Attorney General, may make exceptions to UCMJ procedural rules "as may be required by the unique circumstances of the conduct of military and intelligence operations during hostilities or by other practical need." 10 U.S.C.§ 949a(b). The rules must include certain rights as listed in § 949a(b)(2), but need not include procedural rules listed in § 949a(b)(3). Pursuant to the above authority, the Secretary of Defense published the Manual for Military Commissions (M.M.C.), including the Rules for Military Commissions (R.M.C.) and the Military Commission Rules of Evidence (Mil. Comm. R. Evid.).	The Secretary of Defense may prescribe rules of procedure for military commissions. Such rules may not be inconsistent with the MCA (as amended). Procedural rules for general courts-martial are to apply unless the MCA or UCMJ provide otherwise. Consultation with the Attorney General is required only in cases of exceptions, which continue to be permissible "as may be required by the unique circumstances of the conduct of military and intelligence operations during hostilities or by other practical need." 10 U.S.C. § 949a (as amended). Suppression of certain evidence is a required right rather than an optional rule (see Table 2 specific rights). The right to representation by civilian counsel is included. The procedural rules may no longer provide that evidence shall be admissible if the military judge determines that it would have "probative value to a reasonable person." 10 U.S.C. § 949a(b) (as amended).

Jurisdiction over Persons

General Courts Martial	Military Commissions Act of 2006	Military Commissions Act of 2009
Any offenses made punishable by the UCMJ; offenses subject to trial by military tribunal under the law of war. 10 U.S.C. § 818.	A military commission has jurisdiction to try any offense made punishable by the MCA or the law of war when committed by an alien unlawful enemy combatant before, on, or after September 11, 2001. 10 U.S.C. § 948d(a). Offenses previously codified at 10 U.S.C. §§ 950q-w include the following: murder of protected persons; attacking civilians, civilian objects, or protected property; pillaging; denying quarter; taking hostages; employing poison or similar weapons; using protected persons or property as shields; torture, cruel or inhuman treatment; intentionally causing serious bodily injury; mutilating or maiming; murder in violation of the law of war; destruction of property in violation of the law of war; using treachery or perfidy; improperly using a flag of truce or distinctive emblem; intentionally mistreating a dead body; rape; sexual assault or abuse; hijacking or hazarding a vessel or aircraft; terrorism; providing material support for terrorism; wrongfully aiding the enemy; spying, contempt; perjury and obstruction of justice. 10 U.S.C. § 950v. Conspiracy (§ 950v(b)(28)), attempts (§ 950t), and solicitation (§ 950u) to commit the defined acts are also punishable.	A military commission has jurisdiction over persons subject to the MCA for offenses made punishable by the MCA, arts. 104 and 106 of the UCMJ, or the law of war. Military commissions are expressly authorized to determine their own jurisdiction. 10 U.S.C. § 948d (as amended). (Articles 104 and 106 of the UCMJ, however, state that they do not apply to military commissions under the MCA. 10 U.S.C. §§ 904 & 906). MCA offenses remain otherwise substantially unchanged, except that there is an express requirement that offenses occurred "in the context of and associated with hostilities." 10 U.S.C. § 950p. (as amended). The definition of "cruel or inhuman treatment" is modified to refer to treatment that constitutes a grave breach of common Article 3 of the Geneva Conventions, regardless of where the crime takes place or the nationality of the victim. (The previous definition, which was codified at 10 U.S.C. § 950v(b)(12), referred to 18 U.S.C. § 2340(2).) 10 U.S.C. § 950t(12) (as amended).

Composition

General Courts Martial	Military Commissions Act of 2006	Military Commissions Act of 2009
A military judge and not less than five members, or if requested, except in capital cases, a military judge alone. 10 U.S.C. § 816, R.C.M. 501.	A military judge and at least five members, 10 U.S.C. § 948m; unless the death penalty is sought, in which case no fewer than 12 members must be included.10 U.S.C. § 949m(c). 10 U.S.C. § 949m provides that, in death penalty cases where twelve members are not reasonably available because of physical conditions or military exigencies, the convening authority may approve a commission with as few as 9 members.	No changes.

CHART 2. COMPARISON OF PROCEDURAL SAFEGUARDS

Presumption of Innocence

General Courts Martial	Military Commissions Act of 2006	Military Commissions Act of 2009
If the defendant fails to enter a proper plea, a plea of not guilty will be entered. R.C.M. 910(b). Members of court-martial must be instructed that the "accused must be presumed to be innocent until the accused's guilt is established by legal and competent evidence beyond a reasonable doubt." R.C.M. 920(e). The accused shall be properly attired in uniform with grade insignia and any decorations to which entitled. Physical restraint shall not be imposed unless prescribed by the military judge. R.C.M. 804.	Before a vote is taken on the findings, the military judge must instruct the commission members "that the accused must be presumed to be innocent until his guilt is established by legal and competent evidence beyond reasonable doubt." 10 U.S.C. § 949l. If an accused refuses to enter a plea or pleads guilty but provides inconsistent testimony, or if it appears that he lacks proper understanding of the meaning and effect of the guilty plea, the commission must treat the plea as denying guilt. 10 U.S.C. § 949i.	10 U.S.C. § 949l and 10 U.S.C. § 949i are substantially unchanged.

Right to Remain Silent (Freedom from Coerced Statements)

General Courts Martial	Military Commissions Act of 2006	Military Commissions Act of 2009
Coerced confessions or confessions made in custody without statutory equivalent of	Sections a, b, and d of Article 31, UCMJ, are expressly made inapplicable. These provide that no person subject to the	10 U.S.C. § 948b(d) remains unchanged. Secretary of Defense may provide that confessions
Miranda warning are not admissible as evidence. Art. 31, UCMJ, 10 U.S.C. § 831.Rules of evidence provide that in most cases "an involuntary statement or any derivative evidence therefrom may not be received in evidence against an accused who made the statement if the accused makes a timely motion to suppress or an objection to the evidence under this rule." Mil. R. Evid. 304. The prosecutor must notify the defense of any incriminating statements made by the accused that are relevant to the case prior to the arraignment. Motions to suppress such statements must be made prior to pleading. Mil. R. Evid. 304. Interrogations conducted by foreign officials do not require warnings or presence of counsel unless the interrogation is instigated or conducted by U.S. military personnel. Mil. R. Evid. 305.	UCMJ may compel any person to incriminate himself or interrogate an accused without first informing him of his right to remain silent, and that statements obtained in violation of the above or through other unlawful inducement may not be received in evidence against him in a trial by court-martial. 10 U.S.C. § 948b(d). Secretary of Defense permitted to provide that confessions allegedly elicited through coercion or compulsory self-incrimination that were otherwise admissible were not to be excluded at trial unless except when admission would violate of section 948r. 10 U.S.C. § 949a(b)(2)(C). Section 948r provided that statements elicited through torture may not be entered into evidence except to prove a charge of torture. A statement of the accused obtained prior to the enactment of the DTA through coercion that does not amount to torture was admissible if the military judge found that the "totality of circumstances under which [it] was made renders it reliable and possessing sufficient probative value" and "the interests of justice would best be served" by admission of the statement. Statements taken after passage of the DTA were admissible if the military judge also found that "the interrogation methods used to obtain [them] do not violate the cruel, unusual, or inhumane treatment or punishment prohibited by the Fifth, Eighth, and Fourteenth Amendments to the U.S. Constitution." 10 U.S.C. § 948r. Evidence derived from impermissible interrogation methods is not expressly barred.	allegedly elicited through coercion or compulsory self-incrimination that are otherwise admissible are not to be excluded at trial unless their admission violates section 948r. 10 U.S.C. § 949a(b)(3)(B). Section 948r now provides for the exclusion of statements elicited through torture as well as cruel, inhuman, or degrading treatment prohibited by section 1003 of the DTA (42 U.S.C. § 2000dd), regardless of when the statement was made. hostilities; the accused's age, education level, military training; and the change in place or identity of interrogator between that statement and any prior questioning of the accused. 19 U.S.C. § 949r (as amended). Derivative evidence obtained using coerced statement is not expressly barred.

Freedom from Unreasonable Searches and Seizures

General Courts Martial	Military Commissions Act of 2006	Military Commissions Act of 2009
"Evidence obtained as a result of an unlawful search or seizure ... is inadmissible against the accused ..." unless certain exceptions apply. Mil. R. Evid. 311. "Authorization to search" may be oral or written, and may be issued by a military judge or an officer in command of the area to be searched, or if the area is not under military control, with authority over persons subject to military law or the law of war.	Not provided. Evidence was generally permitted if it was judged to have probative value to a reasonable person, unless it was obtained under circumstances that would render it unreliable. 10 U.S.C. §§ 948r, 949a. Procedural rules may provide that evidence gathered without authorization or a search warrant may be admitted into evidence. 10 U.S.C. § 949a.	The language permitting procedural rules to permit evidence having probative value to a reasonable person was omitted. The Secretary of Defense may provide that "evidence seized outside the United States shall not be excluded from trial by military commission on the grounds that the evidence was not seized pursuant to a search warrant or other authorization." 10 U.S.C. § 949a (as amended)
It must be based on probable cause. Mil. R. Evid. 315. Interception of wire and oral communications within the United States requires judicial application in accordance with 18 U.S.C. §§ 2516 et seq. Mil. R. Evid. 317. A search conducted by foreign officials is unlawful only if the accused is subject to "gross and brutal treatment." Mil. R. Evid. 311(c).		

Effective Assistance of Counsel

General Courts Martial	Military Commissions Act of 2006	Military Commissions Act of 2009
The defendant has a right to military counsel at government expense. The defendant may choose counsel, if that attorney is reasonably available, and may hire a civilian attorney in addition to military counsel. Art. 38, UCMJ, 10 U.S.C. § 838. Appointed counsel must be certified as qualified and may not be someone who has taken any part in the investigation	At least one qualifying military defense counsel is to be detailed "as soon as practicable after the swearing of charges...." 10 U.S.C. § 948k. The accused may also hire a civilian attorney who is a U.S. citizen, is admitted to the bar in any state, district, or possession, has never been disciplined, has a SECRET clearance (or higher, if necessary for a particular case), and agrees to comply with all applicable rules. 10 U.S.C. § 949c(b)(3).	At least one qualifying military defense counsel is to be detailed "as soon as practicable." 10 U.S.C. § 948k. The accused is entitled to select one "reasonably available" military counsel to represent him. The accused is not entitled to have more than one military counsel, but "associate defense counsel" may be authorized pursuant to regulations. 10 U.S.C. §§ 948c, 948k.

or prosecution, unless explicitly requested by the defendant. Art. 27, UCMJ, 10 U.S.C. § 827. The attorney-client privilege is honored. Mil. R. Evid. 502. Defense counsel must be a member of the bar of a federal or state court or authorized by a recognized licensing authority to practice law who is found by the military judge to be qualifed. R.C.M. 502. Once an attorney-client relationship has been formed, defense counsel can withdraw or be excused only at the request of the accused or on good cause shown. R.C.M. 506.	If civilian counsel is hired, the detailed military counsel serves as associate counsel. 10 U.S.C. § 949c(b)(5). No attorney-client privilege is mentioned. Adverse personnel actions may not be taken against defense attorneys because of the "zeal with which such officer, in acting as counsel, represented any accused before a military commission...." 10 U.S.C. § 949b.	10 U.S.C. § 949c, as it relates to the hiring of civilian counsel, remains substantially unchanged. 10 U.S.C. § 949b, prohibiting adverse personnel actions against defense attorneys due to "the zeal with which such officer, in acting as counsel, represented any accused before a military commission ..." also remains unchanged. In capital cases, the accused is entitled to be represented, "to the greatest extent practicable, by at least one additional counsel who is learned in applicable law," who may be a civilian and may be compensated by the government in accordance with regulations. 10 U.S.C. § 949a.

Right to Indictment and Presentment

General Courts Martial	Military Commissions Act of 2006	Military Commissions Act of 2009
The right to indictment by grand jury is explicitly excluded in "cases arising in the land or naval forces."	UCMJ Article 32 hearings are expressly made inapplicable. 10 U.S.C. § 948b(d)(1)(C). Charges and specifications against an accused must be signed by a person subject to UCMJ swearing under oath that	No substantial change to relevant sections of the MCA 2006.
Amendment V. UCMJ Article 32 provides for an inquiry similar to grand jury proceedings in federal criminal court. 10 U.S.C. § 832. Whenever an offense is alleged, the commander is responsible for initiating a preliminary inquiry and deciding how to dispose of the offense. R.C.M. 303-06.	the signer has "personal knowledge of, or reason to believe, the matters set forth therein," and that they are "true in fact to the best of his knowledge and belief." The accused is to be informed of the charges and specifications against him as soon as practicable after charges are sworn. 10 U.S.C. § 948q.	

Right to Written Statement of Charges

General Courts Martial	Military Commissions Act of 2006	Military Commissions Act of 2009
Charges and specifications must be signed under oath and made known to the accused as soon as practicable. Art. 30, UCMJ, 10 U.S.C. § 830.	The trial counsel assigned is responsible for serving defense counsel a copy of the charges upon the accused, in English and, if appropriate, in another language that the accused understands, "sufficiently in advance of trial to prepare a defense." 10 U.S.C. § 948s.	No substantial change to relevant sections of the MCA 2006.

Right to be Present at Trial

General Courts Martial	Military Commissions Act of 2006	Military Commissions Act of 2009
The presence of the accused is required during arraignment, at the plea, and at every	The accused has the right to be present at all sessions of the military commission except deliberation or voting, unless	No substantial change to relevant sections of the MCA 2006. 10 U.S.C. §
General Courts Martial	Military Commissions Act of 2006	Military Commissions Act of 2009
stage of the court-martial unless the accused waives the right by voluntarily absenting him or herself from the proceedings after the arraignment or by persisting in conduct that justifies the trial judge in ordering the removal of the accused from the proceedings. R.C.M. 804.	exclusion of the accused is permitted under § 949d. 10 U.S.C. § 949a(b)(1)(B). The accused may be excluded from attending portions of the proceeding if the military judge determines that the accused persists in disruptive or dangerous conduct. 10 U.S.C. § 949d(e).	949a(b)(2)(B); 10 U.S.C. § 949d(d).

Prohibition against Ex Post Facto Crimes

General Courts Martial	Military Commissions Act of 2006	Military Commissions Act of 2009
Courts-martial will not enforce an ex post facto law, including one that increases the amount of pay to be forfeited for a specific crime. U.S. v. Gorki, 47 M.J. 370 (1997).	Crimes punishable by military commissions under the new chapter are contained in subchapter VII. It includes the crime of conspiracy, which a plurality of the Supreme Court in Hamdan v. Rumsfeld viewed as invalid as a charge of war crimes. 548 U.S. 557 (2006). The act declares that it "codif[ies] offenses that have traditionally been triable by military commissions," and that "because the [defined crimes] (including provisions that incorporate definitions in other provisions of law) are declarative of existing law, they do not preclude trial for crimes that occurred before the date of enactment."	The conspiracy charge remains available under 10 U.S.C. § 950t(29) (as amended). The charge of "material support for terrorism," which the Obama Administration has believes could raise ex post facto implications, is now codified at 10 U.S.C. § 950t(25). 10 U.S.C. § 950p continues to declare that the MCA as amended does not define new crimes, but rather codifies preexisting offenses for trial by military commission, which offenses "have traditionally been triable under the law of war or otherwise triable by military commission," and
	10 U.S.C. § 950p. The statute expressly provides jurisdiction over the defined crimes, whether committed prior to, on or after September 11, 2001. 10 U.S.C. § 948d(a).	therefore "does not preclude trial for offenses that occurred before the date of the enactment ...." 10 U.S.C. § 950p(d). Section 948d continues to provide for jurisdiction over crimes committed "prior to, on or after September 11, 2001," although the offense must have been committed "in the context of and associated with hostilities." 10 U.S.C. § 950p (as amended); 10 U.S.C. § 948d.

Protection against Double Jeopardy

General Courts Martial	Military Commissions Act of 2006	Military Commissions Act of 2009
Double jeopardy clause applies. See Wade v. Hunter, 336 US 684, 688-89 (1949). Art. 44, UCMJ prohibits former jeopardy, provides for jeopardy to attach after introduction of evidence, or in cases resulting in a finding of guilty, after review of the case has been completed. 10 U.S.C. § 844. General court-martial proceeding is	"No person may, without his consent, be tried by a military commission a second time for the same offense." Jeopardy attaches when a guilty finding becomes final after review of the case has been completed. There is no indication when jeopardy attaches in cases that are dismissed without any fault of the accused. 10 U.S.C. § 949h. The United States may not appeal an order or ruling that amounts to a finding of not guilty. 10 U.S.C. § 950d(a)(2).	No substantial change to 10 U.S.C. § 949h. The United States may not appeal any finding of not guilty. 10 U.S.C. § 950d(d)(b). Limitations on the convening authority's ability to revise findings or order a rehearing are unchanged.
considered to be a federal trial for double jeopardy purposes. Double jeopardy does not result from charges brought in state or foreign courts, although court-martial in such cases is disfavored. U. S. v. Stokes, 12 M.J. 229 (C.M.A. 1982). Once military authorities have turned service member over to civil authorities for trial, military may have waived jurisdiction for that crime, although it may be possible to charge the individual for another crime arising from the same conduct. See 54 AM. JUR. 2d, Military and Civil Defense §§ 227-28. In cases in which a rehearing is ordered, the accused may not be tried for any offense of which he was found not guilty, and a sentence cannot be increased unless there is a finding of guilty of an offense not considered in the original proceedings or the sentence prescribed for the offense is mandatory.	The convening authority may not revise findings or order a rehearing in any case to reconsider a finding of not guilty of any specification or a ruling which amounts to a finding of not guilty, or reconsider a finding of not guilty of any charge, unless there has been a finding of guilty under a specification laid under that charge, which sufficiently alleges a violation. The convening authority may not increase the severity of the sentence unless the sentence prescribed for the offense is mandatory. 10 U.S.C. § 950b(d)(2)(B).	
Art. 63, UCMJ, 10 U.S.C. § 863. The United States may not appeal an order or ruling that amounts to a finding of not guilty. Art. 62, UCMJ, 10 U.S.C. § 862.		

Speedy and Public Trial

General Courts Martial	Military Commissions Act of 2006	Military Commissions Act of 2009
In general, accused must be brought to trial within 120 days of the preferral of charges or the imposition of restraint, whichever date is earliest. R.C.M. 707(a). The right to a public trial applies in courts-martial but is not absolute. R.C.M. 806. The military trial judge may exclude the public from portions of a proceeding for the purpose of protecting classified information if the prosecution demonstrates an overriding need to do so and the closure is no broader than necessary. United States v. Grunden, 2 M.J. 116 (CMA 1977).	There is no right to a speedy trial. Article 10, UCMJ, 10 U.S.C. § 810, is expressly made inapplicable to military commissions. 10 U.S.C. § 948b(d). The military judge may close all or part of a trial to the public only after making a determination that such closure is necessary to protect information, the disclosure of which would be harmful to national security interests or to the physical safety of any participant. 10 U.S.C. § 949d(d)	No substantial change to relevant sections of the MCA. 10 U.S.C. § 948b(d); 10 U.S.C. § 949b(c).

Burden and Standard of Proof

General Courts Martial	Military Commissions Act of 2006	Military Commissions Act of 2009
Members of court martial must be instructed that the burden of proof to establish guilt is upon the government and that any reasonable doubt must be resolved in favor of the defendant.	Commission members are to be instructed that the accused is presumed to be innocent until his "guilt is established by legal and competent evidence beyond reasonable doubt"; that any reasonable doubt as to the guilt of the accused must result in acquittal; that reasonable	Instructions for commission members on the burden of and standard of proof are unchanged. 10 U.S.C. § 949l. Two-thirds of the members must concur on a finding of guilty, except in capital cases.

General Courts Martial	Military Commissions Act of 2006	Military Commissions Act of 2009
R.C.M. 920(e).	doubt as to the degree of guilt must be resolved in favor of the lower degree as to which there is no reasonable doubt; and that the burden of proof is on the government. 10 U.S.C. § 949l. Two-thirds of the members must concur on a finding of guilty, except in capital cases. (The death penalty requires a unanimous finding as to guilt as well as sentence). 10 U.S.C. § 949m. The Secretary of Defense may prescribe that the military judge is to exclude any evidence, the probative value of which is substantially outweighed by the danger of unfair prejudice, confusion of the issues, or misleading the members of the commission, or by considerations of undue delay, waste of time, or needless presentation of cumulative evidence. 10 U.S.C. § 949a.	10 U.S.C. § 949m. The provision for the exclusion of irrelevant, cumulative, or prejudicial evidence is expressly made a right of the accused rather than an optional rule subject to the discretion of the Secretary of Defense. 10 U.S.C. § 949a (as amended).

Privilege against Self-Incrimination (Freedom from Compelled Testimony)

General Courts Martial	Military Commissions Act of 2006	Military Commissions Act of 2009
No person subject to the UCMJ may compel any person to answer incriminating questions. Art. 31(a) UCMJ, 10 U.S.C. § 831(a). Defendant may not be	"No person shall be required to testify against himself at a commission proceeding." 10 U.S.C. § 948r(a). While most of Art. 31, UCMJ, relating to compelled self-incrimination, is declared	No substantial change to relevant sections of the MCA 2006. 10 U.S.C. § 948r(b); 10 U.S.C. § 948b(d)(1)(B), 10 U.S.C. § 949l(c).

General Courts Martial	Military Commissions Act of 2006	Military Commissions Act of 2009
compelled to give testimony that is immaterial or potentially degrading. Art. 31(c), UCMJ, 10 U.S.C. § 831(c). No adverse inference is to be drawn from a defendant's refusal to answer any questions or testify at court-martial. Mil. R. Evid. 301(f). Witnesses may not be compelled to give testimony that may be incriminating unless granted immunity for that testimony by a general court-martial convening authority, as authorized by the Attorney General, if required. 18 U.S.C. § 6002; R.C.M. 704.	inapplicable, Art. 31(c), UCMJ, related to immaterial or degrading statements or evidence, applies to all military tribunals. 10 U.S.C. § 948b(d)(1)(B). Adverse inferences drawn from a failure to testify are not expressly prohibited; however, members are to be instructed that "the accused must be presumed to be innocent until his guilt is established by legal and competent evidence." 10 U.S.C. § 949l(c). There does not appear to be a provision for immunity of witnesses, although 18 U.S.C. § 6002 appears to apply.	

Right to Examine or Have Examined Adverse Witnesses (Hearsay and Classified Evidence)

General Courts Martial	Military Commissions Act of 2006	Military Commissions Act of 2009
Rules of Evidence prohibit generally the introduction at trial of statements made out of court to prove the truth of the matter stated unless the declarant is available for cross-examination at trial (hearsay rule).	"Defense counsel may cross-examine each witness for the prosecution who testifies before the commission." 10 U.S.C. § 949c(b)(7). The Secretary of Defense had the authority to establish that hearsay evidence not admissible under the rules of evidence applicable in trial by	The right to cross-examine witnesses remains unchanged. 10 U.S.C. § 949c(b)(6). The Secretary of Defense is permitted to provide that hearsay evidence that would not be admissible at a general court-martial is admissible if adequate

General Courts Martial	Military Commissions Act of 2006	Military Commissions Act of 2009
Mil. R. Evid. 801 et seq. Exceptions exist for cases in which the statement may be presumed to be reliable due to specific circumstances (Rule 803) or the witness is unavailable in court (Rule 804). There is also a "residual exception" (Rule 807), which covers statements not covered under other rules but having similar indicia of trustworthiness. Such statements are admissible if notice is provided to the adverse party sufficient to provide a fair opportunity to prepare to rebut it, and if the military judge determines the statement is more probative of the material fact for which it is offered than other reasonably available evidence and that its admission would serve the interests of justice. Mil. R. Evid. 801 et seq. In capital cases, sworn depositions may not be used in lieu of witness, unless court-martial is treated as non-capital or it is introduced by the	general courts-martial is admissible only if the proponent notifies the adverse party sufficiently in advance of its intention to offer the evidence and the particulars of the evidence (including information on the general circumstances under which the evidence was obtained), unless the party opposing the admission of the evidence "clearly demonstrates that the evidence is unreliable or lacking in probative value." 10 U.S.C. § 949a(b)(2)(E). In the case of classified information, the military judge could authorize the government to delete specified portions of evidence to be made available to the accused, or allow an unclassified summary or statement setting forth the facts the evidence would tend to prove, to the extent practicable in accordance with the rules used at general courts-martial. 10 U.S.C. § 949d(f)(2)(A).	notice is given and the military judge determines that the statement is reliable and is offered as evidence of a material fact, that direct testimony from the witness is not available or would have an adverse impact on military or intelligence operations, and that the general purposes of the rules of evidence and the interests of justice will best be served by admission of the statement into evidence. In determining reliability, the military judge may be obligated to consider the degree to which the statement is corroborated, the indicia of reliability within the statement itself, and whether the will of the declarant was overborne, 10 U.S.C. § 949a(b)(3)(D)(as amended). The burden of persuasion to demonstrate unreliability or lack of probative value appears to be on the profferer of the evidence. (Language providing otherwise was repealed.) The protection of classified information is governed by a new subchapter V, 10 U.S.C. §§ 949p-1 – 949p-7. Subchapter V provides that the government

General Courts Martial	Military Commissions Act of 2006	Military Commissions Act of 2009
defense. Art. 49, UCMJ, 10 U.S.C. § 849.		cannot be compelled to disclose classified information to anyone not authorized to receive it. If the government claims a privilege, the military judge may not authorize the discovery of or access to the classified information unless he determines the evidence is noncumulative, relevant, and helpful to a legally cognizable defense, rebuttal of the prosecution's case, or to sentencing. If the military judge determines disclosure or access is necessary, the military judge must grant the government's request to delete or withhold specified items of classified information; to substitute a summary for classified information; or to substitute a statement admitting relevant facts that the classified information or material would tend to prove, so long as the alternative procedure would provide the accused with substantially the same ability to make a defense. If the prosecution makes a motion for protective measures in camera, the accused has no opportunity to request a reconsideration.

Right to Compulsory Process to Obtain Witnesses and other Evidence (Discovery)

General Courts Martial	Military Commissions Act of 2006	Military Commissions Act of 2009
Defendants before court-martial have the right to compel appearance of witnesses necessary to their defense. R.C.M. 703. Process to compel witnesses in court-martial cases is to be similar to the process used in federal courts. Moreover, the defense and prosecution "shall have equal opportunity to obtain witnesses and other evidence." Art. 46, UCMJ, 10 U.S.C. § 846. In the case of a witness who is not available to testify, but whose testimony is essential to a fair trial, and no adequate substitution for the testimony can be provided, the judge must grant appropriate relief, unless the unavailability of the witness is the fault of the requesting party. R.C.M. 703. There is authority to grant immunity to witnesses in order to compel testimony that may incriminate the witness. 18 U.S.C. § 6002; R.C.M. 704. The prosecution is required to disclose any sworn statements that are material to the case. The government must also provide results or reports of any physical or mental	Defense counsel is to be afforded a reasonable opportunity to obtain witnesses and other evidence, including evidence in the possession of the United States, according to DOD regulations. 10 U.S.C. § 949j(a). The military commission is authorized to compel witnesses under U.S. jurisdiction to appear. 10 U.S.C. § 949j(b). The trial counsel is obligated to disclose exculpatory evidence of which he is aware to the defense, but such information, if classified, is available to the accused only in a redacted or summary form, and only if making the information available is possible without compromising intelligence sources, methods, or activities, or other national security interests. 10 U.S.C. § 949j(d). The military judge may authorize discovery in accordance with rules prescribed by the Secretary of Defense to redact classified information or to provide an unclassified summary or statement describing the evidence. 10 U.S.C. § 949j(c).	Defense counsel is to be afforded a reasonable opportunity to obtain witnesses and other evidence, including evidence in the possession of the United States, in a manner comparable to the opportunity available to a criminal defendant in federal court. As previously, the military commission is authorized to compel witnesses under U.S. jurisdiction to appear. This may include the authority to grant immunity to witnesses whose testimony is self-incriminatory. 10 U.S.C.§ 949j(a)(as amended). Congress emphasized its sense that "the fairness and effectiveness of the military commissions system under chapter 47A of title 10 ... will depend to a significant degree on the adequacy of defense counsel and associated resources for individuals accused, particularly in the case of capital cases," and that "defense counsel in military commission cases, particularly in capital cases, ... should be fully resourced as provided ...." FY2010 NDAA, § 1807. The obligation to disclose exculpatory information is expanded to include mitigating evidence, and the obligation extends beyond information known to the trial counsel to include all information that is known or

General Courts Martial	Military Commissions Act of 2006	Military Commissions Act of 2009
examination of the defendant. Upon the request of the accused, the government must permit the accused to inspect and make copies or photos of tangible objects, buildings or places, within the control of military authorities if the item is material to preparing the defense; the government intends to use the item in its case-in-chief at trial; or the item was obtained from or belongs to the defendant. Trial counsel (the prosecution) must give notice of any witnesses it intends to call at trial. Exculpatory or mitigating evidence known to trial counsel must also be disclosed. R.C.M. 701. Either party can request approval for expert testimony from the convening authority, whose denial can be overridden by the military judge on a finding that such testimony is necessary and relevant. R.C.M. 703(d). Discovery involving classified information is governed by Mil. R. Evid. 505.		reasonably should be known to any government officials who participated in the investigation and prosecution of the case against the defendant. The military judge may authorize trial counsel to disclose such information in a redacted or summary form, and shall authorize such alternative forms evidence when consistent with the interests of justice. 10 U.S.C. § 949j(b)(as amended). The provisions regarding the production of classified information are removed from § 949(d) and revised provisions inserted in new subchapter V, which is to be construed consistent with the Classified Information Procedures Act (18 U.S.C. App.) to the extent that such a construction does not conflict with the revised provisions. 10 U.S.C. § 949p-1 (as added). The military judge is to issue a protection order to prevent the disclosure of any classified information that has been disclosed or otherwise obtained by the accused. 10 U.S.C. § 949p-3 (as added).

Right to Trial by Impartial Judge

General Courts Martial	Military Commissions Act of 2006	Military Commissions Act of 2009
A qualified military judge is detailed to preside over the court-martial. The convening authority may not prepare or review any report concerning the performance or effectiveness of the military judge. Art. 26, UCMJ, 10 U.S.C. § 826. UCMJ Article 37 prohibits unlawful influence of courts-martial through admonishment, censure, or reprimand of its members by the convening authority or commanding officer, or any unlawful attempt by a person subject to the UCMJ to coerce or influence the action of a court-martial or convening authority. Art. 37, UCMJ, 10 U.S.C. § 837.	Military judges must take an oath to perform their duties faithfully. 10 U.S.C. § 949g. The convening authority is prohibited from preparing or reviewing any report concerning the effectiveness, fitness, or efficiency of a military judge. 10 U.S.C. § 948j(a). A military judge may not be assigned to a case in which he is the accuser, an investigator, a witness, or a counsel. 10 U.S.C. § 948j(c). The military judge may not consult with the members of the commission except in the presence of the accused, trial counsel, and defense counsel, nor may he vote with the members of the commission. 10 U.S.C. § 948j(d). Convening authority may not censure, reprimand, or admonish the military judge. No person may attempt to coerce or use unauthorized means to influence the action of a commission. 10 U.S.C. § 949b. The military judge may be challenged for cause. 10 U.S.C. § 949f.	No substantial change to relevant sections of the MCA 2006.

Right to Trial by Impartial Jury

General Courts Martial	Military Commissions Act of 2006	Military Commissions Act of 2009
A military accused has no Sixth Amendment right to a trial by petit jury. Ex Porte Quirin, 317 U.S. 1, 39-40 (1942) (dicta). However, "Congress has provided for trial by members at a court-martial." United States v. Witham, 47 M.J. 297, 301 (1997); Art. 25, UCMJ, 10 U.S.C. § 825. The Sixth Amendment requirement that the jury be impartial applies to court-martial members and covers not only the selection of individual jurors, but also their conduct during the trial proceedings and the subsequent deliberations. United States v. Lambert, 55 M.J. 293 (2001). The absence of a right to trial by jury precludes criminal trial of civilians by court-martial. Reid v. Covert, 354 U.S. 1 (1957); Kinsella v. United States ex rel. Singleton, 361 U.S. 234 (1960).	Military commission members must take an oath to perform their duties faithfully. 10 U.S.C. § 949g. The accused may make one peremptory challenge, and may challenge other members for cause. 10 U.S.C. § 949f. No convening authority may censure, reprimand, or admonish the commission or any member with respect to the findings or sentence or the exercise of any other functions in the conduct of the proceedings. No person may attempt to coerce or, by any unauthorized means, influence the action of a commission or any member thereof, in reaching the findings or sentence in any case. Military commission duties may not be considered in the preparation of an effectiveness report or any similar document with potential impact on career-advancement. 10 U.S.C. § 949b.	No substantial change to relevant sections of the MCA 2006.

Right to Appeal to Independent Reviewing Authority

General Courts Martial	Military Commissions Act of 2006	Military Commissions Act of 2009
The accused may submit matters concerning the findings and the sentence for consideration by the convening authority. The convening authority may approve, disapprove, commute, or suspend the sentence in whole or in part, set aside a finding of guilty or change a finding of guilty to a charge or specification to a finding of guilty to an offense that is a lesser included offense of the offense stated in the charge or specification. Art. 60, UCMJ, 10 U.S.C. § 860. Certain judgments of courts-martial, depending on the severity of the sentence, are directly appealable to the respective Service's Court of Criminal Appeals, which reviews the findings and sentence as approved by the convening authority, considering questions of both fact and law. In the event it sets aside a judgment, it may order a rehearing unless its act was based on insufficiency of	The accused may submit matters for consideration by the convening authority with respect to the authenticated findings or sentence of the military commission. The convening authority must review timely submissions prior to taking action. 10 U.S.C. § 950b. The accused may appeal a final decision of the military commission with respect to issues of law to the Court of Military Commission Review, a new body comprised of appellate military judges who meet the same qualifications as military judges or comparable qualifications for civilian judges. 10 U.S.C. § 950f. Once these appeals are exhausted, the accused may appeal the final decision to the United States Court of Appeals for the District of Columbia Circuit, which is limited to reviewing questions of law regarding "whether the final decision was consistent with the standards and procedures specified in [the MCA] and to the extent applicable, the Constitution and the laws of the United States." D.C. Cir. appellate decisions may be reviewed by the Supreme Court under writ of certiorari. 10 U.S.C. § 950g. Other review by a civilian	No change to 10 U.S.C. § 950b. The accused may appeal a final decision of the military commission with respect to any properly raised issue to the Court of Military Commission Review, a body composed of appellate military judges who meet the same qualifications as military judges or comparable qualifications for civilian judges. 10 U.S.C. § 950f. Once these appeals are exhausted, the accused may appeal the final decision to the United States Court of Appeals for the District of Columbia Circuit, with respect to the findings and sentence as approved by the convening authority and as affirmed or set aside as incorrect in law by the United States Court of Military Commission Review. The appellate court may take action only with respect to matters of law, including the sufficiency of the evidence to support the verdict. D.C. Cir. appellate decisions may be reviewed by the Supreme Court under writ of certiorari.

General Courts Martial	Military Commissions Act of 2006	Military Commissions Act of 2009
evidence in the record to support the findings, in which case it must order a dismissal. Art. 66, UCMJ, 10 U.S.C. § 866. The accused may petition for review of a Court of Criminal Appeals decision to the Court of Appeals for the Armed Forces, a court of civilian judges that is empowered to act only with respect to matters of law. Art. 67, UCMJ, 10 U.S.C. § 867. CAAF decisions, other than denials to hear a case, may be appealed to the Supreme Court through writ of certiorari. Art. 67a, UCMJ, 10 U.S.C. § 867a. The writ of habeas corpus provides the primary means by which those sentenced by military court, having exhausted military appeals, can challenge a conviction or sentence in a civilian court. The scope of matters that a court will address is narrower than in challenges of federal or state convictions. Burns v. Wilson, 346 U.S. 137 (1953).	court, including review on petition of habeas corpus, is expressly prohibited. 10 U.S.C. § 950j (likely unconstitutional under Boumediene v. Bush, 533 U.S. __, 123 S. Ct. 2229 (2008)(holding § 7 of the MCA to be invalid suspension of the writ of habeas corpus)).	10 U.S.C. § 950g. Other review by a civilian court, including review on petition of habeas corpus, is no longer expressly prohibited.

Protection against Excessive Penalties

General Courts Martial	Military Commissions Act of 2006	Military Commissions Act of 2009
Death may only be adjudged for certain crimes where the defendant is found guilty by unanimous vote of court-martial members present at the time of the vote. Prior to arraignment, the trial counsel must give the defense written notice of aggravating factors the prosecution intends to prove. R.C.M. 1004. A conviction of spying during time of war under UMCJ Article 106 carries a mandatory death penalty. 10 U.S.C. § 906.Cruel and unusual punishments are prohibited. Art. 55, UCMJ, 10 U.S.C. § 855. In capital cases, "equal pportunity to obtain witnesses and other evidence" under Art. 46, UCMJ may entitle the accused to expert assistance at the Government's expense . United States v. Kreutzer, 61 M.J. 293 (CAAF 2005). If a sentence extends to death, dismissal, or a dishonorable or bad conduct discharge, that part of the sentence may not be executed until required approval is given and all appeals are exhausted or waived. Art. 71, UCMJ, 10 U.S.C. § 871.	Military commissions may adjudge "any punishment not forbidden by [the MCA] or the law of war, including the penalty of death...." 10 U.S.C. § 948d. A vote of two-thirds of the members present is required for sentences of up to 10 years. Longer sentences require the concurrence of three-fourths of the members present. The death penalty must be approved unanimously on a unanimous guilty verdict. Where the death penalty is sought, a panel of 12 members is required (unless not "reasonably available"). The death penalty must be expressly authorized for the offense, and the charges must have expressly sought the penalty of death. 10 U.S.C. § 949m. An accused who is sentenced to death may waive his appeal, but may not withdraw an appeal. 10 U.S.C. § 950c. The death sentence may not be executed until the commission proceedings have been finally adjudged lawful and the time for filing a writ has expired or the writ has been denied; and the President approves the sentence. 10 U.S.C. § 950i. In capital cases, the accused is not entitled to assistance of counsel with expertise in death penalty cases. 10 U.S.C. § 949a (civilian counsel only authorized if provided at no expense of the government).	No substantial changes, except that in capital cases, the accused is entitled to assistance of counsel with expertise in death penalty cases, which may include civilian counsel paid for by the government. 10 U.S.C. § 949a. Death penalty cases in which 12 panel members are not "reasonably available" may not have fewer than 9 members. 10 U.S.C. § 949m.

End Notes

[1] Detention, Treatment, and Trial of Certain Non-Citizens in the War Against Terrorism §1(a), 66 Fed. Reg. 57,833 (November 16, 2001) (hereinafter "M.O."). President Bush subsequently determined that 20 of the detainees at the U.S. Naval Station in Guantánamo Bay held in connection with the conflict were subject to the M.O., and 10 were eventually charged for trial before military commissions. *See* Press Release, Department of Defense, President Determines Enemy Combatants Subject to His Military Order (July 3, 2003), *available at* http://www.defense.gov/ releases/release.aspx?releaseid=5511. According to the Defense Department, that determination is effectively "a grant of [military] jurisdiction over the person." *See* John Mintz, *6 Could Be Facing Military Tribunals*, WASH. POST, July 4, 2003, at A1. In 2004, nine additional detainees were determined to be eligible. *See* Press Release, Department of Defense, Presidential Military Order Applied to Nine More Combatants (July 7, 2004), *available a* thttp://www.defenselink.mil/releases/r elease. aspx? Releaseid = 7525. In November 2005, five more detainees were charged. *See* Press Release, Department of Defense, Military Commission Charges Approved (November 7, 2005), *available at* http://www.defense.gov/ releases/release.aspx?releaseid=9052.

[2] Rasul v. Bush, 542 U.S. 466 (2004). Persons subject to the M.O. were described as not privileged to "seek any remedy or maintain any proceeding, directly or indirectly" in federal or state court, the court of any foreign nation, or any international tribunal. M.O. at § 7(b). However, the Bush Administration shortly thereafter indicated that defendants were not intended to be precluded from petitioning a federal court for a writ of habeas. *See* Alberto R. Gonzales, *Martial Justice, Full and Fair*, NEW YORK TIMES (op-ed), November 30, 2001. The government did not rely on the M.O. as the legal basis for asserting detainees had no right to pursue writs of habeas corpus, but the Court's opinion served as a warning that military commission verdicts would be subject to collateral review. For a summary of *Rasul* and related cases, see CRS Report RS21884, *The Supreme Court 2003 Term: Summary and Analysis of Opinions Related to Detainees in the War on Terrorism*, by Jennifer K. Elsea.

[3] Title 10 of P.L. 109-148 and Title 14 of P.L. 109-163. The two versions of the Detainee Treatment Act (DTA) were identical as enacted, but subsequent amendments have resulted in some differences in the text.

[4] Hamdan v. Rumsfeld, 548 U.S. 557 (2006), *rev'g* 415 F.3d 33 (D.C. Cir. 2005). For an analysis of the case, see CRS Report RS22466, *Hamdan v. Rumsfeld: Military Commissions in the "Global War on Terrorism,"* by Jennifer K. Elsea.

[5] 10 U.S.C. § 801 *et seq*. Military commissions were said to be authorized pursuant to 10 U.S.C. §§ 821 and 836.

[6] P.L. 109-366, 120 Stat. 2600, codified at chapter 47a of title 10, U.S. Code.

[7] P.L. 109-366 § 7.

[8] Boumediene v. Bush, 533 U.S. 723 (2008). For an analysis of the case, see CRS Report RL33180, *Enemy Combatant Detainees: Habeas Corpus Challenges in Federal Court*, by Jennifer K. Elsea and Michael John Garcia.

[9] Department of Defense, The Manual for Military Commissions ["M.M.C."], January 18, 2007, *available at* http://www.defenselink.mil/news/MANUAL% 20FOR%20MILITARY% 20COMMISSIONS%202007%20signed.pdf.

[10] Press release, Department of Defense, Detainee Convicted of Terrorism Charge at Guantánamo Trial" (March 30, 2007), *available at* http://www.defenselink.mil/releases/ release.aspx? releaseid=10678. Hicks was sentenced to seven years' confinement. As part of his pretrial

agreement, his sentence was limited to nine months confinement to be served in Australia, with six years and three months suspended.

[11] Press release, Department of Defense, Detainee Transfer Announced (Nov. 28, 2008), *available at* http://www.defenselink.mil/releases/release.aspx?releaseid=12372.

[12] Press release, Department of Defense, Detainee Sentenced To Life In Prison (Nov. 3, 2008), *available at* http://www.defenselink.mil/releases/release.aspx?releaseid=12331.

[13] Executive Order 13492, Review and Disposition of Individuals Detained at the Guantánamo Bay Naval Base and Closure of Detention Facilities, 74 Fed. Reg. 4,897 (Jan. 22, 2009) [hereinafter "Executive Order"].

[14] *Id.* at § 4. The Order specifies that the review shall be conducted by the Attorney General (who shall also coordinate the review process), the Secretary of Defense, the Secretary of State, the Secretary of Homeland Security, the Director of National Intelligence, the Chairman of the Joint Chiefs of Staff, as well as other officers or full- or part-time employees of the U.S. government (as determined by the Attorney General, with the concurrence of the relevant department head) with intelligence, counterterrorism, military, or legal expertise.

[15] Press Release, Department of Justice, Ahmed Ghailani Transferred from Guantánamo Bay to New York for Prosecution on Terror Charges (June 9, 2009), *available at* http://www. justice.gov /opa/pr/2009/June/09-ag-563.html.

[16] Peter Finn, *Obama Set to Revive Military Commissions*, WASH. POST, May 9, 2009.

[17] Letter from Robert M. Gates, Secretary of Defense, to Senator Carl Levin, May 15, 2009. A copy is available at http://www.nimj.org/documents/2009%20DoD%20MMC%20C hanges.pdf.

[18] Memorandum from the Detention Policy Task Force to the Attorney General and the Secretary of Defense, July 20, 2009, http://www.nimj.com/display.aspx?base =Military Commissions &ID=255.

[19] Press Release, U.S. Department of Justice, "Departments of Justice and Defense Announce Forum Decisions for Ten Guantánamo Detainees," November 13, 2009, *available at* http://www.justice.gov/opa/pr/2009/November/09-ag1224.html.

[20] *See* Charlie Savage, *Detainees Will Still Be Held, but Not Tried, Official Says*, NY TIMES, Jan. 22, 2010.

[21] *Id.* DOJ has reported that as of March, 2010, 183 detainees remain at Guantánamo . Press Release, Department of Justice, United States Transfers Two Uighur Detainees from Guantánamo Bay to Switzerland (March 24, 2010), *available at* http://www. justice. gov/opa/pr/2010/March/10-ag-301.html.

[22] See CRS Report RL31191, *Terrorism and the Law of War: Trying Terrorists as War Criminals before Military Commissions*, by Jennifer K. Elsea (providing a general background of U.S. history of military commissions).

[23] *See* Hamdan v. Bush, 548 U.S. 557, 595 (2006). In looking at historical precedent, the *Hamdan* Court suggested, it is important to distinguish which type of jurisdiction a military commission is exercising, although the distinction is often blurred. *Id.* at 597 & note 7.

[24] *See* U.S. Army Field Manual (FM) 27-10, The Law of Land Warfare, section 505(e) [hereinafter "FM 27-10"].

[25] *See* WILLIAM WINTHROP, MILITARY LAW AND PRECEDENTS 841-42 (2d ed. 1920)(noting that "in the absence of any statute or regulation," the same principles and procedures commonly govern, though possibly more "liberally construed and applied"); David Glazier, Note, *Kangaroo Court or Competent Tribunal?: Judging the 21st Century Military Commission*, 89 VA. L. REV. 2005 (2003).

[26] 10 U.S.C. § 821. There are only two statutory offenses under the Uniform Code of Military Justice (UCMJ) for which convening a military commission is explicitly recognized: aiding the enemy and spying (in time of war). 10 U.S.C. §§ 904 and 906, respectively. The circumstances under which civilians accused of aiding the enemy may be tried by military tribunal have not been decided, but a court interpreting the article may limit its application to conduct committed in territory under martial law or military government, within a zone of military operations or area of invasion, or within areas subject to military jurisdiction. *See* FM 27-10, *supra* footnote 24, at para. 79(b)(noting that treason and espionage laws are available for incidents occurring outside of these areas, but are triable in civil courts); GEORGE B. DAVIS, A TREATISE ON THE MILITARY LAW OF THE UNITED STATES 417-18 (3d ed. 1913)(arguing that arts. 45 & 46 of the Articles of War, the precursors to 10 U.S.C. §§ 904 & 906, were essentially reliant on martial law to establish jurisdiction over civilians). Spying is not technically a violation of the law of war, but violates domestic law and traditionally may be tried by military commission. *See* FM 27-10, *supra* footnote 24, at para. 77 (explaining that spies are not punished as "violators of the law of war, but to render that method of obtaining information as dangerous, difficult, and ineffective as possible").

[27] For a review of military commission precedent, see David Glazier, *Precedents Lost: The Neglected History of the Military Commission*, 46 VA. J. INT'L L. 5 (2005).

[28] 71 U.S. (4 Wall.) 1 (1867).

[29] Military Commission Order No. 1 ("M.C.O. No. 1"), *reprinted at* 41 I.L.M. 725 (2002). A revision was issued August 31, 2005. The Department of Defense (DOD) subsequently released ten "Military Commission Instructions" ("M.C.I. No. 1-10") to elaborate on the set of procedural rules to govern military tribunals. The instructions set forth the elements of some crimes to be tried by military commission, established guidelines for civilian attorneys, and provided other administrative guidance and procedures for military commissions.

[30] *See* ACTL, Supplemental Report on Military Commissions for the Trial of Terrorists, October 2005, online at http://www.actl.com/AM/Template.cfm? Section=Home&template= /CM/ ContentDisplay.cfm&ContentID=2152.

[31] The Bush Administration did not explicitly use this authority; instead, it characterized the prisoners as "enemy combatants" detained pursuant to the law of war. *See, e.g.*, Response of the United States to Request for Precautionary Measures - Detainees in Guantánamo Bay, Cuba to the Inter-American Commission on Human Rights, Organization of American States 25 (2002)("It is humanitarian law, and not human rights law, that governs the capture and detention of enemy combatants in an armed conflict.")

[32] *See* Bruce Zagaris, *U.S. Defense Department Issues Order on Military Commissions*, 18 No. 5 INT'L ENFORCEMENT L. REP 215 (2002) (citing comments by former DOD chief counsel William J. Haynes II to a New York Times reporter).

[33] *See* Neil A. Lewis, *Two Prosecutors Faulted Trials For Detainees*, NY TIMES, August 1, 2005, at A1.

[34] P.L. 109-366, codified as amended by P.L. 111-84 at chapter 47a of title 10, U.S. Code. Unless otherwise noted, the terms "Military Commissions Act" or "MCA" (without specifying the year enacted) in this report refer to the amended version of the act as codified in title 10.

[35] 10 U.S.C. § 948h.

[36] Available at http://www.defenselink.mil/news/Apr2007/Reg_for_Trial_by_mcm.pdf.

[37] MCA § 4 (adding to 10 U.S.C. § 836(a) the words "except as provided in chapter 47A of this title" and to § 836(b) the words "except insofar as applicable to military commissions established under chapter 47A of this title").

[38] 10 U.S.C. § 948a (as added by the MCA).

[39] MCA § 4 (amending 10 U.S.C. §§ 821(jurisdiction of general courts-martial not exclusive), 828 (detail or employment of reporters and interpreters), 848 (power to punish contempt), 850(a) (admissibility of records of courts of inquiry), 904 (aiding the enemy), and 906 (spying)). The 2009 MCA amendments, Title XVIII of P.L. 111-84, enable military commissions under chapter 47A to try alien enemy unprivileged belligerents for violating 10 U.S.C. §§ 904 and 906, but did not amend 10 U.S.C. §§ 904 & 906 to reflect the change.

[40] 10 U.S.C. § 948b(d)(2).

[41] For a discussion of criticism related to the M.O. and M.C.O. No. 1, see CRS Report RL31600, *The Department of Defense Rules for Military Commissions: Analysis of Procedural Rules and Comparison with Proposed Legislation and the Uniform Code of Military Justice*, by Jennifer K. Elsea; NATIONAL INSTITUTE OF MILITARY JUSTICE, ANNOTATED GUIDE: PROCEDURES FOR TRIALS BY MILITARY COMMISSIONS OF CERTAIN NON-UNITED STATES CITIZENS IN THE WAR AGAINST TERRORISM 10-11(2004)(hereinafter "NIMJ").

[42] M.O. § 1(e) (finding such tribunals necessary to protect the United States and for effective conduct of military operations).

[43] A privileged belligerent is defined " an individual belonging to one of the eight categories enumerated in Article 4 of the Geneva Convention Relative to the Treatment of Prisoners of War," 10 U.S.C. § 948a(6).

[44] 10 U.S.C. § 948a(7). Prior to the 2009 amendments, any alien "unlawful enemy combatant" was subject to jurisdiction, which was defined to mean: (i)a person who has engaged in hostilities or who has purposefully and materially supported hostilities against the United States or its co-belligerents who is not a lawful enemy combatant (including a person who is part of the Taliban, Al Qaeda, or associated forces); or (ii) a person who, before, on, or after the date of the enactment of the Military Commissions Act of 2006, has been determined to be an unlawful enemy combatant by a Combatant Status Review Tribunal or another competent tribunal established under the authority of the President or the Secretary of Defense.

Previous 10 U.S.C. § 948a(1). The definition applies to military commission jurisdiction, and does not describe who can be detained under the AUMF. Some judges in the U.S. District Court for the District of Columbia have adopted a more restrictive definition to describe such persons, who were termed "enemy combatants" by the Bush Administration. *See* Mattan v. Obama, 618 F. Supp.2d 24 (D.D.C. 2009) (Government's detention authority covers individuals who are "part of" enemy forces, but does not extend to those who "supported" such forces, although evidence of such support would be considered in determining whether a detainee should be considered "part of" the forces); Hamlily v. Obama, 616 F. Supp. 2d 63 (D.D.C. 2009) (neither AUMF nor the law of war authorizes government's detention of individual who substantially supports, but is not part of, targeted organization, nor to those who have only directly supported hostilities); Gherebi v. Obama, 609 F. Supp.2d 43 (D.D.C.2009) (President has the authority to detain persons who were "part of, or substantially supported, the Taliban or al-Qaeda forces that are engaged in hostilities against the United States or its coalition partners, provided that the terms 'substantially supported' and 'part of' are interpreted to encompass only individuals who were members of the enemy organization's armed forces, as that term is intended under the laws of war, at the time of their capture.").

[45] The definition applies to military commission jurisdiction, and does not describe who can be detained under the AUMF. Some judges in the U.S. District Court for the District of Columbia have adopted a more restrictive definition to describe such persons, who were termed "enemy combatants" by the Bush Administration. *See* Mattan v. Obama, 618 F. Supp.2d 24 (D.D.C. 2009) (Government's detention authority covers individuals who are "part of" enemy forces, but does not extend to those who "supported" such forces, although evidence of such support would be considered in determining whether a detainee should be considered "part of" the forces); Hamlily v. Obama, 616 F. Supp. 2d 63 (D.D.C. 2009) (neither AUMF nor the law of war authorizes government's detention of individual who substantially supports, but is not part of, targeted organization, nor to those who have only directly supported hostilities); Gherebi v. Obama, 609 F. Supp. 2d 43 (D.D.C. 2009) (President has the authority to detain persons who were "part of, or substantially supported, the Taliban or al-Qaeda forces that are engaged in hostilities against the United States or its coalition partners, provided that the terms 'substantially supported' and 'part of' are interpreted to encompass only individuals who were members of the enemy organization's armed forces, as that term is intended under the laws of war, at the time of their capture.").

[46] For analysis of the authority to detain U.S. citizens, see CRS Report RL31724, *Detention of American Citizens as Enemy Combatants*, by Jennifer K. Elsea.

[47] 10 U.S.C. § 948a(9).

[48] *See, e.g., Ex parte* Milligan, 71 U.S. (4 Wall.) 2 (1866); Duncan v. Kahanamoku, 327 U.S. 304 (1945).

[49] 317 U.S. 1 (1942).

[50] *See* Department of Defense (DOD) Fact Sheet, "Combatant Status Review Tribunals," *available at* http://www.defenselink.mil/news/Jul2004/d20040707factsheet.pdf. CSRT proceedings are modeled on the procedures of Army Regulation (AR) 190-8, Enemy Prisoners of War, Retained Personnel, Civilian Internees and Other Detainees (1997), which establishes administrative procedures to determine the status of detainees under the Geneva Conventions and prescribes their treatment in accordance with international law. It does not include a category for "unlawful" or "enemy" combatants, who would presumably be covered by the other categories.

[51] *See* Josh White and Shailagh Murray, *Guantánamo Ruling Renews The Debate Over Detainees*, WASH. POST, June 6, 2007, at A3.

[52] United States v. Khadr, CMCR 07-001 (September 24, 2007), *available online* at http://www.defenselink.mil/news/ Sep2007/KHADR%20Decision%20(24%20Sep%2007)(25%20pages).pdf.

[53] *Id.* at 13.

[54] Gates letter, *supra* footnote 17.

[55] 10 U.S.C. § 950p(c).

[56] 10 U.S.C. § 948d.

[57] Military Commission Instruction (M.C.I.) No. 2, Crimes and Elements for Trials by Military Commission. M.C.I. No. 2 was published in draft form by DOD for outside comment. The final version appears to have incorporated some of the revisions, though not all, suggested by those who offered comments. *See* NATIONAL INSTITUTE OF MILITARY JUSTICE, MILITARY COMMISSION INSTRUCTIONS SOURCEBOOK 95 (2003) [hereinafter "SOURCEBOOK"].

[58] Crimes against the law of war listed in M.C.I. No. 2 were: 1) Willful Killing of Protected Persons; 2) Attacking Civilians; 3) Attacking Civilian Objects; 4) Attacking Protected Property; 5) Pillaging; 6) Denying Quarter; 7) Taking Hostages; 8) Employing Poison or Analogous Weapons; 9) Using Protected Persons as Shields; 10) Using Protected Property as Shields; 11) Torture; 12) Causing Serious Injury; 13) Mutilation or Maiming; 14) Use of Treachery or Perfidy; 15) Improper Use of Flag of Truce; 16) Improper Use of Protective Emblems; 17) Degrading Treatment of a Dead Body; and 18) Rape.

[59] Crimes "triable by military commissions" included 1) Hijacking or Hazarding a Vessel or Aircraft; 2) Terrorism; 3) Murder by an Unprivileged Belligerent; 4) Destruction of Property by an Unprivileged Belligerent; 5) Aiding the Enemy; 6) Spying; 7) Perjury or False Testimony; and 8) Obstruction of Justice Related to Military Commissions. Listed as "other forms of liability and related offenses" are: 1) Aiding or Abetting; 2) Solicitation; 3) Command/Superior Responsibility - Perpetrating; 4) Command/Superior Responsibility - Misprision; 5) Accessory After the Fact; 6) Conspiracy; and 7) Attempt.

[60] *See* M.C.I. No. 2 § 3(A) ("No offense is cognizable in a trial by military commission if that offense did not exist prior to the conduct in question.").

[61] International armed conflicts are governed primarily by the Hague Convention No. IV Respecting the Laws and Customs of War on Land, Oct. 18, 1907, 36 Stat. 2277 ("Hague Convention"), and the Geneva Conventions. Non-international armed conflicts are not covered by the Hague Convention, and are covered only by Common Article 3 of the Geneva Conventions. However, some international criminal tribunals have worked to define war crimes applicable in non-international armed conflicts. For example, Article 3 of the Statute governing the International Criminal Tribunal for the former Yugoslavia (ICTY) includes the following as violations of the laws or customs of war in non-international armed conflict. Such violations shall include, but not be limited to: a) employment of poisonous weapons or other weapons calculated to cause unnecessary suffering; b) wanton destruction of cities, towns or villages, or devastation not justified by military necessity; c)attack, or bombardment, by whatever means, of undefended towns, villages, dwellings, or buildings; d) seizure of, destruction or wilful damage done to institutions dedicated to religion, charity and education, the arts and sciences, historic monuments and works of art and science; e) plunder of public or private property. UN Doc. S/Res/827 (1993), art. 3. The ICTY Statute and procedural rules are available at http://www.un.org/icty/ legaldoc-e/index.htm. The Trial Chamber in the case Prosecutor v. Naletilic and Martinovic, (IT-98-34)March 31, 2003, interpreted Article 3 of the Statute to cover specifically: "(i) violations of the Hague law on international conflicts; (ii) infringements of provisions of the Geneva Conventions other than those classified as grave breaches by those Conventions; (iii) violations of [Common Article 3] and other customary rules on internal conflicts, and (iv) violations of agreements binding upon the parties to the conflict" *Id.* at para. 224. *See also* Prosecutor v. Tadic, (IT-94-1) (Appeals Chamber), Decision on the Defence Motion for Interlocutory Appeal on Jurisdiction, October 2, 1995, para. 86-89. The Appeals Chamber there set forth factors that make an offense a "serious" violation necessary to bring it within the ICTY's jurisdiction: (i) the violation must constitute an infringement of a rule of international humanitarian law; (ii) the rule must be customary in nature or, if it belongs to treaty law, the required conditions must be met ...(iii) the violation must be "serious," that is to say, it must constitute a breach of a rule protecting important values, and the breach must involve grave consequences for the victim....(iv) the violation of the rule must entail, under customary or conventional law, the individual criminal responsibility of the person breaching the rule. *Id.* at para. 94.

[62] Hamdan v. Rumsfeld, 548 U.S. 557, 611 (2006).

[63] M.M.C., *supra* note footnote 9, at IV-11-12. The comment on the crime "intentionally causing serious bodily injury" states that "For the accused to have been acting in violation of the law of war, the accused must have taken acts as a combatant without having met the requirements for lawful combatancy." With respect to the crime "destruction of property in violation of the law of war," the M.M.C. states that "A "violation of the law of war," may be established by proof of the status of the accused as an unlawful combatant or by proof of the character of the property destroyed, or both." *Id.* at IV-13.

[64] Civil War records contain many examples of military commission cases against persons who, although not members of "any lawfully organized or authorized force at war with the United States," participated in the killing of other persons, including soldiers, "contrary to the laws and customs of war." *See, e.g.* Trial of Smith Crim, General Order (G.O.) 151, May 26, 1863 (trial of civilian in Missouri for murder of a U.S. Army officer); Trial of Thomas J. Caldwell and others, G.O. 267, Aug. 3, 1863 (trial of guerrilla for murder of U.S. soldier as well as loyal citizens in Missouri). However, the fact that specifications of the charges often included reference to the defendant being "a citizen of the United States and owing allegiance thereto" or that the act took place "within the lines occupied by the lawfully authorized military force of the United States" suggests that the actual legal basis for the charge was a state of martial law or military occupation rather than the law of war as it applies to belligerents.

[65] The U.S. Civil War was considered to be governed by the rules of international warfare as far as combatant immunity and related concepts were concerned. *See, e.g.,* Trial of T.E. Hogg and others, G.O. 52, HQ, Department of the Pacific, June 27, 1865, *reprinted in* [Series II] 7 WAR OF THE REBELLION: OFFICIAL RECORDS OF THE UNION AND CONFEDERATE ARMIES ("OFFICIAL RECORDS") 674, 677 (1899) ("[C]ivil wars are not distinguishable from other wars as to belligerent and neutral rights ... in such contests the principles of public law in relation to belligerents must govern, and all the rights which a state of war gives to public enemies are to be allowed to the respective parties engaged in them.")(quoting "Stevenson to Palmerston"); General Order No. 1, HQ, Dept. of the Missouri, Jan. 1, 1862, *reprinted in* [Series I] 8 OFFICIAL RECORDS at 476-78. With respect to the current conflict against Al Qaeda, the Supreme Court in *Hamdan* held that Common Article 3 applies, interpreting "conflict not of an international nature" in the definition "in contradistinction to a conflict between nations," which the Geneva Conventions designate a "conflict of international character." 548 U.S. 557, 630 (2006).

[66] *See, e.g.,* Prosecutor v. Pavle Strugar, Case No. It-01-42-A (Appeals Chamber), Judgment, July 17, 2008, para. 172 ("In order to prove cruel treatment as a violation of Common Article 3 ... the Prosecution must prove beyond a reasonable doubt that the victim of the alleged offence was a person taking no active part in the hostilities"); Prosecutor v. Kvocka *et al.*, Case No. IT-98-30/1 (Trial Chamber), November 2, 2001, para. 124: ("An additional requirement for Common Article 3 crimes under Article 3 of the Statute is that the violations must be committed against persons 'taking no active part in the hostilities.'"), *aff'd.* Case No. IT-98-30/1-A (Appeals Chamber), Feb. 28, 2005; Prosecutor v. Jelisic, Case No. IT-95-10 (Trial Chamber), December 14, 1999, para. 34 (Common Article 3 protects "[p]ersons taking no active part in the hostilities" including persons "placed *hors de combat* by sickness, wounds, detention, or any other cause."); Prosecutor v. Blaskic, Case No. IT-95-14 (Trial Chamber), March 3, 2000, para. 180 ("Civilians within the meaning of Article 3 are persons who are not, or no longer, members of the armed forces. Civilian property covers any property that could not be legitimately considered a military objective.").

[67] Prosecutor v. Kvocka *et al.* (The elements of the "murder" offense vary depending on whether it is charged as a violation of the laws and customs of war or a crime against humanity).

[68] *See* KNUT DÖRMANN, ELEMENTS OF WAR CRIMES UNDER THE ROME STATUTE OF THE INTERNATIONAL CRIMINAL COURT 383 (2003) (describing elements common to crimes under article 8(2)(c) of the Rome Statute of the International Criminal Court).

[69] *See id.* at 476 (describing elements of "killing or wounding treacherously a combatant adversary" under article 8(2)(e)(ix) of the Rome Statute).

[70] United States v. Khadr, Ruling on Defense Motion to Dismiss Charge One for Failure to State an Offense and for Lack of Subject Matter Jurisdiction (D-008) (April 21, 2008). Military Commission orders through June 1, 2009, are available from the National Institute of Military Justice, 1 Military Commission Reporter, http://www.nimj.com/ documents/ reporter_june%2019_i.pdf.

[71] United States v. Jawad, Ruling on Defense Motion to Dismiss – Lack of Subject Matter Jurisdiction (D-007) (September 24, 2008) (rejecting prosecution argument that 'murder in violation of the law of war' is identical to the charge of 'murder by an unprivileged belligerent'). Two other judges reached similar conclusions. *See* U.S. Congress, House Committee on the Judiciary, Subcommittee on the Constitution, Civil Rights, and Civil Liberties, *Proposals for Reform of the Military Commissions System*, 111th Cong., 1st sess., June 30, 2006 (prepared testimony of former Guantánamo military defense attorney Maj. David Frakt, USAFR).

[72] *See* CHARLES ROSCOE HOWLAND, A DIGEST OF OPINIONS OF THE JUDGE ADVOCATES GENERAL OF THE ARMY, 1071-72 (1912); *id.* at 1072 & note 1 (noting that 1873 military commission trying Modoc Indians for 'a treacherous killing of an enemy during a truce' charged the offense as "murder in violation of the law of war"); Trial of Henry Wirz, General Court Martial Order (G.C.M.O.) no. 607, Nov. 6, 1865, *reprinted in* [Series II] 8 OFFICIAL RECORDS OF THE UNION AND CONFEDERATE ARMIES 784, 786 (1899) (Confederate officer charged for "murder in violation of the laws and customs of war" for shooting death of prisoner of war); Trial of James W. Duncan, G.C.M.O. 153, June 8, 1866 *reprinted in* [Series II] 8 OFFICIAL RECORDS 926 (1899) (employee "in the rebel military service" charged with "murder in violation of the laws of war" for beating death of prisoner).

[73] *See* cases listed *supra* note 64; Trial of Frank B. Gurley, G.C.M.O. no. 505, Sept. 6, 1865, *reprinted in* [Series II] 8 OFFICIAL RECORDS 741 (Judge Advocate General approved conviction of "citizen" not "lawfully in the services of the so-called Confederate States" for murder of U.S. general officer where accused could not provide proof of Confederate commission). Gurley was, despite his death sentence, exchanged as a prisoner of war, to the consternation of the Judge Advocate General, *see id.* at 742. Military commission trials of persons not in the service of the Confederate government, including those tried for guerrilla activities in during periods of martial law, were later held invalid by civil courts on the basis that civil courts were open when the trials took place. *In re* Murphy, 17 F. Cas. 1030 (1867); District Court v. Commandant of Fort Deleware, 25 F. Cas. 590 (1866); *In re* Egan, 8 F. Cas. 367 (1866); Thompson v. Wharton, 70 Ky. 563 (Ky. 1870). Military detention of such persons without trial was also held to be unlawful. Johnson v. Jones, 44 Ill. 142 (Ill. 1867); Carver v. Jones, 45 Ill. 334 (Ill. 1867).

[74] For military commission trials against Filipinos for cruelty to U.S. soldiers, see U.S. Congress, Senate Committee on the Philippines, *Affairs in the Philippine Islands*, 57th Cong., 1st sess., April 10, 1902, S.Hrg. 57-331, 1340 *et seq.* (Washington: GPO, 1902). Sometimes the

charge was listed as "murdering prisoners in violation of the laws of war" or similar language.

[75] In one case in which an accused was tried for both types of murder, the difference appears to be that simple murder applied to the killing of Filipino scouts and other officials in the employ of the United States (outside of ordinary combat), while the murder of civilians suspected to be spies was "in violation of the laws of war." *Id.* at 1249-50.

[76] *Id.* at 1362 (reprinting G.O. 171, July 13, 1901). It was also noted that the accused had not himself fired a weapon. The judge advocate went on to note that under the circumstances, conspiracy to commit the crime (murder, in violation of the laws of war) would not be warranted, either, but that the accused might have been found guilty of being a "war traitor" to the military government. In another case, a sentence for "murder" of a town official as well as "violations of the laws of war" for attacking a U.S. garrison was disapproved because "[t]he accused was a regularly commissioned officer of the hostile army engaged in a contemplated attack upon the enemy under the orders of his officers." *Id.* at 1231-32 (reprinting G.O., 197, July 27, 1901). That the participants had covered their uniforms and weapons during the operation was excused as a "ruse de guerre," and the killing of the official justified by his resistance to being taken prisoner. *Id.*

[77] 10 U.S.C. § 950v(b)(25)(incorporating the definition found in 18 U.S.C. § 2339A).

[78] United States v. Hamdan, Ruling on Motion to Dismiss (Ex Post Facto) D-012 (July 14, 2008), *available at* http://howappealing.law.com/ HamdanRulingMotions ToDismissExPostFacto. Pdf.

[79] 71 U.S. (4 Wall.) 2 (1866). Lambdin Milligan and others were tried by military commission for conspiracy and "violations of the law of war," among other offenses, for participating in a secret armed organization opposed to the Union's efforts to prevent the secession of southern states and planning to use force in aid of the rebellion. G.O. 27, HQ District of Indiana (May 9, 1865), *reprinted in* [Series II], vol. 8 OFFICIAL RECORDS 543 - 49. The Supreme Court, while not disputing military commission jurisdiction over violations of the "laws and usages of war," stated those laws and usages "... can never be applied to citizens in states which have upheld the authority of the government, and where the courts are open and their process unobstructed." 71 U.S. at 121. By treating the case as one related to the legitimacy of martial law, the Court implicitly rejected the government's position that such activities, when committed by unprivileged belligerents, were amenable to military jurisdiction as violations of the law of war. *Compare id. with Ex parte* Quirin, 317 U.S. 1 (1941) (military commission jurisdiction appropriate for German saboteurs who breached U.S. coastal defenses despite absence of martial law).

[80] *See* cases listed *supra* note 73.

[81] G.O. 4, HQ Dept. of the Missouri (Jan. 16, 1864) 7 (accused was convicted and banished to Iowa on a charge of "harboring and feeding guerrillas"); G.O. 164, HQ, Dept. of the Missouri 8 (Sept. 8, 1864) (conviction of "harboring and feeding guerrillas" as well as "giving aid and comfort to rebel enemies ... "); G.O. 236, HQ, Dept. of the Missouri 8 (Dec. 26, 1864) ("harboring and feeding guerrillas").

[82] U.S. Congress, Senate Committee on the Philippines, *Affairs in the Philippine Islands*, 57th Cong., 1st sess., April 10, 1902, S.Hrg. 57-331 (Washington: GPO, 1902), pp. 1943-1946 (Statement explaining martial law and reprint of proclamation by Gen. Arthur McArthur of Dec. 10, 1900). It appears that the terms "martial law" and the "law of hostile [or belligerent] occupation" were used interchangeably.

[83] U.S. Congress, Senate Committee on Armed Services, *Military Commissions*, 111th Cong., 1st sess., July 7, 2009 (Submitted statement of David Kris, Assistant Attorney

General)("[T]here are serious questions as to whether material support for terrorism or terrorist groups is a traditional violation of the law of war. The President has made clear that military commissions are to be used only to prosecute law of war offenses. Although identifying traditional law of war offenses can be a difficult legal and historical exercise, our experts believe that there is a significant risk that appellate courts will ultimately conclude that material support for terrorism is not a traditional law of war offense, thereby reversing hard-won convictions and leading to questions about the system's legitimacy.")

[84] Mohammed Jawad was originally charged with attempted murder in violation of the law of war and attempt to cause serious bodily injury. Both charges have since been dropped. Charge sheets are available at http://www.defenselink.mil/news/commissions.html.

[85] *See* WINTHROP, *supra* footnote 25, at 773 (the law of war "prescribes the rights and obligations of belligerents, or ... define[s] the status and relations not only of enemies—whether or not in arms—but also of persons under military government or martial law and persons simply resident or being upon the theatre of war, and which authorizes their trial and punishment when offenders"); *id* at 836 (military commissions have valid jurisdiction only in theater of war or territory under martial law or military government).

[86] Some may argue that no war has a specific deadline and that all conflicts are in a sense indefinite. In traditional armed conflicts, however, it has been relatively easy to identify when hostilities have ended; for example, upon the surrender or annihilation of one party, an annexation of territory under dispute, an armistice or peace treaty, or when one party to the conflict unilaterally withdraws its forces. *See* GERHARD VON GLAHN, LAW AMONG NATIONS 722-730 (6th ed. 1992).

[87] *See* Human Rights First, Trial Under Military Order, A Guide to the Final Rules for Military Commissions (revised May 2006)[hereinafter "HRF"], *available at* http://www.humanrightsfirst.org/us_law/PDF/detainees/trials_under_order0604.pdf; *See* Leila Nadya Sadat, *Terrorism and the Rule of Law*, 3 WASH. U. GLOBAL STUD. L. REV. 135, 146 (2004) (noting possibly advantageous domestic aspects of treating terrorist attacks as war crimes, but identifying possible pitfalls of creating a new international legal regime).

[88] 10 U.S.C. § 948d.

[89] 10 U.S.C. § 950p(d).

[90] United States v. Hamdan, Ruling on Motion to Dismiss (Res Judicata) (April 2, 2008).

[91] 10 U.S.C. § 949m.

[92] 10 U.S.C. § 948j.

[93] *See* M.C.O. No. 1 § 3(C) (asserting jurisdiction over participants in commission proceedings "as necessary to preserve the integrity and order of the proceedings").

[94] Rule for Military Commissions (R.M.C.) 809. An updated Manual for Military Commissions has not been released since the eneactment of the 2009 MCA.

[95] *See* 10 U.S.C. § 848. This section is made inapplicable to military commissions in chapter 47a by MCA § 4.

[96] 10 U.S.C. § 949j. P.L. 111-84 § 1807 expresses the sense of Congress that: 1)the fairness and effectiveness of the military commissions system under chapter 47A of title 10, United States Code (as amended by section 1802), will depend to a significant degree on the adequacy of defense counsel and associated resources for individuals accused, particularly in the case of capital cases, under such chapter 47A; and 2)defense counsel in military commission cases, particularly in capital cases, under such chapter 47A of title 10, United States Code (as so amended), should be fully resourced as provided in such chapter 47A.

[97] *Id.*

[98] R.M.C. 703.

[99] *See* 10 U.S.C. § 847. It is unclear how witnesses are "duly subpoenaed" for military commissions established under the UCMJ. 10 U.S.C. § 846 empowers the president of a court-martial to compel witnesses to appear and testify and to compel production of evidence, but this statutory authority does not explicitly apply to military commissions. The subpoena power extends to "any part of the United States, or the Territories, Commonwealth and possessions."

[100] R.M.C. 703; R.C.M. 703.

[101] DAVID SCHLEUTER, MILITARY CRIMINAL JUSTICE: PRACTICE AND PROCEDURE § 11-2(D)(2) (5th ed. 1999); United States v. Bennett, 12 M.J. 463 (C.M.A. 1982).

[102] R.M.C. 611(d).

[103] *Hamdan*, 647-51 (Kennedy, J. concurring).

[104] Gregory S. McNeal, *Beyond Guantánamo, Obstacles and Options*, 103 NW. U. L. REV. COLLOQUY 29, 32 (2008) (blaming "conflicting statutory provisions" for perceived undue influence at military commissions under the MCA).

[105] *See id.* at 34; U.S. Congress, House Committee on the Judiciary, Subcommittee on the Constitution, Civil Rights, and Civil Liberties, *Proposals for Reform of the Military Commissions System*, 111th Cong., 1st Sess., July 30, 2009 (statement of Peter R. Masciola, USAFG, Chief Defense Counsel Office of Military Commissions-Defense Washington, DC), available at http://judiciary.house.gov/hearings /pdf/Masciola090730.pdf.

[106] United States v. Hamdan, Ruling on Motion to Dismiss (Unlawful Influence) (D-026) (May 9, 2008) (Ordering substitute legal advisor be appointed for reviewing the case); United States v. Jawad, Ruling on Motion to Dismiss – Unlawful Influence (D-004) (Aug. 14, 2008) (finding the Legal Advisor's public expression of support for the military commission process and alignment with the prosecution to have "compromised the objectivity necessary to dispassionately and fairly evaluate the evidence and prepare the post-trial recommendation," consequently disqualifying the legal advisor from carrying out post-trial responsibilities in the case); United States v. al Darbi, Ruling on Defense Motion to Dismiss (D-011) (October 2, 2008) (denying as moot request for relief, while noting activities of previous Legal Advisor may have compromised objectivity in necessary to fairly evaluate evidence and prepare post-trial recommendation).

[107] United States v. Khadr, Ruling on Defense Motion to Dismiss (D-076) (Aug. 15, 2008) (denying relief where military judge was replaced after expiration of recall to active duty);

[108] 10 U.S.C. § 950g. Previously, appeals could challenge only whether "the final decision was consistent with the standards and procedures specified" in the MCA, and "to the extent applicable, the Constitution and the laws of the United States."

[109] 10 U.S.C. § 948q.

[110] 10 U.S.C. § 949i.

[111] 10 U.S.C. § 949a(b).

[112] *See* Globe Newspaper Co. v. Super. Ct., 457 U.S. 596, 602 (1982)(newspaper had standing to challenge court order closing portions of criminal trial).

[113] United States v. Hershey, 20 M.J. 433 (C.M.A.1985), *cert. denied*, 474 U.S. 1062 (1986); United States v. Grunden, 2 M.J. 116 (C.M.A.1977). The press has standing to challenge closure of military justice proceedings. ABC, Inc. v. Powell, 47 M.J. 363, 365 (1997).

[114] Pell v. Procunier, 417 U.S. 817, 822-24 (1974).

[115] *See* Juan R. Torruella, *On the Slippery Slopes of Afghanistan: Military Commissions and the Exercise of Presidential Power*, 4 U. PA. J. CONST. L. 648, 718 (2002) (noting that

proceedings held at the Guantánamo Bay Naval Station may be *de facto* closed due to the physical isolation of the facility).

[116] *See* Press-Enterprise Co. v. Superior Court of California, 464 U.S. 501 (1984).

[117] 10 U.S.C. § 949d(d).

[118] *E.g.*, United States v. Hamdan, Protective Order #3 (June 4, 2008).

[119] 10 U.S.C. § 949p-7.

[120] 10 U.S.C. § 839.

[121] That the accused could be excluded from portions of own trial and prevented from learning what evidence was introduced was among the factors that the *Hamdan* Court found most troubling about the military commissions established pursuant to President Bush's M.O. 548 U.S. at 614.

[122] 10 U.S.C. § 949d(d).

[123] United States v. Khadr, Ruling on Defense Motion for Appropriate Relief (D-015) (Feb. 21, 2008).

[124] R.M.C. 804 (discussion).

[125] 10 U.S.C. § 948k.

[126] 10 U.S.C. § 949c(b); R.M.C. 804.

[127] 10 U.S.C. § 949a(b)(2)(D). The military judge can revoke the accused's right to self-representation if the accused fails to conduct his defense within the relevant rules and decorum applicable in military commission trials. Prior to the 2006 MCA, M.C.I. No. 4 required detailed defense counsel to "defend the accused zealously within the bounds of the law ... notwithstanding any intention expressed by the accused to represent himself." M.C.I. No. 4 § 3(C).

[128] M.C.O. No. 1 § 4(C).

[129] 10 U.S.C. § 949c(b)(2).

[130] Regulation for Trial by Military Commissions, Para. 9-2. The accused may request a specific JAG officer from the cadre of officers assigned to the Defense Counsel's Office, but does not have a right to choose. The Rules for Military Commissions, Rule 506 was amended to provide the accused an opportunity to choose military defense counsel from among military counsel assigned to the Office of Military Commissions as defense counsel. Gates letter, *supra* footnote 17.

[131] 10 U.S.C. § 949c(b)(4).

[132] R.M.C. 501.

[133] R.M.C. 506(c).

[134] 10 U.S.C. § 949c(b).

[135] 10 U.S.C. § 949c, R.M.C. 502(d)(3).

[136] Regulation for Trial by Military Commissions, Para. 9-5(c).

[137] Mil. R. Evid. 502.

[138] *See* M.C.O. No. 3, "Special Administrative Measures for Certain Communications Subject to Monitoring." The required affidavit and agreement annexed to M.C.I. No. 3 was modified to eliminate the following language: "I understand that my communications with my client, even if traditionally covered by the attorney-client privilege, may be subject to monitoring or review by government officials, using any available means, for security and intelligence purposes. I understand that any such monitoring will only take place in limited circumstances when approved by proper authority, and that any evidence or information derived from such communications will not be used in proceedings against the Accused who made or received the relevant communication."

[139] M.C.I. No. 5, Annex B § II(J).

[140] Regulation for Trial by Military Commissions, Figure 9.2. Affidavit and Agreement by Civilian Defense Counsel, II(J).

[141] U.S. CONST. Amdt. VI applies in courts-martial. *E.g.* United States v. Scheffer, 523 U.S. 303 (1998).

[142] Maryland v. Craig, 497 U.S. 836, 845 (1990).

[143] The Military Rules of Evidence (Mil. R. Evid.) are contained in the Manual for Courts-Martial (M.C.M.), established as Exec. Order No. 12473, Manual for Courts-Martial, United States, 49 Fed. Reg 17,152, (April 23, 1984), as amended. The M.C.M. also contains the procedural rules for courts-martial, known as the Rules For Courts-Martial (R.C.M.).

[144] Mil. R. Evid. 402.

[145] Mil. R. Evid. 403 (relevant evidence may be excluded "if its probative value is substantially outweighed by the danger of unfair prejudice, confusion of the issues, or misleading the members, or by considerations of undue delay, waste of time, or needless presentation of cumulative evidence").

[146] *See* R.C.M. 701(a)(6).

[147] Mil. R. Evid. 505 provides procedures similar to the Classified Information Protection Act (CIPA) that applies in civilian court.

[148] Hamdan v. Rumsfeld, 548 U.S. 557, 635 (2006)(while accepting that the government "has a compelling interest in denying [the accused] access to certain sensitive information," stating that "at least absent express statutory provision to the contrary, information used to convict a person of a crime must be disclosed to him"). The Court viewed the international law of war to be incorporated by Congress into the UCMJ language authorizing military commissions.

[149] 10 U.S.C. § 949a.

[150] 10 U.S.C. § 949j.

[151] 10 U.S.C. § 846.

[152] 10 U.S.C. § 949p-1(b).

[153] 10 U.S.C. § 949j. The prosecution is obligated to provide, as soon as practicable, information that is known or reasonably should be known to the prosecution or any government officials who participated in the investigation that tends to negate or mitigate the guilt of the accused of an offense charged or to impeach the credibility of a witness whom the government intends to call at trial. As soon as practicable after a finding of guilt, the prosecution is required to disclose any other information that might reasonably be viewed as mitigating factors for sentencing.

[154] 10 U.S.C. §§ 949p-(1-7). Where potential evidence is classified, trial counsel is to work with the original classification authority to declassify the information to the maximum extent possible, but decisions not to declassify are not subject to review by the military judge. 10 U.S.C. § 949p-1(c).

[155] 10 U.S.C. § 949p-4.

[156] 10 U.S.C. § 949p-1(a).

[157] M.C.O. No. 1, § 6 (defining "Protected Information" to include classified or classifiable information, information protected "by law or rule from unauthorized disclosure," information that could endanger trial participants, intelligence and law enforcement sources, methods or activities, or "information concerning other national security interests").

[158] 10 U.S.C. §§ 948a(2) & 949p-1.

[159] 10 U.S.C. § 949p-4(a).

[160] *Id.*

[161] 10 U.S.C. § 949p-4(b).

[162] 10 U.S.C. § 949a(c)(3). Under the military commissions established by the 2006 MCA, evidence was admissible if the commission deemed it to have "probative value to a reasonable person." Previous 10 U.S.C. § 949a(b)(2)(a). This standard was met if "a reasonable person would regard the evidence as making the existence of any fact that is of consequence to a determination of the commission action more probable or less probable than it would be without the evidence." Mil. Comm. R. Evid. 403. At courts-martial, evidence is admitted if it is "relevant," meaning "tending to make the existence of any fact that is of consequence to the determination of the action more probable or less probable than it would be without the evidence." Mil. R. Evid. 401. The elimination of the "probative value to a reasonable person" standard by the 2009 MCA means that the "relevant" standard from the rules of courts martial will likely apply, but because the definition assigned by the Secretary of Defense to "probative value to a reasonable person" under the 2006 MCA was virtually identical to the meaning of "relevant" in the Military Rules of Evidence, and because the right to exclude irrelevant evidence was included in the rules, there will likely be no practical difference. ("Probative" differs from "relevant" in that relevance includes an element of materiality to an issue, where "probative" simply means "tends to prove" a fact, whether or not the fact is material to the case).

[163] 10 U.S.C. § 949a(b)(2)(F). Under the 2006 MCA, this right could be (and was) included in the procedural rules at the discretion of the Secretary of Defense.

[164] Gates letter, *supra* footnote 17.

[165] 10 U.S.C. § 948r(c).

[166] 10 U.S.C. § 948r(d).

[167] Mil. Com. R. Evid. 304(d).

[168] Mil. Com. R. Evid. 304(f).

[169] United States v. Jawad, ruling on Defense Motion to Suppress Out-of-Court Statements of the Accused to Afghan Authorities (D-022) (October 28, 2008).

[170] Mil. R. Evid. 304.

[171] United States v. Jawad, ruling on Defense Motion to Suppress Out-of-Court Statements of the Accused Made While in U.S. Custody (D-021) (November 19, 2008).

[172] "Military officially drops charges against Mohammed Jawad," *McClatchy* , July 31, 2009, online edition.

[173] Mil. R. Evid. 801-807 provide procedures for determining the admissibility of hearsay evidence in courts-martial. It is unclear how, under the MCA, it is to be determined whether certain hearsay evidence would be admissible in a general court-martial.

[174] 10 U.S.C. § 949a(b)(3)).

[175] 10 U.S.C. § 949a(2)(E) (rules that may be prescribed by the Secretary of Defense).

[176] Gates letter, *supra* footnote 17.

[177] Mil. R. Evid. 803 (exceptions for which the availability of the declarant is immaterial); Mil. R. Evid. 804 (exceptions applicable when declarant is unavailable); Mil. R. Evid. 807 (residual exception, which permits all other hearsay not covered by express exceptions when there are "equivalent circumstantial guarantees of trustworthiness" and the military judge determines the statement relates to a material fact, is more probative to that fact than other reasonably obtainable evidence, and that its introduction into evidence "serves the general purposes of the rules and the interest of justice").

[178] Mil. Comm. R. Evid. 803(b)(2).

[179] Mil. Comm. R. Evid. 803(c) (as modified).

[180] Defined in 10 U.S.C. § 948a(4) as "[a]ny information or material that has been determined by the United States Government pursuant to statute, Executive order, or regulation to require

protection against unauthorized disclosure for reasons of national security" and "restricted data, as that term is defined in section 11y of the Atomic Energy Act of 1954 (42 U.S.C. 2014(y))."

[181] 10 U.S.C. § 949d(f)(3).

[182] *Id.*

[183] *Id.*

[184] *Cj* Crane v. Kentucky, 476 U.S. 683 (1986)(evidence about the manner in which a confession was obtained should have been admitted as relevant to its reliability and credibility despite court's determination that the confession was voluntary and need not be suppressed).

[185] *Cf.* Ohio v. Roberts, 448 U.S. 56, 66 (1980)(admissibility of hearsay evidence), *but cf.* Crawford v. Washington, 541 U.S. 36 (2004)("Admitting statements deemed reliable by a judge is fundamentally at odds with the right of confrontation.... [The Confrontation Clause] commands ... that reliability be assessed in a particular manner: by testing in the crucible of cross-examination.").

[186] M.M.C. at III-26.

[187] Mil. Comm. R. Evid. 505(f). Similar procedures are permitted in courts-martial. Mil. R. Evid. 505(j).

[188] Mil. Comm. R. Evid. 505(g). This rule is virtually identical to Mil. R. Evid. 505(h).

[189] Mil. R. Evid. 505.

[190] P.L. 96-456, Oct. 15, 1980, codified at 18 U.S.C. App.

[191] 10 U.S.C. § 948d.

[192] 10 U.S.C. § 949s.

[193] *See* Jess Bravin, *Military Tribunal Brings Knots, Too*, WALL ST. J., March 15, 2010.

[194] The MCA permits the death penalty for convictions of murder of a protected person or murder in violation of the law of war, or spying; and if death results, any of the following crimes: attacking civilians, taking hostages, employing poison or similar weapon, using protected persons as a shield, torture or cruel or inhuman treatment, intentionally causing serious bodily injury, maiming, using treachery or perfidy, hijacking or hazarding a vessel or aircraft, terrorism, and conspiracy to commit any of the crimes enumerated in 10 U.S.C. § 950v.

[195] 10 U.S.C. § 949m.

[196] An accused sentenced to death may neither waive his right to appeal nor withdraw an appeal. 10 U.S.C. § 950c.

[197] 10 U.S.C. § 950i(b)-(c).

[198] 10 U.S.C. § 950i(b).

[199] 10 U.S.C. § 950i(d).

[200] R.M.C. 1001(b)(2). Otherwise, aggravating factors are similar to those listed in R.C.M. 1001(b)(5)(D) for courts-martial.

[201] R.M.C. 1001(c)(2)(D). The trial counsel may rebut the statement. This procedure does not appear to differ substantially from that used in courts-martial.

[202] R.M.C. 1004(c).

[203] M.C.I. No. 9 § 4(C).

[204] 10 U.S.C. § 950f.

[205] 10 U.S.C. § 859; 10 U.S.C. § 950a(a).

[206] 10 U.S.C. § 950g. No collateral attack on the verdict was permitted under the MCA 2006. 10 U.S.C. § 949j(b) previously provided that: Except as otherwise provided in this chapter and notwithstanding any other provision of law (including section 2241 of title 28 or any other habeas corpus provision), no court, justice, or judge shall have jurisdiction to hear or

consider any claim or cause of action whatsoever, including any action pending on or filed after the date of the enactment of the Military Commissions Act of 2006, relating to the prosecution, trial, or judgment of a military commission under this chapter, including challenges to the lawfulness of procedures of military commissions under this chapter.

[207] 10 U.S.C. § 950g.

[208] R.M.C. 1102(b).

[209] R.M.C. 1105.

[210] R.M.C. 1106.

[211] R.M.C. 1107.

[212] R.M.C. 1102A.

[213] R.M.C. 1107(e).

[214] R.M.C. 1107(f)(5).

[215] R.M.C. 1111. Courts-martial findings are first forwarded to the Judge Advocate General of the particular service for legal review, R.C.M. 1112.

[216] R.M.C. 1201.

[217] R.M.C. 1210.

[218] M.C.O. No. 1 § 5(P). The finding was to become final when "the President or, if designated by the President, the Secretary of Defense makes a final decision thereon pursuant to Section 4(c)(8) of the President's Military Order and in accordance with Section 6(H)(6) of [M.C.O. No. 1]." *Id.* § 6(H)(2).

[219] *See* CRS Report RL33688, *The Military Commissions Act of 2006: Analysis of Procedural Rules and Comparison with Previous DOD Rules and the Uniform Code of Military Justice.*

[220] 10 U.S.C. § 949h.

[221] 10 U.S.C. § 950b(d)(2)(B).

[222] R.M.C. 1102(c).

[223] *Id.* At courts-martial, sessions to increase the severity of a sentence are permitted only if the sentence is mandatory. R.C.M. 1102(c).

[224] 10 U.S.C. § 948q.

[225] 10 U.S.C. § 948s.

[226] R.M.C. 307.

[227] *Id.*

[228] RM.C. 602.

[229] *Id.*

[230] M.O. § 7(e).

[231] R.M.C. 907.

[232] *See also* CRS Report R40932, *Comparison of Rights in Military Commission Trials and Trials in Federal Criminal Court*, by Jennifer K. Elsea.

In: The Military Commissions Act...
Editors: J. Segel, Soto Kimura
ISBN: 978-1-61470-072-2

Chapter 2

COMPARISON OF RIGHTS IN MILITARY COMMISSION TRIALS AND TRIALS IN FEDERAL CRIMINAL COURT*

Jennifer K. Elsea

SUMMARY

The Obama Administration's decision to try certain detainees and other terrorist suspects in federal criminal court, including those accused of conspiring to commit the 9/11 terrorist attacks and the man arrested after a failed aircraft bombing on Christmas day, and to try other detainees by military commission, has focused attention on the procedural differences between trials in federal court and those conducted under the Military Commissions Act, as recently amended. Some who are opposed to the decision argue that bringing detainees to the United States for trial poses a security threat and risks disclosing classified information, or could result in the acquittal of persons who are guilty. Others have praised the decision as recognizing the efficacy and fairness of the federal court system and have voiced confidence in the courts' ability to protect national security while achieving justice that will be perceived as such among U.S. allies abroad. Some continue to object to the planned trials of detainees by military commission, despite the amendments Congress enacted as Title XVIII of the National Defense Authorization Act for

* This is an edited, reformatted and augmented version of a Congressional Research Service 7-5700, R40932 publication, dated April 6, 2010.

Fiscal Year 2010, P.L. 111-84, because they say it demonstrates a less than full commitment to justice or that it casts doubt on the strength of the government's case against those detainees. Seven bills have been introduced to prohibit federal trial or to require military commission trials for certain classes of suspected terrorists, or to authorize their detention, H.R. 4111, H.R. 4463, H.R. 4127, H.R. 4738, S. 2977, H.R. 4588, and H.R. 4556. One bill, H.R. 4415, would authorize the President to determine which persons are subject to detention or military commission trial as unlawful enemy combatants. One bill in the Senate, S. 2943, would require the Attorney General to consult with the Director of National Intelligence as well as the Secretaries of Defense and Homeland Security prior to proceeding against a terrorism suspect in the criminal justice system.

This report provides a brief summary of legal issues raised by the choice of forum for trying accused terrorists and a table comparing selected military commissions rules under the Military Commissions Act, as amended, to the corresponding rules that apply in federal court.

INTRODUCTION

The Obama Administration's decision to try certain detainees and other terrorist suspects in federal criminal court, including those accused of conspiring to commit the 9/11 terrorist attacks and a man who tried to bring down a commercial aircraft on Christmas Day, 2009, while continuing to try other detainees by military commission, has focused attention on the procedural differences between trials in federal court and those conducted under the Military Commissions Act, as amended. Some who are opposed to the decision argue that bringing detainees to the United States for trial poses a security threat and risks disclosing classified information, or could more readily result in the acquittal of persons who are guilty. In addition, some have argued that terrorists captured in the United States could better be exploited for intelligence purposes if they are kept out of the criminal justice system. Others have praised the decision as recognizing the efficacy and fairness of the federal court system and have voiced confidence in the courts' ability to protect national security while achieving justice that will be perceived as such, particularly among U.S. allies abroad. They argue that terrorist suspects subjected to criminal trial in federal court have been subject to interrogation for intelligence purposes without undermining the government's ability to win a guilty verdict. Some continue to object to the planned trials of detainees by military commission, despite the amendments Congress enacted as Title XVIII of the National Defense Authorization Act for Fiscal Year 2010 (Military Commissions Act of 2009), P.L. 111-84, because they say it demonstrates a less than full commitment to justice or that it casts doubt on the strength of the government's case against those detainees.

The plan to transfer five "high value detainees" to New York for trial in federal court has been placed on hold due to resistance from Congress and some New York officials. A number of bills have been introduced that would effectively force the Administration to use military commissions to try certain classes of individuals (see below). The Administration opposed an earlier effort to restrict funds for federal trials, arguing that:

> We believe that it would be unwise, and would set a dangerous precedent, for Congress to restrict the discretion of either department to fund particular prosecutions. The exercise of prosecutorial discretion has always been and should remain an Executive Branch function. We must be in a position to use every lawful instrument of national power—including both courts and military commissions—to ensure that terrorists are brought to justice and can no longer threaten American lives.[1]

This report provides a brief summary of legal issues raised by the choice of forum for trying accused terrorists and a table comparing authorities and composition of the federal courts to those of military commissions. A second table compares selected military commissions rules under the Military Commissions Act, as amended by the Military Commissions Act of 2009, to the corresponding rules that apply in federal court. This table follows the same order and format used in CRS Report RL31262, *Selected Procedural Safeguards in Federal, Military, and International Courts*, to facilitate comparison with safeguards provided in international criminal tribunals. For similar charts comparing military commissions as envisioned under the MCA, as passed in 2006, to the rules that had been established by DOD for military commissions and to general military courts-martial conducted under the Uniform Code of Military Justice (UCMJ), see CRS Report RL33688, *The Military Commissions Act of 2006: Analysis of Procedural Rules and Comparison with Previous DOD Rules and the Uniform Code of Military Justice*, by Jennifer K. Elsea. For additional analysis of issues related to the disposition of Guantanamo detainees, including possible trials in federal or military courts, see CRS Report R40139, *Closing the Guantanamo Detention Center: Legal Issues*, by Michael John Garcia et al. For information about legislation with relevance to Guantanamo detainees, see CRS Report R40754,

Guantanamo Detention Center: Legislative Activity in the 111th Congress, by Anna C. Henning.

BACKGROUND

On January 22, 2009, President Barack Obama issued an Executive Order requiring that the Guantanamo detention facility, which continues to house just under 200 aliens detained in connection with post-9/11 military operations, be closed no later than a year from the date of the Order.[2] The Order establishes a task force to review all Guantanamo detentions to assess whether each detainee should continue to be held by the United States, be transferred or released to another country, or be prosecuted by the United States for criminal offenses. Ongoing military commissions were essentially halted during this review period, although some pretrial proceedings have continued to take place. One detainee, Ahmed Ghailani, was transferred in June to the Southern District of New York for trial in federal court on charges related to his alleged role in the 1998 East Africa Embassy bombings.[3]

President Obama's Detention Policy Task Force[4] issued a preliminary report July 20, 2009, reaffirming that the White House considers military commissions to be an appropriate forum for trying some cases involving suspected violations of the laws of the war, although federal criminal court would be the preferred forum for any trials of detainees.[5] The disposition of each case referred for criminal prosecution is to be assigned to a team comprised of DOJ and DOD personnel, including prosecutors from the Office of Military Commissions. The report also provided a set of criteria to govern the disposition of cases involving Guantanamo detainees. In addition to "traditional principles of federal prosecution," the protocol identifies three broad categories of factors to be taken into consideration:

- Strength of interest, namely, the nature and gravity of offenses or underlying conduct; identity of victims; location of offense; location and context in which individual was apprehended; and the conduct of the investigation.
- Efficiency, namely, protection of intelligence source and methods; venue; number of defendants; foreign policy concerns; legal or evidentiary problems; efficiency and resource concerns.

- Other prosecution considerations, namely, the extent to which the forum and offenses that can be tried there permit a full presentation of the wrongful conduct, and the available sentence upon conviction.

On November 13, 2009, Attorney General Holder announced his decision to transfer the five "9/11 conspirators," who include Khalid Sheikh Mohammed, Walid Muhammed Salih Mubarak Bin Attash, Ramzi Bin Al Shibh, Ali Abdul-Aziz Ali, and Mustafa Ahmed Al Hawsawi, to the Southern District of New York to stand trial.[6] Five other detainees are to be tried by military commission. These include Omar Khadr, a Canadian citizen captured as a teenager and charged before a military commission for allegedly throwing a hand grenade that killed a U.S. medic in Afghanistan; Abd al-Rahim al-Nashiri, whose military commission charges related to the October 2000 attack on the USS Cole were previously withdrawn in February; Ahmed Mohammed Ahmed Haza al Darbi, who is accused of participating in an al-Qaeda plot to blow up oil tankers in the Straits of Hormuz, and two other detainees about whom no further information was given.

As the deadline for closing the detention facility at Guantanamo passed unmet, the Obama Administration reportedly completed its assessment, determining that about 50 of the detainees held there will continue to be held without trial, that around 40 detainees will be prosecuted in military commission or federal court, and that the remaining 110 detainees will be released once a suitable country has agreed to take each of them.[7] However, the transfer of 30 detainees of Yemeni nationality was stymied because an al Qaeda affiliate in Yemen is suspected to have been behind the Christmas bombing attempt.[8]

FORUM CHOICE FOR TERROR SUSPECTS

U.S. law provides for the trial of suspected terrorists, including those captured abroad, in several ways. Those who are accused of violating specific federal laws are triable in federal criminal court. Provisions in the U.S. Criminal Code relating to war crimes and terrorist activity apply extraterritorially and may be applicable to some detainees.[9] Those accused of violating the law of war or committing the offenses enumerated in the Military Commissions Act (MCA), as amended by the Military Commissions Act of 2009,[10] may be tried by military commissions under the MCA, or by general court-martial under the UCMJ.[11]

The procedural protections afforded to the accused in each of these forums may differ. The MCA authorizes the establishment of military commissions with jurisdiction to try alien "unprivileged enemy belligerents"[12] for offenses made punishable by the MCA or the law of war. Notwithstanding the recent amendments to the MCA, which generally enhance due process guarantees for the accused, critics continue to question their constitutionality.

One issue that has been raised by proponents of the use of military commissions is the concern that federal criminal courts would endow accused terrorists with constitutional rights they would not otherwise enjoy. The MCA does not restrict military commissions from exercising jurisdiction within the United States, and the Supreme Court has previously upheld the use of military commissions against "enemy belligerents" tried in the United States under procedural rules that differed from the federal rules.[13] The Supreme Court has not settled the question regarding the extent to which constitutional guarantees apply to aliens detained at Guantanamo, making any difference in rights due to location of the trials difficult to predict. Some view the unpredictability of the Supreme Court's acceptance of the military commission procedures as a factor in favor of using civilian trial courts.

Sources of Rights

The Fifth Amendment to the Constitution provides that "no person shall be ... deprived of life, liberty, or property, without due process of law." Due process includes the opportunity to be heard whenever the government places any of these fundamental liberties at stake. The Constitution contains other explicit rights applicable to various stages of a criminal prosecution. Criminal proceedings provide both the opportunity to contest guilt and to challenge the government's conduct that may have violated the rights of the accused. The system of procedural rules used to conduct a criminal hearing, therefore, serves as a safeguard against violations of constitutional rights that take place outside the courtroom, for example, during arrests and interrogations.

The Bill of Rights applies to all citizens of the United States and all aliens within the United States.[14] However, the methods of application of constitutional rights, in particular the remedies available to those whose rights might have been violated, may differ depending on the severity of the punitive measure the government seeks to take and the entity deciding the case. The jurisdiction of various entities to try a person accused of a crime could have a profound effect on the procedural rights of the accused. The type of judicial review available also varies and may be crucial to the outcome.

International law also contains some basic guarantees of human rights, including rights of criminal defendants and prisoners. Treaties to which the United States is a party are expressly made a part of the law of the land by the Supremacy Clause of the Constitution[15] and may be codified through implementing legislation,[16] or in some instances, may be directly enforceable by the judiciary.[17] International law is incorporated into U.S. law,[18] but does not take precedence over statute. The law of war, a subset of international law, applies to cases arising from armed conflicts (i.e., war crimes).[19] It remains unclear how the law of war applies to the current hostilities involving non-state terrorists, and the nature of the rights due to accused terrorist/war criminals may depend in part on their status under the Geneva Conventions. The Supreme Court has ruled that Al Qaeda fighters are entitled at least to the baseline protections applicable under Common Article 3 of the Geneva Conventions,[20] which includes protection from the "passing of sentences and the carrying out of executions without previous judgment pronounced by a regularly constituted court, affording all the judicial guarantees which are recognized as indispensable by civilized peoples."[21]

Federal Court

The federal judiciary is established by Article III of the Constitution and consists of the Supreme Court and "inferior tribunals" established by Congress.[22] It is a separate and co-equal branch of the federal government, independent of the executive and legislative branches, designed to be insulated from the public passions. Its function is not to make law, but rather to interpret law and decide disputes arising under it. Federal criminal law and procedures are enacted by Congress and codified primarily in title 18 of the U.S. Code. The Supreme Court promulgates procedural rules for criminal trials at the federal district courts, subject to Congress's approval. These rules, namely the Federal Rules of Criminal Procedure (Fed. R. Crim. P.) and the Federal Rules of Evidence (Fed. R. Evid.), incorporate procedural rights that the Constitution and various statutes demand. The tables provided at the end of this report cite relevant rules or court decisions, but make no effort to provide an exhaustive list of authorities.

There is historical precedent for using federal courts to try those accused of terrorism or war related offenses, including some that might under some circumstances be characterized as "violations of the law or war." The U.S. Constitution empowers Congress to "define and punish Piracies and Felonies committed on the high Seas, and Offences against the Law of Nations."[23] The First Congress provided for the punishment of persons who committed murder or robbery or the like on the high seas, declaring that each offender was to be "taken and adjudged to be a pirate and felon and being thereof convicted," would be sentenced to death.[24] In 1798, Attorney General Charles Lee advised Secretary of State Timothy Pickering that federal courts were fully competent to try and punish pirates, whether U.S. citizens or aliens.[25] Federal courts exercised jurisdiction in many such cases.[26]

More recently, several high-profile prosecutions involving terrorism abroad have resulted in federal convictions. The 1985 hijacking of the *Achille Lauro* by Palestinian Liberation Organization (PLO) terrorists resulted in the federal conviction of a Lebanese suspect on charges of aircraft piracy and hostage-taking, notwithstanding the defendant's claim to have been merely following military orders.[27] Federal courts also handled prosecutions related to the 1993 bombing of the World Trade Center in New York City, the 2000 bombing of the U.S.S. Cole in the Gulf of Aden, and the 1998 U.S. Embassy bombings in Africa.

The Department of Justice has compiled a list of terrorism trials conducted since 2001,[28] and reports a total of 403 unsealed convictions from September 11, 2001 to March 18, 2010.[29] Around 60% of these convictions are charged under criminal code provisions that are not facially terrorism offenses, including such offenses as fraud, immigration violations, firearms offenses, drug-related offenses, false statements, perjury, obstruction of justice, and general conspiracy charges under 18 U.S.C. § 371, some of which may not have law-of-war analogs that would permit their trial by military commissions.[30] The remaining 40 % are what the Justice Department labels "Category I Offenses" for the purposes of its report, which covers crimes that are directly related to international terrorism. These crimes include

- Aircraft Sabotage (18 U.S.C. § 32)
- Animal Enterprise Terrorism (18 U.S.C. § 43)
- Crimes Against Internationally Protected Persons (18 U.S.C. §§ 112, 878, 1116, 1201(a)(4))
- Use of Biological, Nuclear, Chemical or Other Weapons of Mass Destruction (18 U.S.C. §§ 175, 175b, 229, 831, 2332a)
- Production, Transfer, or Possession of Variola Virus (Smallpox) (18 U.S.C. § 175c)

- Participation in Nuclear and WMD Threats to the United States (18 U.S.C. § 832)
- Conspiracy Within the United States to Murder, Kidnap, or Maim Persons or to Damage Certain Property Overseas (18 U.S.C. § 956)
- Hostage Taking (18 U.S.C. § 1203)
- Terrorist Attacks Against Mass Transportation Systems (18 U.S.C. § 1993)
- Terrorist Acts Abroad Against United States Nationals (18 U.S.C. § 2332)
- Terrorism Transcending National Boundaries (18 U.S.C. § 2332b)
- Bombings of Places of Public Use, Government Facilities, Public Transportation Systems and Infrastructure Facilities (18 U.S.C. § 2332f)
- Missile Systems designed to Destroy Aircraft (18 U.S.C. § 2332g)
- Production, Transfer, or Possession of Radiological Dispersal Devices (18 U.S.C. § 2332h)
- Harboring Terrorists (18 U.S.C. § 2339)
- Providing Material Support to Terrorists (18 U.S.C. § 2339A)
- Providing Material Support to Designated Terrorist Organizations (18 U.S.C. § 2339B)
- Prohibition Against Financing of Terrorism (18 U.S.C. § 2339C)
- Receiving Military-Type Training from an FTO (18 U.S.C. § 2339D)
- Narco-Terrorism (21 U.S.C. § 1010A)
- Sabotage of Nuclear Facilities or Fuel (42 U.S.C. § 2284)
- Aircraft Piracy (49 U.S.C. § 46502)
- Violations of IEEPA (50 U.S.C. § 1705(b)) involving E.O. 12947 (Terrorists Who Threaten to Disrupt the Middle East Peace Process); E.O. 13224 (Blocking Property and Prohibiting Transactions With Persons Who Commit, Threaten to Commit, or Support Terrorism or Global Terrorism List); and E.O. 13129 (Blocking Property and Prohibiting Transactions With the Taliban)[31]

Military Commissions

The Constitution empowers Congress to declare war and "make rules concerning captures on land and water,"[32] to define and punish violations of the "Law of Nations,"[33] and to make regulations to govern the armed forces.[34]

The power of the President to convene military commissions flows from his authority as Commander in Chief of the Armed Forces[35] and his responsibility to execute the laws of the nation.[36] Under the Articles of War and subsequent statute,[37] the President has at least implicit authority to convene military commissions to try offenses against the law of war.[38] The authority and objectives underlying military courts-martial and military commissions are not coextensive.[39] Rather than serving the internally directed purpose of maintaining discipline and order of the troops, the military commission is externally directed at the enemy as a means of waging successful war by punishing and deterring offenses against the law of war. Military commissions have historically been used in connection with military government in cases of occupation or martial law where ordinary civil government was impaired.

Jurisdiction of military commissions is limited to time of war and to trying offenses recognized under the law of war or as designated by statute.[40] While case law suggests that military commissions could try U.S. citizens as enemy belligerents,[41] the Military Commissions Act permits only aliens to be tried. The United States first used military commissions to try enemy belligerents accused of war crimes during the occupation in Mexico in 1847, and made heavy use of them in the Civil War and in the Philippine Insurrection.[42] However, prior to President Bush's Military Order of 2001 establishing military commissions for certain alien terrorism suspects, no military commissions had been convened since the aftermath of World War II. As non-Article III courts, military commissions have not been subject to the same constitutional requirements that are applied in Article III courts.[43] The Military Commissions Act authorizes the Secretary of Defense to establish regulations for military commissions in accordance with its provisions.

PROPOSED LEGISLATION IN THE 111TH CONGRESS

Six bills have been introduced to require military commission trials for certain classes of suspected terrorists or prohibit their prosecution in federal court. H.R. 4463, the "Military Tribunals for Terrorists Act of 2010," would require that any foreign national who "has engaged in conduct constituting an offense relating to a terrorist attack" against persons or property in the United States or against U.S. personnel or property abroad and who is subject to jurisdiction under the MCA be tried by military commission. H.R. 4127 would make military commissions the mandatory forum for trying all persons subject to jurisdiction under the MCA by amending 10 U.S.C. § 948c to require that alien unprivileged enemy belligerents who are "subject to trial for any alleged conduct for which a term of incarceration or the death penalty may be sought or obtained" may only be tried by such commissions. H.R. 4588, the "Detainee Trials at Gitmo Act" would mandate that those presently detained at Guantanamo Bay be tried there by military commission, if at all, and would keep the detention facility open indefinitely. H.R. 4111 would prohibit the Department of Justice from prosecuting any "unprivileged enemy combatant"[44] for any offense, apparently regardless of where such persons are tried. H.R. 4556 and S. 2977 would prohibit the use of any funds by the Department of Justice to prosecute those accused of conspiracy connected with the September 11 attacks in an article III court. H.R. 4738 would prohibit federal trials of those individuals at any DOD owned or controlled facility within the United States, its territories or possessions.

Another bill, H.R. 4415, the "Terrorist Detention and Prosecution Act of 2010" does not address where suspected terrorists are to be prosecuted, but would amend the MCA to add a new category of unlawful enemy combatant (reversing the change in terminology to "alien unprivileged enemy belligerent" introduced by the 2009 amendment to the MCA, 10 U.S.C. § 948a(7)) and providing the President express authority to detain "for military purposes" all categories of unlawful enemy combatants (including U.S. citizens) until he determines they no longer pose a threat to the United States or its allies. The new category would consist of anyone the President determines

(i) is closely associated with or has provided material support to al Qaeda or any other organization dedicated to committing acts of terrorism against the United States;
(ii) has taken up or conspired to take up arms on behalf of al Qaeda; and
(iii) has committed or conspired to commit acts of terrorism in the United States or against American citizens or targets, regardless of the location of the individual's capture.

S. 2943 would require the Attorney General to consult with the Director of National Intelligence as well as the Secretaries of Defense and Homeland Security and the Director of the National Counterterrorism Center prior to proceeding against a terrorism suspect in the criminal justice system, including by conducting a custodial interrogation. The Attorney General would have the authority to proceed over the objection of any of these officials only with the President's express approval.

Comparison of Authorities and Procedural Rights

The following tables provide a comparison of the military commissions under the revised Military Commissions Act and standard procedures for federal criminal court under the Federal Rules of Criminal Procedure and the Federal Rules of Evidence. *Chart 1* compares the legal authorities for establishing both types of tribunals, the jurisdiction over persons and offenses, and the structures of the tribunals. *Chart 2,* which compares procedural safeguards incorporated in the MCA to those applicable in federal criminal cases, follows the same order and format used in CRS Report RL31262, *Selected Procedural Safeguards in Federal, Military, and International Courts*, *Selected Procedural Safeguards in Federal, Military, and International Courts*, by Jennifer K. Elsea, in order to facilitate comparison of the those tribunals to safeguards provided in the international military tribunals that tried World War II crimes at Nuremberg and Tokyo, and contemporary ad hoc tribunals set up by the UN Security Council to try crimes associated with hostilities in the former Yugoslavia and Rwanda. For a comparison with previous rules established under President George W. Bush's Military Order, refer to CRS Report RL33688, *The Military Commissions Act of 2006: Analysis of Procedural Rules and Comparison with Previous DOD Rules and the Uniform Code of Military Justice*.

Chart 1. Comparison of Rules

Authority

Federal Criminal Court	Military Commissions Act of 2009
U.S. Constitution, Article III, establishing the Judiciary; Article 1, § 8.	U.S. Constitution, Article I, § 8, in particular, cl. 10, "To define and punish Piracies and Felonies committed on the high Seas, and Offences against the Law of Nations;" cl. 11, "To declare War, grant Letters of Marque and Reprisal, and make Rules concerning Captures on Land and Water"; and cl. 14 (Necessary and Proper Clause).

Procedure

Federal Criminal Court	Military Commissions Act of 2009
Most criminal offenses are defined and criminal procedure established in Title 18, U.S. Code. The Federal Rules of Criminal Procedure (Fed. R. Crim. P.) are set forth as an appendix to Title 18.	The Secretary of Defense may prescribe rules of procedure for military commissions. Such rules may not be inconsistent with the MCA (as amended). Procedural rules for general courts-martial are to apply unless the MCA or UCMJ provide otherwise. Consultation with the Attorney General is required only in cases of exceptions, which are permissible "as may be required by the unique circumstances of the conduct of military and intelligence operations during hostilities or by other practical need." 10 U.S.C. § 949a .

Jurisdiction over Persons

Federal Criminal Court	Military Commissions Act of 2009
Varies depending on criminal statute. Generally applies to U.S. nationals and aliens within the United States or within the Special Territorial and Maritime Jurisdiction of the United States (SMTJ) as defined in 18 U.S.C § 7. Aliens are covered under some, but not all, definitions of the SMTJ. In particular, the areas outside the territories of the United States apply to aliens only if a U.S. national is a perpetrator or victim of the offense. Statutes may apply to extraterritorial conduct of U.S. nationals, or more rarely, certain aliens.	Alien unprivileged enemy belligerents are subject to trial by military commission. 10 U.S.C. § 948c. The term "unprivileged enemy belligerent" is defined to mean "an individual (other than a privileged belligerent) who has engaged in hostilities against the United States or its coalition partners; or has purposefully and materially supported hostilities against the United States or its coalition partners...." or an individual who was a member of Al Qaeda at the time the offense occurred.
	"Privileged belligerent" is defined in terms of the Geneva Convention Relative to the Treatment of Prisoners of War (GPW) Art. 4. 10 U.S.C. § 948a(6-7).

Jurisdiction over Offenses

Federal Criminal Court	Military Commissions Act of 2009
Offenses described by statute, typically defined in Title 18, U.S. Code.	A military commission has jurisdiction to try any offense made punishable by the MCA or the law of war when committed by an alien unlawful enemy combatant that occurred "in the context of and associated with hostilities," whether before, on, or after September 11, 2001. Military commissions are expressly authorized to determine their own jurisdiction. 10 U.S.C. § 948. Offenses listed in 10 U.S.C. § 950t include the following: murder of protected persons; attacking civilians, civilian objects, or protected property; pillaging; denying quarter; taking hostages; employing poison or similar weapons; using protected persons or property as shields; torture, cruel or inhuman treatment; intentionally causing serious bodily injury; mutilating or maiming; murder in violation of the law of war; destruction of property in violation of the law of war; using treachery or perfidy; improperly using a flag of truce or distinctive emblem; intentionally mistreating a dead body; rape; sexual assault or abuse; hijacking or hazarding a vessel or aircraft; terrorism; providing material support for terrorism; wrongfully aiding the enemy; spying, contempt; perjury and obstruction of justice. Conspiracy, attempts, and solicitation to commit the defined acts are also punishable. 10 U.S.C. § 950t.

Composition

Federal Criminal Court	Military Commissions Act of 2009
A federal judge and twelve jurors, unless a jury trial is waived by the defendant. Fed. R. Crim. P. 23.	A military judge and at least five members, 10 U.S.C. § 948m; unless the death penalty is sought, in which case no fewer than 12 members must be included. 10 U.S.C. § 949m(c). In death penalty cases where twelve members are not reasonably available because of physical conditions or military exigencies, the convening authority may approve a commission with as few as 9 members. 10 U.S.C. § 949m

CHART 2. COMPARISON OF PROCEDURAL SAFEGUARDS

Presumption of Innocence

U.S. Constitution	Federal Criminal Court	Military Commissions Act of 2009
"The principle that there is a presumption of innocence in favor of the accused is the undoubted law, axiomatic and elementary, and its enforcement lies at the foundation of the administration of our criminal law." Coffin v. United States, 156 U.S. 432, 453 (1895).	If the defendant fails to enter a proper plea, a plea of not guilty will be entered. Fed. R. Crim. P. 11(a). Defendant is entitled to jury instructions explaining that guilt must be proved on the evidence beyond a reasonable doubt. Taylor v. Kentucky, 436 U.S. 478 (1978). Defendant is entitled to appear in court without unnecessary physical restraints or other indicia of guilt, such as appearing in prison uniform, that may be prejudicial to jury. See Holbrook v. Flynn, 475 U.S. 560 (1986).	Before a vote is taken on the findings, the military judge must instruct the commission members "that the accused must be presumed to be innocent until his guilt is established by legal and competent evidence beyond reasonable doubt." 10 U.S.C. § 949l. If an accused refuses to enter a plea or pleads guilty but provides inconsistent testimony, or if it appears that he lacks proper understanding of the meaning and effect of the guilty plea, the commission must treat the plea as denying guilt. 10 U.S.C. § 949i.

Right to Remain Silent (Freedom from Coerced Statements)

U.S. Constitution	Federal Criminal Court	Military Commissions Act of 2009
"No person ... shall be compelled in any criminal case to be a witness against himself ...." Amendment V.	Incriminating statements made by defendant under duress or without prior Miranda warning are inadmissible as evidence of guilt in a criminal trial. Miranda v. Arizona, 384 U.S. 436 (1966). Before a jury is allowed to hear evidence of a defendant's confession, the court must determine that it was voluntarily given. 18 U.S.C. § 3501.	Sections a, b, and d of Article 31, UCMJ, is expressly made inapplicable to military commission trials under the MCA, as amended. These provide that no person subject to the UCMJ may compel any person to incriminate himself or interrogate an accused without first informing him of his right to remain silent, and that statements obtained in violation of the above or through other unlawful inducement may not be received in evidence against him in a trial by court-martial. 10 U.S.C. § 948b(d). Confessions allegedly elicited through
		coercion or compulsory self-incrimination that are otherwise admissible are not to be excluded at trial unless their admission violates section 948r. 10 U.S.C. § 949a(b)(2)(C). Statements elicited through torture or cruel, inhuman, or degrading treatment prohibited by 42 U.S.C. § 2000dd are inadmissible except against a person accused of torture or such treatment, regardless of whether the statement was made prior to the enactment of that provision. No statement of the accused is admissible at trial unless the military judge finds that the statement is reliable and Not provided. The Secretary of Defense may provide that "evidence seized outside the United States shall not be excluded from trial by military commission on the grounds that the evidence was not seized pursuant to a search warrant or other authorization." 10 U.S.C. § 949a.sufficiently probative; and that the statement was made "incident to lawful conduct during military operations at the point of capture or

U.S. Constitution	Federal Criminal Court	Military Commissions Act of 2009
		during closely related active combat engagement" and the interests of justice would best be served by admission of the statement into evidence; or that the statement was voluntarily given, taking into consideration all relevant circumstances, including military and intelligence operations during hostilities; the accused's age, education level, military training; and the change in place or identity of interrogator between that statement and any prior questioning of the accused. 10 U.S.C. § 948r. Evidence derived from impermissible interrogation methods is not barred.

Freedom from Unreasonable Searches and Seizures

U.S. Constitution	Federal Criminal Court	Military Commissions Act of 2009
"The right of the people to be secure ... against unreasonable searches and seizures, shall not be violated; and no Warrants shall issue, but upon probable cause..." Amendment IV.	Evidence, including derivative evidence, gained through unreasonable searches and seizures may be excluded in court. Boyd v. United States, 116 U.S. 616 (1886); Nardone v. United States, 308 U.S. 338 (1938); Fed. R. Crim. P. 41. A search warrant issued by a magistrate on a showing of probable cause is generally required for law enforcement agents to conduct a search of an area where the subject has a reasonable expectation of privacy, including searches and seizures of telephone or other communications and emissions of heat and other phenomena detectable with means other than human senses. Katz v. United States, 389 U.S. 347 (1967). Evidence resulting from overseas searches of American property by foreign officials is admissible unless foreign police conduct shocks judicial conscience or participation by U.S. agents is so substantial as to render the action that of the United States. United States v. Barona, 56 F.3d 1087 (9th Cir. 1995). Searches of alien property overseas are not necessarily protected by the Fourth	Not provided. The Secretary of Defense may provide that "evidence seized outside the United States shall not be excluded from trial by military commission on the grounds that the evidence was not seized pursuant to a search warrant or other authorization.

U.S. Constitution	Federal Criminal Court	Military Commissions Act of 2009
	Amendment. United States v. Verdugo-Urquidez, 494 U.S. 259 (1990). The Fourth Amendment's warrant requirement does not govern searches conducted abroad by United States agents. In the Terrorist Bombings of U.S. Embassies in East Africa, 552 F.3d 157 (2d. Cir. 2008).	

Effective Assistance of Counsel

U.S. Constitution	Federal Criminal Court	Military Commissions Act of 2009
"In all criminal prosecutions, the accused shall enjoy the right ... to have the Assistance of Counsel for his defence." Amendment VI.	Defendants in criminal cases have the right to representation by an attorney at all stages of prosecution. The defendant may hire an attorney or, if indigent, have counsel appointed at the government's expense. If two or more codefendants are represented by one attorney, the court must inquire as to whether a conflict of interest exists. Fed. R. Crim. P. 44. Conversations between attorneys and clients are privileged. Fed. R. Evid. 501. Procedures for ensuring adequate representation of defendants are outlined at 18 U.S.C. §§ 3005 (capital cases) and 3006A.	At least one qualifying military defense counsel is to be detailed "as soon as practicable." 10 U.S.C. § 948k. The accused is entitled to select one "reasonably available" military counsel to represent him. The accused is not entitled to have more than one military counsel, but "associate defense counsel" may be authorized pursuant to regulations. 10 U.S.C. §§ 948c, 948k. The accused may also hire a civilian attorney who 1) is a U.S. citizen, 2) is admitted to the bar in any state, district, or possession, 3) has never been disciplined, 4) has a SECRET clearance (or higher, if necessary for a particular case), and 5) agrees to comply with all applicable rules. 10 U.S.C. § 949c(b)(3). If civilian counsel is hired, the detailed military counsel serves as associate counsel. 10 U.S.C. § 949c(b)(5). No attorney-client privilege is mentioned.

U.S. Constitution	Federal Criminal Court	Military Commissions Act of 2009
		Adverse personnel actions may not be taken against defense attorneys because of the "zeal with which such officer, in acting as counsel, represented any accused before a military commission...." 10 U.S.C. § 949b. In capital cases, the accused is entitled to be represented, "to the greatest extent practicable, by at least one additional counsel who is learned in applicable law," who may be a civilian. 10 U.S.C. § 949a.

Right to Indictment and Presentment

U.S. Constitution	Federal Criminal Court	Military Commissions Act of 2009
"No person shall be held to answer for a capital, or otherwise infamous crime, unless on a presentment or indictment of a Grand Jury, except in cases arising in the land or naval forces, or in the Militia, when in actual service in time of War or public danger ...." Amendment V.	Where the accused is in danger of being subjected to an infamous punishment if convicted, he has the right to insist that he shall not be tried except on the accusation of a grand jury. Ex parte Wilson, 114 U.S. 417 (1885); Fed. R. Crim. P. 7. Jurors must be selected from a fair cross section of the community; otherwise, an accused can challenge the indictment. 28 U.S.C. §§ 1861 et seq. Once an indictment is given, its scope may not be increased. Ex parte Bain, 121 U.S. 1 (1887). (Amendments to an indictment must undergo further grand jury process.)	UCMJ Article 32, which provides for impartial pretrial hearings prior to referral of a matter to general court-martial, is expressly made inapplicable. 10 U.S.C. § 948b(d)(1)(C). Charges and specifications against an accused are to be signed by a person subject to UCMJ swearing under oath that the signer has "personal knowledge of, or reason to believe, the matters set forth therein," and that they are "true in fact to the best of his knowledge and belief." The accused is to be informed of the charges and specifications against him as soon as practicable after charges are sworn. 10 U.S.C. § 948q.

Right to Written Statement of Charges

U.S. Constitution	Federal Criminal Court	Military Commissions Act of 2009
"In all criminal prosecutions, the accused shall enjoy the right ... to be informed of the nature and cause of the accusation; ..." Amendment VI.	Defendant is entitled to be informed of the nature of the charge with sufficiently reasonable certainty to allow for preparation of defense. Cook v. United States, 138 U.S. 157 (1891).	The trial counsel assigned is responsible for serving counsel a copy of the charges upon then accused, in English and, if appropriate, in another language that the accused understands, "sufficiently in advance of trial to prepare a defense." 10 U.S.C. § 948s.

Right to Be Present at Trial

U.S. Constitution	Federal Criminal Court	Military Commissions Act of 2009
The Confrontation Clause of Amendment VI guarantees the accused's right to be present in the courtroom at every stage of his trial. Illinois v. Allen, 397 U.S. 337 (1970).	The language, history, and logic of Rule 43 support a straightforward interpretation that prohibits the trial in absentia of a defendant who is not present at the beginning of trial. Crosby v. United States, 506 U.S. 255, 262 (1993); Fed. R. Crim. P. 43. When defendant knowingly absents himself from court during trial, court may "proceed with trial in like manner and with like effect as if he were present." Diaz v. United States, 223 U.S. 442, 455 (1912).	The accused has the right to be present at all sessions of the military commission except deliberation or voting, unless exclusion of the accused is permitted under § 949d. 10 U.S.C. § 949a(b)(1)(B). The accused may be excluded from attending portions of the proceeding if the military judge determines that the accused persists in disruptive or dangerous conduct. 10 U.S.C. § 949d(e).

Prohibition against Ex Post Facto Crimes

U.S. Constitution	Federal Criminal Court	Military Commissions Act of 2009
No ... ex post facto law shall be passed." Art. I, § 9, cl. 3.	Congress may not pass a law punishing conduct that was not a crime when perpetrated, increasing the possible sentence for a crime, or reducing the government's evidentiary burden. Calder v. Bull, 3 Dall. (3 U.S.) 386 (1798); Ex Parte Garland, 4 Wall (71 U.S.) 1867.	The MCA expressly provides jurisdiction over the defined crimes, whether committed prior to, on or after September 11, 2001. 10 U.S.C. § 948d. The act declares that, because it codifies offenses that "have traditionally been triable under the law of war or otherwise triable by military commission," the subchapter defining offenses "does not preclude trial for offenses that occurred before the date of the enactment of this subchapter, as so amended." 10 U.S.C. § 950p. Crimes punishable by military commissions under the new chapter are contained in subchapter VII.
		It includes the crime of conspiracy, which a plurality of the Supreme Court in Hamdan v. Rumsfeld viewed as invalid as a charge of war crimes. 548 U.S. 557 (2006).

Protection against Double Jeopardy

U.S. Constitution	Federal Criminal Court	Military Commissions Act of 2009
"... nor shall any person be subject for the same offence to be twice put in jeopardy of life or limb; ..." Amendment V. Subject to "dual sovereign" doctrine, that is, federal and state courts may prosecute an individual for the same conduct without violating the clause.	Jeopardy attaches once the jury is sworn or where there is no jury, when the first evidence is presented. If the trial is terminated after jeopardy has attached, a second trial may be barred in a court under the same sovereign, particularly where it is prosecutorial conduct that brings about the termination of the trial. Illinois v. Somerville, 410 U.S. 458 (1973).	"No person may, without his consent, be tried by a military commission [under the MCA] a second time for the same offense." Jeopardy attaches when a guilty finding becomes final after review of the case has been completed. 10 U.S.C. § 949h. The United States may not appeal an order or ruling that amounts to a finding of not guilty. 10 U.S.C. § 950d(b). The convening authority may not revise findings or order a rehearing in any case to reconsider a finding of not guilty of any specification or a ruling which amounts to a finding of not guilty, or reconsider a finding of not guilty of any charge, unless there has been a finding of guilty under a specification
		laid under that charge, which sufficiently alleges a violation. The convening authority may not increase the severity of the sentence unless the sentence prescribed for the offense is mandatory. 10 U.S.C. § 950b(d).

Speedy and Public Trial

U.S. Constitution	Federal Criminal Court	Military Commissions Act of 2009
"In all criminal prosecutions, the accused shall enjoy the right to a speedy and public trial, ..." Amendment VI.	Defendant is entitled to jury instructions clarifying that the prosecution has the burden of presenting evidence sufficient to prove guilt beyond a reasonable doubt. Cool v. United States, 409 U.S. 100 (1978). Jury verdicts must be unanimous. Fed. R. Crim. P. 31.	Commission members are to be instructed that the accused is presumed to be innocent until his "guilt is established by legal and competent evidence beyond reasonable doubt"; that any reasonable doubt as to the guilt of the accused must result in acquittal; that reasonable doubt as to the degree of guilt must be resolved in favor of the lower degree as to which there is no reasonable doubt; and that the burden of proof is on the government. 10 U.S.C. § 949l. Two-thirds of the members must concur on a finding of guilty, except in capital cases (which must be unanimous) and cases involving confinement for more than ten years. 10 U.S.C. § 949m. The Secretary of Defense must prescribe that the military judge is to exclude any evidence, the probative value of which is substantially outweighed by the danger of unfair prejudice, confusion of the issues, or misleading the members of the commission, or by considerations of undue delay, waste of time, or needless presentation of cumulative evidence.

Privilege against Self-Incrimination (Freedom from Compelled Testimony)

U.S. Constitution	Federal Criminal Court	Military Commissions Act of 2009
"No person ... shall be compelled in any criminal case to be a witness against himself..." Amendment V.	Defendant may not be compelled to testify. Jury may not be instructed that guilt may be inferred from the defendant's refusal to testify. Griffin v. California, 380 U.S. 609 (1965). Witnesses may not be compelled to give testimony that may be incriminating unless given immunity for that testimony. 18 U.S.C. § 6002.	"No person shall be required to testify against himself or herself at a proceeding of a military commission under this chapter." 10 U.S.C. § 948r. No person subject to the UCMJ may compel any person to make a statement or produce evidence before any military tribunal if the statement or evidence is not material to the issue and may tend to degrade him. 10 U.S.C. § 831(c).

U.S. Constitution	Federal Criminal Court	Military Commissions Act of 2009
		Adverse inferences drawn from a failure to testify are not expressly prohibited; however, members are to be instructed that "the accused must be presumed to be innocent until his guilt is established by legal and competent evidence." 10 U.S.C. § 949l. There does not appear to be a provision for immunity of witnesses, although 18 U.S.C. § 6002 may apply to military commissions.

Right to Examine or Have Examined Adverse Witnesses (Hearsay Prohibition, Classified Information)

U.S. Constitution	Federal Criminal Court	Military Commissions Act of 2009
"In all criminal prosecutions, the accused shall enjoy the right ... to be confronted with the witnesses against him; ...." Amendment VI.	Rules of Evidence prohibit generally the introduction at trial of statements made out of court to prove the truth of the matter stated unless the declarant is unavailable for cross-examination at trial (hearsay rule). Fed. R. Evid. 801 et seq. The government is required to disclose to defendant any relevant evidence in its possession or that may become known through due diligence. Fed. R. Crim. P. 16. The use of classified information is governed by the Classified Information Procedures Act (CIPA, codified at 18 U.S.C. App. 3). CIPA recognizes the	"Defense counsel may cross-examine each witness for the prosecution who testifies before a military commission under this chapter." 10 U.S.C. § 949c. The Secretary of Defense is permitted to provide that hearsay evidence that would not be admissible at a general court-martial is admissible if adequate notice is given and the military judge determines that the statement is reliable and is offered as evidence of a material fact, that direct testimony from the witness is not available or would have an adverse impact on military or intelligence operations,

U.S. Constitution	Federal Criminal Court	Military Commissions Act of 2009
	government's entitlement to prevent the disclosure of classified information, even where it is material to the defense. However, in such cases the court is empowered to dismiss the indictment against the defendant or impose other sanctions as may be appropriate. The United States may ask the court to permit the substitution of a statement admitting relevant facts that the specific classified information would tend to prove or of a summary of the specific classified information. The court is required to grant the government's motion if it finds that the statement or summary will provide the defendant with substantially the same ability to make his defense as would disclosure of the specific classified information.	and that the general purposes of the rules of evidence and the interests of justice will best be served by admission of the statement into evidence. In determining reliability , the military judge may be obligated to consider the degree to which the statement is corroborated, the indicia of reliability within the statement itself, and whether the will of the declarant was overborne, 10 U.S.C. § 949a(b)(3)(D) The burden of persuasion to demonstrate unreliability or lack of probative value appears to be on the profferer of the evidence. (Language providing otherwise was repealed). The protection of classified information is governed by a new subchapter V, 10 U.S.C. §§ 949p-1 – 949p-7. Subchapter V provides that the government cannot be compelled to disclose classified information to anyone not to sentencing authorized to receive it. If the government claims a privilege, the military judge may not authorize the discovery of or access to the classified information unless he determines the evidence is noncumulative, relevant,

U.S. Constitution	Federal Criminal Court	Military Commissions Act of 2009
		and helpful to a legally cognizable defense, rebuttal of the prosecution's case, or to sentencing. If the military judge determines disclosure or access is necessary, the military judge must grant the government's request to delete or withhold specified items of classified information; to substitute a summary for classified information; or to substitute a statement admitting relevant facts that the classified information or material would tend to prove, so long as the alternative procedure would provide the accused with substantially the same ability to make a defense. If the prosecution makes a motion for protective measures in camera, the accused has no opportunity to request a reconsideration.

Right to Compulsory Process to Obtain Witnesses (Discovery)

U.S. Constitution	Federal Criminal Court	Military Commissions Act of 2009
"In all criminal prosecutions, the accused shall enjoy the right ... to have compulsory process for obtaining witnesses in his favor, ..." Amendment VI.	Defendants have the right to subpoena witnesses to testify in their defense. The court may punish witnesses who fail to appear. Fed. R. Crim. P. 17. The prosecution is required to disclose defendant's statements, whether written or oral, that are material to the case. The government must also provide results or reports of any physical or mental examination of the defendant. Upon a defendant's request, the government must permit the defendant to inspect and make copies or photos of tangible objects, buildings or places, within the government's control if the item is material to preparing the defense; the government intends to use the item in its case-in-chief at trial; or the item was obtained from or belongs to the defendant. At the defendant's request, the government must provide a written summary of any expert testimony that the government intends to use during its case-in-chief at trial. Fed. R. Crim. P. 16 The government must also give notice of any witnesses it intends to depose, generally permitting the defendant to attend the deposition. Fed. R. Crim. P. 15	Defense counsel is to be afforded a reasonable opportunity to obtain witnesses and other evidence, including evidence in the possession of the United States, according to DOD regulations. The military judge is authorized to compel witnesses under U.S. jurisdiction to appear. The trial counsel is obligated to disclose exculpatory evidence of which he is aware to the defense, along with mitigating evidence, evidence that reasonably tends to impeach the credibility of a government witness who is to be called at trial. The trial counsel is deemed to be aware of information that is known or reasonably should be known to any government officials who participated in the investigation and prosecution of the case 10 U.S.C. § 949j.

Right to Trial by Impartial Judge

U.S. Constitution	Federal Criminal Court	Military Commissions Act of 2009
"The Judicial Power of the United States, shall be vested in one supreme Court, and in ... inferior courts .... The Judges ... shall hold their Offices during good Behaviour, and shall ... receive ... a Compensation, which shall not be diminished during their Continuance in Office." Article III § 1.	The independence of the judiciary from the other branches was established to ensure trials are decided impartially, without the "potential domination by other branches of government." United States v. Will, 449 U.S. 200, 217-18 (1980). Judges with a pecuniary interest in the outcome of a case or other conflicts of interest are disqualified and must recuse themselves. 28 U.S.C. § 455.	Military judges must take an oath to perform their duties faithfully. 10 U.S.C. § 949g. The convening authority is prohibited from preparing or reviewing any report concerning the effectiveness, fitness, or efficiency of a military judge. 10 U.S.C. § 948j(f). A military judge may not be assigned to a case in which he is the accuser, an investigator, a witness, or a counsel. 10 U.S.C. § 948j(c). The military judge may not consult with the members of the commission except in the presence of the accused, trial counsel, and defense counsel, nor may he vote with the members of the commission. 10 U.S.C. § 948j(d). Convening authority may not censure, reprimand, or admonish the military judge. No person may attempt to coerce or use unauthorized means to influence the action of a commission. 10 U.S.C. § 949b. The military judge may be challenged for cause. 10 U.S.C. § 949f.

Right to Trial by Impartial Jury

U.S. Constitution	Federal Criminal Court	Military Commissions Act of 2009
"The Trial of all Crimes, except in Cases of Impeachment, shall be by Jury; ...." Art III § 2 cl. 3. "In all criminal prosecutions, the accused shall enjoy the right to a ... trial, by an impartial jury of the state ...." Amendment VI.	The pool from which juries are drawn must represent a fair cross section of the community. Taylor v. Louisiana, 419 U.S. 522 (1975). There must further be measures to ensure individual jurors selected are not biased (i.e., the voir dire process). Lewis v. United States, 146 U.S. 370 (1892); see Fed. R. Crim. P. 24 (peremptory challenges). The trial must be conducted in a manner designed to avoid exposure of the jury to prejudicial material or undue influence. If the locality of the trial has been so saturated with publicity about a case that it is impossible to assure jurors will not be affected by prejudice, the defendant is entitled to a change of venue. Irvin v. Dowd, 366 U.S. 717 (1961).	Military commission members must take an oath to perform their duties faithfully. 10 U.S.C. § 949g. The accused may make one peremptory challenge, and may challenge other members for cause. 10 U.S.C. § 949f. No convening authority may censure, reprimand, or admonish the commission or any member with respect to the findings or sentence or the exercise of any other functions in the conduct of the proceedings. No person may attempt to coerce or, by any unauthorized means, influence the action of a commission or any member thereof, in reaching the findings or sentence in any case. Military commission duties may not be considered in the preparation of an effectiveness report or any similar document with potential impact on career advancement. 10 U.S.C. § 949b.

Right to Appeal to Independent Reviewing Authority

U.S. Constitution	Federal Criminal Court	Military Commissions Act of 2009
"The Privilege of the Writ of Habeas Corpus shall not be suspended, unless when in Cases of Rebellion or Invasion the public Safety may require it" Article I § 9 cl. 2. There is no express requirement for appellate review. Appellate courts may exercise jurisdiction only where Congress has authorized it. E.g. Liberty Mut. Ins. Co. v. Wetzel, 424 U.S. 737 (1976).	Originally, the writ of habeas corpus permitted collateral attack upon a prisoner's conviction only if the sentencing court lacked subject matter jurisdiction. It later evolved into an avenue for the challenge of federal and state convictions on other due process grounds, to determine whether a prisoner's detention is "contrary to the Constitution or laws or treaties of the United States." 28 U.S.C. §§ 2241 et seq. Federal appellate courts may review the final decisions of district courts as well as certain interlocutory orders. 28 U.S.C. §§ 1291-92	The accused may submit matters for consideration by the convening authority with respect to the authenticated findings or sentence of the military commission. The convening authority must review timely submissions prior to taking action. 10 U.S.C. § 950b. The accused may appeal a final decision of the military commission with respect to any properly raised issue to the Court of Military Commission Review, a body composed of appellate military judges who meet the same qualifications as military judges or comparable qualifications for civilian judges. 10 U.S.C. § 950f. Once these appeals are exhausted, the accused may appeal the final decision to the United States Court of Appeals for the District of Columbia Circuit, with respect to the findings and sentence as approved by the convening authority and as affirmed or set aside as incorrect in law by the United States Court of Military Commission Review. The appellate court may take action only with respect to matters of law, including the sufficiency of the evidence to support the verdict. D.C. Cir. appellate decisions may be reviewed by the Supreme Court under writ of certiorari. 10 U.S.C. § 950g. Other review by a civilian court, including review on petition of habeas corpus, is no longer expressly prohibited.

Protection against Excessive Penalties

U.S. Constitution	Federal Criminal Court	Military Commissions Act of 2009
"Excessive bail shall not be required, nor excessive fines imposed, nor cruel and unusual punishments inflicted." Amendment VIII.	The death penalty is not per se unconstitutional, but its discriminatory and arbitrary imposition may be, and the death penalty may not be automatic. See Gregg v. Georgia, 428 U.S. 153 (1976); 18 U.S.C.§ 3592 (mitigating /aggravating circumstances). When the death penalty may be imposed, the defendant shall be provided a list of potential jurors and witnesses, unless the court finds that such action might jeopardize the life or safety of any person. 18 U.S.C. § 3432. A special hearing is held to determine whether the death sentence is warranted. 18 U.S.C. § 3593. In capital cases, the accused is entitled to assistance of at least 2 counsel, one of whom has expertise in death penalty cases. Counsel in such cases have free access to the accused at all reasonable hours. The defendant is allowed to make any proof in his defense that he can produce by lawful witnesses, and is entitled to have the same process to compel witnesses to appear as is ordinarily granted to the prosecution. 18 U.S.C. § 3005 The court must stay a death sentence if the defendant appeals the conviction or sentence. Fed. R. Crim. P. 38.	Military commissions may adjudge "any punishment not forbidden by [the MCA], including the penalty of death when specifically authorized...." 10 U.S.C. § 948d. A vote of two-thirds of the members present is required for sentences of up to 10 years. Longer sentences require the concurrence of three-fourths of the members present. The death penalty must be approved unanimously on a unanimous guilty verdict. Where the death penalty is sought, a panel of 12 members is required (unless not "reasonably available"). The death penalty must be expressly authorized for the offense, and the charges must have expressly sought the penalty of death. 10 U.S.C. § 949m. An accused who is sentenced to death may waive his appeal, but may not withdraw an appeal. 10 U.S.C. § 950c. The death sentence may not be executed until the commission proceedings have been finally adjudged lawful and the time for filing a writ has expired or the writ has been denied. The President must approve the sentence. 10 U.S.C. § 950i. In capital cases, the accused is entitled to assistance of counsel with expertise in death penalty cases, which may include civilian counsel paid for by the government. 10 U.S.C. § 949a.

End Notes

[1] Letter from Attorney General Eric Holder and Defense Secretary Robert Gates to Senators Reid and McConnell, October 30, 2009, *available online* at http://www.justice.gov /cjs/docs/graham-amendment.pdf.

[2] Executive Order 13492, "Review and Disposition of Individuals Detained at the Guantanamo Bay Naval Base and Closure of Detention Facilities," 74 *Federal Register* 4897, January 22, 2009.

[3] For information about the Ghailani case and other federal court cases involving putative enemy combatants, see CRS Report R41156, *Judicial Activity Concerning Enemy Combatant Detainees: Major Court Rulings*, by Jennifer K. Elsea and Michael John Garcia.

[4] This entity was created by Executive Order 13493, "Review of Detention Policy Options," 74 *Federal Register* 4901 (January 22, 2009).

[5] Memorandum from the Detention Policy Task Force to the Attorney General and the Secretary of Defense, July 20, 2009, http://www.nimj.com/display.aspx?base=MilitaryCommissions &ID=255.

[6] Press Release, U.S. Department of Justice, "Departments of Justice and Defense Announce Forum Decisions for Ten Guantanamo Detainees," November 13, 2009, *available at* http://www.justice.gov/opa/pr/2009/November/09-ag1224.html.

[7] *See* Charlie Savage, *Detainees Will Still Be Held, but Not Tried, Official Says*, NY TIMES, January 22, 2010. Since the November 2009 announcement, more than 30 detainees have been transferred to other countries.

[8] *Id.*

[9] *See, e.g.,* 18 U.S.C. chapter 113B (terrorism-related offenses); 18 U.S.C. § 2441 (war crimes).

[10] Title XVIII of the National Defense Authorization Act for Fiscal Year 2010, P.L. 111-84.

[11] *See* 10 U.S.C. § 818 (jurisdiction of general court-martial over any person triable under the law of war). The jurisdiction of common law military commissions under the UCMJ is also preserved to try "offenders or offenses that by statute or by the law of war may be tried by military commissions, provost courts, or other military tribunals." 10 U.S.C. § 821. No proposals have been floated to use general courts-martial or military commissions under the UCMJ to try Guantanamo detainees. This report will discuss federal court trials and trials under the Military Commissions Act of 2009.

[12] This term replaces "alien unlawful enemy combatant" who were subject to jurisdiction under the Military Commissions Act of 2006.

[13] *See Ex parte* Quirin, 317 U.S. 1, 31 (upholding military commissions used to try eight German saboteurs in the United States).

[14] Zadyvydas v. Davis, 533 U.S. 678, 693 (2001). ("the Due Process Clause applies to all 'persons' within the United States, including aliens, whether their presence here is lawful, unlawful, temporary or permanent"); Wong Wing v. United States, 163 U.S. 228, 238 (1896) ("all persons within the territory of the United States are entitled to the protection guarantied by [the Fifth and Sixth Amendments], and ... aliens shall not be held to answer for a capital or other infamous crime, unless on a presentment or indictment of a grand jury, nor be deprived of life, liberty, or property without due process of law").

[15] U.S. CONST. art. VI ("[A]ll Treaties ... shall be the Supreme Law of the Land; ...").

[16] *See, e.g.* 18 U.S.C. § 2441 (War Crimes Act).

[17] Treaty provisions that are self-executing are binding on the courts in the absence of implementing legislation. *See* RESTATEMENT (THIRD) OF FOREIGN RELATIONS § 113 (1987). Most human rights treaties, however, are not likely to be held self-executing.

[18] *Id.* § 111.

[19] For a brief explanation of the sources of the law of war, see generally CRS Report RL31191, *Terrorism and the Law of War: Trying Terrorists as War Criminals before Military Commissions*, by Jennifer K. Elsea.

[20] Hamdan v. Rumsfeld, 548 U.S. 557, 630 (2006).

[21] The Geneva Convention Relative to the Treatment of Prisoners of War, August 12, 1949, art. 3 § 1(d), 6 U.S.T. 3317). The identical provision is included in each of the four Geneva Conventions and applies to any "conflict not of an international character." The majority declined to accept the President's interpretation of Common Article 3 as inapplicable to the conflict with Al Qaeda and interpreted the phrase "in contradistinction to a conflict between nations," which the Geneva Conventions designate a "conflict of international character."

[22] U.S. CONST. art. III, § 1.

[23] U.S. CONST. art .I, § 8, cl. 10.

[24] Act of April 30, 1790, 1 Stat. 112. Current statutes provide for life imprisonment for piracy as defined by the law of nations, 18 U.S.C. § 1651; for citizens engaged in hostilities against the United States, *id.* § 1652; for aliens taken on the high seas making war against the United States in violation of a treaty, *id.* § 1653. Lesser punishments are available for other piracy or privateering offenses under chapter 81 of title 18, U.S. code.

[25] 1 Op. Att'y. Gen. 83-84 (1798) (recommending that accused pirates be tried in New Jersey). *See also* 1 Op. Att'y Gen 185 (1815) (those committing piratical acts outside the jurisdiction of any state should be tried in the federal district where the offender is apprehended or first brought after capture).

[26] *See, e.g.* United States v. Palmer, 16 U.S. (3 Wheat.) 610 (1818); United States v. Holmes, 18 (5 Wheat.) 412 (1820); United States v. Furlong, 18 U.S. (5 Wheat.) 184 (1820) (jurisdiction over offenses committed using U.S. vessel); Miller v. United States, 88 F.2d 102.(9th Cir. 1937); Daeche v. United States, 250 F. 566 (2d Cir. 1918) (defendants were accused of conspiring to aid Germany by attaching to munition bearing ships in U.S. waters "infernal machines which would explode while they were on the high seas"). *See also* The Ambrose Light, 25 F. 408 (S.D.N.Y. 1885) (depredations on the high seas committed without authority of from any sovereign power is piracy under the law of nations).

[27] United States v. Yunis, 924 F.2d 1086 (D.C. Cir. 1991).

[28] *See* Fact Sheet, Statistics on Unsealed International Terrorism and Terrorism-Related Convictions, *available online at* http://www.justice.gov/cjs/docs/terrorism-convictions-statistics.html.

[29] http://www.justice.gov/cjs/docs/terrorism-convictions-statistics.pdf.

[30] Some of the offenses, categorized as Category II offenses in the report are comparable to offenses under the MCA, such as Arsons and Bombings (18 U.S.C. §§ 842(m), 842(n), 844(f), 844(I)); Killings in the Course of Attack on a Federal Facility (18 U.S.C. § 930(c)); Genocide (18 U.S.C. § 1091); Destruction of Communication Lines (18 U.S.C. § 1362); Sea Piracy (18 U.S.C. § 1651); Wrecking Trains (18 U.S.C. § 1992); Destruction of National Defense Materials, Premises, or Utilities (18 U.S.C. § 2155); Violence against Maritime Navigation and Maritime Fixed Platforms (18 U.S.C. §§ 2280, 2281); Torture (18 U.S.C. § 2340A); War Crimes (18 U.S.C. § 2441); International Traffic in Arms Regulations (22 U.S.C. § 2778); Destruction of Interstate Gas or Hazardous Liquid Pipeline Facilities (49 U.S.C. § 60123(b)).

[31] *Id* at Annex A.

[32] U.S. CONST. art. I, § 8, cl. 11.

[33] *Id*. art. I, § 8, cl. 10.

[34] *Id.* art. I, § 8, cl. 14.

[35] *Id.* art. II, § 2, cl. 1.

[36] *Id.* art. II, § 3.

[37] The Articles of War were re-enacted at 10 U.S.C. § 801 *et seq.* as part of the UCMJ. Although there is no case law interpreting the UCMJ as authorizing military commissions, the relevant sections of the UCMJ, which recognize the concurrent jurisdiction of military commissions to deal with "offenders or offenses designated by statute or the law of war," are essentially identical to the corresponding language in the Articles of War. *See* 10 U.S.C. § 821.

[38] *Ex parte* Quirin, 317 U.S. 1 (1942).

[39] *See* WILLIAM WINTHROP, MILITARY LAW AND PRECEDENTS 831 (2d ed. 1920) (describing distinction between courts-martial and military tribunals).

[40] 10 U.S.C. § 821. Statutory offenses for which military commissions may be convened are limited to aiding the enemy, 10 U.S.C. § 904, and spying, 10 U.S.C. § 906. These offenses are explicitly included in the MCA.

[41] *See Ex parte* Quirin, 317 U.S. 1 (1942).

[42] For more information about the history of military commissions in the United States, see CRS Report RL31191, *Terrorism and the Law of War: Trying Terrorists as War Criminals before Military Commissions*, by Jennifer K. Elsea. For more information about the jurisdiction of military commissions, see CRS Report R40752, *The Military Commissions Act of 2006 (MCA): Background and Proposed Amendments*, by Jennifer K. Elsea.

[43] *See Ex parte* Quirin, 317 U.S. at 38; *Ex parte* Milligan, 71 U.S. (4 Wall.) 2, 123 (1866) (noting a servicemember "surrenders his right to be tried by the civil courts").

[44] "Unprivileged enemy combatant" is defined by reference to 10 U.S.C. § 948a(7), which currently provides a definition for "unprivileged enemy belligerent."

In: The Military Commissions Act…
Editors: J. Segel, Soto Kimura
ISBN: 978-1-61470-072-2

Chapter 3

TESTIMONY OF PETER R. MASCIOLA COLONEL, UNITED STATES AIR FORCE – ANGUS CHIEF DEFENSE COUNSEL DEPARTMENT OF DEFENSE, OFFICE OF MILITARY COMMISSIONS HOUSE JUDICIARY COMMITTEE, SUBCOMMITTEE ON THE CONSTITUTION, CIVIL RIGHTS, AND CIVIL LIBERTIES*

30 July, 2009

INTRODUCTION

I thank Chairman Nadler and the Members of the Subcommittee on the Constitution, Civil Rights, and Civil Liberties for allowing me to testify on a topic of critical importance to the fairness of any future military commissions system – the provision of adequate resources to the defense to ensure trials that produce verdicts that are both reliable and fair to the accused. I will also have a few words to say about the standard of fairness that should be applied to

* This is an edited, reformatted and augmented version of testimony given by Peter R. Masciola, Colonel, United States Air Force – ANGUS Chief Defense Counsel, before Subcommittee on the Constitution, Civil Rights, and Civil Liberties publication, on July 30, 2009.

military commission trials: compliance with both Common Article 3 of the Geneva Conventions and the United States Constitution. Because the latter topic has received the most attention from witnesses before this and other committees and subcommittees of both the House and the Senate, however, my testimony today is primarily devoted to the issue of defense resources, which to date has received far too little attention.

I am the fourth Chief Defense Counsel to come before the Congress as you debate the fourth iteration of these military commissions. I am therefore the fourth Chief Defense Counsel to talk to you about the fundamental and fatal flaws of the military commission system as it is currently constituted, and, in the present case, as it has been passed by the Senate. I hope to be the last. If the problems I identify today are finally addressed in the present legislation, it will go a long way toward "leveling the playing field" between the defense and prosecution in the military commissions in a way that finally brings this system into line with other American court systems, both civilian and military, and thus makes its claim to fairness far more legitimate than it ever has been in the past. VADM MacDonald set the right standard in his testimony before the House and Senate Armed Services Committees. Trial by military commission should be trials that we would expect for our own soldiers, sailors, airmen and marines.

I emphasize at the outset that I am testifying solely as The Chief Defense Counsel on behalf of the Office of Military Commission-Defense and not on behalf of any accused, as I am prevented by regulation from representing any individual charged in the military commissions. In addition, my testimony today should not be construed as an endorsement of the adoption of a military commissions system, nor should it be construed to suggest that the problems mentioned are the only deficiencies in the current or proposed system. Finally, given my role as Chief Defense Counsel, my testimony does not represent an endorsement or approval of any policy or the legal sufficiency of any action on behalf of the Government, and should not be cited as such.

Defense Resources in the Military Commissions: Problems and Solutions

In two recent memoranda to the Administration, I have detailed many ways that the commissions' current resourcing policies have prevented detailed defense counsel from carrying out their mission. *See* Memorandum for the General Counsel of the Department of Defense (13 July 2009) ("13 July Memo") (Exh. A hereto);[1] Memorandum to the Attorney General of the United States and General Counsel of the Department of Defense (9 June 2009) ("9 June Memo") (Exh. C hereto). These memoranda cover a wide range of crucial issues in the current resourcing system that make adequate representation of the accused difficult at best and in many cases, impossible.

Because these memoranda discuss the covered topics in factual and legal detail, in the testimony that follows I focus primarily on the structural issues that the memoranda do not address and otherwise simply highlight the most important aspects of memoranda topics. Please consider these memoranda incorporated by reference into this testimony, and read the individual sections of the below testimony in conjunction with the relevant memorandum section.

In each of the following subsections, I describe one of the problems that the current resourcing policies have created and, where appropriate, recommend at the end of the section an amendment to the current Senate bill to address that problem, either with specific legislative language and/or with a description of the conditions that a sufficient legislative fix must meet. Where the nature of the problem makes it more appropriately addressed at the regulatory rather than legislative level, I have suggested that language be included in the appropriate legislative reports identifying the problem and directing the Department of Defense or other regulatory agency to issue regulations that address and resolve the issue.

The Principle of "Equality of Arms"

The military commission system, like the court-martial system under the Uniform Code of Military Justice ("UCMJ") and prosecution in federal court, is an adversarial system of justice that is premised on the belief that the most reliable way of finding the truth of a criminal charge is to allow the government and the accused to present their clashing versions of the evidence of the crime. It is a given that no such system can either achieve reliable results or guarantee fairness unless the accused has an equivalent ability to investigate and present his defense as does the prosecution to investigate and prove its charges. As the United States Supreme Court put it, "[w]e recognized long ago that mere access to the courthouse doors does not by itself assure a proper functioning of the adversary process, and that a criminal trial is fundamentally unfair if the State proceeds against an indigent defendant without making certain that he has access to the raw materials integral to the building of an effective defense." *Ake v. Oklahoma*, 470 U.S. 68, 77 (1984).

In the court-martial system, this fundamental principle of "equality of arms" is embodied in UCMJ Art. 46 (10 U.S.C. § 846), which provides that the defense "shall have equal opportunity to obtain witnesses and other evidence" as the prosecution and the court-martial. In federal court, the principle is embodied in the Criminal Justice Act ("CJA"), which guarantees that all services "necessary for adequate representation" shall be provided to defendants unable to pay for them. 18 U.S.C. § 3006A(e).

The Military Commissions Act of 2006 ("current MCA") deliberately deviated from this model by allowing the accused, in direct contrast to the parallel UCMJ provision, only a "*reasonable* opportunity to obtain witnesses and other evidence" – that is, neither an "equal opportunity," nor the services "necessary" to obtain "adequate" access under the CJA model. *See* current 10 U.S.C. § 949j(a). This change from traditional military practice was a clear message to the Secretary of Defense, the Convening Authority, and the military judges that the UCMJ rule of "equality of arms" should not apply in the commissions, with results that can be seen in the below discussion and attached exhibits.

Inexplicably, although the Senate Armed Services Committee Report to the proposed MCA amendments refers to the problem of defense resources, the bill reported out and subsequently passed by the Senate maintains the current MCA's "reasonable opportunity" standard for defense access to evidence and witnesses. Expressions of concern in Committee Reports, however well intentioned, are not enough in this situation. The simplest solution is to restore the language of Art. 46, and amend the language of proposed § 949j(a)(1) to eliminate the current language and substitute the first sentence of Article 46 (as suitably modified by changing "court-martial" to "military commission"): "The trial counsel, the defense counsel, and the military commission shall have equal opportunity to obtain witnesses and other evidence in accordance with such regulations as the President may prescribe." Apart from its fundamental fairness, this is a standard with a long history of application in military courts with which all JAGC members and military judges are familiar, and thus can be inserted in the present system without fear of confusion.

Solution: Amend proposed § 949j(a)(1) as follows:

a) "IN GENERAL.—(1) Defense counsel *in* a *military* commission under *this chapter shall* have a *reasonable opportunity to obtain*

> *witnesses and other* evidence as provided *in* regulations prescribed_*by the* Secretary *of* Defense. *The trial counsel, the defense counsel, and the military commission shall have equal opportunity to obtain witnesses and other evidence in accordance with such regulations as the President may prescribe.*

The Military Commission Convening Authority: An Untenable Dual Role

Many of the problems associated with the funding of the defense in the commissions is a result of the untenable and inherently conflicted role of the Convening Authority ("CA"), a position that is established by statute under both the current MCA and Senate bill. *See* current 10 U.S.C. § 948h; proposed § 948h. The reality is that significant defense resourcing issues will continue to arise unless this fundamental structural flaw in the system is resolved.

Some background in conventional military law is required to understand the nature of the problem with the CA structure and how this problem arose in the formulation of the military commissions. It must be recalled that the military justice system serves a disciplinary, as well as strictly-speaking criminal, function within the military. Thus, under the UCMJ, courts-martial are convened by a commanding officer when a serious disciplinary problem, which sometimes rises to the level of criminal behavior, occurs in his command unit. In such cases, the commander convenes a court-martial of some type (depending on the seriousness of the offense), which then hears the case against the accused service member. This gives the convening authority, just because he is also the commander of the unit, the dual responsibility of not only enforcing the law but of defending the rights of the service member under his or her command. In the strictly military context, that makes sense, given the fact that the commander/convening authority in courts-martial is the officer in charge of ensuring the good order and discipline of his entire unit, including not only the accused but the prosecution (and often the witnesses) as well. In this situation, such centralized control of the case on both the prosecution and defense sides makes some sense as a matter of logic, as well as of the simple reality that the court-martial takes place in a military unit in which the convening authority, as commanding officer, is the ultimate military authority and promotes military discipline and efficiency.

Neither logic nor military reality compels any such centralization of prosecution and defense control in the hands of a single individual in the military commissions system. To say the obvious, the Convening Authority in the military commissions is not responsible for the "good order and discipline" of the Guantanamo detainees. Indeed, even Joint Task Force-Guantanamo, the military unit responsible for guarding and administering the Guantanamo prison camps, is an entirely separate military entity under a separate command that does not answer to the Convening Authority. Nor is there any military or otherwise natural necessity for the Convening Authority to hold ultimate power over funding of both the prosecution and defense. The Office of Military Commissions - Convening Authority is entirely a creature of Congressional and Department of Defense regulation, headed by a political appointee (who is currently a civilian). This structure could be entirely overhauled with no damage to either the prosecutorial or defense functions. Indeed, as we explain below, if constituted logically – that is, by separating the prosecutorial and defense functions – such an overhaul would enormously enhance the fairness of the entire system.

In any event, despite the absence of any logic or necessity, the conventional military role of the Convening Authority is replicated under the current military commission system, with disastrous consequences for the defense, and nothing in the Senate bill purports to change this situation. In part by statute but mostly by regulation, the Convening Authority is currently responsible, on one hand, for the ultimate decision to proceed with charging and trial of the accused (Regulation for Trial by Military Commission ("RTMC") § 4-1), ultimate acceptance or rejection of pretrial agreements (the military term for plea bargains) (RTMC § 12-1), and initial review and correction of all convictions (current 10 U.S.C. § 950b) – all prosecutorial or quasi-prosecutorial functions. At the same time, the Convening Authority is responsible for all of the most critical defense resource and funding decisions: the initial decision whether or not the defense is entitled to retain and fund defense experts at government expense (RTMC § 13-7); the initial decision to authorize travel funding of all witnesses (which, given the location of the accused and trials in Guantanamo Bay, is tantamount to virtual veto power over the presentation of most witnesses) (RTMC § 13-2); and to provide for interpretation and translation service for the defense (current 10 U.S.C. § 9481(b), RTMC § 7-3(c)).

This structure has had two consequences for the defense, both of which are unjustified by any military or other need, and both of which have rendered the process fundamentally unfair.

The first consequence is that, because the Convening Authority is the *de facto* chief prosecutor as well as the arbiter of defense resources, defense requests have not been ruled upon with even a semblance of fairness or objectivity. As of 21 July 2009, of the 56 requests for expert assistance filed in 11 cases, only nine have been granted. *See* Table, "Expert Requests filed by OMC-D Counsel to the Convening Authority" (Exh. B hereto). Not a single request made by detailed counsel in the four capital cases among these has been granted. That statistic alone is astonishing, given the special need for mitigation specialists and other experts in capital cases, which has been recognized by both the United States Supreme Court and the Court of Appeals for the Armed Forces, as well as by authoritative guidelines for competent representation and resourcing of capital cases. *See* Guidelines for Appointment and Performance of Defense Counsel in Death Penalty Cases (February 2003 revision) ("ABA Guidelines"); Guidelines for the Administration of the Criminal Justice Act and Related Statutes (promulgated by the Administrative Office of the Federal Judiciary and approved by the Judicial Conference of the United States) ("AO Guidelines"); *see generally* 13 July Memo (Exh. A), at 3-4, 5-12.

Even these data are misleading. Of the nine requests that have been granted, seven have been in the single case of *United States v. Khadr*. In all of the other cases, which include four capital defendants, only two experts have been authorized, and one of these was granted only after the intervention of the military judge. The underlying reality is thus that while the defense in the other 10 cases combined have received one grant and 41 denials; the defense in *Khadr* has received seven grants and only six denials.

The disparity between the treatment of Mr. Khadr and the other accused is highly significant and damning to, at a minimum, the appearance of fairness of the CA's actions. The accused in the *Khadr* case is a Canadian, and the former legal advisor to the Convening Authority, BG Hartmann (who was disqualified from further participation in *Khadr* and two other cases for unlawful influence or the appearance thereof), stated in testimony before the commission that during the pendency of the *Khadr* case he met with and thereafter provided regular updates to representatives of the Canadian government on the progress of the case.[2] My office is not aware of any other such regular contacts between the CA's office and the home governments of any of the other current accused, none of whom are from Western countries. The inevitable danger of this kind of inside contact by an accused's interested and sympathetic home government is that not just "updates" but influence is involved. In this case, that is a danger that at least gives the appearance of having come to fruition on the evidence of the disparity between the CA's treatment of Khadr's expert requests when compared to those of the other accused. No system that makes, or even appears to make, the provision of resources to the defense dependent on extraneous diplomatic and political considerations can possibly be considered fair. Whether or not the accused have the resources they need to prepare for trial should not be a function of their passport or their home government's relationship with the United States.

The second significant consequence of making the CA the source for defense resources is that simply filing a request to the CA requires our defense teams to lay out, in detail, defense strategy and privileged materials that the CA freely shares with the prosecution. Moreover, in practice, the prosecutors have enjoyed a vote on whether or not defense counsel requests will be granted. If the request is not granted, defense counsel must submit on the record filings with the military judge to reverse the CA's decision. As a result, the defense is forced to make the Hobson's choice between seeking needed expert assistance or protecting privileged information.

Moreover, the need to appeal the CA's decision to the military judge in virtually every case has made the proceedings grossly inefficient and has led to significant delays even if the defense requests are ultimately granted.

With regard to the logic of defense resourcing, military commissions far more resemble federal court prosecutions than they do courts-martial. Both military commissions and federal court prosecutions serve purely criminal functions where the government is in an exclusively adversarial position to the accused. Military commissions serve no military-disciplinary functions and the accused lack any status that would constitute membership in or service to the government. Accordingly, military commission applications for defense resources should be made on the same terms as federal applications -- on a purely *ex parte* basis. See 18 U.S.C. § 3006A(e)(1)("Counsel for a person who is financially unable to obtain investigative, expert, or other services necessary for adequate representation may request them in an *ex parte* application."); *see generally* the discussion of this problem in the 9 June Memo (Exh. C), at 2-3.

In short, the joined prosecutorial and defense functions of the current CA structure is unjustified by any military or other necessity and has proved, both in theory and, very clearly in practice, fundamentally unfair. Indeed, this structure is the source of most of the other resourcing problems discussed below and in the 13 July (Exh. A) and 9 June Memos (Exh. C).

Solutions: Any solution to this problem must meet the criterion of separating the defense resourcing functions of the position of CA from all of its other duties under the statute, and creating a firewall that prevents the CA (or any other DoD or other official affiliated with the prosecutorial functions of the government) from influencing the function of defense resourcing. In the federal system, this is the norm, and is achieved by administering the defense's resources and funding through an agency of the federal judiciary – the Administrative Office of the Federal Courts – which is in a different branch of government than the prosecution.

Assuming that that degree of separation is impossible, the solution to the problem will have to resolve the issue of how a defense funding agency within the same Department of government can be made truly independent of the rest of the Departmental agencies. Because the Office of the CA and especially its role in defense resourcing is primarily a creation of DoD regulation, a new defense funding agency itself could be established at the regulatory level. Nevertheless, there are legislative changes that can establish the principles of separation and independence that will require the regulatory scheme to avoid the concerns articulated above.

One possibility is amending proposed § 949b(a) (which prohibits unlawful influence) along the following lines (deletions are struck-through; insertions are italicized):

"(a) IN GENERAL.—(1) No authority convening a military commission under this chapter may censure, reprimand, or admonish the military commission, or any member, military judge, *the defense resource funding authority*, or counsel thereof, with respect to the findings or sentence adjudged by the military commission, or with respect to any other exercises of its or their functions in the conduct of the proceedings.

(2)"No person may attempt to coerce or, by any unauthorized means, influence—

(a) the action of a military commission under this chapter, or any member thereof, in reaching the findings or sentence in any case;
(b) the action of any convening, approving, or reviewing authority with respect to their judicial acts; or
(c) the exercise of professional judgment by trial counsel or defense counsel; or
(d) the action or decision making of the defense resource funding authority with respect to its acts authorizing or funding defense resources.

(3) The provisions of this subsection shall not apply with respect to—

a) general instructional or informational courses in military justice if such courses are designed solely for the purpose of instructing members of a command in the substantive and procedural aspects of military commissions; or
b) statements and instructions given in open proceedings by a military judge or counsel;or
c) requests by defense counsel to the defense resource funding authority for the authorization or funding of defense resources for use in cases to which they have been detailed.

Language along these lines, especially with an accompanying explanation in the legislative record, would go some distance in requiring the establishment of a "defense resource funding authority" within the Department of Defense with the kind of independence from outside influences – including prosecutorial and political influences – that have plagued the current system.

Finally, the problem of prosecutorial involvement and interference with defense resource requests, to the extent not covered by the above amended unlawful influence provision, could be addressed by inserting language equivalent to that of 18 U.S.C. § 3006A(e)(1)("Counsel for a person who is financially unable to obtain investigative, expert, or other services necessary for adequate representation may request them in an *ex parte* application.") into proposed § 949j(a)(1), which, after the amendment suggested in the first section, would result in the following amended language:

"(a) IN GENERAL.—(1) Defense *counsel in a military*_commission under *this chapter shall have* a reasonable *opportunity to obtain witnesses* and *other* evidence as provided *in* regulations prescribed *by* the Secretary *of* Defense. *The trial counsel, the defense counsel, and the military commission shall have equal opportunity to obtain witnesses and other evidence in accordance with such regulations as the President may prescribe. Defense counsel may request the authorization or funding of resources from the defense resource funding authority in an ex parte application.*

The Special Problem of Capital Cases

Congress has recognized that capital cases pose a special need for resources since the passage of the original federal Crimes Act of 1790, in which it authorized, uniquely in capital cases, the appointment of two counsel, one of whom was required to be "learned in the law," and counsels' right to meet with their clients at all reasonable hours. That special capital provision has been carried forward with only minor modifications to the present day in the form of 18 U.S.C. § 3005, which provides in relevant part that the judge in a capital case "shall promptly, upon the defendant's request, assign 2 such counsel, of whom at least 1 shall be learned in the law applicable to capital cases, and who shall have free access to the accused at all reasonable hours." Other provisions of federal law, both by their terms and as interpreted by the federal judiciary's rulings and its funding Guidelines promulgated by its Administrative Office, similarly recognize the special need for mitigation specialists, experts, investigators, and other special defense services in capital cases.

These topics are covered in detail in the attached 13 July and 9 June Memos (Exhs. A and C), and rather than repeat myself I will simply incorporate those discussions by reference and highlight some the most important points here. In sum, a capital defense team that meets current professional standards of practice, as embodied in the Guidelines for Appointment and Performance of Defense Counsel in Death Penalty Cases (February 2003 revision), the Guidelines for the Administration of the Criminal Justice Act and Related Statutes (promulgated by the Administrative Office of the Federal Judiciary and approved by the Judicial Conference of the United States), the Supplementary Guidelines for the Mitigation Function of Defense Teams in Death Penalty Cases (2008) and relevant Supreme Court precedents requires the following (see ABA Guidelines 4.1 ("The Defense Team and Supporting Services") and 10.4 ("The Defense Team"):

a) At least two defense counsel, one of whom is "death qualified" within the meaning of the ABA Guidelines and "learned in the law applicable to capital cases" within the meaning of 18 U.S.C. § 3005. In those cases in which a death-qualified JAGC member "learned in the law applicable to capital cases" is not available, then a civilian "learned counsel" should be appointed and funded by the government to serve in that role.

b) A mitigation investigator, who is qualified to perfonn the duties described in Commentary (B) to ABA Guideline 4.1 and the Supplementary Guidelines for the Mitigation Function of Defense Teams in Death Penalty Cases (2008), selected by lead defense counsel.

c) A professional investigator trained in and competent to perfonn the special duties associated with the investigation of death penalty cases pursuant to ABA Guideline 10.7 ("Investigation"), selected by lead defense counsel.
d) At least one mental health expert competent to diagnose and, if necessary, treat mental health issues presented by the client, selected by lead defense counsel
e) An expert in the accused's native culture, selected by lead defense counsel
f) f. At least one translator and interpreter fully competent to provide translation and interpretation services between the client's native language and English, selected and/or approved by lead defense counsel.
g) A privilege team.
h) When requested by the client, a foreign attorney familiar with the client's culture to serve as a member of the defense team.

All of these resources should be made available to the accused from the time that charges are preferred. Because of the enormous amount of preliminary work involved in capital cases, provision of these experts and services should not wait until the capital referral – in fact doing so will ordinarily cause significant delays in the proceedings.

The degree to which the CA has fallen woefully short of these professional norms and standard federal-court practices in the military commission capital cases is suggested by the attached Table, "Expert Requests filed by OMC-D Counsel to the Convening Authority" (Exh. B). As noted above, the CA has denied every single request for a mitigation specialist or expert made by every capital defense team that has sought one. Apart from the denials of the requests for mitigation specialists, she has denied a request for a mental health expert to assist in a competence evaluation of a capital accused to whom the government was administering anti-psychotic drugs prior to counsel's appearance, whom a panel of court-appointed government mental health experts found to be mentally ill, and for whom the military judge himself had ordered a competency hearing *sua sponte*.

This record of denials is, to say the least, inconsistent with current military practice under the UCMJ, in which there has been a growing recognition of the need for special resources in capital cases. Whether this trend is the result of the fact that eight of the last nine military death sentences have been overturned on appeal or some other reason, it is clear that military justice now recognizes that special resourcing of the defense is required if capital cases have a chance of being tried in a manner that meets appellate standards. Most recently, in a far less complex case than those being tried in the commissions, the Court of Appeals for the Armed Forces ruled that it violated the Due Process Clause to deny a capital accused the services of a mitigation specialist, noting that "because there is no professional death penalty bar in the military services, it is likely that a mitigation specialist may be the most experienced member of the defense team in capital litigation." *United States v. Kreutzer*, 61 MJ. 293, 298 n.7 (CAAF 2005). It is inconceivable that the present cases fail to meet the *Kreutzer* standard, yet in every case the Convening Authority has denied the request for a mitigation specialist.

Nevertheless, for the reasons explained above, the real point of comparison and measure of fairness of the commissions is the federal courts system. (Indeed, this is the standard implicit in the President's decision, for those Guantanamo detainees who are to be prosecuted, to try them either in federal court or by military commission – courts-martial are not an option.) Thus, to fully comprehend the magnitude of the unfairness of the CA's treatment of the capital cases, these denials should be compared with the initial funding order in the now-federal court case of *United States v. Ghailani* (*Ex Parte* Order, *United States v. Ahmed Khalfan Ghailani*, 98 Cr 1023 (LAK), U.S. District Court, Southern District of New York, 25 June 2009; Exh. D hereto). Ghailani was originally an accused in the military commissions, with capital charges preferred against him that were eventually referred non-capitally to a commission for trial. He was recently transferred for trial to federal court, and, in parallel fashion, has been charged with capital crimes but the Department of Justice has not yet decided whether or not to seek the death penalty against him. Despite the uncertainty of whether his case will ultimately be treated capitally, the judge issued the attached funding order providing for extensive resources – including 300 hours of a mitigation expert's time at the rate of $100 per hour -- given the mere possibility that the case will end up capital, and prior to the defense counsel even being required to submit a budget. This, moreover, is a standard order issued at the outset of all such capital cases in the Federal District Court for the Southern District of New York; it is not based on demonstrated need in the particular case but on the federal court's experience with the expert and funding needs in such cases as a general matter.

The disparity between Mr. Ghailani's treatment in the commissions (he was denied a mitigation specialist by the CA along with another request for a privilege team prior to being transferred) and the treatment he and other capital (and potentially capital) defendants receive in federal courts poses an enormous challenge to the legitimacy and the credibility of the entire military commissions system. The President's Detainee Task Force is currently deciding whether to charge individuals, capitally and noncapitally, in federal courts or the commissions. Under present circumstances, given the monumental disparity in defense resources between the two systems of capital prosecution, how can a decision to try a capital defendant in the commissions be viewed as anything but a government decision to increase the chances of achieving a death sentence by providing him with a third-rate or worse defense? Given this disparity, how can such a system ever be fair, or be viewed as fair by an outside observer?

Solutions: Any solution to these problems must begin with the restructuring of the CA functions as described above, to ensure that the funding decisions in all cases, including the capital cases, receive the impartial consideration of the defense's real needs and the relevant professional norms and guidelines that they would receive in federal court. But it will also require a genuine commitment on the part of the Administration not to allow this disparity to continue, and to bring its support for the defense function in the commissions up to the norms of other legitimate American courts. The TJAGs all testified before the House Armed Services Committee that they opposed the Administration's "preference" for federal court prosecution on exactly these grounds – that no such preference will be necessary if the military commissions are made just as fair and just as legitimate as federal courts. Unless the disparate treatment of defense resourcing between commission cases generally, capital and noncapital, and parallel cases in federal court is rectified, that standard cannot be met. In the present circumstances, it is the capital cases in which the commissions' egregious failure by this measure is most evident.

Along with a change of CA structure and a change of commitment at the Department of Defense level, however, there are amendments to the Senate bill that are necessary to enable capital cases in the commissions to achieve the kind of fairness and reliability that federal court capital prosecutions provide. In particular, the primary requirement of "learned" or "death-qualified" counsel on the capital defense team cannot presently be met by JAGC attorneys alone. As the Court of Appeals for the Armed Services has recognized, "there is no professional death penalty bar in the military services," *Kreutzer*, *supra*, for the simple reason that that there are too few capital cases in the military for JAGC members to gain the experience necessary to become death-qualified.

In my office today, there are two death-qualified attorneys – a civilian who was hired specifically because of his capital experience as a resource counsel, and a Navy reservist who was called up after the capital cases were fully staffed. Neither are detailed to any of the capital defense teams, in part because I need them to remain conflict-free with the capital defendants so that they can advise them all even-handedly. As a result, none of the military lawyers detailed to the capital cases are death-qualified under the ABA standards or "learned" within the meaning of 18 U.S.C. § 3005. In an effort to provide the representation to their clients that they are well-aware is required, these fine attorneys have sought out the services of "learned" civilian co-counsel with extensive experience in capital cases in the civil courts. To date, these civilian attorneys have either been funded by non-governmental organizations or, in some cases, not at all, acting – to the extent that they have been able to afford it – on a *pro bono* basis.

This is an untenable situation, since these civilian attorneys will not be able to continue in their current capacities, especially as these cases become more active again. The correct solution – the one adopted in 18 U.S.C. § 3005 – is to appoint and pay these civilian attorneys on a contract basis during the term of the case, as is currently done in federal capital cases under § 3005 and the Criminal Justice Act. As currently enacted, however, and as proposed under the Senate bill, the government is forbidden to pay civilian attorneys serving as commissions defense attorneys, no matter how necessary they are for the adequacy of the accused's capital defense. Both current and proposed § 949a(b)(2)(C) by its terms only entitles an accused to a civilian attorney "if provided at no expense to the Government." I note that this is unfair not only as a matter of guaranteeing capital defendants the representation they need, but by the measure of "equality of arms" as well. The commission prosecution teams – and the capital HVD prosecution teams in particular – are largely staffed by Department of Justice attorneys, that is, by civilians who are being paid by the government.

One amendment to the Senate bill that would solve this problem would be to amend § 949a(b)(2)(C) as follows:[3]

"(2) Notwithstanding any exceptions authorized by paragraph (1), the procedures and rules of evidence in trials by military commission under this chapter shall include, at a minimum, the following rights:

....

"(C) *(i) When none of the charges preferred against the accused are capital, t*To be represented before a military commission by civilian counsel if provided at no expense to the Government, and by either the defense counsel detailed or by military counsel of the accused's own selection, if reasonably available, *or (ii) when any of the charges preferred against the accused are capital, to be represented before the military commission by at least two counsel, one of whom is learned in the law applicable to capital cases within the meaning of 18 U.S.C. § 3005 who, if necessary, may be a civilian compensated pursuant to regulations prescribed by the Secretary of Defense. Subject to these requirements, the accused may be represented by detailed defense counsel, military counsel of the accused's own selection, if reasonably available, or by civilian counsel provided at no expense to the Government.* [4]

Resource Problems Common to All Cases, Capital and Noncapital

As I explain in the 13 July Memo (Exh. A), even the noncapital cases in the office are extraordinarily complex and require unusual resourcing, far beyond what is typical either in courts-martial or even federal criminal prosecutions. *See* 13 July Memo, at 5, 15-19. Foreign, non-English speaking clients; extraterritorial crimes requiring international travel, all the difficulties of investigations on foreign, non-English-speaking territories, and coordinating interaction and cooperation with the Department of State; and clients who are naturally suspicious of Americans in uniform after many of them were abused, sometimes seriously, by other Americans wearing the uniform – these are not obstacles that most defense attorneys usually face. Accordingly, as I state in the 13 July Memo, in my view an adequate defense team in a noncapital case in my office is composed, at a minimum, of the following individuals:

a) Two defense counsel, one of whom is experienced in complex criminal litigation, and preferably with experience in defending foreign defendants charged with extraterritorial crimes.
b) A professional investigator competent to perform the special requirements of extraterritorial investigations, selected by lead defense counsel.
c) A mental health expert competent to diagnose and, if necessary, treat mental health issues presented by the client, selected by lead defense counsel.

d) An expert in the accused's native culture, selected by lead defense counsel.
e) At least one translator and interpreter fully competent to provide translation and interpretation services between the client's native language and English, selected and/or approved by lead defense counsel.
f) A privilege team.
g) When requested by the client, a foreign attorney familiar with the client's culture to serve as a member of the defense team.

The justifications for these particular team members are provided in the 13 July and 9 June Memos (Exhs. A and C) and I will not repeat them here. Suffice it to say that almost all of the many difficulties that the detailed attorneys have experienced in fulfilling these requirements has stemmed from the recalcitrance of the CA, who has been no more forthcoming with requests for, for example, privilege teams than she has been with the expert requests. The privilege team denials, which are documented and explained in the 13 July Memo (Exh. A), at 17) have made representation of clients particularly difficult, especially in the HVD cases where the TS//SCI materials are concentrated. It has led to defense counsel in effect walking a high-wire with no safety net whenever the have needed to submit classified material in connection with motions or even speak about it in court. Counsel have even been threatened with prosecution for such statements.

Among the issues discussed in my memoranda, I think it is important to highlight the problem of client access created by the over-classification of defense-relevant materials, up to and including the very words that the HVD accused speak, a security environment that separates attorneys from their clients both physically and psychologically, insofar as the accused are subjected to "security measures" every time they are taken from their cells to see the attorneys that are reminiscent of the abuse they suffered previously at the hands of Americans, and the virtual impossibility of getting experts the chance to meet, assess and/or treat the clients in many cases. Moreover, the abysmal state of the translation and interpretation services creates another difficulty in making access meaningful even when it occurs at all. While the issue of client access is discussed under the "Capital Case" heading in the 13 July memo (Exh. A) (at 12-15), because it is a particular problem in capital cases where there is an increased needs to develop a relationship with the client and obtain expert access, it is a problem that is experienced across the board, in every case. Many of the restrictions are so inhibiting with so little justification or rational explanation that, as I state in the memo, they arguably rise to the level of deliberate interference with the attorney-client relationship – certainly, at a minimum, their continued existence despite our many pleas, complaints and motions demonstrates deliberate indifference to the needs of defense attorneys to establish and maintain client relationships. None of this is good for the commission process, as any trial judge, prosecutor or appellate judge who has had to work with a *pro se* case can tell you. Why the government would want to buy this trouble is unclear, since these policies are unlikely to help any convictions stand up on review.

The problem of inadequate investigation resources is also one that appears under the "Capital" heading in the 19 July Memo but affects the fairness of the noncapital cases as well. Along with the issues raised in the 19 July Memo, there is a persistent "inequality of arms" on the investigation front that has been particularly evident in the government's differential access to witnesses and databases. It should go without saying that the defense has the right to obtain information about its own and the government's case outside the discovery process – that is, by legitimate investigatory and intelligence-gathering means. In fact, however, databases and witnesses to which the military investigators and intelligence analysts had routine access when they were detailed in the court-martial context have been foreclosed in the commissions arena. For example, the majority of personnel on our intelligence analysis team have been affirmatively denied access to various intelligence databases routinely used by members of their profession, even though they had the appropriate security clearances and "need to know" mandate.

The prosecution, on the other hand, does not suffer the same handicaps. Denials to defense analysts included requests for access to the Joint Detainee Information Management System (JDIMS), even though OMC-P and DoD OGC attorneys appear to have had access to selected JDIMS information through a file transfer protocol site at least since May of 2009. They have similarly been denied requests for specific information (RFI) submitted through the typical intelligence processes, and have been referred back to the prosecution or to databases for which their access had not been approved. The prosecution and attorneys who support habeas litigation in the DoD Office of General Counsel have the ability to submit RFIs to the Joint Intelligence Group at JTF-GTMO, for questions such as the circumstances under which statements were made by a detainee or information supporting factual assertions use to determine enemy combatant status. Our intelligence analysts are denied any ability to submit such requests as part of their inherent investigatory function.

Prosecutorial control of information is another structural problem faced by investigators and attorneys alike. Defense counsel have been unable to obtain authorization to interview government witnesses, including interrogators responsible for extracting statements from their clients in detention. By withholding such authorization, the prosecution can effectively shield itself from defense arguments that the statements were obtained by cruel, inhumane or degrading treatment, or otherwise under conditions that made the statements involuntary or unreliable. In another case, defense counsel requested contact information for overseas witnesses known to the prosecution in preparation for travel to a predominantly traditional Muslim state cited by the U.S. State Department for a risk of terrorism, indiscriminate attacks on tourists and Westerners, and serious levels of crime. The prosecutors refused to give defense counsel the contact information they possessed, and the military judge in the case denied a request to order the prosecution to provide this information. Military defense counsel were left to seek out and locate the witnesses themselves, additionally and unnecessarily jeopardizing their personal safety.

Some of these problems could be solved by an independent defense resource funding authority that took defense needs seriously (provision of privilege teams); others will require policy changes within the DoD or by JTF-GTMO (equality of investigator access and meaningful client access). There are two problems, however, that require amendments to the proposed Senate bill to fix.

The first is the many issues my office has had with the both the quality and number of translators and interpreters provided to detailed counsel under the auspices of the CA. *See* 13 July Memo (Exh. A), at 16-17. By statute, the CA is responsible for the provision of interpretation services to the defense. Proposed § 948l(b). Its language should be amended to delete references to "defense counsel" and the "accused," and responsibility for the provision of these services should be assigned to the independent defense resource funding agency:

"(b) INTERPRETERS.—Under such regulations as the Secretary of Defense may prescribe, the convening authority of a military commission under this chapter may detail to or employ for the military commission interpreters who shall interpret for the military commission, and, as necessary, for trial counsel and defense counsel for the military commission, and for the accused."

Second, under proposed § 949c(b)(3)(A), an accused cannot be represented by a civilian unless that civilian is a United States citizen. For reasons discussed in the 13 July Memo (Exh. A) (at 17-18), this limitation is not justifiable and works a very real hardship on many accused and on their detailed counsel as well, who virtually always find it a benefit to their own relationship with the client to serve as counsel with an attorney from the accused's home country or culture. This subsection, and the related subsection § 949c(b)(3)(B), which requires membership in the bar of a state, federal territory or federal court as a related requirement, should be deleted from the Senate bill.

How Should the Fairness of Any Military Commissions System Be Judged?

To date, interested parties have offered various overall measures of fairness by which to test and justify any new commissions system. The TJAGs recently testified before the House Armed Service Committee that they believed that Common Article 3 of the Geneva Conventions, and no other body of law, was the correct legal standard that the new commissions must meet. The Administration, through DoD General Counsel Jeh Johnson and DOJ National Security Division head David Kris, has suggested that if the military commissions do not satisfy some ill-defined notion of constitutional "general due process," then federal courts may strike them down. Navy TJAG VADM Bruce MacDonald, in his testimony before both Senate and House Armed Services Committee, provided an informal measure: Any new commissions system must be one that we would feel comfortable in trying our own servicemen and women for violations of the law of war.

My position, and the official position of my office, is that the Commissions must meet the standards of both Common Article 3 and the United States Constitution as a whole. Because this stakes out a position somewhat different, and more stringent, than the other parties, I want to briefly discuss my reasons for believing that this standard is the correct one. Those reasons are both historical and logical, apart from the strictly-speaking legal basis for the argument. Those legalities are being fought out in commissions, so today I will address the historical and logical reasons to believe that the Constitution applies in full to the proposed military commissions.

(1) The Actual History of Military Commissions

First, understanding those reasons requires an understanding of the institution of the military commission in greater historical depth than others have generally supplied. Air Force TJAG Lt. Gen. Rives, for example, cited the history of military commissions several times in explaining his general support for the Senate bill in his testimony in the House Armed Services Committee, but his citations only reached back to World War II and the *Quirin* and *Yamashita* cases that upheld two of the more well-known (or notorious) of that period's commission verdicts. The military commission existed, however, for 100 years before World War II, since their inception in General Winfield Scott's General Order 20 issued in connection with his invasion of Mexico during the Mexican war, and when that history is included in the analysis, the picture of what military commissions actually stand for changes dramatically.

I obviously cannot tell that whole story here in any detail, and so will only review those aspects demonstrating that the current assumptions about the historical role and practices of military commissions underlying the TJAGs and Administration's positions are fundamentally inaccurate and at odds with their actual history.[5] In particular, this actual history demonstrates that those aspects of the Senate bill that continue to embrace procedural rules that are in patent conflict with our constitutional traditions – including the provisions permitting the introduction of coerced statements and otherwise inadmissible hearsay – are deeply inconsistent with the history and actual practice of military commissions.

The genuine history and practice of military commissions demonstrates two general propositions that have been entirely lost in the current debates:

a) A commitment to constitutional values embodied in the common law of evidence, including in particular (i) a prohibition on the admission of coerced (involuntary) statements and (ii) a prohibition on the admission of hearsay (except for the common law hearsay exceptions); and
b) A commitment to conform to court-martial procedures.

These propositions may appear strange if one is accustomed to hearing the current Senate bill's variations from constitutional norms justified on the basis of "battlefield evidence" and "military necessity." In fact, however, this use of "military necessity" is completely at odds with the original meaning of "military necessity" as it was used in connection with military commissions. The traditional justification for the use of military commissions was indeed based on "military necessity," but that term had nothing whatsoever to do with "battlefield evidence" and similar notions. Rather, from Gen. Winfield Scott's original Mexican War commissions forward, the "military necessity" for the use of commissions has been jurisdictional, and not based on any putative need for admitting otherwise patently inadmissible evidence. The jurisdictional necessity for the use of military commissions was based on the severe limitations placed on the jurisdiction of courts-martial until Congressional revision of the Articles of War in the 1912-1916 period. As a result of these limitations, civilians and enemy combatants could (with certain limited exceptions) generally not be tried in courts-martial in situations of military occupation (e.g., General Scott's march through Mexico), under martial law (e.g., military governance of parts of border states during the Civil War), and in battlefield situations involving the capture of enemy combatants who violated the law of war (i.e., "law of war military commissions" such as those established by the original MCA of 2006 and carried forward by the current proposed amendments).

The need created by that jurisdictional gap was the actual meaning of "military necessity" until the notion began to be employed by the previous Administration as a justification for commission procedures that violated the Constitution and Common Article 3 of the Geneva Conventions. *See e.g.* Benet, *A Treatise on Military Law and the Practice of Courts-Martial, 6th ed.*, Chapter XV, "Military Commissions") (1868); Winthrop, *Digest of the Opinions of the Judge Advocate General* 325 (1880), among other sources. Proof that this jurisdictional problem was the meaning of "military necessity" is provided by the fact that, with extremely limited exceptions (and none relevant to the present legislation), military commissions consistently followed the same procedures as courts-martial. Indeed, as the below points demonstrate, the one thing that the phrase "military necessity" has clearly *not* meant is that military commissions can deviate from court-martial practice in a manner that violates the Constitution as a matter of course.

First, for 100 years, it was a cardinal principle of military commissions that they followed the procedural and evidentiary rules of courts-martial. The conformity of military commission practice with court-martial evidence rules is particularly telling, because both courts-martial and commissions followed the common law of evidence. As a result, military commissions, like courts-martial, imposed an absolute bar on the use of coerced statements and any hearsay that fell outside the scope of one of the accepted exceptions to the hearsay rule.

By way of example, during the Spanish-American War numerous military commission trials were conducted in the Phillipines during the Phillipine insurrection against American rule. These commissions were convened mid-way in the 100 year history between General Scott's original commissions and the World War II commissions upon which the former Administration, and now the current Administration as well, relies to justify its approach to commission procedures. These commissions and their rules were characteristic of the conduct of commissions during this entire history, and are cited solely as examples. Similar examples from General Scott's military commissions and "councils of war" (his name for what we would now call "law of war military commissions") could also be cited.

The precedents and rulings from the Phillipine insurrection demonstrate that, traditionally, military commissions were not only dedicated to remarkable standards of impartiality and fairness in the face of a bloody and brutal enemy, but specifically committed to the constitutional values that underlie the common law of evidence, values which are overturned in the current MCA and proposed Senate bill.

For instance, in one case – involving the murder of five United States soldiers -- a commission conviction was overturned for failure to abide by the hearsay rules:

> "In th[is] case the surprising error occurs of admitting as evidence the report of a board of officers, which had investigated the cause of disappearance of the soldiers. . .. Every officer, even of a year's service, should be presumed to know that mere written ex parte statements are wholly inadmissible as evidence, and grossly irregular in a capital case."

Headquarters, Division of the Philippines, Gen. Order No. 36 (Feb. 19, 1902) (emphasis added). This statement, from a military commission over 100 years ago, is an embarrassment to the hearsay provisions of the Senate bill.

The history speaks in the same voice when it comes to the admissibility of involuntary statements. Such statements were inadmissible under the common law of evidence as inherently unreliable (this evidentiary rule was the precursor of the modern constitutional requirement of voluntariness), and, accordingly, military commissions have traditionally been equally vigilant about the prohibition on coerced statements, requiring proof of voluntariness before they were admitted in evidence, and being reversed when they failed to abide by that rule. *See e.g.* Headquarters, Division of the Philippines, Gen. Order No. 232 (Aug. 22, 1901), in 2 Charges of Cruelty, Etc. to the Natives of the Philippines, S. Doc. 57-1 No. 205 Pt. 2 (1902), at 363.

In sum, the actual history and tradition of the military commission stands for something quite different than how it has been presented over the past eight years. As one commission summed up its understanding of its role:

> "That it is better that many guilty men should escape punishment than an innocent one suffer is too well grounded in the administration of justice to pass unheeded by military commissions. So, too, it is better that no person, innocent or guilty, should be convicted unfairly, in violation of his legal rights and privileges, or in defiance of the well-established and equitable laws of evidence without which the evolution of [our] system of law and justice would be impossible."

Headquarters, Division of the Philippines, Gen. Order No. 365 (Nov. 25, 1901), in 2 Charges of Cruelty, Etc. to the Natives of the Philippines, S. Doc. 57-1 No. 205 Pt. 2 (1902), at 305.

As against this 100 year-long consistent history of respect for the rule of law and constitutional values in military commissions, proponents of the controversial and unconstitutional deviations from court-martial procedure have generally focused solely on two World War II precedents: *Ex parte Quirin*, 317 U.S. 1 (1942), and *In re Yamashita*, 327 U.S. 1 (1946). But, as the leading historical work on military commissions has definitively demonstrated, these precedents are historical anomalies. See David Glazier, "Precedents Lost: The Neglected History of the Military Commission," 46 Va. J. Int'l L. 5 (2005). It is worth noting that, after *Korematsu v. United States*, 323 U.S. 214 (1944), these are two of the most harshly criticized of the Supreme Court's precedents in the past 100 years.

Most important, that criticism has come from the Supreme Court itself, leaving the precedential status of both cases – at least insofar as they stand for the constitutionality of military commissions that deviate from the practices of courts-martial in ways that facially violate the Constitution – very much in doubt. *See e.g. Boumediene v. Bush*, 128 S.Ct. 2229, 2271 (2008) ("[T]he procedures used to try General Yamashita have been sharply criticized by Members of this Court. *See Hamdan*, 548 U.S., at 617, 126 S.Ct. 2749; *Yamashita*, *supra*, at 41- 81, 66 S.Ct. 340 (Rutledge, J., dissenting). We need not revisit [Yamashita and Qurin], however."); *Hamdan v. Rumsfeld*, 126 S.Ct. 2749, 2774 (2006) ("We have no occasion to revisit *Quirin*'s controversial characterization of Article of War 15 as congressional authorization for military commissions."); id., 126 S.Ct. at 2788-9 ("The procedures and evidentiary rules used to try General Yamashita near the end of World War II deviated in significant respects from those then governing courts-martial.. . .

The force of that precedent, however, has been seriously undermined by post-World War II developments. . . . The most notorious exception to the principle of uniformity, then, has been stripped of its precedential value."); *Hamdi v. Rumsfeld*, 542 U.S. 507, 569 (2004) (Scalia, J., joined by Stevens, J., dissenting) ("The case [*Quirin*] was not this Court's finest hour.").

Because they are in effect a new system of criminal justice that deliberately dispenses with protections embodied in the Constitution for well over 200 years, there is little doubt that any convictions arising from the new military commissions -- especially any capital convictions -- will be reviewed by the Supreme Court as a matter of course. It is a gamble at best that *Quirin* and *Yamashita*, insofar as they suggest that the fact that the mere invocation of "military necessity" – especially given the misuse to which that term has been put – will be enough to justify these kinds of wholesale and (as demonstrated above) unprecedented changes in American military justice – will withstand renewed scrutiny by today's Court. See e.g. *United States v. Robel*, 389 U.S. 258, 263 (1967) ("[T]he phrase 'war power' cannot be invoked as a talismanic incantation to support any exercise of congressional power which can be brought within its ambit."). Congress thus proceeds at its own risk if the discredited history of the World War II military commissions will be sufficient to uphold the current Senate bill.

(2) It is Entirely Illogical to Apply the Rules of "Battlefield Evidence" and Other Battlefield Conditions to Court Proceedings that Take Place Many Years and Thousands of Miles Away from the Battlefield

In his testimony before the House Armed Services Committee, VADM MacDonald suggested that the TJAGs' proposed "reliability" test would incorporate the traditional voluntariness as one factor. That voluntariness factor, however, would be subject to a "sliding scale," whereby the further away from the battlefield the interrogation took place, the more important voluntariness became as a determining factor of the "reliability" test. Specifically, VADM MacDonald testified, in his view, all statements taken in Guantanamo should be evaluated under the voluntariness test alone because of these interrogations' distance – presumably in both time and location – from the battlefield.

There is a real logic to VADM MacDonald's analysis of the TJAGs' "reliability" test, but it is unclear why he limited this logic to the question of voluntariness alone. In fact, the farther away in time and distance from a battlefield a trial occurs, the less sense it makes to deviate from the traditional constitutional norms that govern any other criminal trials in this country. Indeed, one of the traditional limitations on the jurisdiction of "law of war" military commissions like those at issue in the Senate bill was the requirement that they actually be conducted on the battlefield itself and before the end of the war, because that geographical and temporal proximity to war-time conditions were the only possible justification for those deviations from court-martial procedure that sometimes occurred in military commissions, despite the general rule of following court-martial practice whenever possible. *See e.g.* Winthrop, *Military Law and Precedents* 836-841 (2nd ed. 1920); *Hamdan*, 126 S.Ct. at 2777 & n.29.

These criteria are not arbitrary; they were designed by common law courts to ensure that military commissions remain the exception rather than the rule of criminal adjudication, and are limited to only those exigent situations where they are actually necessary to the conduct of the military's mission. As the Supreme Court put it, these prerequisites were "designed to ensure that a military necessity exists to justify the use of this extraordinary tribunal." *Hamdan*, 126 S.Ct. at 2777.

These criteria are thus logical as well as historical. As VADM MacDonald recognized, the further away in time and space from the battlefield that a trial occurs, the less justification there is for holding trials conducted as if the bombs were falling and the only evidence available for use is that obtained, to use his example, by soldiers' kicking doors down and questioning enemy insurgents at the point of a rifle. That is hardly the case with respect either to the current military commissions or the amended versions provided by the Senate bill. In every respect, these trials will resemble, from the perspective of military exigency or "necessity," a trial in any other jurisdiction in the United States.

Thus, MCA tribunals serve a very different purpose than do genuine law-of-war military commissions. As the Supreme Court has explained the law-of-war commission, "its role is primarily a factfinding one – to determine, typically on the battlefield itself, whether the defendant has violated the law of war." *Hamdan*, 126 S.Ct. at 2776. That is, genuine law-of-war commissions are convened only after perpetrators are caught red-handed on the battlefield (as in *Yamashita*) or behind the lines (as in *Quirin*). Its function is thus limited to the relatively minimal "factfinding" required to assure the military commander (who, being "typically on the battlefield itself," is in no position to guarantee more than this) that the accused is in fact subject to his war-crime jurisdiction and in fact perpetrated the crime. That underlying reality explains both the extremely brief time period between capture and trial typical of the World War II commissions, as well as the far less formal evidentiary and procedural rules employed by genuine commissions.

The MCA military commissions, by contrast, are held far away from the exigencies of the battlefield, and long enough after the crime that there is more than enough time – as the current commission cases amply demonstrate – for traditional law-enforcement fact-finding techniques, including both traditional law-enforcement interrogations and other more sophisticated methods typical of modern prosecutions in other American criminal courts. How and why the logic of the battlefield should apply to proceedings that in every way resemble ordinary court proceedings in which the Constitution governs is a mystery to which no boilerplate invocation of "military necessity" or "battlefield evidence" provides more than a fig-leaf of an answer.

In short, because there is no logical reason *not* to treat military commission trials like the fundamentally ordinary criminal trials that they are ("ordinary," at least, in every sense that matters to the only legitimate justifications for deviation from the Constitution and court-marital procedure), the Constitution ought to apply to them equally as well as every other criminal trial. VADM MacDonald's logic proves more, perhaps, than he intended, but it remains a valid basis for invoking the entire Constitution, and not just the constitutional proscription against the use of involuntary statements, once trials are as removed from the battlefield in time and space as the trials contemplated by the Senate bill.

CONCLUSION

In summary, any revised military commissions statute must provide the defense adequate resources to ensure trials that produce verdicts that are both reliable and fair to the accused.

Equality of arms between prosecution and defense must be the norm. The standard of fairness that should be applied to military commission trials is compliance with both Common Article 3 of the Geneva Conventions and the United States Constitution in full. Any new commissions system must be one that we would feel comfortable in trying our own servicemen and women for violations of the law of war. An accused should not be given fewer rights or opportunity to defend himself by virtue of a prosecutor's choice of forum - that is the antithesis of a "regularly constituted court."

Peter R. Masciola
Colonel, USAFG
Chief Defense Counsel

Attachments:

(a) Letter from Col Peter R. Masciola, Chief Defense Counsel, OMC, to Mr. Jeh Johnson, General Counsel of the Department of Defense, and Mr. Eric Holder, Attorney General of the United States, dated 13 July 2009, Re: Request for Adequate Resources
(b) Expert Requests filed by OMC-D Counsel to the Convening Authority, dated 21 July 2009
(c) Letter from Col Peter R. Masciola, Chief Defense Counsel, OMC, to Mr. Jeh Johnson, General Counsel of the Department of Defense, and Mr. Eric Holder, Attorney General of the United States, dated 9 June 2009, Re: Request for Adequate Resources
(d) *Ex Parte* Order, *United States v. Ahmed Khalfan Ghailani*, 98 Cr 1023 (LAK), U.S. District Court, Southern District of New York (25 June 2009)

Cc:
Mr. Jeh Johnson
Mr. Paul Koffsky LTG Scott Black
Lt Gen Jack Rives
VADM Bruce MacDonald
BGen James Walker Colonel Mark Martins Mr. Brad Wiegmann Mr. David Kris
AG Eric Holder

End Notes

[1] I have omitted the attachments to the 13 July memo itself because they are all included as separate exhibits to this testimony.

[2] BG Hartman's testimony was as follows:

Q [LCDR KUEBLER]: Sir, have you had any communications with any officials of the Canadian government concerning the Khadr case?
A [BG HARTMANN]: Yes.
Q [LCDR KUEBLER]: And who would that be, sir?

A [BG HARTMANN]: Bernard Lee is at the Canadian embassy here in the United States, and I've spoken with him a few times. And then there was a meeting among--there was a meeting in, I believe, it was in the summer of 2007, I believe there was a meeting with the legal advisor to the Foreign Ministry--Canadian Foreign Ministry and then he had two other people with him, one of whom was a military person, another person I do not recall, and then Mr. Lee was there as well.

Q [LCDR KUEBLER]: What were--was the subject matter of those meetings?

A [BG HARTMANN]: It was just one meeting. It was just a general--don't recall the subject matter exactly. It was just a general introduction for me because, I think, I only had been in the job for 2 weeks when this happened, very, very shortly after I arrived. I don't remember the entir-- anything about the content of the conversations except that it was about Mr. Khadr.

Q [LCDR KUEBLER]: Who initiated----

A [BG HARTMANN]: And just in general the--just in general the process that we were going through and that--how the military commissions process worked.

Q [LCDR KUEBLER]: Who initiated the meeting, sir?

A [BG HARTMANN]: I don't know who initiated the meeting. I was invited to it.

Q [LCDR KUEBLER]: Were there other DoD or administration officials present?

A [BG HARTMANN]: Mr. Paul Nye was there, who was the person that I generally spoke with inside the Office of General Counsel, and I believe Mr. John Bellinger was there from the State Department.

Q [LCDR KUEBLER]: And your conversations with Mr. Lee, sir, what were they related to?

A [BG HARTMANN]: Generally, they had been just updates. If Mr. Lee has a question about something that appears in the press, he'll call and ask. And if he learns about a motion and the motion has been released, he may ask me to provide that to him or something like that.

Q [LCDR KUEBLER]: And you have provided motions to Mr. Lee?

A [BG HARTMANN]: To the extent that they've been released to the public, yes.

United States v. Omar Khadr, Transcript of Rule of Military Commission 803 Session (13 August 2008), at 600- 601.

[3] Military courts have, to date, resisted the appointment of paid civilian counsel in capital cases (although there is some precedent for it, *see e.g. United States v. Curtis*, 33 M.J.101, 109 n.11 (C.M.A. 1991) (authorizing funding of military defense counsel "for use in their discretion to obtain the assistance of 'death qualified' civilian counsel, to retain expert consultants, or otherwise prepare their case"), as I have already explained, the nature of courts-martial is unlike other courts insofar as it has a disciplinary component and the participants in the court-martial – prosecutor, defense attorney, military judge, and convening authority – typically share a common military culture and sense of common commitment. Given these differences from federal court, it is not surprising that historically military courts have not seen the need for funding of nonmilitary counsel.

[4] Alternatively, a solution that would leave the structuring of the "learned counsel" provisions in the hands of the regulatory authority of the Secretary of Defense, could amend the same subsection with the following language:

"(C) To be represented before a military commission by civilian counsel if provided at no expense *to the* Government *pursuant to regulations prescribed by the Secretary of Defense*, and by either the defense counsel detailed or by military counsel of the accused's own selection, if reasonably available.

This amendment would leave the Secretary to issue regulations that, for example, provided for hourly payment to death-qualified, civilian "learned counsel" in capital cases but not to civilian attorneys in noncapital cases or civilian co-counsel in capital cases who were not "learned" (or payment to "non-learned" civilians at a lower rate).

[5] For that full picture, I recommend the article by David Glazier, a 20-year active-duty Navy Commander-turned law professor who has gone into this history with the greatest scholarly depth. David Glazier, "Precedents Lost: The Neglected History of the Military Commission," 46 Va. J. Int'l L. 5 (2005).

In: The Military Commissions Act…
Editors: J. Segel, Soto Kimura
ISBN: 978-1-61470-072-2

Chapter 4

STATEMENT OF MAJOR DAVID J. R. FRAKT, USAFR OFFICE OF MILITARY COMMISSIONS – OFFICE OF THE CHIEF DEFENSE COUNSEL PREPARED TESTIMONY TO THE SUBCOMMITTEE ON THE CONSTITUTION, CIVIL RIGHTS AND CIVIL LIBERTIES COMMITTEE ON THE JUDICIARY UNITED STATES HOUSE OF REPRESENTATIVES*

THE MILITARY COMMISSIONS AND THE ABANDONMENT OF THE RULE OF LAW

By David J. R. Frakt, Lt Col (sel.), USAFR[1 2]

July 30, 2009

---

* This is an edited, reformatted and augmented version of a Prepared Testimony given by Major David J. R. Frakt, before Subcommittee on the Constitution, Civil Rights and Civil Liberties Committee on the Judiciary United States House of Representatives, on July 30, 2009.

I. Introduction

Chairman Conyers, Subcommittee Chairman Nadler, Ranking Member Sensenbrenner, members of the Subcommittee, thank you for giving me the opportunity to testify on this important subject, a subject with which I have been deeply engaged for the past couple of years.

The purpose of this hearing, as I understand it, is to consider whether military commissions are an appropriate, legitimate forum for prosecuting suspected terrorists and war criminals currently detained at Guantanamo Bay, Cuba, and other individuals who may be captured in the ongoing conflict with Al Qaeda and the Taliban. Assuming the answer to be yes, or that, regardless of the answer, military commissions are likely to continue to be utilized, a further purpose of this hearing is to determine what changes should be made to the Military Commissions Act of 2006 (MCA) to ensure that military commissions are regularly constituted courts which comport with our international treaty obligations, the law of war and the due process requirements of the U.S. Constitution. More specifically, are the amendments to MCA included in the Senate version of the 2010 National Defense Authorization Act sufficient to address the shortcomings of the MCA as enacted, or are more or different changes required to ensure that military commissions will provide fair, just trials which will withstand court challenges on appeal and be accepted as legitimate by the American public and the international community?

Before I answer these two critically important questions, let me first briefly explain my relevant experience which qualifies me to try to answer these questions. After graduating from Harvard Law School in 1994, and clerking for a year for the Honorable Monroe G. McKay of the U.S. Tenth Circuit Court of Appeals, I received a direct commission into the U.S. Air Force Judge Advocate General's Corps. I served on active duty from September 1995 to April 2005. During this time, my primary practice areas were military justice and international and operational law. In the spring of 2005, I transitioned into the Air Force Reserves, and started a second career as a law professor. At Western State University College of Law, I have taught criminal law, criminal procedure, evidence, professional responsibility (legal ethics), and a seminar on international war crimes, all courses which proved highly relevant when I was mobilized to active duty in April 2008 to serve as a military defense counsel with the Office of Military Commissions, Office of the Chief Defense Counsel. In the fall of 2008, I taught a seminar as an adjunct professor at Georgetown Law Center entitled "Terrorism as a War

Crime: Military Commissions and Alternative Approaches" as part of their National Security Law program. In 2007, I began an intensive study of the Military Commissions Act of 2006 and the implementing regulations published by the Secretary of Defense in the Manual for Military Commissions (which includes the Rules for Military Commissions or RCMs, the Military Commission Rules of Evidence or MCREs, and the list of crimes and elements), which culminated in the publication of a law review article comparing the rules and procedures of military commissions and courts-martial. 3 In January 2008, I answered a DoD-wide solicitation for volunteers to serve as defense counsel in military commissions and I was selected for the position in February 2008. I was mobilized to active duty in late April 2008 and promptly was detailed as lead defense counsel in two referred cases, *U.S. v. Mohammed Jawad* and *U.S. v. Ali Hamza al Bahlul*. I was engaged in extensive pre-trial litigation in the military commissions from May 2008 through September 2008 in both cases, including several multi-day motion hearings.[4] In October 2008, Mr. al Bahlul became the third and final detainee to be tried by military commission at Guantanamo. He was convicted and sentenced to life in prison in early November 2008. I was his sole defense counsel at trial. His case has now been turned over to appellate counsel to file an appeal.

As you are undoubtedly aware, there have been a number of recent developments in Mr. Jawad's case. The military commission was originally scheduled to go to trial in January 2009, but due to an interlocutory appeal filed by the prosecution, his case was delayed. Because the military commissions, including appeals pending before the Court of Military Commission Review were suspended by Executive Order of President Obama in late January, the CMCR has stayed its decision until September 17, 2009. Although I completed my active duty tour in early June 2009, I continue to represent Mr. Jawad in my capacity as a Reserve JAG officer. Along with the ACLU, I also represent Mr. Jawad in his *habeas corpus* petition in U.S. District Court for the District of Columbia where we have been actively seeking Mr. Jawad's release from his illegal detention. Two weeks ago, in response to a motion to suppress, the government conceded that every statement made by Mr. Jawad since his arrest on December 17, 2002, was the product of torture. Accordingly, the District Court Judge, the Honorable Ellen Huvelle, suppressed the statements. Last Friday, July 24th, the Department of Justice filed a notice with the court that the United States no longer considers Mr. Jawad detainable under the laws of war. They informed the Court that Mr. Jawad would be transferred out of the maximum security prison where he has been held for six and half years into a less restrictive detention camp for detainees eligible for release. An order granting the writ of habeas corpus and ordering Mr. Jawad's immediate release is expected shortly. We are hopeful that Mr. Jawad will soon be repatriated to Afghanistan and reunited with his family. In short, as both a scholar and practitioner, I have substantial experience to bring to bear on the issues being considered by this committee.

As we ponder the questions before us, I think it is important to review where we are now and how we got to this point. As the Administration considers reviving the military commissions and Congress considers various revisions to the Military Commissions Act, everyone should have a clear understanding of why the military commissions of the Bush Administration were created and where they went wrong.

II. The Abandonment of the Rule of Law

One point on which all sides should be able to agree is that the military commissions of the Bush Administration were a catastrophic failure. The military commissions clearly failed to achieve their intended purpose. After more than seven years and hundreds of millions of dollars wasted, the military commissions yielded only three convictions, all of relatively minor figures. Not a single terrorist responsible for the planning or execution of a terrorist attack against the United States was convicted. Two of the convicted, David Hicks and Salim Hamdan, received sentences of less than one year and were subsequently released. The third trial, of my client Mr. al Bahlul, although yielding a life sentence, was far from a triumph for the military commissions. There were several problematic aspects of this trial, not the least of which was the fact that several members of Mr. Hicks' jury were actually recycled for this military commission. More disturbing was the denial of Mr. al Bahlul's statutory right of self-representation. Mr. al Bahlul, a low-level Al Qaeda media specialist, wanted to represent himself before the military commissions and this request was granted by the military judge at the arraignment, Army Colonel Peter Brownback. Soon thereafter, Col. Brownback was involuntarily retired from the Army and replaced. The new judge revoked Mr. al Bahlul's *pro se* status, although he knew that Mr. al Bahlul had refused to authorize me, his appointed military defense counsel, to represent him. As a result, there was no defense presented; Mr. al Bahlul was convicted of all charges and received the maximum life sentence.

Why, with the entire resources of the Department of Defense, the Justice Department and the national intelligence apparatus at their disposal, were the military commissions such an abysmal failure? The answer is simple: the military commissions were built on a foundation of legal distortions and outright illegality. The rules, procedures and substantive law created for the commissions were the product of, or were necessitated by, the wholesale abandonment of the rule of law by the Bush Administration in the months after 9/11. In the United States of America, any such legal scheme is ultimately doomed to fail.

If we review the origins of the military commissions, a clear picture emerges of an intentional disregard for existing legal norms. Perhaps the first indication that the rule of law was to be abandoned was in President Bush's Military Order of November 13, 2001.[5] In this document, President Bush found: "it is not practicable to apply in military commissions . . . the principles of law and the rules of evidence generally recognized in the trial of criminal cases in the United States district courts." In other words, what we consider essential for a fair trial for *us* would not be required for *them*. How did the Administration know, two months after 9/11, before a single major terrorist suspect had been caught, and before a single prosecutor had reviewed a single piece of evidence, that it would be impracticable to prosecute terrorism cases using existing rules and procedures? They didn't, of course. But having made this unsupported finding, President Bush and his senior advisors set out to make it a reality.

Another major step in the abandonment of the rule of law came on February 7, 2002, when President Bush issued another order,[6] this time announcing that the Geneva Conventions would not apply to those detained in the War on Terror, who were labeled with the new and misleading term "unlawful enemy combatants." The President held not only that such persons were not entitled to be treated as prisoners of war, but also, shockingly, that they were not even legally entitled to be treated humanely. With a stroke of the pen, the President wiped out the principle source of the law of war and the entire existing legal framework for the treatment of persons captured in an armed conflict and replaced it with a policy preference for humane treatment, which could be readily discarded whenever it interfered with military or intelligence operations. The decision that humane treatment was not required created unnecessary confusion about what was permissible and cleared the way for the approval of a vast array of patently illegal and highly coercive "enhanced interrogation techniques" to be employed upon the detainees.

The abandonment of the rule of law was compounded by the decision to house the "unlawful enemy combatants" at Guantanamo Bay, Cuba, and to turn the detention facilities there into a legal black hole, a place where detainees were not even entitled to be informed of the basis for their detention, much less challenge it. Indeed, the Bush Administration, regrettably aided and abetted by Congress, made a determined (and for several years, successful) effort to prevent detainees from gaining access to courts or legal representation. In an environment with no judicial oversight or meaningful avenues for redress, the detainees were simply at the mercy of their captors -- and the captors were not in a merciful mood. The extraordinary pressure to produce "actionable intelligence" coupled with the vengeful mood of the times led inexorably to shameful abuses of detainees.[7]

In 2002 and 2003, as senior Bush Administration officials drafted the rules for the President's military tribunals, they were aware of several important pieces of information about the detainees at Guantanamo. First, despite claims by high-level officials, including Secretary Rumsfeld, that the detainees represented "the worst of the worst," in reality, the vast majority of the detainees had no tangible connection with Al Qaeda, and even fewer had any provable role in any terrorist attack. Many of the detainees were completely innocent of any wrongdoing, and had simply been turned in for bounty, or were caught in the wrong place at the wrong time. The worst that could be said about many of them was that they had fought against the U.S. and Coalition forces that had invaded Afghanistan, conduct that, under the laws of war, would not be considered a war crime. A small group of those captured were likely guilty of terrorism crimes, but not crimes of war. The Administration was also keenly aware that, to the extent that there was some evidence of criminal acts by a small fraction of the detainees, much, if not most, of this evidence had been developed through highly coercive interrogations, which would not be admissible in a regular court of law.

The drafters of the original military commission rules[8] resolved each of these problems by rewriting the law. First, the rules of evidence were rewritten to allow the introduction of coerced statements and to eliminate the rules barring the fruits of torture and abuse. Second, the drafters classified as "war crimes" conduct, such as conspiracy and terrorism crimes that are violations of regular criminal law but had never previously been recognized as covered by the laws of war, largely because the laws of war rightly apply to the narrow context of armed conflict. They also created a number of "new" war crimes based on the alleged status of a person, rather than on conduct that actually violates the laws of war.[9] The most egregious examples of these were the invented crimes "Murder by an Unprivileged Belligerent," and "Destruction of Property by an Unprivileged Belligerent" which appeared in the original commission's list of offenses. These provisions made killing U.S. soldiers, destroying military property, or attempting to do so, a war crime. In other words, the U.S. declared that it was a war crime to fight, regardless of whether the fighters comply with the laws of war.

After protracted litigation, the original military commissions were invalidated by the Supreme Court in *Hamdan v. Rumsfeld* in the summer of 2006 before anyone was ever convicted. With nearly five years wasted, there was a great rush to put a new legal system in place. Within months, "new and improved" military commissions were authorized by Congress through the Military Commissions Act of 2006 (MCA). While these legislatively created commissions were undoubtedly an improvement over those created by Presidential decree, the hastily drafted and poorly considered MCA still incorporated some of the key distortions and departures from the rule of law featured in the invalidated version. Most disturbingly, Congress retained the rules of evidence (with minor variations) that permitted coerced evidence to be introduced. Congress also retained the full list of war crimes (again with minor variations), including the invented ones, and even added new ones, such as the flexible catch-all "material support to terrorism."

The Obama Administration has now acknowledged that material support is not a traditional war crime, calling into question all three of the convictions thus far attained. (Mr. Hicks, Mr. Hamdan and Mr. al Bahlul were all convicted of material support. For Mr. Hicks and Mr. Hamdan, it was the only crime of which they were convicted.) Although the military commissions were purportedly modeled on the Uniform Code of Military Justice, the best features of that system, such as the robust pretrial investigation required by Article 32 of the Uniform Code of Military Justice (UCMJ) and equal access by the prosecution and the defense to evidence and witnesses, were removed or weakened. The implementing regulations produced by the Secretary of Defense,[10] which could have corrected or mitigated some of the glaring problems with the legislation, served only to exacerbate them. [11]

Despite the widespread criticism of the MCA by the international community, legal scholars and non-governmental organizations, identifying the myriad shortcomings of the military commissions, the Bush Administration was determined to press ahead with the military commissions and convict as many detainees as possible. It was the hope and deliberate strategy of the administration that if the military commissions were well underway by the time the next Administration assumed office, with several trials completed and convictions duly rendered (the Administration did not foresee or accept the possibility of acquittals[12]), the commissions would be difficult to derail.

This "spray and pray"[13] strategy might have succeeded but for one factor the Bush Administration never anticipated: many of the military lawyers assigned the roles of prosecutors, defense counsel and judges in the military commissions refused to put aside their ethical obligations and their training in the rule of law. Many of these judge advocates, officers with decades of expertise in the law of war, considered the military commissions an affront to the military justice system to which they had devoted their careers. Ethical and courageous military prosecutors, such as former Chief Prosecutor Colonel Morris Davis and Lieutenant Colonel Darrel Vandeveld, who took their oaths to defend the Constitution seriously, resigned rather than be party to trials using coerced evidence or to allow political considerations to interfere with their prosecutorial judgment. Professional military judges refused to be bullied into endorsing the Administration's strained interpretations of the law of war. Tenacious military defense counsel challenged the government at every turn, exposing the many flaws in this concocted legal system and the disgraceful brutality with which their clients had been treated. Through patient, professional advocacy both inside and outside the commissions, these lawyers managed to put the brakes on the military commission freight train and slow the proceedings to the point where it was a simple matter for President Obama to suspend them almost immediately after assuming office. This suspension period allows us an opportunity for reasoned debate about the shortcomings of the military commissions and their efficacy and utility.

Although I have become known as a fierce critic of the military commissions, I want to make it clear that am not opposed to military commissions as a general matter, but rather am opposed to military commissions in their current form. I am a strong proponent of military justice and have no concerns about the military's ability to provide a fair trial, even for our worst enemies, given a fair set of rules and procedures. In my law review article, I did not propose to abolish the military commissions, but rather suggested a number of legislative and regulatory changes to convert them into a viable, acceptable legal system. After practicing in the military commissions, I developed some additional concerns with the military commissions which also would require legislative action to address. (These concerns are addressed in some detail below.) Although I still believe it is theoretically possible to amend the MCA to create valid commissions, the best solution would simply be to repeal the MCA and start over to create military commissions that are not just loosely based on the UCMJ and Manual for Courts-Martial, but are virtually identical. Any proposed deviation from court-martial procedure would have to be carefully scrutinized to ensure that it was truly necessary and appropriate and not merely an effort to favor the prosecution. Any deviations, individually and cumulatively, from the rules and procedures for general courts-martial should be minimal, and must not significantly detract from the overall fairness of the proceedings. In my view, had we adopted a military commissions scheme that truly mirrored the rules and procedures for general courts-martial, as was already authorized under federal law in 2001, we would not be in the position we find ourselves in today. The military commissions would have succeeded in providing fair trials and would not have been plagued by endless delays, challenges and setbacks.

Recognizing that it is highly unlikely that the Military Commissions Act will be repealed, and that the preferred approach of the Administration and Congress appears to be to revise it, there are a number of amendments that I would recommend.

III. Recommended Revisions to the MCA

A. Admissibility of Coerced Statements

First and foremost, it is of the utmost importance that the military commissions categorically bar the admission of coerced evidence. The proposal in the Senate NDAA to amend § 948r to preclude the admissibility of statements made as a result of cruel, degrading and inhumane interrogation methods does not go far enough because it still allows for the admission of coerced statements so long as the government disputes "the degree of coercion," and a judge determines its reliability and that "the interests of justice would best be served" by admission of the statement. This entire provision is built on false premises. There are no circumstances where "the interests of justice would best be served" by the introduction of involuntary statements. One significant reason that involuntary statements are inadmissible is because, as a category, such statements are not reliable. I concur with the Administration's view that due process standards apply to military commissions and endorse the proposal of the administration to require a voluntariness standard for the admissibility of all statements. The use of a voluntariness standard, a standard which pre-dates Miranda v. Arizona, would not mean that soldiers should be required to administer Miranda or Article 31, UCMJ warnings on the battlefield, or that evidence would necessarily be excluded for lack of a rights advisement. Rather, a totality of the circumstances test would be employed to determine if a statement was voluntary.

B. Derivative Evidence

Congress must also restore the ban on evidence derived from coerced, involuntary statements. When the Secretary of Defense promulgated the Military Commission Rules of Evidence, the derivative evidence rule was omitted from MCRE 304. Thus, although MCRE prohibits the introduction of statements which are the product of torture and limits the introduction of coerced statements, it does not prohibit the introduction of evidence derived from an interrogation in which torture, coercion, or cruel, degrading and inhumane interrogation methods were used. This evidentiary loophole creates a powerful incentive to use unauthorized abusive interrogation methods. MCRE 304 should be amended to mirror Military Rule of Evidence 304 which states simply "an involuntary statement or any derivative evidence therefrom may not be received in evidence against an accused who made the statement if the accused makes a timely motion to suppress or an objection to the evidence under this rule."

C. Hearsay Evidence

Congress should significantly restrict the use of hearsay evidence to conform military commission procedures to those utilized in federal criminal court and general courts-martial. The hearsay rules currently in effect under the MCA create a presumption in favor of hearsay and inappropriately place the burden on the opposing party to prove the unreliability of the hearsay, The proposed revision to § 949a.(b)(3)(D) in the Senate NDAA goes a long way toward improving this rule and bringing the rule in line with federal practice, but still permits a greater degree of hearsay evidence than is justifiable, creating a potential for unfairness and unnecessarily infringing on the right of confrontation. This provision should be further amended to require that hearsay admitted under any special military or intelligence necessity exception must be "more probative on the point for which it is offered than other evidence which the proponent can procure through reasonable efforts."

D. Choice of Counsel

The MCA currently requires that the accused be represented by military counsel. The Obama Administration has recently proposed a rule change which purports to give greater choice of counsel to the accused. However, the accused is still required to have an appointed military defense lawyer. This provision for the right to request individual military defense counsel does bring military commission practice more in line with court-martial practice, but does nothing to address the real problem of choice of counsel: most of the accused are unwilling to be represented by American military lawyers. I experienced this myself. I was appointed to represent Mr. Ali Hamza al Bahlul, but he refused to accept me as his attorney, as he had rejected several other previously assigned military counsel. It was not personal. It was simply that he was Al Qaeda and I was the enemy. The refusal to accept the representation of the detailed defense counsel has been a major source of delay in the military commissions and has placed several military counsel in untenable ethical quandaries. The requirement to be represented by military counsel has caused several defendants to seek to represent themselves, which has also caused significant delay and logistical problems. Of course, the rules permit accused who have the resources to also hire a civilian counsel at their own expense, but such counsel must be U.S. citizens. The requirement of U.S. citizenship is unjustifiable and should be eliminated. Non-U.S. citizens may represent U.S. service members in courts-martial. In fact, non-citizens may serve in the U.S. Armed Forces. It is particularly unfair when attorneys from our coalition partners, such as Canada, the U.K. and Australia, are ineligible to represent detainees from their home countries. The citizenship requirement should be replaced with a rule permitting foreign counsel but requiring them to have proficiency in English and to be admitted to practice in at least one U.S. jurisdiction. Of course, the foreign counsel must also be eligible for a visa and meet other security requirements.

E. Pretrial Investigation

The MCA eliminated one of the best features of the military justice system, the Article 32 pretrial investigation. Article 32 of the UCMJ, sets forth the requirements of a "thorough and impartial investigation" prior to referral of charges to a General Court-Martial. Under Article 32, a neutral, experienced investigating officer, typically a senior JAG officer, investigates the charges, determines if there are reasonable grounds to believe the offenses were committed by the accused, explores potential legal and evidentiary issues, and makes recommendations as to the appropriate disposition of the charges. The Article 32 investigation also provides an opportunity for the defense to receive a significant amount of discovery early in the process. Article 32 investigations frequently help to winnow out weak or duplicative charges and narrow the issues for trial; they can also facilitate pre-trial agreements. The lack of any pretrial investigation is a serious limitation on the due process available in military commissions, and gives far too much power to the prosecution. It is contrary to both domestic and international practice for serious offenses (including capital offenses) to be referred to trial without any independent review. In federal court, a grand jury indictment is required for any felony. State courts require either a grand jury or a preliminary hearing in front of a judge. International war crimes tribunals such as the ICC and ICTY require approval from the pre-trial chamber. A pretrial investigation requirement modeled on Article 32 and Rule for Court-Martial 405 should be incorporated into the MCA.

F. Statutes of Limitation

There are no statutes of limitation in the MCA, even where the comparable offense under the UCMJ or federal law carries a statute of limitation. This enables disparate treatment of non-citizens tried in military commissions. This should be remedied to ensure that there are reasonable statutes of limitation in place for non-capital offenses. Provision for tolling the statute of limitations until an offense is discovered or until a suspect is captured may be appropriate.

G. Speedy Trial

There is no real requirement for a speedy trial under the MCA. The MCA specifically makes inapplicable the speedy trial requirements of the UCMJ14 which require that a service member placed in pretrial confinement be charged and brought to trial promptly (within 120 days) or released. Since the detainees are ostensibly detained under the law of war, which permits combatants to be removed from the battlefield for the duration of the conflict, requiring a detainee to be charged or released within 120 days would be unreasonable. However, the government should not be able to hold detainees indefinitely before charging them, especially when the government is aware of chargeable offenses. Once a detainee in custody is suspected of involvement in a chargeable offense, there should be some reasonable window of time in which the government must bring charges, or forfeit the opportunity to do so. This time limit could be extended by the commission for good cause shown, such as the discovery of new evidence, the necessity to wait for another trial to conclude, or while awaiting evidence to be declassified.

There is a speedy trial requirement under R.M.C. 707 requiring a military commission to be assembled within 120 days of service of charges, but this requirement has proven to be illusory because the government can withdraw charges without prejudice and re-prefer them at any time, thereby granting itself a fresh 120 days. The government has repeatedly taken advantage of this provision. The MCA should be amended to close this loophole and prevent gamesmanship by the prosecution.

H. Credit for Pretrial Detention and Illegal Pretrial Punishment

The Rules for Military Commission do not include a provision found in Rules for Court-Martial 305(k) which provide for administrative credit for time served in pretrial detention. In *U.S. v. Hamdan*, the U.S. argued that no credit should be given for pretrial detention. The military judge, Captain Keith Allred, disagreed, and awarded credit for a significant period of the time served by Mr. Hamdan. The MCA should be amended to make it clear that the judge has the power to award this credit. Rule for Court-Martial 305(k) and military case law also authorize military judges to provide extra credit "for each day of pretrial confinement that involves. . . unusually harsh circumstances." This rule was omitted from the Rules for Military

Commission. In two rulings by Colonel Stephen Henley in response to pretrial motions in *U.S. v. Jawad*, Judge Henley indicated that he believed this remedy to be available in military commissions. [15] Congress should affirm this power through an appropriate amendment to the MCA.

I. Discovery and Production of Evidence and Witnesses

The military commissions have been plagued by slow, incomplete and inadequate discovery on the part of the government, which has resulted in needless delay while motions to compel discovery are litigated. Routine discovery requests have gone unanswered for months. The prosecution has even gone so far as to claim that they have no obligation under the MCA to respond in writing to defense discovery requests.

In my view, part of the problem is that the MMC weakens the discovery requirements which exist in courts-martial. Instead of guaranteeing "an equal opportunity to interview witnesses and inspect evidence" as R.M.C. 701(b)(5)(3) does, the equivalent Rule for Military Commissions promises only that "no party may unreasonably impede the access of another party to a witness or evidence." Similarly, § 949j. of the MCA requires that "defense counsel shall have a *reasonable* opportunity to obtain witnesses and other evidence" where in courts-martial, R.C.M. 703(a) states that both sides "shall have *equal* opportunity to obtain witnesses and evidence." There is no justification for the weakening of this rule, which clearly provides an advantage to the prosecution.

In practice, the defense has been hampered by the requirement to submit all witness requests through the prosecution and all requests for expert witnesses to the Convening Authority, Susan Crawford, who routinely denied defense requests regardless of their merits. Merely replacing the current Convening Authority will not resolve the systemic unfairness of the current scheme. The defense needs to have an independent budget to hire experts and independent subpoena power.

The Senate NDAA proposal amends the MCA to strengthen the requirement to turn over exculpatory evidence. This is a welcome proposal as exculpatory evidence has repeatedly been withheld by the prosecution.

J. Age Limitations and the Treatment and Prosecution of Juvenile Detainees

The MCA does not contain any age limitation. Theoretically, anyone captured who meets the definition of an "unlawful enemy combatant" ("unprivileged enemy belligerent" in the Senate NDAA version) can be tried by military commission. Two juvenile detainees, Omar Khadr, aged 15 at the time of capture, and my client Mohammed Jawad, possibly as young as 12 at the time of capture according to his family and the government of Afghanistan, have had charges referred to trial by military commission. Mr. Khadr was rapidly approaching trial at the time the military commissions were suspended by President Obama. It appears, based on the government's recent concession that Mr. Jawad is no longer detainable under the laws of war, that the military commission charges against him will be withdrawn. I believe the omission of an age limitation in the MCA was an unintentional oversight by Congress and that Congress did not intend for juveniles to be subjected to trial by military commission. There is not a single mention of "minors" "child soldiers" or "juveniles" in the legislative history of the MCA. One possible reason for the oversight is that the UCMJ, upon which the MCA is based, does not include an age limit. However, since jurisdiction under the UCMJ is limited to military members and one may not join the Armed Forces until the age of 18,[16] court-martial jurisdiction is necessarily limited to adults.

If Congress did not intend for juveniles to be subject to military commissions, then this oversight must be corrected. Child soldiers, even those who perpetrate atrocities, are recognized under international law primarily as victims of war. There is no international precedent for treating child soldiers as war criminals. The United States should not be the first country in the world to prosecute child soldiers. Authorizing juveniles to be subject to the MCA arguably violates our treaty obligations under the Optional Protocol to the Convention on the Rights of the Child on the Involvement of Children in Armed Conflict. This treaty, entered into force on February 12, 2002, requires that state parties accord to child soldiers "all appropriate assistance for their physical and psychological recovery and their social reintegration." Omar Khadr and Mohammed Jawad have been housed in adult facilities and denied any opportunities for rehabilitation and reintegration. The MCA has no provisions to take into account the age of juveniles and the only sentencing option is confinement. Subjecting child soldiers to possible life imprisonment is incompatible with the requirement to provide child soldiers with rehabilitation and reintegration.

K. Substantive Crimes and Elements

Many commentators, myself included, believe that there is a serious *ex post facto* or retroactivity problem with the MCA because it authorizes trial for offenses not previously punishable under the law of war. The MCA, at § 950p, declares, inaccurately, that "the provisions of this subchapter codify offenses that have traditionally been triable by military commissions." Thus, according to the MCA:

Because the provisions of this subchapter. . . are declarative of existing law, they do not preclude trial for crimes that occurred before the date of the enactment of this chapter.

The proposed revision of the MCA recognizes that there is considerable debate over whether several of the listed offenses were traditionally triable under the law of war, and proposes this caveat: "To the extent that the provisions of this subchapter codify offenses that have traditionally been triable under the law of war or otherwise triable by military commission, this subchapter does not preclude trial for offenses that occurred before the date of. . . enactment." In essence, this proviso acknowledges the possibility that courts may find some listed offenses in the MCA were not traditionally law of war offenses. However, the Senate NDAA version still retains all of the offenses of the original MCA, even those widely acknowledged to be new crimes.

Allowing detainees to be tried for offenses in military commissions which are not traditional war offenses creates a strong possibility either that the charges will be dismissed by the trial judge or that the convictions will be reversed on appeal. The more prudent course of action would be to remove those offenses from the MCA which were not clearly recognized war crimes prior to the enactment of the MCA. There have been several recent comprehensive codifications of the laws of war which list law of war offenses, most notably the Rome Statue of the International Criminal Court. The U.S. had a significant role in developing the list of war crimes in the Rome Statue and in defining the elements of those offenses. There are several offenses in the MCA which do not appear in the Rome Statute or in other recent codifications of the law of war, including terrorism, conspiracy, and material support for terrorism. None of these offenses have been traditionally been triable under the law of war.[17] All should be deleted from the Military Commissions Act.

In addition to removing offenses which are not traditional law of war offenses, Congress should clarify the meaning of certain offenses to remove ambiguity. In particular, Congress should clarify the vaguely defined offense of "murder in violation of the law of war." This offense replaced the invented offense of "murder by an unprivileged belligerent" in the list of offenses created by Executive Order of President Bush. Although the title and definition of this offense are clearly different from the predecessor offense, government prosecutors interpreted this offense to be identical to the offense of "murder by an unprivileged belligerent." Several defendants at the military commissions have been charged with the offense of "murder in violation of the law of war" and/or solicitation or conspiracy to commit this offense. The prosecution's theory, advanced in several military commissions, was that all murders committed by an "unlawful combatant" or "unprivileged belligerent" violated the law of war. Their claim was that the mere status of being an "unlawful combatant" was sufficient to establish a violation of the law of war and that no other law of war violation need be proven. This interpretation of the statute finds no support in the law of war and was emphatically rejected by three different judges (Captain Keith Allred, USN; Colonel Stephen Henley, USA; and Colonel Ronald Gregory, USAF) in three different military commissions (Hamdan, Jawad and al Bahlul). The clearest expression of this can be found in Judge Henley's ruling in *U.S. v. Jawad.*[18] According to Judge Henley:

> 10 U.S.C. § 950v(b)(15) states that "Any person subject to this chapter who intentionally kills one or more persons, including lawful combatants, in violation of the law of war shall be punished by death or such other punishment as a military commission under this chapter may direct." Thus, there is a dual requirement for the government to prove beyond reasonable doubt (1) that the [attempted] killings in this case were committed by an unlawful enemy combatant AND (2) that the method, manner or circumstances used violated the law of war. . .
>
> If Congress intended to make any murder committed by an unlawful enemy combatant a law of war violation, they could have said so. . . .
>
> Proof the Accused is an unlawful enemy combatant, by itself, is insufficient to establish that the attempted murders in this case were in violation of the law of war.

Unsatisfied with this explanation, which undercut their entire theory of criminality, the government filed a motion for reconsideration of this ruling.[19] Once again, Judge Henley found the government arguments "unpersuasive":

> Congress did not intend to make every murder committed by an alien unlawful enemy combatant or every murder of a lawful combatant by an

> unlawful combatant a law of war violation. As the Military Commission held in its September 24, 2008 ruling, there is a dual requirement for the Government to prove beyond reasonable doubt (1) that the [attempted] killings in this case were committed by an alien unlawful enemy combatant AND (2) that the method, manner or circumstances used violated the law of war. The propriety of the charges in this case must be based on the nature of the act and not merely on the status of the Accused at the time of the alleged offenses. In other words, proof that the Accused is an alien unlawful enemy combatant alone will be insufficient at trial to find the alleged acts of attempted murder in this case were in "in violation of the law of war." The Military Commission's position is consistent with case precedent, international law and Congressional intent.

The government attempted to resurrect the theory of the meaning of "murder in violation of the law of war" in the trial of Mr. al Bahlul, in their proposed jury instructions. Colonel Gregory, the military judge, rejected the government's proposed jury instructions and substituted instructions based on Judge Henley's ruling in *U.S. v. Jawad.* Despite the repeated rejection of their theory, the government has continued to charge detainees with this crime, or allow charges previously referred to go forward despite a complete lack of any evidence of a violation of the law of war. Congress could resolve this situation and eliminate any ambiguity about legislative intent by providing a definition for "in violation of the law of war" in the MCA. This phrase appears in the offense of "destruction of property in violation of the law of war" and "intentionally causing serious bodily injury" as well. I recommend adding a definition to § 948a as follows:

IN VIOLATION OF THE LAW OF WAR – The term 'in violation of the law of war' means in a method or manner or under circumstances which violate the law of war. The mere status of being an unprivileged enemy belligerent, without more, is insufficient to establish that an act was 'in violation of the law of war'.

IV. Conclusion

In short, the revisions of the MCA in the SASC proposal fall well short of what is required to transform the deeply flawed MCA into a law Americans can be proud of. The suggestions I have provided above are just a partial list of many aspects of the MCA that require revision.

However, by adopting these recommendations and others proposed by the witnesses on this panel and others who have testified before this committee, the Military Commissions Act could be modified to create a fair, legitimate legal system to try law of war offenses.

The question this committee, and the rest of Congress, must consider is whether there is any point in continuing with military commissions. As President Obama has stated, military commissions are a legitimate forum in which to try offenses under the law of war, but this begs the question of whether there are any law of war offenses to try. If one were to review the charges brought against all of the approximately 25 defendants charged in the military commissions, as I have, one would conclude that 99% of them do not involve traditionally recognized war crimes. Rather, virtually all of the defendants are charged with non-war crimes, primarily criminal conspiracy, terrorism and material support to terrorism, all of which are properly crimes under federal criminal law, but not the laws of war. In fact, in my estimation, there has been only one legitimate war crime charged against any Guantanamo detainee, the charge of "perfidy" against Abdal-Rahim Al-Nashiri for his alleged role in the attack on the U.S.S. Cole in October 2000. But even though perfidy is a traditional offense under the law of war, convicting Mr. Al-Nashiri of this offense requires accepting the dubious legal fiction that the United States was at war with Al Qaeda nearly a year before 9/11, for the law of war only applies during a war. In fact, most of the offenses with which the so-called "high value detainees" are charged relate to events which occurred on or before 9/11, when the U.S. was not involved in an armed conflict with Al Qaeda. Perhaps more to the point, Mr. Al- Nashiri was also charged with several other non-law of war offenses arising out of the same conduct, including multiple charges carrying the death penalty, making the charge of perfidy redundant. The Senate bill acknowledges that it includes non law of war offenses in §948b "This chapter establishes procedures governing the use of military commissions. . .for violations of the law of war *and other offenses triable by military commission.*" (emphasis added)

If there are no real war crimes to prosecute, are there any good reasons to continue with military commissions? The Bush Administration's motive for creating military commissions was to establish a forum in which American standards of due process did not apply and convictions could be obtained for terrorism crimes (not law of war offenses) under summary procedures using evidence which would not be admissible in a regular court of law. The Obama Administration has now rightly concluded that Constitutional due process standards should apply to military commissions, and that normal rules of evidence should apply. Modifying the military commissions to comport with due process and the rule of law will mean eliminating the very reason for their existence. Partially amending them with some minor cosmetic changes will result only in many more years of protracted litigation.

Among the over two hundred detainees still at Guantanamo, there are perhaps a few dozen who have committed serious offenses. I have yet to hear any compelling reason why any of these men could not be prosecuted under existing law in Federal Court. As the recent report by Human Rights First conclusively demonstrates,[20] the federal courts are open, and have a long track record of successful prosecutions of terrorism crimes. Military commissions have not proven to be faster, more efficient or less costly than the alternative. The logistical difficulties in trying cases in Guantanamo have proven to be incredibly vexing. With Guantanamo slated to be closed in the next six months, the military commissions will have to be relocated and a whole new infrastructure created to support the commissions. This could further delay the commissions for months or even years. Military lawyers, unlike federal prosecutors and federal public defenders, have no special expertise in prosecuting or defending complex international terrorist conspiracies. The entire military commissions experiment has been a massive drain on DoD resources and personnel at a time when the military can least afford it.

The only other reason I have heard advanced for the use of military commissions is the belief that a person who could not be successfully prosecuted in Federal Court because of evidentiary problems might be successfully prosecuted in a military commission. Those who make this argument are essentially conceding that military commissions do not and should not provide the same due process as a regularly constituted American court.

The desire to achieve convictions at all costs is simply not an acceptable basis for the creation of an alternative legal system. The reason that the military commissions failed, indeed, the primary mistake of the entire "War on Terror" was the pervasive abandonment of the rule of law by the prior administration. We must not repeat the mistakes of the past and continue to cut corners. We must remember that this war is ultimately a war about ideas and values. True American values guarantee justice and fairness for all, even for the vilified and unpopular. If there are terrorists and war criminals to be tried, let's do it the old-fashioned way, in a fair fight in a real court with untainted evidence. America is better than the last eight years. It is time to prove it to the world, and to ourselves. Thank you.

End Notes

[1] Lead Defense Counsel, Office of Military Commissions-Defense and Associate Professor of Law and Director, Criminal Law Practice Center, Western State University College of Law, Fullerton, California.

[2] The views expressed herein are my own, and do not reflect the views of the Air Force, the Office of Military Commissions, or the Department of Defense.

[3] David J. R. Frakt, *An Indelicate Imbalance: A Critical Comparison of the Rules and Procedures for Military Commissions and Courts-Martial*, 34 Am. J. Crim L. 315 (2007).

[4] For further information about my experience as a Guantanamo defense lawyer and these two cases, see, David J. R. Frakt, *Closing Argument at Guantanamo: The Torture of Mohammad Jawad* 22 Harvard Human Rights Journal 1 (2009); David J. R. Frakt, *The Difficulties of Defending Detainees*, 48 Washburn Law Journal 381 (2009); see also, *The Guantanamo Lawyers: Inside a Prison Outside the Law,* edited by Mark Denbeaux and Jonathan Hafetz (NYU Press, forthcoming October 2009).

[5] Military Order of November 13, 2001—Detention, Treatment, and Trial of Certain Non-Citizens in the War Against Terrorism, 66 Fed. Reg. 57833 (Nov. 13, 2001).

[6] President's Memorandum to the Vice President et al. regarding Humane Treatment of al Qaeda and Taliban Detainees (Feb. 7, 2002), (Homeland Security Digital Library), *available at* http://www.pegc.us/archive/White_House/bush_memo_20020207_ed.pdf.

[7] See generally, Inquiry into the Treatment of Detainees in U.S. Custody, Report of the Senate Armed Services Committee, available at:_http://armed-services.senate.gov/Publications/Detainee%20 Report%20inal_April%2022%202009.pdf; see also, Philippe Sands, *Torture Team* (2008); Jordan J. Paust, *Beyond The Law: The Bush Administration's Unlawful Responses in the "War" on Terror* (2007); Jane Mayer, *The Dark Side: The Inside Story of How the War on Terror Turned into a War on American Ideals* (2008).

[8] See, Dep't pf Defense, Military Commission Order No. 1: Procedures for Trials by Military Commissions of Certain Non-United States Citizens in the War Against Terrorism (March 21, 2002) (Homeland Security Digital Library).

[9] Military Comm'n Instruction No. 2, Crimes and Elements for Trials by Military Commission, 32 C.F.R. § 11.6 (2005).

[10] U.S. Dep't of Defense, Manual for Military Commissions (Jan. 18, 2007); U.S. Dep't of Defense, Regulation for Trial by Military Commissions (April 27, 2007).

[11] See generally, David J. R. Frakt, *An Indelicate Imbalance: A Critical Comparison of the Rules and Procedures for Military Commissions and Courts-Martial*, 34 Am. J. Crim L. 315 (2007).

[12] See, Ross Tuttle, Rigged Trials at Gitmo, The Nation, (February 20, 2008) in which the following quotation was attributed by the Chief Prosecutor Colonel Morris Davis to DoD General Counsel William J. Haynes IV, "Wait a minute, we can't have acquittals. If we've been holding these guys for so long, how can we explain letting them get off? We can't have acquittals. We've got to have convictions."

[13] This expression was used by a senior Guantanamo official, Brig Gen Gregory Zanetti, in testimony before the military commission in U.S. v. Jawad to describe the push to bring as many cases to trial as possible. See, Jane Sutton, "Guantanamo Trials Put Generals At Odds" Reuters, August 13, 2008 ("The strategy seemed to be spray and pray, let's go, speed, speed, speed," Army. Brig. Gen. Gregory Zanetti said. "Charge 'em, charge 'em, charge 'em and let's pray that we can pull this off.").

[14] Article 10, UCMJ states "When any person subject to this chapter is placed in arrest or confinement prior to trial, immediate steps shall be taken to inform him of the specific wrong of which he is accused and to try him or to dismiss the charges and release him."

[15] Ruling on Defense Motion to Dismiss – Torture of the Detainee (D-008), 1 Military Commission Reporter 334, 336-37 (2008), "the Commission finds other remedies are available to adequately address the wrong inflicted upon the Accused, including, but not limited to, sentence credit towards any approved period of confinement.") Ruling available at_http://www.defenselink.mil/news/Ruling%20D-008.pdf; Ruling on Defense Motion to Dismiss – Lack of Personal Jurisdiction: Child Soldier (D-012), 1 Military Commission Reporter 338, 341 at n. 13(2008)("Nothing precludes the defense from requesting relief from the Military Commission for housing the accused while a juvenile with adult detainees, providing inadequate physical and psychological resources to a confined juvenile and any other actions that may constitute unlawful pretrial punishment of the Accused. Such relief may include, but is not limited to, specific sentence credit towards any approved period of confinement.") Ruling available at http://www.defenselink.mil/news/RULING% 20D-012% 0(child%20soldier).pdf.

[16] Seventeen year olds may enlist with the permission of a parent. However, service members are ineligible to serve in a theater of war until they turn 18, precluding the possibility of committing a war crime as a juvenile.

[17] The Administration has acknowledged that material support for terrorism is not a traditional law of war offense.

[18] Ruling on Defense Motion to Dismiss, Lack of Subject Matter Jurisdiction (D-007), 1 Military Commission Reporter 331, 332 (2008) available at:_http://www.defenselink.mil/new s/RULING% 20D007%20(subject%20matter% 20 jurisdiction) 20(2).pdf;

[19] Ruling on Government Motion for Reconsideration (D-007), 1 Military Commission Reporter 347, 348 (2008). Available at: http://www.defenselink.mil/news/d20081104 J awadD007 Reconsider. \pdf

[20] In Pursuit of Justice: Prosecuting Terrorism Cases in the Federal Courts (2008) and 2009 Update and Recent Developments available at http://www.humanrightsfirst. org/us_ law/prosecute/

In: The Military Commissions Act...
Editors: J. Segel, Soto Kimura
ISBN: 978-1-61470-072-2

Chapter 5

PROPOSALS TO REFORM THE MILITARY COMMISSIONS SYSTEM TESTIMONY OF EUGENE R. FIDELL PRESIDENT, NATIONAL INSTITUTE OF MILITARY JUSTICE AND SENIOR RESEARCH SCHOLAR IN LAW AND FLORENCE ROGATZ LECTURER IN LAW, YALE LAW SCHOOL HEARING BEFORE THE SUBCOMMITTEE ON THE CONSTITUTION, CIVIL RIGHTS AND CIVIL LIBERTIES COMMITTEE ON THE JUDICIARY U.S. HOUSE OF REPRESENTATIVES*

July 30, 2009

Chairman Nadler, Ranking Member Sensenbrenner, Chairman Conyers, and Members of the Subcommittee:

---

* This is an edited, reformatted and augmented version of testimony given by Eugene R. Fidell President, National Institute of Military Justice and Senior Research Scholar in Law and Florence Rogatz Lecturer in Law, Yale Law School before the United States House of Representatives on Hearing Before the Subcommittee on the Constitution, Civil Rights and Civil Liberties Committee on the Judiciary, on July 30, 2009.

Thank you for inviting me to testify about military commissions.

I am a Senior Research Scholar and Florence Rogatz Lecturer in Law at Yale Law School, where I have taught military justice since 1993. I am also president of the National Institute of Military Justice, a nonprofit organization founded in 1991 to advance the fair administration of justice in the armed forces and to foster improved public understanding of military justice. NIMJ has been deeply involved in military commission issues since shortly after President George W. Bush revived them in November 2001. We have published an annotated guide to the original military commission rules, four volumes of Military Commission Instructions Sourcebooks, and, earlier this month, the first volume of the Military Commissions *Reporter,* which collects all of the commissions' rulings from 2006 to 2009. We have presented congressional testimony on several occasions and have filed numerous amicus curiae briefs. We have sent observers to Guantanamo to attend and report on military commission hearings. We do not represent individuals, and neither NIMJ nor I have ever personally represented a Guantanamo detainee or military commission defendant.

I would like to make four basic points.

First, military commissions are not "normal," and we must never lose sight of that. Although they have been used in a variety of contexts since the Mexican War, they plainly are not one of the brighter chapters in our legal tradition—unless you think the mass hanging of Indians in Minnesota or the military trial of the Lincoln Conspirators while the local courts here were open was a good thing. Other doubtful chapters include the use of military commissions in our effort to suppress the Philippine Insurrection and the unfair proceedings against General Yamashita after World War II.

Military commissions remain a far cry from the familiar process of military justice that we employ in ensuring good order and discipline within our armed forces. They are an even farther cry from trials in our federal district courts. Those courts—the jewel in the crown of our legal system—have earned the respect not only of our own people but of fair-minded observers around the globe. Public confidence in the administration of justice is a key element of our national strategy to defeat terrorism. That means public confidence both here and abroad. We cannot get from where we are now to where we need to be by trying to fashion a "reformed" military commission system 3.0.

Earlier this year, President Obama spoke of military commissions (among other things) at the National Archives. His remarks unfortunately could be interpreted as suggesting that commissions are a normal part of the fabric of

American law. The temptation to do so should be resisted, for reasons I set forth in an op-ed in *The New York Times*. I request that it be made a part of the hearing record. Without suggesting that the history of military commissions is all negative, they have too often been put to uses of which we have little reason to be proud. We must remain alert to the danger that they will, by degrees, become normal rather than a disfavored exception.

Second, and as a corollary to the first, every effort should be made to ensure that military commissions, assuming they are ever to be used, are used no longer than is strictly justified. This means careful policing both at the beginning and the end of the pertinent time-frame. Only if the very limited conditions warranting military commissions have been met should they be employed, and then they should be terminated once the need has passed. Any military commission legislation should therefore be subject to a sunset provision. Military commissions should never be a permanent feature of our legal system. Remember: we got along without them for over half a century following World War II, despite our involvement in numerous armed conflicts, large and small.

Third, every aspect of military commissions should be governed by a policy to limit rather than to expand their use. Thus, the jurisdictional definitions, both as to what kinds of conduct would be subject to trial by military commission (in other words, subject matter jurisdiction) and as to who should be subject to such trial (personal jurisdiction), should be as narrow as possible. If an offense is not known to the law of armed conflict, such as conspiracy, "material support" or spying, try it in some other forum. Any doubt should be resolved against, rather than for, the exercise of jurisdiction by these exceptional courts. If we do not apply this stringent test at every turn, you will have created a "national security court" in camouflage. I do not believe our country is ready for such courts.

Fourth, even if a case and an individual are plausibly within the jurisdiction of a military commission, the strongest preference must be given to available trial options in the Article III courts. The recent Sense of the Senate resolution favoring trials by military commission has the telescope turned in precisely the wrong direction. It is fortunate that the resolution lacks the force of law.

In 2006, I testified before the Senate Armed Services Committee that Congress should insist that no case be tried by a military commission unless the Attorney General has personally certified that it could not be tried in district court. That still seems to be the best approach, and I hope the current Administration will apply it or something like it. However, it is important to stress that mere prosecutorial difficulty or inconvenience or embarrassment to the government arising from a district court prosecution cannot be enough to justify resort to the extraordinary process of a military commission. Only when the politically-accountable Attorney General assures the country, with particularity, that a given case lies outside the complex web of PATRIOT Act-era or earlier civilian criminal law prohibitions should charges be referred to a military commission.

The process described in the Detention Policy Task Force's July 20, 2009 protocol on Determination of Guantanamo Cases Referred to Prosecution falls short. It speaks of "feasibility" of prosecution in federal court, but the preference for civilian trial is merely a presumption, and one that can be overridden based on broad factors that leave far too much to discretion: "strength of interest," "efficiency" and "other prosecution considerations." For example, "evidentiary problems that might attend prosecution in the other jurisdiction" enables forum-shopping that should be rejected. Similarly, it is difficult to see why the fact that the armed forces have sunk investigative costs in a case should play any role in deciding whether an offense should be tried in a military commission rather than in district court. This is not to suggest congressional micromanagement of prosecutorial decisions, as these are quintessentially within the ken of the Executive given the President's duty under Article II, § 3 of the Constitution, to "take Care that the Laws be faithfully executed." Still, Congress can and should impose limits rather than permit a matter as sensitive as this to be so unstructured.

In 2006, Congress enacted the Military Commissions Act under tremendous pressure from the White House and, as far as I could determine as an observer of the passing scene, out of concern for permitting the subject to be made an issue in that year's congressional elections. The result was most unwise. It left us with the traditional military justice system which permits war crimes to be tried by general courts-martial, a set of military commissions for trying war crimes by lawful combatants, and yet another set of military commissions for trying war crimes (and other offenses) by unlawful combatants.

The result is senseless. We don't need two flavors of military commissions; indeed, we may not even need one. I would therefore advise that the MCA be repealed and if military commissions prove necessary, let them conform with general court-martial procedures and rules subject to a very few exceptions such as dispensing with the need for a pretrial investigation. The current arrangement, whereby three distinct systems exist, is needlessly complex and an open invitation for yet more years of litigation.

Two weeks ago I prepared some notes on aspects of the Senate bill (as it then stood) that might have been improved.

I ask that my slightly updated version be made part of the record. Even if all of the questions in those notes were resolved in the manner indicated, I would still restore the (pre-MCA) status quo ante. And in any event I would encourage the Subcommittee as well as those who will be responsible for both the administration and judicial review of any future military commissions to bear in mind the four basic points set out in this testimony as a way to minimize the insult to our constitutional system.

I will be happy to respond to your questions.

EUGENE R. FIDELL is Senior Research Scholar and Florence Rogatz Lecturer in Law at Yale Law School, where he teaches military justice, among other subjects. He also serves as president of the National Institute of Military Justice, a nonprofit organization affiliated with the American University Washington College of Law. He served on active duty as a judge advocate in the U.S. Coast Guard from 1969 to 1972 and is co-author, with Prof. Elizabeth Lutes Hillman and Colonel Dwight H. Sullivan, of MILITARY JUSTICE: CASES AND MATERIALS (LexisNexis 2007). He is of counsel to the Washington firm Feldesman Tucker Leifer Fidell LLP.

June 14, 2009,
Op-Ed Contributor

THE TROUBLE WITH TRIBUNALS

By Eugene R. Fidell

In a Manhattan courtroom last week, the first Guantanamo detainee to face a trial in a civilian court pleaded not guilty. President Obama has indicated that other terrorism cases will likewise be tried in the federal courts, but that does not necessarily spell the end for military commissions. In a speech at the National Archives in May, he confirmed that the commission system won't be abolished, merely revised.

Whether his proposed changes will substantially improve the military commissions and increase public confidence in the commissions' administration of justice will be the subject of debate in the coming months and years. There is, however, a more fundamental question: the president's assertion that military commissions have long played a respectable role in American legal history.

The history is more ambiguous than many have assumed, and is not one of which we have much reason to be proud. Let's consider the high points typically cited.

A board of general officers conducted an inquiry into the spying case of Maj. John Andre, a British officer, in 1780. Whether that board or the one convened in another Revolutionary War spying case constituted a military commission is open to doubt. At the time, of course, the country was an actual battleground and there were not yet any civilian federal courts. But these inquiries were isolated events and hardly a solid starting point for an entire system of justice.

Fast forward more than half a century to the Mexican-American War. Gen. Winfield Scott, who commanded the American contingent in southern Mexico, found his forces in a partial legal vacuum, as the Articles of War — the Army predecessor of the Uniform Code of Military Justice — did not cover non-military offenses. He had no alternative but to create a system of military commissions to try both American soldiers and enemy civilians.

Congress did not even acknowledge Scott's system until 1862, when it did so backhandedly: the legislation dealing with the position of judge advocate general simply noted his duty to review military commission cases.

During the Civil War and Reconstruction, military commissions were used in a variety of settings. Famously, the Supreme Court forbade their use in states that had not seceded and in which the courts were open. In the South, however, civilian courts were closed or could not be relied on to prosecute offenders against the Union.

A commission was actually convened to try the conspirators in the Lincoln assassination. Why? The Civil War was for all practical purposes over by then and it was almost certainly the wrong impulse not to trust the District of Columbia's courts.

Military commissions were occasionally used during the so-called Indian wars. An 1862 commission trial after a Sioux uprising in Minnesota led to the largest mass hanging in Anierican history, even after Abraham Lincoln spared a number of those who had been condemned. Is the genocidal war our country waged against the original inhabitants a chapter of which we are proud?

We used military commissions in the aftermath of the Spanish-American War. But our efforts to suppress the Philippine insurrection of 1898 were brutal and in service of a blatantly imperialistic cause; and whether these commissions were conducted fairly or not, the setting is not one to be held out as a model for the 21st century. At least those commissions were conducted in the field — unlike the Guantanamo commissions.

Many Americans have heard of the military commission that convened in 1942 to try eight German saboteurs. But few are aware that a major reason the case was tried by commission rather than in the federal courts was that federal law at the time did not prescribe harsh enough penalties for what they had attempted to do. That is obviously not so today, thanks to the Patriot Act and other legislation passed since World War II.

In its review of the saboteurs' case, Ex parte Quirin, the Supreme Court did sustain the military commission's jurisdiction — but, in a discomfiting move, did not even release its legal reasoning until months after six of the Germans had been electrocuted. Though the ruling was unanimous, Justice Felix Frankfurter declared that Quirin was "not a happy precedent."

Other commissions were held in the aftermath of World War II. Gen. Tomoyuki Yamashita, the Japanese commander in Manila, was hanged after an appallingly unfair military commission trial. Here again, at least his case was held overseas, not in territory over which the United States had full power to use its regular courts.

In 1950, Congress passed the Uniform Code of Military Justice, which substantially upgraded the military justice system and reduced the disparities among the disciplinary laws governing the various branches of the armed forces. From 1951, when the code took effect, until 2001, when President George W. Bush set the stage for the Guantanamo tribunals, we did perfectly well without military commissions, despite numerous armed conflicts, large and small — and despite a growing engagement with terrorism.

This is not to say that no military commission has ever been conducted fairly or in a worthy cause. At times the commissions' work has been acceptable, especially when they applied general court-martial standards. Nonetheless, the history of our military commissions brings little credit on our country. We should not invoke that history without recognizing the combination of doubtful goals and missed opportunities to use other forums. The coming new-and-improved model of military commissions — our third effort in less than a decade — is unlikely to inspire confidence here or abroad in our administration of justice.

There is a second point to be made concerning President Obama's recent speech. At no point did he give a detailed explanation of why military commissions had to be used rather than the federal district courts, or why some detainees will have full procedural safeguards in federal court while others will be afforded fewer rights before a military commission.

This is not a matter to be addressed generically. Rather, it is incumbent on the administration to state why any particular case cannot be tried in the federal courts. Those courts are open, and have demonstrated that they can try terrorists in ways that bring honor on our country and fully respect our legal values.

The issue is not whether it is easier or more convenient to use military commissions, but whether the conduct sought to be punished is literally outside the complex web of criminal provisions Congress has enacted over the years, including the Patriot Act.

President Obama justifiably reminded his audience at the National Archives that the last administration left the country with a terrible, and terribly complicated, legal mess. His personal commitment to the rule of law cannot be doubted. Nonetheless, unless his administration explains why specific cases cannot be prosecuted in the federal courts, it will have done no better than its predecessor on a pivotal threshold issue.

Eugene R. Fidell teaches military law at Yale Law School.

S. 1390, National Defense Authorization Act for Fiscal Year 2010 Notes on § 1031, Military Commissions

1) Section 948b(d): why exclude application of the speedy trial rule and UCMJ art. 31?
2) Section 948c: overbroad definition of persons subject to trial by military commission. This would confer jurisdiction over persons who have never been on the battlefield, for nontraditional war crimes like material support and terrorism.
3) Section 948d would permit military commissions to try spying charges

4) Section 948j makes no provision for terms of office for military judges, in contrast to Army regulations that provide for 3-year terms for military judges in courts-martial.
5) Section 948r would permit evidence obtained by means of cruel, inhuman, and degrading treatment so long as it's reliable and not a product of one of the specific methods noted in § 1003 of the Detainee Treatment Act.
6) Section 949a(b) authorizes the Secretary of Defense to depart from general court-martial procedures under a very fuzzy standard ("unique circumstances of the conduct of military and intelligence operations during hostilities or by other practical need"). Any guaranteed opportunity for public comment before submission to Congress? *See §* (d) (last page).
7) Section 949a(b)(2) is unclear: does the accused have a right to probe the government's non-live evidence by interrogatories or other means of discovery?
8) Section 949a(b)(3)(D) allows the use of hearsay evidence that would never be admitted in a general court-martial or district court, and well beyond the parameters actually applied in international criminal tribunals such as the International Criminal Tribunal for the Former Yugoslavia.
9) Section 949d(c)(4) seems to depart from general court-martial procedures for classified information. Why is any departure necessary? Why is there no provision for dismissal if the military judge finds there is no adequate substitute and the information is deemed essential to the defense?
10) Section 949j erects a "reasonable opportunity" standard in place of UCMJ art. 46's "equal opportunity" standard for access to witnesses and other evidence. Why the difference? The military commissions had denied the defense access to high- value detainees. Will that denial continue to be possible under the amendments? If so, why?
11) Section 950f provides for review as of right by the Court of Appeals for the Armed Forces. If enemy combatants are entitled to this, why not our own military personnel, who (except for those sentenced to death) must show "good cause" under the UCMJ. This part of the bill is good, but raises a question as to why most court-martial appellants cannot even seek certiorari from the Supreme Court (because the Court of Appeals has denied discretionary review). Congress should pass this provision, but it would be a disgrace to do so without putting

GIs' cases on the same footing with respect to eligibility for Supreme Court review. *See S.* 357 (Sen. Feinstein); H.R. 569.

12) Section 950p(c) permits military commission trials only if the offense is committed in the context of and associated with armed conflict. This loose standard could sweep in non-battlefield conduct not subject to trial by military tribunals under the law of armed conflict.
13) Section 950u: four Justices in *Hamden* did not believe conspiracy is a crime under the law of armed conflict. Including it is a misuse of the military commission as an institution.
14) What new matter in the amendments made by § 1031 addresses the specific problems of independence of trial and defense counsel that have repeatedly arisen under the MCA?

INDEX

C

D

N

O

P

Q

R

S

Y

The Internationalization of Small Firms

This book explores the role of network relationships in the internationalization of small knowledge-intensive firms, by drawing on case-study research carried out in the Bangalore software industry. The book is concerned with small firm growth and the accelerated internationalization of young, small firms – a phenomenon that has attracted widespread research attention over the past decade at the intersection of entrepreneurship, international business and strategy.

Prashantham's study focuses on the value of a strategic approach and highlights the importance of recognizing and leveraging network relationships. It also analyses the idea of using technology from a relational, and not merely transactional, perspective. Other key themes include the significance of location and the role of the entrepreneur. The author also explores the notion that endowment of ties does not automatically result in internationalization unless proactively influenced. The propensity of small knowledge-intensive firms to develop and grow through forging network relationships and the resourcefulness with which entrepreneurial firms can (and do) internationalize is a key lesson learnt from this volume.

This cutting-edge book is particularly relevant to advanced students and academics with an interest in international business and entrepreneurship and will also benefit researchers involved with small business and new technology management.

Dr Shameen Prashantham is a Lecturer at the Centre for Internationalization and Enterprise Research at the University of Glasgow's Department of Management.

Routledge studies in small business

Edited by David J. Storey

Centre for Small and Medium Sized Enterprises, Warwick Business School, UK.

1 **Small Firm Formation and Regional Economic Development**
Edited by Michael W. Danson

2 **Corporate Venture Capital**
Bridging the equity gap in the small business sector
Kevin McNally

3 **The Quality Business**
Quality issues and smaller firms
Julian North, Robert A. Blackburn and James Curran

4 **Enterprise and Culture**
Colin Gray

5 **The Financing of Small Business**
A comparative study of male and female small business owners
Lauren Read

6 **Small Firms and Network Economies**
Martin Perry

7 **Intellectual Property and Innovation Management in Small Firms**
Edited by Robert A. Blackburn

8 **Understanding the Small Family Business**
Edited by Denise E. Fletcher

9 **Managing Labour in Small Firms**
Edited by Susan Marlow, Dean Patton and Monder Ram

10 **The Foundations of Small Business Enterprise**
Gavin C. Reid

11 **The Internationalization of Small Firms**
A strategic entrepreneurship perspective
Shameen Prashantham

The Internationalization of Small Firms

A strategic entrepreneurship perspective

Shameen Prashantham

Routledge
Taylor & Francis Group
LONDON AND NEW YORK

First published 2008
by Routledge
2 Park Square, Milton Park, Abingdon, Oxon, OX14 4RN

Simultaneously published in the USA and Canada
by Routledge
270 Madison Ave, New York NY 10016

Routledge is an imprint of the Taylor & Francis Group, an informa business

Transferred to Digital Printing 2009

Typeset in Times by Wearset Ltd, Boldon, Tyne and Wear

British Library Cataloguing in Publication Data
A catalogue record for this book is available from the British Library

Library of Congress Cataloging in Publication Data
A catalog record for this book has been requested

ISBN10: 0-415-43177-8 (hbk)
ISBN10: 0-203-94052-0 (ebk)

ISBN13: 978-0-415-43177-4 (hbk)
ISBN13: 978-0-203-94052-5 (ebk)

To my wife, Deepali

Contents

Illustrations

Figures

Tables

Foreword

The subjects of the internationalization of small- and medium-sized enterprises (SMEs) and international entrepreneurship are very exciting and topical ones. In particular the growth of the global knowledge economy is associated with the emergence of many intellectual capital-intensive SMEs, whose adventurous and entrepreneurial strategies may lead to early and rapid internationalization and globalization. These phenomena are not confined to industrialized countries, with India in the forefront of developments, as this volume, drawing on research undertaken in the Bangalore software industry, reveals very clearly and forcefully. The main premise of the volume is that *networks and social capital enable resourceful internationalization*, and its principal contributions lie in improving our understanding of the development of social capital, the leveraging of social capital and the management of social capital portfolios.

It gives me particular pleasure to pen this Foreword since I was privileged to be the principal supervisor for Dr Shameen Prashantham's Doctoral research, and the volume draws substantially on his Doctoral studies. While the PhD process is never easy and Shameen encountered his fair share of challenges along the way, I became increasingly aware that here was an academic star in the making. This view was reinforced by his mature and polished performance at his Viva, the External Examiner for which was Professor Shaker Zahra, a distinguished scholar in the field of SME internationalization, entrepreneurship and strategy. Shameen states that this volume 'represents his "baby steps" in academia' – this may be so, but, like the early internationalizing SMEs he studies, we can anticipate a rapid and accelerated pace of academic development characterized by more radical steps in future! Indeed the final chapter of the volume on *Future Research Directions* suggests some of the ways this may occur, namely through integrating innovation into SME internationalization research and through consideration of the role of MNCs as a source of social capital to local knowledge-intensive SMEs. Enjoy these initial stimulating contributions to the internationalization of entrepreneurial firms … with much more to follow.

Stephen Young, Professor of International Business
Co-Director, Centre for Internationalisation & Enterprise Research,
University of Glasgow

Preface

That I would develop a research interest in small firm internationalization is perhaps almost inevitable given that, at the turn of the century, I came into contact as a graduate student with renowned internationalization scholars who were generating exciting work on the internationalization of small knowledge-intensive firms in settings as diverse as Britain, Germany and the United States. When I decided to embark on a PhD, I was caught up in the wave of interest in this area.

There were certain distinctive elements that I sought to bring into my doctoral research, with a view to making a unique contribution. I sought to simultaneously (a) examine an emerging economy context (namely, the Indian software industry) which I was sure could yield novel insights, (b) incorporate a contemporary perspective by taking into cognizance the enabling role of technology, and (c) drawing upon both economics and sociology, delve deeply into the role of social capital arising from network relationships of internationalizing small firms.

The work in this volume represents my "baby steps" in academia – in other words, writings based on my preliminary conceptualization and fieldwork which, in the European tradition, focused on qualitative case studies.[1] It explores the role of network relationships in the internationalization of small knowledge-intensive firms, by drawing on case-study research carried out in the Bangalore software industry. The research is, in general, concerned with small firm growth and, more specifically, with accelerated internationalization of young, small firms, a phenomenon that has attracted widespread research attention for over a decade now. The book highlights the propensity of small knowledge-intensive firms to develop and leverage network relationships and thereby, the resourcefulness with which entrepreneurial firms can (and do) internationalize.

The primary audience comprises academics and doctoral students with an interest in the internationalization of entrepreneurial firms. Additionally, there is useful material to supplement core texts in postgraduate courses on internationalization. Furthermore, there are hopefully useful messages for thoughtful entrepreneurs and policy-makers, especially those based in emerging economies, where the opportunity for small firm internationalization has never been greater.

Aside from the introductory and concluding chapters, the eight other papers in the volume were not intentionally written as chapters of a book and therefore there is some repetition of themes, citations and methodology sections. However, these eight papers offer substantial portions that do not overlap and in general, provide internally consistent ideas. Moreover, the papers were previously published in journals (six) or edited volumes (two), indicating thereby that they benefited from rigorous peer review and critique. Also, in most cases, a previous version had been presented at a conference, resulting in useful feedback from colleagues.

And so, it is my hope that when considered cumulatively, the whole is greater than the sum of the parts, and that the conceptualization and empirical findings presented in this volume informs and provokes further developments in an exciting research stream that I have the good fortune to continue to work on.

Shameen Prashantham

Acknowledgements

There have been important influences on my development as a researcher on small firm internationalization and international entrepreneurship. Foremost is Steve Young whom I was fortunate enough to have as doctoral supervisor. As many previous doctoral students of his will attest, I could not have asked for a better mentor. I am grateful for his wise counsel during my doctoral studies and for his collaboration on research papers (including one in this volume). I am also delighted to be continuing to pursue this stream of research as a lecturer within the Centre for Internationalization and Enterprise Research at the University of Glasgow that he co-directs along with another esteemed colleague Marian Jones. Others who helped me enormously during my doctoral studies include Maureen Berry who instilled in me my interest in small knowledge-intensive firms and co-authored a couple of my very first papers (included in this volume) and Pavlos Dimitratos from whom I have learned much about the craft of academic research. I would be remiss not to acknowledge Christine Donald and Jane Brittin, who were a great source of support in numerous ways during the doctoral research process.

There are others who have also contributed to my early development in academia. I thank Shaker Zahra, who was a provocative and thorough external examiner who has subsequently helped me enormously in honing my skills as a researcher and writer. Léo-Paul Dana has been a major source of encouragement and of writing opportunities – which led to a couple of the papers included in the volume. Many scholars have generously provided me valuable feedback on my work at conferences and elsewhere, notably Rod McNaughton who also co-authored one of the papers in the volume and Kevin Ibeh who was my internal examiner and a forerunner in highlighting the importance of small firm internationalization in developing economies. My first academic job as post-doctoral research fellow under the auspices of the Advanced Institute of Management helped me strengthen my knowledge of strategic management through my work with Gerry Johnson, whose encouragement and support has helped me to continue progressing my internationalization research as well, for which I am very grateful indeed.

Most of the work in this volume could not have been written without the access I had to four fascinating small software firms in Bangalore. I am grateful to their dynamic entrepreneurs who shared so freely of their time and stories. Many industry experts in Bangalore, who are acknowledged by name in my doctoral thesis, were similarly generous with their time and views. During the initial stages of my inquiry in Bangalore, I was provided hospitality and administrative support by Vertebrand Management Consulting and am thankful to its CEO Raghu Viswanath and his colleagues for the intellectually stimulating environment that they provided. My good friends C.G. Srividya and Nidhi Bassi helped enormously with providing me useful contacts in Bangalore and expert advice on my research methodology, respectively – I thank my pals, Ramesh Kumar and Neeraj Bassi for marrying such good wives! Incidentally, my initial research in Bangalore coincided with my getting married to Deepali who then, and since, has been the wind beneath my wings as I have embarked on the journey of an academic researcher and for which reason I can think of no one more appropriate to dedicate this book to. I am also ever grateful for the constant support that I have received from my family, especially my brother and parents and in-laws.

Finally, I express my gratitude to the various publishers who granted me the permission to reproduce my work in this volume. Other than minor modifications for consistency of formatting, no changes have been made. The original publication details and acknowledgement of permission to reprint the papers in this volume are provided below:

Chapter 2: Prashantham, S. and Berry, M.M.J. (2004) 'The small knowledge-intensive firm: a conceptual discussion of its characteristics and internationalization', *International Journal of Entrepreneurship and Innovation Management*, 4(2/3): 150–158. © 2004 Inderscience Enterprises Ltd. Reprinted with kind permission of Inderscience Ltd.

Chapter 3: Prashantham, S. (2005) 'Toward a knowledge-based conceptualization of internationalization', *Journal of International Entrepreneurship*, 3(1): 37–52. © 2005 Springer Science + Business Media, Inc. Reprinted with kind permission of Springer Science and Business Media.

Chapter 4: Prashantham, S. and Berry, M.M.J. (2004) 'The Internet and the internationalization of small knowledge-intensive firms: a conceptual approach', in M.V. Jones and P. Dimitratos (eds) *Emerging Paradigms in International Entrepreneurship*, Northampton, MA: Edward Elgar, 192–213. Reprinted with kind permission of Marian V. Jones and Pavlos Dimitratos, and of Edward Elgar Publishers Ltd.

Chapter 5: Prashantham, S. (2004) 'Indian perspectives of International entrepreneurship', in L.P. Dana (ed.) *The Handbook on Research in International Entrepreneurship*, Northampton, MA: Edward Elgar, 481–498. Reprinted with kind permission of Léo-Paul Dana, and of Edward Elgar Publishers Ltd.

Chapter 6: Prashantham, S. (2004) 'Local network relationships and the internationalization of small knowledge-intensive firms', *Copenhagen Journal of Asian Studies*, 19: 5–26. Reprinted with kind permission of the Asia Research Centre, Copenhagen Business School.

Chapter 7: Prashantham, S. (2006) 'Foreign network relationships and the internationalization of small knowledge-intensive firms', *International Journal of Entrepreneurship and Innovation Management*, 6(6): 542–553. © 2006 Inderscience Enterprises Ltd. Reprinted with kind permission of Inderscience Ltd.

Chapter 8: Prashantham, S. and Young, S. (2004) 'The Internet and the internationalization of small knowledge-intensive firms: promises, problems and prospects', *International Journal of Entrepreneurship and Small Business*, 1(1/2): 153–175. © 2004 Inderscience Enterprises Ltd. Reprinted with kind permission of Inderscience Ltd.

Chapter 9: Prashantham, S. and McNaughton, R.B. (2006) "Facilitating links between MNC Subsidiaries and SMEs: The Scottish Technology and Collaboration (STAC) initiative', *International Business Review*, 15: 447–462. © 2006 Elsevier Ltd. Reprinted with kind permission of Elsevier Ltd.

Abbreviations

B2B	Business-to-Business
BoP	Balance of Payment
CEO	Chief Executive Officer
CII	Confederation of Indian Industry
CMM	Capability Maturity Model
DoE	Department of Electronics
EDI	Electronic Data Interchange
EO	Entrepreneurial Orientation
ERP	Enterprise-wide Resource Planning
FDI	Foreign Direct Investment
GATT	General Agreement on Tariffs and Trade
HR	Human Resources
ICT	Information and Communication Technology
INV	International New Venture
IOR	Inter-Organizational Relationship
IT	Information Technology
ITES	Information Technology Enabled Services
KBV	Knowledge-Based View
KIF	Knowledge-Intensive Firm
MBA	Master in Business Administration
MIT	Ministry of Information Technology
MNC	Multinational Corporation
MNE	Multinational Enterprise
MO	Marketing Orientation
NASSCOM	National Association of Software Service Companies
NBD	New Business Development
NPD	New Product Development
PC	Personal Computer
PSU	Public Sector Undertaking
R&D	Research & Development
RFI	Request for Information
RFID	Radio Frequency Identification
RFP	Request for Proposal

SEI	Software Engineering Institute
SKIF	Small Knowledge-Intensive Firm
SME	Small- and Medium-sized Enterprise
STAC	Scottish Technology and Collaboration
STPI	Software Technology Parks of India
TiE	The Indus Entrepreneurs
UK	United Kingdom
UNDP	United Nations Development Programme
US	United States
USA	United States of America
VPN	Virtual Private Network
Y2K	Year 2000

Part I

Conceptual underpinnings

1 Resourceful internationalization

> It is resourcefulness, not the mere amount or even types of resources, that matters.
>
> (Zahra 2005: 21)

Internationalization: a strategic entrepreneurship perspective

Firms operating in international markets today seek competitive advantage. It has been suggested that if international business scholars agree on a 'big question' for the field, it ought to concern explanations of the differential performance of internationalizing firms – that is, 'What determines the international success and failure of firms' (Peng 2004: 99). Competitive advantage is at the very core of strategic management and an issue of interest to many researchers who focus on internationalization. Internationalization, after all, is 'a major dimension of the ongoing strategy process of most business firms' (Melin 1992: 101). Ultimately, successful internationalization is pointless if it does not help firms achieve greater strategic performance.

Today, it is widely recognized that international expansion can no longer be deemed the exclusive domain of the established multinational corporations (MNCs) (Wright and Ricks 1994; Zahra 2005). Despite a general preoccupation with large multinational enterprises, recent years have seen a surge in the study of internationalization of the smaller firm, especially in knowledge-intensive industries (Etemad and Wright 2003; Peng 2001). While Young (1987) was among the first to highlight the emerging importance of the internationalization of knowledge-intensive smaller firms, such interest caught on fairly rapidly within the international business field as evident from the following observation by Wright and Ricks (1994: 699) seven years later on significant trends in international business research:

> Another, even newer thrust of research activity is *international entrepreneurship* and the internationalization of *small business*. In the emerging global environment, entrepreneurs and their businesses become less limited

> to domestic markets. Even small firms are entering the realm of international business.... International players in the world of tomorrow will no longer be limited to big business.

It was, coincidentally, in the same year that Oviatt and McDougall (1994) profoundly influenced internationalization researchers with their ideas on the accelerated internationalization of international new ventures, resulting in considerable research activity over the subsequent decade (Zahra 2005). Thus Wright and Ricks' words have proved to be prophetic.

Scholars whose pioneering efforts seek to foster a research agenda at the strategy/entrepreneurship interface suggest that the internationalization of smaller firms is a topic that can be fruitfully examined from a strategic entrepreneurship perspective. Hitt *et al.* (2001) identify internationalization – along with external networks, resources/organizational learning and innovation – as a naturally occurring domain in strategic entrepreneurship. Smaller firms lack the resources of their large counterparts. Yet many are able to successfully leverage limited resources in an enterprising yet sensible manner. It is therefore appropriate that research on the internationalization of small and new firms be approached from *both* strategic and entrepreneurial perspectives.

Hitt *et al.* (2001: 480) note, 'Entrepreneurship is about creation; strategic management is about how advantage is established and maintained from what is created.... Wealth creation is at the heart of both entrepreneurship *and* strategic management.' Scholars have pointed out the need for an entrepreneurial mindset as they engage with risks and dangers presented by international expansion (Oviatt and McDougall 1994). Equally, attention has been drawn to the importance of a strategic orientation (Welch and Welch 1996) in relation to the key choices to be made in terms of market selection, entry mode choice and timing of entry. A strategic entrepreneurship perspective is consistent with internationalizing small firms' need to 'punch above their weight', as it were, and resourcefully use their limited means to internationalize (Zahra 2005).

Other scholars echo the call for integrating strategic and entrepreneurial perspectives. Venkatraman and Sarasvathy (2001) colourfully argue that strategic management and entrepreneurship are incomplete without the other – much as Romeo would be incomplete without a balcony, and vice versa! Shane (2003) discusses the need for entrepreneurial strategies that synthesize opportunity recognition and strategic choice. McGrath and McMillan (2000) call for strategists to adopt an entrepreneurial mindset. As such, these two fields are seen as offering mutually beneficial perspectives (Zahra and Dess 2001).

The three other domains of strategic entrepreneurship identified by Hitt *et al.* (2001) can all be related to resourceful internationalization. There are certain *resources* that firms need to possess themselves. The influence of Penrose (1959), whose work inspired the resource-based view of the firm (e.g. Barney 1991), is evident in the small firm internationalization literature. In particular, knowledge is seen as a vital resource (Wiklund and Shepherd 2003). As Yli-Renko *et al.* (2002: 280) observe, 'Given the importance of knowledge as a central value-adding resource of firms, it is not surprising that the current dominant theories on the internationalization process of new and small firms treat knowledge as a central enabling and driving resource.' Reflecting the wider literature that emphasizes the role of market and technological knowledge with respect to smaller firms (Wiklund and Shepherd 2003), the internationalization literature documents the role of market knowledge as a regulator of resources (Johanson and Vahlne 1977) and of technological knowledge as an enabling resource (Oviatt and McDougall 1994). An important complementary perspective to the resource/knowledge-based view is that of *organizational learning*. As Hitt *et al.* (2001: 483) assert, 'Knowledge is generated through organizational learning.' Both traditional (e.g. Johanson and Vahlne 1977) and more recent (e.g. Sapienza *et al.* 2006) perspectives of internationalization highlight the importance of learning (Cyert and March 1963). Linking this notion with that of external networks above, a significant potential outcome for internationalizing firms is that 'social capital facilitates learning' (Hitt *et al.* 2001: 482); in other words, 'external networks can be valuable because they provide the opportunity to learn new capabilities' (Hitt *et al.* 2001: 481). The role of resources and organizational learning in small firm internationalization is considered in this volume (see Chapter 3).

A key manifestation of knowledge and learning, including via social capital, is in terms of *innovation*. The literature is replete with exhortations for firms to succeed at innovation. The significance of innovation is evident from Hitt *et al.*'s (2001: 481) suggestion that innovation 'is considered by many scholars and managers to be critical for firms to compete effectively in domestic and global markets'. The role of innovation in internationalization is evident, at least implicitly, in the literature. McDougall and Oviatt's (2000) definition of international entrepreneurship identifies cross-border innovation as a component. Also, innovation can be expected to precede international expansion given that 'the capability to develop and introduce new products is a primary driver of a successful global strategy' (Hitt *et al.* 2001: 484). Finally, parallels have been identified between the processes of innovation and internationalization – in other words, internationalization is an innovative process (Johanson and Vahlne 1992; Knight and Cavusgil 2004). While the importance of innovation is unmistakably acknowledged in this volume, its role in small firm internationalization is, in the main, implicit; indeed, a major call in the concluding chapter is for future research to take innovation into account more explicitly.

Of all the domains of strategic entrepreneurship, perhaps none is more relevant to small firms' resourceful internationalization than *external networks*, the focus of this volume. External networks are an important means by which internationalizing firms are able to augment their limited resource base. As Hitt *et al.* (2001: 481) observe, 'the greatest value of networks for entrepreneurial firms is the provision of resources and capabilities needed to compete effectively in the marketplace.' This notion is expanded upon presently. Thus, in terms of the four domains of strategic entrepreneurship, this volume is primarily concerned with the relationship between external networks and internationalization. This introductory chapter explores some key themes on the role of networks in internationalization, to set the tone for the rest of the volume.

Networks and internationalization

A long-standing tradition, perhaps originating with Johanson and Mattsson's (1988) network model of internationalization, has emphasized the role of interorganizational relationships in the internationalization process. Recently, internationalization scholars have drawn on social capital theory to conceptualize and study this phenomenon (e.g. Coviello 2006). Social capital emanating from network relationships provides internationalizing small and new firms with vital network resources (Gulati 1999). In this volume, social capital is taken to mean 'the sum of the actual and potential resources embedded within, available through, and derived from the network of relationships possessed by an individual or social unit. Social capital thus comprises both the network and the assets that may be mobilized through that network' (Nahapiet and Ghoshal 1998: 243). The rationale for the choice of this definition is threefold. First, this definition is conducive for research on firm-level social capital, including social capital derived from inter-firm relationships, which is the focus in the present volume. Second, this definition is integrative of previous work, which is useful given the diversity of views on social capital; for instance, it combines both the public and private good perspectives and is neutral on social capital typologies (Adler and Kwon 2002; Inkpen and Tsang 2005). Third, Nahapiet and Ghoshal's (1998) definition – along with their ideas – establishes a relationship between social capital and knowledge wherein repeated and intensive social interaction facilitates the transfer of knowledge (Yli-Renko *et al.* 2001; Zahra *et al.* 2000). This approach therefore sits harmoniously with the knowledge-based view of the firm, which is dominant in the internationalization literature (see Chapter 3).

According to Portes (1998), it was Bourdieu (1986: 248) who provided the first systematic analysis of social capital, which he defined as 'the aggregate of the actual or potential resources which are linked to possession of a durable network of more or less institutionalized relationships of mutual acquaintance or recognition'. That one kind of social tie (e.g. friendship) can achieve a different purpose (e.g. work-related advice) is a long-held belief in sociology (Portes 1998). Social relations – as distinct from market or hierarchical relations – underlie social capital. Of course, market or hierarchical relations may, over the course of time through repeated interaction, yield social relations – and therefore social capital (Adler and Kwon 2002). The social capital concept has formalized the notion that benefits can be derived from social ties and encapsulated it in a manner that has attracted considerable interest beyond the confines of sociology. For the purposes of the present discussion, the key facet of social capital is that it allows small firms to achieve levels of internationalization and performance that they would not have been able to achieve on their own. In other words, *social capital enables resourceful internationalization*.

A number of scholars have acknowledged the role of network relationships and social capital in small firm internationalization. With regard to the emergent body of work on accelerated internationalization, Johanson and Vahlne (2003: 83–84) observe that 'a common feature of much of this research is that it places attention on networks and network relationships when trying to understand and explain the rapid internationalization of the firms'. They go on to suggest that 'there is a need for new and network-based models of internationalization' (Johanson and Vahlne 2003: 84). In similar vein, Oviatt and McDougall (2005a: 544) acknowledge that 'network analysis has been a powerful framework for international entrepreneurship researchers' and that 'networks help entrepreneurs identify international opportunities, establish credibility, and often lead to strategic alliances and other cooperative strategies'. Also, as Zahra (2005: 24) notes, 'Building relationships and gaining access to existing networks can help to shorten and expedite INVs' learning.'

Three facets of network relationships or social capital, with respect to internationalizing small firms, seem especially relevant and are echoed in the following chapters of this volume. These facets, discussed briefly below, are

1 the development of social capital;
2 the leverage of social capital;
3 the management of portfolios of social capital.

Developing social capital

As Coviello (2006) has recently pointed out, new ventures have certain network relationships that can play a significant role in initial market entry. It would seem likely that such founding relationships can have path-dependent consequences in terms of the subsequent development of the firm. Initial network relationships are often directly attributable to the entrepreneur and/or top management team (McDougall *et al.* 1994). Over time, however, additional network relationships can – and indeed, must – be built. These relationships will likely influence subsequent international expansion. Oviatt and McDougall (2005a) argue that initially strong ties are important to ventures but over time a set of weak ties are more likely to provide information and opportunities that facilitate accelerated internationalization. As the portfolio of network relationships expands, and especially as the ventures' confidence and capabilities grow (Coviello and Munro 1997), international growth accrues.

However, network relationships are not easy to come by and cannot be taken for granted. Research at the strategy/entrepreneurship interface suggests that ventures can develop the capability to replenish extant network relationships (i.e. its stock of social capital) with the addition of new ties (Hitt *et al.* 2001). However, while ventures' network range, density and centrality are bound to increase over time (Coviello 2006), they must overcome key barriers and be able to achieve visibility, efficiency and intimacy with respect to their network of relationships.

Achieving *visibility* is an important challenge for the smaller firm. A large established MNC seeking strategic alliances is quite different from a small, often young, firm attempting to establish network relations. While there are specific smaller social networks within a given milieu wherein even smaller firms *can* gain visibility, this requires time and effort and often it is the entrepreneur who bears the burden of networking activity that must be undertaken if the smaller firm is to become, and remain, well known among key actors. Difficulty arises from these firms' liability of foreignness (Zaheer 1995) – which has been viewed by some scholars as a symptom of deficient international social capital (Arenius and Autio 2005) – and liability of smallness (and of newness, for young firms). As Zahra (2005: 23) suggests, in relation to international new ventures (INVs),

> INVs usually experience three types of liability. The first relates to their newness and inexperience, which limits their access to resources and existing networks. Newness raises questions in the minds of other stakeholders about INVs' credibility and potential viability. The second liability stems from their size, as many INVs are small. This limits the slack resources of INVs and, as a result, their ability to withstand the challenges of internationalization. The third and final liability arises from the foreignness of INVs, which means that they have to work hard to overcome barriers to entry, build links to their customers and suppliers, and gain the acceptance of potential customers.

The next aspect of developing social capital can be referred to as the achievement of *efficiency* in relationships, once they are formed. The point being made here is that social capital is more likely to result when a firm is seen to be efficient and competent in its interactions. Efficiency in carrying out its part in a transaction or engagement ensures that a firm instills confidence and trust in the other actor(s) involved. As Gulati (1995: 92) notes, trust is built over time through repeated interactions. Implicit in this assertion is the importance of small firms ensuring that they 'deliver': that is, do a good job of whatever it is that has been undertaken. Initial interactions and impressions can be particularly important in establishing the reliability of the firm as an efficient player.

Finally, not in all but in some cases, it becomes possible and appropriate for small firms to build *intimacy* with the other actor(s). Intimacy implies knowledge about the other actor(s), which in turn increases the odds that any assistance provided is timely and relevant. Frequent interactions over time lead to stronger ties (Granovetter 1973) which can yield useful benefits (Krackhardt 1992). Even moderate levels of intimacy in relatively weaker ties can lead to the exchange of useful information and trade leads (Coviello 2006; Oviatt and McDougall 2005a). An important case of network relationship where intimacy can be particularly valuable is that of the involved customer, defined as 'a customer who regularly makes purchases … and with whom the relationship also involves considerable interaction and information exchange and the discussing of past, present and future needs' (Yli-Renko *et al.* 2002: 293). Such relationships can be a valuable source of technological knowledge (Yli-Renko *et al.* 2001), thereby resulting in useful innovation and internationalization outcomes.

Leveraging social capital

As noted, the initial network relationships of a small internationalizing venture can often be attributed to the entrepreneur and/or top management team. The extent to which a firm is initially endowed with social capital can vary greatly. The work of Bourdieu (1986), for instance, would suggest that ventures where the top management team is drawn from the elites of society – marked by attendance at prestigious educational institutions, for example – possess greater stocks of social capital. Certainly in the context of management education, the popular press emphasizes the importance of connections that are fostered at business schools through an MBA degree, implying that alumni networks from top educational institutions constitute a valuable source of social capital.

Similarly, another determinant of the stock of social capital that a firm is endowed with is the prior professional affiliations of the founding team. Former employees and colleagues can be an important source of information and advice (Nebus 2006). Also, as with educational institutions, former employers can signal pedigree which in turn helps to overcome barriers to social capital, such as a lack of visibility, while seeking to form network relationships (e.g. with banks). Finally, friends and family cannot be discounted as an important source of social capital. A variety of studies by entrepreneurship scholars (e.g. Davidsson and Honig 2003) indicates that family and friendship ties can result in tangible help in the form of start-up capital as well as intangible assistance (e.g. moral support). Thus, in a variety of ways, a small firm may be well endowed with social capital.

A well-endowed stock of social capital of itself, however, cannot guarantee success for the firm. Rather, social capital must often be 'leveraged' in order to yield useful network resources such as information (Gulati 1999). Small firms seem to vary in their capability to leverage social capital through, for instance, integrating knowledge within and outside its boundaries or adeptly tapping into a relatively small set of network relationships with a view to achieving initial successes (Lorenzoni and Lipparini 1999). Building upon these successes, such firms could expand further, adding additional ties to their portfolio of network relationships in the process.

However, it is also conceivable for smaller firms to have a sizeable number of network relationships and yet fail to utilize them effectively. This would occur for a variety of reasons. One, the top management team may not actively recognize these relationships as a valuable resource. Two, the top managers may be bashful when it comes to asking for help. Three, the managers may make suboptimal requests of network relationships. For instance, weak ties may be better used in obtaining novel information while strong ties may be more likely to yield timely assistance (Granovetter 1973). If, however, top managers have inappropriate expectations that all ties, whether strong or weak, will yield timely help, then they are likely to face disappointment in their interactions with less intimate associates.

It is noteworthy that the main emphasis in terms of leveraging social capital is on *active*, rather than passive, utilization of network relationships. This would be reflected in the difference between consciously attending a carefully selected set of industry conferences in order to build and maintain visibility and failing to do so. This active utilization suggests that there is virtue in communicating, within key close relationships, the nature of assistance that would be truly beneficial. What it certainly does *not* imply is that phoney or opportunistic behaviour in relation to building networks will yield fruit. At best, such efforts can lead to positive outcomes in the short term. In the medium to long term, such behaviour will destroy social capital. Furthermore, cultural differences and nuances will likely have to be taken into account while interacting with other actors. Persistence in making a request may be appreciated in one culture and frowned upon in another. Thus efforts to leverage social capital have to be accompanied by cross-cultural sensitivity.

Finally, it is suggested that the leveraging of social capital is likely to yield useful *learning* outcomes. As noted earlier, social capital can facilitate the creation and acquisition of market and technological knowledge, thereby leading to useful innovation and internationalization outcomes. Social capital fosters trust and decreases barriers to the exchange and combination of new knowledge (Nahapiet and Ghoshal 1998). This is likely to be increasingly the case as firms develop their visibility, efficiency and intimacy vis-à-vis their networks of relationships.

Managing social capital portfolios

Building upon the idea that network relationships differ in their characteristics and potential benefits, it would seem that firms possess *portfolios* of different network relationships. There are various ways of identifying social capital types. Granovetter (1973) differentiated between strong and weak ties which primarily differ in terms of their degree of intimacy and frequency of interaction. Putnam and Goss (2002) distinguish bonding from bridging social capital. According to Putnam and Goss (2002: 11), ‘Bonding social capital brings together people who are like one another in important aspects (ethnicity, age, gender, social class, and so on), whereas bridging social capital refers to social networks that bring together people who are unlike one another.’ In other words, bonding social capital pertains to social groups that are homogenous or similar; bridging social capital pertains to heterogeneous or dissimilar groups (Putnam 2000).

In the context of small firm internationalization, there exist important differences between network relationships in the local milieu and those in international markets. In other words, geographic location of social capital (local/domestic versus foreign/overseas) is another important dimension that differentiates between social capital types in a small firm’s social capital portfolio.

Again, the entrepreneur or top management team is often crucial in determining the extent of local and overseas network relationships that a small firm possesses. When these individuals have studied and/or worked abroad, they may have access to network connections that yield valuable social capital (McDougall *et al.* 1994). Furthermore, friends and family may live abroad, constituting a valuable source of coethnic social capital.

However, in general, small firms are likely to have a greater number of local network relationships compared to their network relationships in international markets. The latter are therefore coveted connections and the first instinct of small firms appears to be to look overseas to its existing network relationships (Johanson and Vahlne 2003) and to make further efforts (e.g. via trade missions) to develop further connections. Such an intuitive preference for overseas or foreign network relationships is understandable. Indeed, foreign network relationships do yield valuable benefits in terms of international expansion. Coviello and Munro's (1997) insightful research into the evolution of small firms' international growth patterns as a consequence of their network relationships suggests that initial relationships with large customers can be especially valuable in providing a breakthrough in initial international market entry. In some cases clients may themselves expand internationally, in the process providing new international business opportunities for the internationalizing small firm (Bell 1997). Network relationships in international markets can yield valuable information and leads, as well as advice (e.g. on the timing of market entry) that may be difficult to obtain elsewhere. Internet technology makes communication with network relationships easier and so valuable opportunities, information and advice can emanate from social capital in international markets.

The above benefits of international networks notwithstanding, the value of *local* network relationships ought not to be overlooked. There may be a tendency to do so, however, in the context of internationalization given firms' instincts to look beyond its own national boundaries for valuable networks (Johanson and Vahlne 2003). Yet, the local milieu is crucial in terms of providing the inputs that go into the creation of globally mobile offerings in the first place (Fernhaber *et al.* 2003). In other words, for small knowledge-intensive firms (SKIFs), the local milieu is ultimately associated with innovation, resources and learning (Hitt *et al.* 2001). Where agglomeration leads to specialization, small firms may also benefit from reputation effects and access to infrastructure. Intriguingly, local milieus also attract MNCs to set up local subsidiaries (Birkinshaw and Hood 2000), which constitute a potential source of social capital that could lead to interesting possibilities, both locally and internationally (see the Chapter 10 for a fuller discussion of this idea).

The important point here is that small firms must take a holistic perspective in recognizing their wider portfolio of network relationships, which could have potential direct and indirect benefits – both in international markets and in the local milieu. Taking a portfolio approach increases the odds that firms will have realistic expectations of network ties without becoming overly reliant on any. It could also provide an antidote against negative effects of social capital such as groupthink or overembeddedness (Yli-Renko *et al.* 2001). Internationalizing small firms that curb their instinct to look for social capital exclusively in international markets are likely not to overlook valuable resources in their own backyard, as it were.

The contents of this volume

The themes discussed hitherto recur in the remaining chapters, which are concerned with conceptual underpinnings, exploratory insights (based on case-study findings) and future research directions.

In relation to *conceptual underpinnings*, Chapter 2 makes the point that network relationships constitute a key driver of the internationalization of SKIFs. This is found to be entirely consistent with the nature of these firms; their resource-poverty and proclivity for innovation make the leverage of network relationships crucial. Chapter 3 presents a synthesis of the internationalization literature and highlights the ways in which network relationships could influence small firm internationalization. In addition to the internationalization opportunities that emanate from networks, it is posited that network relationships (and the resultant social capital) lead to market knowledge and knowledge-intensity, which in turn influence internationalization. In other words, knowledge may mediate the role of network relationships in the internationalization of SKIFs. Chapter 4, the final conceptual chapter, develops the argument that information technologies, such as the Internet, could facilitate the internationalization of SKIFs. It is suggested that the Internet will be particularly influential in the internationalization of SKIFs when applied to enhancing their visibility, efficiency and intimacy in the context of their network relationships, which may be either local and spatially concentrated or foreign and spatially dispersed. The chapter notes in conclusion that most prior research has been conducted in advanced economy settings.

Indeed, a key distinguishing point about this volume is the empirical setting which the subsequent four chapters that discuss *exploratory insights* are based upon – the software industry in Bangalore. Most of the extant literature deals with advanced economy contexts. The Bangalore software industry is, by contrast, based within a developing economy – clearly of growing interest to scholars – and has yet achieved prominence for its international orientation and, increasingly, technological excellence. This empirical setting has certain unique features that emphasize resourcefulness. There are accentuated resource constraints. In a developing economy context, there are greater challenges to overcome, and hence highly entrepreneurial behaviour is required given the limited size of the domestic market and the environmental hostility manifested through frustrations with infrastructural shortcomings and bureaucratic red tape. This challenge, in turn, accentuates the resource constraint commonly associated with SKIFs. Consequently, reliance on network relationships is likely to be particularly high.

Also, the reliance on network relationships is further strengthened by cultural factors in an Asian context such as the Bangalore software industry, given the well-known emphasis on relational capital in Asia. As Hitt *et al.* (2002: 354) note:

> In the West (i.e. North America, Western Europe), business dealings have been largely based on the concept of transactions. However, in most Asian societies, they are based on relationships. For example, when an executive is regarded as successful in Western societies, s/he is often described as wealthy. However, an executive of similar success in China is referred to as well connected.

Finally, the Bangalore software industry has acquired prominence as an important base for multinational corporations to set up subsidiaries, not merely to exploit the Indian market for technology but also to tap into its innovative milieu. This is consistent with the notion of the 'metanational' – firms that learn from the rest of the world and redeploy the acquired knowledge (e.g. innovation or new technologies) on a global basis. Thus unique opportunities for local network relationships to be utilized by SKIFs exist in Bangalore.

The above factors collectively provide a unique setting in which entrepreneurial firms could demonstrate (or not) resourcefulness in their internationalization activity. The empirical insights begin with Chapter 5, a chapter that points out the dearth of published research on the internationalization of SKIFs in a developing economy context. It provides an overview of an interesting setting, the Indian software industry, in which research can be undertaken to address this shortcoming. Additionally, the four case-firms are briefly introduced. Chapter 6, based on the four case studies, highlights the role played by network relationships that are local and spatially concentrated, which can be seen as an important resource in enhancing international competitiveness. It is seen, however, that the benefits accruing from location in a reputable software cluster like Bangalore can be easily overlooked and not exploited actively, a danger to be guarded against. In Chapter 7, the role played by network relationships that are based outside a firm's home country is examined. Like local network relationships, they constitute an important resource for a small knowledge-intensive firm, often leading to their entering or consolidating a presence in foreign markets. Entrepreneurs are seen to be particularly vital in, and burdened with, developing and maintaining foreign network relationships. The final chapter based on the four case studies, Chapter 8, reports the role of the Internet in the internationalization of SKIFs in Bangalore and brings together several of the themes discussed in the preceding chapters. The hope for enhanced internationalization prospects that the Internet provides is reiterated; some evidence of this comes from a preliminary exercise that finds a significant correlation between the quality of Internet application and international growth among 30 small Bangalore-based software firms. Equally, however, the scope to do more by way of applying the Internet to facilitate internationalization is also noted. An evolutionary approach to sophistication of the application of the Internet appears to exist.

The final section seeks to draw attention to *future directions* in terms of research on small firm internationalization. A key theme in the final two chapters (Chapters 9 and 10) is the potential role of MNCs as a source of social capital to internationalizing small firms. The penultimate chapter (Chapter 9) presents a brief case study of public policy efforts – within my own current local mileu, namely, Scotland – that seek to foster the links between MNCs and small- and medium-sized enterprises (SMEs). Clearly, MNCs can play an important role in small firm internationalization, in both advanced economies like Scotland and emerging economies like India, particularly given the importance of innovation to many internationalizing small firms. The concluding chapter expands on these ideas and calls for the explicit incorporation of technological innovation in future studies of small firm internationalization. It is suggested that the role of MNC links can be even greater when both internationalization and innovation outcomes are taken into account in concert.

As such, this volume should make it clear that small firm internationalization constitutes an 'entrepreneurial strategy' (Lu and Beamish 2001: 565) and that research in this area has the potential to gain from, and contribute to, the wider conversation at the intersection of strategy and entrepreneurship, especially with respect to the role of network relationships to foster strategic entrepreneurship on the part of the internationalizing small firm.

2 Networks and internationalization

Prashantham, S. and Berry, M.M.J. (2004) 'The small knowledge-intensive firm: a conceptual discussion of its characteristics and internationalization', *International Journal of Entrepreneurship and Innovation Management*, 4(2/3): 150–158.

Abstract

This conceptual chapter seeks to answer the research question: What are the determinants of internationalization in small knowledge-intensive firms (SKIFs)? It does so by establishing the meaning of the term 'small knowledge-intensive firm', by synthesizing literature from the small firm and knowledge-intensive firm literatures, and then subsequently marrying this definition with internationalization literature to yield a conceptual framework involving such key influences on internationalization as firm size, knowledge-intensity, the entrepreneur and environment. In each of these aspects, network relationships are seen to be influential. Implications of this discussion include the importance for SKIFs to prioritize and nurture network relationships, while seeking to strike a balance between strategy-making and responding opportunistically to new possibilities that emerge through these relationships.

Introduction

There has been growing interest in the internationalization of small knowledge-intensive firms (SKIFs) and while much good work has been done in this area – which this chapter cites – a nagging problem has been the non-standard use of the term 'small knowledge-intensive firm', which has rendered comparisons across most studies difficult. Further, it is argued here, the findings from many of these studies is actually seen to be much more meaningful when considered in the light of an in-depth understanding of the nature and characteristics of the SKIF. Thus, this conceptual chapter seeks to answer a research question that has been posed before: What are the determinants of internationalization in SKIFs? However, it does so differently – by seeking first to establish the meaning of the term 'small knowledge-intensive firm', by synthesizing literature from the small firm and knowledge-intensive firm literatures, and then subsequently marrying this definition with literature on small firm internationalization. It is in this definition-led approach to the subject that the contribution of this chapter to the extant body of literature lies. This chapter is structured as follows: the next section discusses the definition of a SKIF; the following section highlights four influences – derived from the definition – on SKIFs' internationalization; the penultimate section focuses on network relationships and their role in SKIFs' internationalization; and the final section draws out managerial, theory- and policy-related implications.

Defining a small knowledge-intensive firm (SKIF)

While categorizing firms in terms of size, the primary variable utilized is number of employees (see, e.g., Hadjimanolis 2000b). The US Small Business Administration defines a small- and medium-sized enterprise (SME) as one with fewer than 500 employees (Carlsson 1999: 107). The European Union defines a small firm as one with fewer than 50 employees (Wiklund and Shepherd 2001). In certain studies a lower limit is used as well: for example, in a study of Cypriot firms, small firms are defined as those with between ten and 50 employees (Hadjimanolis 2000b); a similar definition has been used in a study of Irish firms (McNamee *et al.* 2000). The most common understanding of a 'small firm' appears to be one with fewer than 100 employees (Brock 2000), and this understanding of a small firm will be adopted for this chapter.

The term 'knowledge-intensive firm' (KIF) has by no means a unique and universally understood meaning and has been somewhat ambiguous (Robertson and Hammersley 2000). It has superseded the terms 'high-technology firm' and 'technology-based firm' in studies about software firms. Alvesson (1995) has defined a knowledge-intensive firm as 'a company where most work can be said to be of an intellectual nature and where well-qualified employees form the major part of the workforce'. Elkjaer (2000: 344) sees a KIF as 'a company of knowledge workers' where 'human competencies are the main assets'. According to Robertson and Hammerlsey (2000: 241), 'KIFs have always been in the business of managing knowledge – knowledge being their primary asset and source of competitive advantage'. Autio *et al.* (2000) define knowledge-intensity as 'the extent to which a firm depends on the knowledge inherent in its activities and outputs as a source of competitive advantage', a view accepted by McNaughton (2001). Examples of knowledge-intensive disciplines include software (McNaughton 2001), law, accountancy, management consulting, advertising (Robertson and Hammersley 2000), engineering and computer consulting firms (Elkjaer 2000).

A synthesis of the above literature leads to the following definition of a SKIF:

> *A small knowledge-intensive firm is one that has fewer than 100 employees, the majority of whom comprise a highly qualified workforce which is its most important resource and is engaged in knowledge work – meaning that knowledge is inherent in the firm's main activities – as its central preoccupation.*

Influences on the internationalization of SKIFs

Drawing on the foregoing definition of a SKIF, four influences on the internationalization of SKIFS can be identified, explicitly or implicitly: size (smallness), knowledge-intensity, the environment and the entrepreneur.

Smallness: Three characteristics of small firms that are prominent in the literature are their *innovation*, *informality* and *interaction* with other actors. Small firms play an important role in innovation (Almeida 1999) and have been described as agents of change (Audretsch 1999), creators of radical innovation (Acs *et al.* 1999) and carriers of new ideas (Carlsson 1999). Small firms have a tendency to specialize in a niche area, which may even lead to their internationalization (Acs *et al. 1*999). It may, however, be pointed out that some small firms – even new ventures – are not innovative (Zahra and Neubaum 1998). Strategy-making in small firms can be very different from that in large firms (Manimala 1992b), is often informal and flexible (Carlsson 1999; Hadjimanolis 2000a) and has a short-run, opportunistic focus on operational, rather than strategic, issues (Bhide 1994). Of course, exceptions to the rule do exist (Berry 1998; Berry and Taggart 1998; Hadjimanolis 2000b; Manimala 1992b). Small firms are resource-poor, and external relationships can be vital to a small firm's viability and compensate for resources it lacks in (McNamee *et al.* 2000), as well as facilitate knowledge-building (Almeida 1999) and, therefore, innovation. These relationships may be available through regional networks which lead to opportunities for exploration and exploitation of new knowledge, local sourcing of resources and job-related information flows that allows for inter-firm mobility of labour (Almeida 1999; Saxenien 1990).

Knowledge-intensity: Knowledge-intensive firms have a propensity to be *born global*, that is, international virtually from inception. Berry *et al.* (2001) have pointed out that for knowledge-intensive firms, their key markets are often spread across geographies and yet concentrated in the triad economies of North America, Western Europe and Japan, and, consequently, these firms tend to focus on global niches, in which they must compete successfully in order to remain viable. Clearly, the motivation to internationalize – and that too at a rapid pace – is understandable. Not surprisingly then, SKIFs have constituted several instances – although not the only ones – of firms that have been international virtually from inception, which have been variously referred to as 'born globals', 'new international ventures' and 'global start-ups' (Knight and Cavusgil 1996; McDougall *et al.* 1994; Oviatt and McDougall 1994, 1997; Rennie 1993; Shrader *et al.* 2000;). This is often in contradiction to, and inconsistent with, the traditional stage theories (Bell 1995; Coviello and McAuley 1999; Coviello and Munro 1997; Crick and Jones 2000).

Environment: SKIFs operate in environments with rapidly changing technology, increasing research costs, ever shortening product life cycles and consequently greater uncertainty compared to manufacturing firms (Bell 1995; Jones 1999; McNaughton 2001; Young 1987), which accentuate the need for and impact of networking (Coviello and Munro 1997). This may also impact firms' appropriability of technology and lead them to seek strategic alliances (Rao and Klein 1994). As noted, markets for SKIFs tend to be concentrated, generally within the triad markets of North America, Western Europe and Japan (Bell 1995; Young 1987). This may prompt SKIFs based in less-advanced economies to seek symbiotic or collaborative relationships for market and technology access (Fontes and Coombs 1995, 1997). Also, instances of SKIFs internationalizing as a consequence of client followership in these triad markets have been reported (Bell 1995; O'Farrell *et al.* 1998). While these markets have attracted many SKIFs from developing economies, these entrepreneurs often fear the challenge of competing internationally (Bartlett and Ghoshal 2000). Further, SKIFs operate in markets marked by intensive competitiveness. This too is sometimes a driver for firms to seek alliances and network relationships and may have a bearing – with a view to protecting knowledge-based assets – on the choice of foreign market entry modes, which are often multiple or integrated (Brouthers *et al.* 1996; McNaughton 1996; McNaughton and Bell 2001). Of course, a hostile environment – marked by strong rivalry (Athreye 2001), for instance – could also be a driver of greater innovation on the part of small firms (Hadjimanolis 2000b; Zahra and Neubaum 1998).

Entrepreneur: While no particular personality trait is 'truly' entrepreneurial (Bhide 1994), the business-related characteristics of the entrepreneur have a strong bearing on the internationalization of small firms (Aaby and Slater 1989; Chetty and Hamilton 1993; Leonidou and Katsikeas 1996; Welch and Luostarinen 1988); this is particularly true in relation to firms that are international from inception (Madsen and Servais 1997). Three aspects of the entrepreneur that particularly matter for SKIFs' internationalization are his or her *knowledge*, *intent* and *networks*. The entrepreneur's technical domain of knowledge is very likely to determine the niche area that the firm focuses in while his or her business knowledge – including international experience and knowledge of foreign languages – will impact on decisions of market selection, entry mode and timing of entry. In terms of intent, an entrepreneur's strategic orientation (Berry 1996) and international orientation (Aaby and Slater 1989), or 'global mindset' (Berry 1998), will similarly influence the SKIF's attitude and approach to internationalization. As for networks, the entrepreneur brings to the table experience and contacts that influence the location and networking potential of the firm (Almeida 1999).

The internationalization of SKIFs: role of network relationships

A common thread running through the literatures on the small firm, knowledge-intensive firms and entrepreneurship, as seen in the preceding sections, can be termed as the role of network relationships, that is, relationships with customers, suppliers, competitors, alliance partners, universities, government bodies, industry associations and so on. The motivations for these, as seen, include resource-dependence and competitive considerations.

International entrepreneurship scholars Dana *et al.* (2000, 2001) have recently highlighted the role of network relationships in small firm internationalization, as an emerging paradigm (Wright and Dana 2003). This echoes Johanson and Mattson's (1988) argument that network relationships, which may exist across borders (Johanson and Mattsson 1988) or be spatially bound (Enright 1999; Porter 1990), influence internationalization decisions of firms.

Based on the foregoing discussion, this is likely to be especially true for SKIFs, and evidence for this is available in the literature; indeed, network relationships have been found to accelerate the internationalization of small firms and specifically SKIFs (Bell 1995; Coviello and Munro 1995, 1997). Coviello and Munro's (1995, 1997) work suggested that networks lead to rapid internationalization across several markets, new market opportunities, identification of potential partners, restructuring of relationships through power-play by firms including acquisition of some firms and emergence of dominant players. Key internationalization issues identified in relation to networks are impact on market selection, relative influence of other firms, evolution of power and control, interconnectedness, effect on growth and outsourcing of marketing (given the resource scarcity of smaller firms). Other impacts of the network were seen on the marketing aspect; these included: the ability of firms to focus on new product development (i.e., their core competency, while other members in the network dealt with marketing), evolution of relationships from distributorships to subsidiaries, and perception of a need for marketing intelligence and planning. The role of networks acquires significance when SKIFs specialize (Carlsson 1999). In some cases a large firm may dominate while in others there are a large number of small firms; strategic alliances may be entered into (Rao and Klein 1994) or the lead taken from key clients (Bell 1995; O'Farrell *et al. 1*998). Thus, network relationships are significant – both facilitating and constraining – for competitive advantage in general and internationalization in particular (Bell 1995; Johanson and Mattsson 1988).

To summarize, by deriving a coherent definition of a SKIF, four key elements can be identified which influence SKIFs' internationalization: their size, knowledge-intensity, environment and entrepreneur (Figure 2.1). The interplay between these elements is further moderated by network relationships, which are found to be vital when considering the elements individually and collectively. As mentioned earlier, this definition-led approach vindicates and renders more meaningful the strand of the internationalization literature which has highlighted the relevance of network relationships, especially in the case of SKIFs.

Implications

The foregoing discussion leads to important implications for entrepreneurs and managers in SKIFs, in terms of marketing. These include the need for them to prioritize meaningfully among their network relationships and accordingly allocate the time and energy that is invested in each. Having done so, they should network proactively; this would mean setting up face-to-face meetings, in both professional and social settings as appropriate. They should actively consider the prospect of driving their firms to specialize in areas of technical and market strength and collaborate with other players, including SKIFs, having complementary technical and marketing strengths. An element of choice certainly exists in how firms respond to opportunities arising from their network relationships and a balancing act is required between strategy-making and

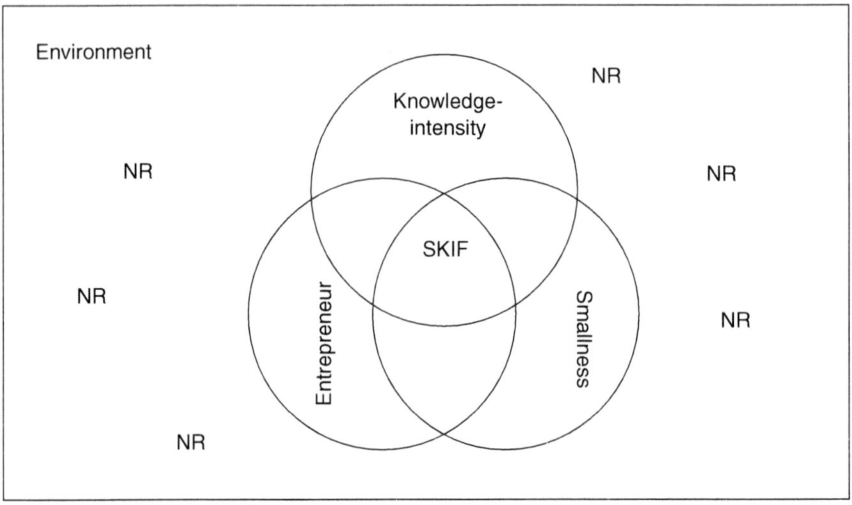

Figure 2.1 Determinants of the internationalization of small knowledge-intensive firms.

opportunism. Attention is drawn to the resource constraints that SKIFs face and therefore their managers should explore efficient and effective options such as the application of Internet technology to their marketing and internationalization efforts.

In terms of theory-building, it should be evident that consensus and clarity do not exist among researchers in relation to defining terms such as ‘small firms’ and ‘knowledge-intensive firms’, and this lack of uniformity will hinder the progress of the development of theory. Greater collaborative efforts will thus have to be undertaken by scholars with an interest in SKIFs. Specific research avenues that could be undertaken include studying the impact of Internet technology application on SKIFs’ network relationships, the role of network relationships in SKIFs’ internationalization in a developing economy context and differences between the impact of spatially bound and geographically dispersed network relationships of SKIFs on their internationalization.

Policy-makers should facilitate the setting up of networks for SKIFs with a view to promoting their internationalization. Such arrangements will lead to contacts, which in turn could result in knowledge development, joint marketing activity and potentially long-term network relationships. Specifically, activities that could be undertaken by governments include mentoring programmes in collaboration with internationalization experts and consultants, organizing training seminars which also provide networking opportunities and offering subsidized foreign trips to key markets. It is important that policy-makers adopt a persistent approach that allows concerted networking over a period of time, something that may not always happen if discontinuity in policy accompanies changes in government.

3 Knowledge and internationalization

Prashantham, S. (2005) 'Toward a knowledge-based conceptualization of internationalization', *Journal of International Entrepreneurship*, 3(1): 37–52.

Abstract

This conceptual chapter contributes to the internationalization literature in response to previous criticisms by enabling the integration of apparently contradictory strands of the literature and incorporation of the potential role of the Internet. Knowledge is at the core of received wisdom on internationalization. This is consistent with the notion that internationalization represents an innovation of the firm and often entails decision-making under conditions of uncertainty, for both of which knowledge is vital. Given the link between knowledge and internationalization, apparent tensions in the literature can be resolved by recognizing its different types, consequently varying roles and diverse sources. Furthermore, network relationships – of growing significance in the literature – yield social capital, which in turn leads to knowledge acquisition and creation; thus it is worthwhile to integrate knowledge and social capital perspectives. Finally, consistent with the knowledge-based approach adopted in the chapter, the application of Internet technology is conceptualized in terms of information effects such as information dissemination, acquisition and sharing which could lead to enhanced internationalization, knowledge and social capital, respectively.

Introduction

Internationalization, commonly understood to be the process of adapting firms' operations to international environments (Calof and Beamish 1995: 116), is an issue of importance for firms; it often results in vital growth (Luostarinen 1980), useful learning outcomes (Zahra *et al.* 2000) and enhanced financial performance (Lu and Beamish 2001). Recent focus on the internationalization of the smaller firm has resulted in a growing overlap of interest between international business and entrepreneurship researchers (Coviello and Jones 2004; McDougall and Oviatt 2000; Oviatt and McDougall 2005b). While these scholars have made considerable progress in taking forward the internationalization literature, issues that have not been satisfactorily addressed as yet include its fragmentary nature and the need to take recent technological developments on board (Andersen 1993; Melin 1992; Singh and Kundu 2002).

This conceptual chapter therefore seeks, first, to integrate, by drawing on the emerging knowledge-based view of the firm from the strategy literature, two dominant yet apparently contradictory strands of the small firm internationalization literature: the internationalization process model (Johanson and Vahlne 1977) and international new venture perspective (Oviatt and McDougall 1994). Thereafter, (whilst still dealing with the first concern – the fragmentary nature of the internationalization literature), the chapter seeks to further strengthen its integrative approach, by also considering the role of network relationships in internationalization, on the basis of social capital theory, owing to its link with knowledge formation (Nahapiet and Ghoshal 1998). Finally, in order to address the second concern (i.e. the need to incorporate recent technological developments), the chapter considers the rise of Internet technology and, consistent with the knowledge-based approach adopted in the chapter, identifies three information effects of the Internet and their potential impact on internationalization. The subsequent discussion examines these three issues, in turn, and is followed by a concluding section on implications for further research and managerial practice. It may be noted that this chapter does not aim to provide a comprehensive survey of the internationalization literature, but rather focuses on certain key seminal ideas, thus encouraging a more holistic and up-to-date (having taken into account recent technological developments) approach to research on small firm internationalization.

Knowledge and internationalization

Knowledge is at the core of received wisdom on internationalization. In the 1970s, international business scholars, notably Johanson and colleagues[1] (Johanson and Vahlne 1977; Johanson and Wiedersheim-Paul 1975), argued that a firm's market knowledge determines its internationalization, of which three dimensions are conspicuous: international market selection, entry mode choice and pace of internationalization (Jones and Coviello 2005). Such knowledge regulates the resources committed to a foreign market, a notion that has been supported in the literature (Eriksson *et al.* 1997). With respect to market selection, Johanson and colleagues postulated that psychic distance distorts the acquisition of market knowledge and therefore foreign markets that are initially selected will be psychologically proximate to the firm's domestic market. In terms of mode choice, a firm was envisaged as traversing a sequential set of stages, from indirect exporting at one end of the spectrum to wholly owned production-oriented subsidiaries at the other. As for pace, the manifestation of this model was anticipated to be incremental international expansion following a period of domestic growth. However, many empirical studies of firms' internationalization behaviour, especially in technology-based knowledge-intensive sectors, contradicted all three predictions (Andersen 1993). That is, these firms were international virtually from inception, entering psychically distant markets through high-commitment modes from an early stage in their life cycle. In the 1990s, this led to a different perspective among certain US-based entrepreneurship scholars, notably McDougall and colleagues[2] (McDougall *et al.* 1994; Oviatt and McDougall 1994). Their views were seen as a challenge to Johanson and Vahlne's thesis.

However, in relating key notions from the internationalization literature to the emerging knowledge-based view (KBV) of the firm in the strategy literature, a fruitful basis for synthesizing these apparently disparate views, at least partially, can be found. A useful overview of the KBV is provided by Grant (2002) according to whom:

> [t]he emerging 'knowledge-based view of the firm' is not a theory of the firm in any formal sense. It is more a set of ideas about the existence and nature of the firm that emphasize the role of knowledge.

He identifies certain assumptions on which this view is based: (a) the great importance of knowledge as a productive resource, (b) the variation in transferability of knowledge – it is high for explicit knowledge and low for tacit knowledge (skills, know-how, and contextual knowledge); knowledge-intensive industries may therefore enjoy increasing returns, (c) knowledge is more expensive to create than replicate, leading to potential economies of scale, (d) specialization leads to greater efficiency in knowledge creation and storage and (e) the requirement, often, for many types of knowledge in firms' operations. Distinction is drawn between the creation and application of knowledge: while the former requires specialized skills, the latter calls for diverse ones. Knowledge management has emerged as a subject of great interest to managers all over the world and is a central issue posed by the KBV.

While KBV is informed by a variety of perspectives, it draws heavily on Penrose's (1959) theory of the growth of the firm. Penrose posited that a firm's knowledge to productively integrate resources into higher-level capabilities determines its growth. Several scholars have developed their ideas further in the 1990s. Strongly echoing Penrose, Spender (1994) has argued that competitive advantage is not merely explained by individual resources but by a different type of resource – knowledge; this refers to the *coordination* of resources, which inheres in the activity itself and therefore the firm (rather than its individual members). Thus, competitive advantage has come to be seen as based on knowledge, not raw materials; consequently firms create and sustain competitive advantage by protecting valuable knowledge through preventing its migration and reducing its imitability (Liebeskind 1996). Similar notions are expressed by Demsetz (1991: 172), who conceptualizes firms as 'repositories of specialized knowledge and of the specialized inputs required to put this knowledge to work', and by Kogut and Zander (1993: 627), who proffer the 'notion of the firm as a repository of social knowledge that structures cooperative action'.

That knowledge is a necessary driver in the successful internationalization of the firm becomes clear in the light of the notion that internationalization constitutes a form of innovation (Bilkey and Tesar 1977; Simmonds and Smith 1968), of which knowledge is a vital source (Penrose 1959). Furthermore, knowledge is vital in dealing with environmental uncertainties that characterize internationalization (Liesch and Knight 1999) and informing decisions on market selection, mode choice and pace of internationalization (Young *et al.* 1989). Given the link between knowledge and internationalization, the apparent tension between the perspectives of Johanson and Vahlne and that of Oviatt and McDougall can be mitigated by recognizing the Penrosian roots in both perspectives, albeit with differing emphases (Sapienza *et al.* 2003; Yli-Renko *et al.* 2002). These differences primarily pertain to the *type* of knowledge emphasized in each approach, the *role* that knowledge plays in internationalization, and the *sources* of the knowledge. For Johanson and Vahlne, the type of knowledge that is vital is market knowledge,[3] and the role it plays is regulating the resources committed to a foreign market by the firm; by extension, a lack of market knowledge is a significant obstacle for firms' internationalization (Eriksson *et al.* 1997). Its main source is the firm itself, through its experience of foreign operations (Johanson and Wiedersheim-Paul 1975) and (as recently emphasized) network relationships (Johanson and Vahlne 2003). Oviatt and McDougall's perspective differs from this view in that, in addition to market knowledge, there is an emphasis on the role of (technological) knowledge-intensity in internationalization; consequently software and biotechnology firms, to cite two popular examples, have been noted for their proactive and early internationalization. In other words another type of knowledge – (technological) knowledge-intensity – is highlighted which plays a separate role from resource-regulation, that of an enabling resource leading to the firm's globally mobile offerings in the marketplace. Support for the notion that knowledge-intensive firms internationalize with greater market diversity and more involved modes (Zahra *et al.* 2000) and earlier in their life cycle (Autio *et al.* 2000) can be seen in the literature.

Furthermore, Oviatt and McDougall explicitly identify the entrepreneur as a vital source of a firm's knowledge resources, from prior professional experience (see also McDougall *et al.* 1994). In other words, while Johanson and Vahlne emphasized Penrose's *managerial* knowledge, Oviatt and McDougall focused on her *entrepreneurial* knowledge concept (Sapienza *et al.* 2003; Yli-Renko *et al.* 2002). Sapienza *et al.* (2003) correctly note that 'implicitly, the core of the difference in the two views is that Johanson and Vahlne do not see prior, individual experience as mitigating firm-level aversion to new markets'. Yet, this is perplexing in the light of observations made by some of Johanson's colleagues, at the time of the original Uppsala model, that the 'pre-export' experience of individual decision-makers – who might often be the entrepreneur – can greatly influence a firm's internationalization decisions (Wiedersheim-Paul *et al.* 1978). This inexplicable oversight of individual entrepreneurs' role can, however, now be rectified by extending the sources of a firm's market knowledge and knowledge-intensity to include the firm itself, its network relationships and individual decision-makers or entrepreneurs. More recently, extending Oviatt and McDougall's views, Reuber and Fischer (1997) have highlighted the important role of the prior international experience of the top management team as a whole. In summary, both traditional internationalization process and international new venture perspectives, though apparently contradictory in their

Table 3.1 Knowledge and internationalization: a synthesis

Types	*Theory*	*Role*	*Sources*
Market knowledge	Penrose's managerial knowledge	Resource regulator	• Firm (Johanson and Vahlne 1977) • Entrepreneur (McDougall *et al.* 1994)
Knowledge-intensity	Penrose's entrepreneurial knowledge (Sapienza *et al.* 2003)	Enabling resource (Yli-Renko *et al.* 2002)	• Top management team (Reuber and Fischer 1997) • Network relationships (Oviatt and McDougall 1994; Johanson and Vahlne 2003)

manifestations, have sufficient commonality in the knowledge-based view underpinning each to warrant an integrative approach that includes a wider set of knowledge types, role and sources than included in either approach taken on its own. This integration is summarized in Table 3.1.

The foregoing constructs can also be fruitfully considered in the context of organizational capabilities[4] (Teece *et al.* 1997). Differential resources, particularly knowledge, are seen to explain firms' performance (Barney 1991) and capabilities (Prahalad and Hamel 1990). Knight and Cavusgil (2004: 126) note that 'knowledge is the most important resource, and the integration of individuals' specialized knowledge is the essence of organizational capabilities'. Thus the notion of organizational capabilities further accentuates the vital significance of knowledge, which is further captured by Johanson and Vahlne's (2003: 90) assertion that 'an important implication of the process view of internationalization is that development, integration, and transfer of knowledge should be regarded as a critical aspect of [the] strategic management of internationalization'.

There would seem to be a mutually reinforcing effect between knowledge and organizational capabilities. On the one hand, organizational capabilities enable firms to create and leverage knowledge (Eisenhardt and Martin 2000), as urged by Johanson and Vahlne (2003). On the other hand, the creation of new knowledge by firms leads to the development of organizational capabilities (Nelson and Winter 1982). As stated by Knight and Cavusgil (2004: 126), 'The idiosyncratic knowledge base acquired by following pathways gives rise to organizational capabilities.' Thus there is, as Tallman and Fladmoe-Linquist (2002) note, a capability-leveraging and a capability-building aspect to the international expansion of firms; both outcomes can be expected, potentially resulting in a virtuous cycle.

Such capabilities as learning (Fiol and Lyles 1985) and absorptive capacity (Cohen and Levinthal 1990) are highly complementary to the present discussion. Internationalizing firms need to be adept at learning to enhance their stock of market knowledge and knowledge intensity. Closely related is the aspect of absorptive capability, which is the ability of a firm to recognize, assimilate and apply information from the external environment and influences its ability to enhance market knowledge in the context of internationalization (Eriksson and

Chetty 2003). Indeed, considerable work by international business scholars in the tradition of Johanson and Vahlne (e.g. Blomstermo *et al.* 2004; Eriksson *et al.* 1997) has focused on learning by internationalizing firms. Similarly, and furthermore, the work of some entrepreneurship scholars extending Oviatt and McDougall's work has focused on learning both as an antecedent (e.g. Autio *et al.* 2000) and as a consequence (e.g. Zahra *et al.* 2000) of internationalization; this is consistent with Tallman and Fladmoe-Linquist's (2002) capability-leverage and capability-building, noted above. Thus, complementary to the knowledge-based conceptualization of internationalization espoused in the present discussion is the notion of organizational capabilities, where the importance of a firm's capacity to learn and absorb new information (and subsequently, knowledge) is paramount.

Social capital, knowledge and internationalization

Having established a knowledge-based conceptualization of internationalization, the discussion now turns to network relationships, whose role in internationalization has acquired significance in the literature in recent years (Holm *et al.* 1996; Johanson and Mattsson 1988; Oviatt and McDougall 1994). Integrating network approaches with the 'mainstream' models of internationalization has in fact been strongly advocated recently by the very scholars whose work is highlighted in this chapter (Johanson and Vahlne 2003; McDougall and Oviatt 2003). Furthermore, the value of invoking social capital theory in the context of this chapter's knowledge-based conceptualization of internationalization lies in recent developments in the strategy literature,[5] which suggests that social capital leads to the creation and acquisition of knowledge (Nahapiet and Ghoshal 1998; Tsai and Ghoshal 1998; Yli-Renko *et al.* 2001). Of course, firms must have the organizational capability to leverage inter-firm relationships effectively (Lorenzoni and Lipparini 1999).

The primary tenet of social capital theory is that benefits accrue to actors from their social networks (Burt 1992; Coleman 1988). This applies to a business context as well, and a firm's network relationships can, and often do, yield social capital to it. 'Social capital' is a broad umbrella term, which is variously defined; in this chapter, the definition of Nahapiet and Ghoshal (1998: 243) is adopted, according to whom social capital is 'the sum of the actual and potential resources embedded within, available through, and derived from the network of relationships possessed by an individual or social unit'. In the context of internationalization, social capital could emanate from a variety of network relationships, including those with customers, suppliers, distributors and strategic partners (Yli-Renko *et al.* 2002). As noted, the internationalization literature has highlighted the importance of these relationships; such research can, however, be enhanced in terms of its theoretical rigour by utilizing a social capital perspective.

Information, influence and solidarity have been identified as key benefits arising as a consequence of social capital (Adler and Kwon 2002). Of these, in the context of internationalization, information is the most significant (Liesch and Knight 1999) and has been referred to as a network resource – that is, a resource that resides not within a firm's boundaries, but rather in inter-firm relationships (Gulati 1999). This notion is useful in terms of theorizing, as it allows for Penrosian and social capital theories to be creatively combined, resulting in greater explanatory power for ensuing research frameworks. Lee *et al.* (2001: 616) argue that such an integration is appropriate, given that (resource-constrained) firms 'develop firm-specific assets while obtaining complementary external resources through their social networks'.

Information-related benefits arising from social capital include access to new information, timeliness of information, and referrals (Burt 1992). Furthermore, social capital can result in enhanced volume, diversity and richness of information for actors (Koka and Prescott 2002). The notion that social capital enhances knowledge (Nahapiet and Ghoshal 1998) is thus consistent with the view that social capital often results in information benefits, given the strong relationship between information and knowledge, which is evident from Liebeskind's (1996) definition of knowledge as 'information whose validity has been established through tests of proof'. The role of network relationships in providing access to knowledge may be greater in dynamic environments, such as those that characterize knowledge-intensive industries (Grant 1996).

The application of social capital theory to the multinational enterprise context and internationalization phenomenon is relatively recent. In terms of the former, Kostova and Roth (2003) have argued that social capital in multinational subsidiaries, when transformed from a private to a public good, has significant potential to influence headquarters-subsidiary and other intra-organizational relationships. In terms of the latter (which is more directly linked to this chapter), a pioneering study is the case-based research of Arenius (2002) [see also Jones (2003) for a summary]. She has proposed that a new venture's social capital positively influences its speed of internationalization, international diversification, success of international market entry and international growth. Another vital contribution is made by Yli-Renko *et al.* (2002) who demonstrated empirically that social capital positively influences market knowledge and knowledge intensity, which in turn positively influence the firm's international growth, an indicator internationalization performance (Manolova and Manev 2004). Given that their research builds upon the same bases of the present discussion – the work of Johanson and Vahlne (1977) and Oviatt and McDougall (1994) – we extend their ideas to internationalization more broadly (i.e. in terms of market selection, mode choice and pace) and summarize the foregoing synthesis of the internationalization in Figure 3.1.

Internet technology, social capital, knowledge and internationalization

While authors such as Yli-Renko *et al.* (2002) and Sapienza *et al.* (2003) have made significant progress in developing a knowledge-based view of

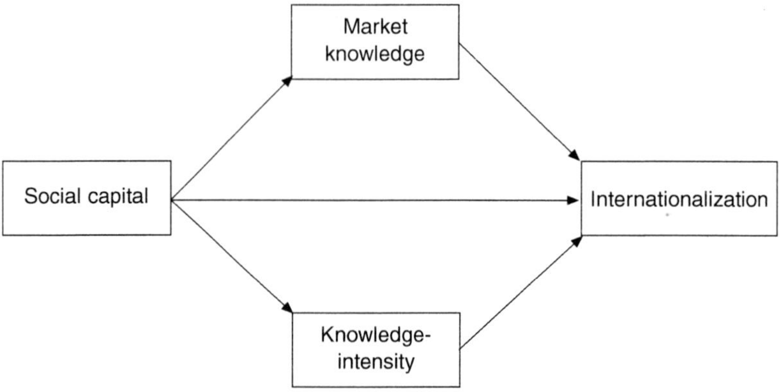

Figure 3.1 Social capital, knowledge and internationalization.

internationalization that is enriched by social capital, they – as also Johanson and Vahlne as well as Oviatt and McDougall – have thus far failed to explicitly incorporate in their approaches recent developments in information technology such as the Internet. Indeed, despite recognition of the vital importance of the Internet to business in general (Afuah 2003) and to the specific context of internationalization in particular (Quelch and Klein 1996), surprisingly little progress has been made in incorporating the role of the Internet in the mainstream internationalization literature; perhaps this shortcoming will be mitigated as more empirical studies (e.g. Berry and Brock 2004; Prashantham and Young 2004) of this phenomenon emerge. In any case, considering the role of the Internet in internationalization is important. As Porter (2001: 64) notes, 'The key question is not whether to deploy Internet technology – companies have no choice if they want to stay competitive – but how to deploy it.'

Therefore, this final section of the conceptual discussion seeks to incorporate the role of the Internet in internationalization. The knowledge-based conceptualization developed thus far in this chapter makes this possible through the link between information and knowledge, noted earlier (Liebeskind 1996). As noted by Sampler (1998), the emergence of the Internet has made information an increasingly important resource for firms. Thus irrespective of whether or not e-commerce transactions are carried out, the Internet offers firms an information-intensive environment, allowing them to disseminate, acquire and share information. These applications could lead to, respectively, enhanced internationalization (in terms of market diversity and pace), knowledge and social capital, as discussed below.

Information dissemination: The Internet allows firms to disseminate information about themselves to potentially any part of the world. Kobrin (2001: 688) asserts that '[c]yberspace and e-commerce are intrinsically international'. On similar lines, Kotha *et al.* (2001: 776) suggest that '[i]n principle, an Internet firm gains immediate access to international customers by virtue of launching a website'. The underlying principle behind these new possibilities is described by Evans and Wurster (1997) as the 'blowing up' of the trade-off between reach and richness of communication. In other words, a firm could either communicate intimately with a small audience (e.g. a salesman interacting with a prospective customer) or superficially with a large audience (e.g. a commercial on national television). The Internet, however, allows firms to provide in-depth and interactive (i.e. rich) content to a potentially global audience (i.e. reach) using a Web site. It should thus be theoretically possible for information dissemination to result in unsolicited orders from abroad, and therefore in greater market diversity, less involved entry modes and more rapid internationalization (Quelch and Klein 1996); indeed as a consequence of this, one study found that small firms with Web sites perceived themselves to be engaging in 'border-crossing' (Walczuch, van Braven and Lundgren 2000). Although the notional instant global presence was at the heart of early excitement regarding the Internet, a more realistic perspective now prevails. For instance, a Web site or hub site (Kaplan and Sawhney 2000) will attract traffic only if proactively promoted (Hoffman and Novak 2000); furthermore, despite the Internet's global reach, country-specific Web sites may be required in key markets (Kotha *et al.* 2001) and the importance of physical presence is seen to be virtually undiminished in many respects (Leamer and Storper 2001). Nonetheless, internationalization is likely to be facilitated by the Internet (Berry and Brock 2004; Prashantham and Young 2004).

Information acquisition: A corollary to information dissemination is the acquisition of information through Internet technology. Although the following observation was made in relation to customers, it applies equally to the internationalizing small firm: the Internet 'expands the potential (credible) sources of information that is available' (Parasuraman and Zinkhan 2002: 286). Firms can access much information about existing and prospective foreign markets, which is of immense value in the context of internationalization (Liesch and Knight 1999), through relevant Web sites such as specialist search engines. Thus the Internet has the potential to enhance aspects of a firm's market knowledge. A firm's own Web site can be used to capture information from customers, business partners and other visitors to the site through database technology that can then yield, for example, a nuanced understanding of international market segments (Davenport *et al.* 2001). Further, information for specific tasks or transactions can be acquired from suppliers, customers or distributors through Internet-supported supply chain management applications (Evans and Wurster 1997; Porter 2001).

Information sharing: Perhaps the most significant aspect of the Internet is interactivity (Hoffman and Novak 1996), which allows firms to exchange information. In the context of internationalizing small firms, Singh and Kundu (2002: 680) suggest that as a consequence of Internet technology, such firms 'have a unique set of advantages based on network resources, open accessibility, innovative entrepreneurship, and *information sharing*' [emphasis added]. Intranets and extranets constitute important tools for information exchange, in which context Parasuraman and Zinkhan (2002: 288) observe that 'organizations now have an opportunity to use information technology and information systems to make closer connections with their relational partners'. Another tool is Internet-supported groupware, the use of which is patently evident in the active exchange of information among open-source software developers (von Krogh 2003), suggesting that certain knowledge-intensive firms are particularly likely to adopt such technology. Also of relevance to such firms is the suggestion that Internet technology offers 'a powerful platform for collaborating with customers on innovation' (Sawhney *et al.* 2003: 77). It may be noted, however, that the vital importance of face-to-face contact cannot be discounted; as Leamer and Storper (2001: 641) observe, the Internet 'allows long distance "conversations" but not "handshakes" '. The foregoing discussion is summarized in Table 3.2.

In terms of the Internet, as with the knowledge constructs discussed earlier, organizational capabilities such as the internationalizing firm's ability to learn (Fiol and Lyles 1985) are vital, given the rapid changes in information technology. Furthermore, the Internet literature emphasizes the importance of a customer-led approach in applying new technology. Thus borrowing from the marketing literature, market orientation, which has received widespread attention as a predictor of firms' performance (Hult and Ketchen 2001; Kohli and Jaworski 1990), is a useful ability for internationalizing firms to cultivate. Kohli *et al.* (1993: 467) define marketing orientation as 'the organizationwide generation of market intelligence pertaining to current and future needs of customers, dissemination of intelligence horizontally and vertically within the organization,

Table 3.2 The Internet and internationalization: information applications

	Internet properties	*Internet tools*	*Internationalization effects*
Information dissemination	'Explosion' of reach and richness (Evans and Wurster 1997); so, intrinsically international (Kobrin 2001)	• Web site (Hoffman and Novak 2000; Kotha *et al.* 2001) • Business-to-business 'hub' site (Kaplan and Sawhney 2000)	International growth (Quelch and Klein 1996; Singh and Kundu 2002)
Information acquisition	Information-intensity and expanded sources of credible information (Parasuraman and Zinkhan 2002)	• Other Web sites (Parasuraman and Zinkhan 2002) • Own database-driven Web site (Davenport *et al.* 2001)	Enhanced market knowledge (Liesch and Knight 1999; Parasuraman and Zinkhan 2002)
Information sharing	Interactivity (Hoffman and Novak 1996)	• Intranet/extranet (Parasuraman and Zinkhan 2002) • Groupware (Sawhney *et al.* 2003)	Enhanced social capital (Sawhney and Zabin 2002)

and organizationwide action or responsiveness to market intelligence'. Such an approach, in combination with a learning orientation, can facilitate internationalizing firms' efforts to obtain insights through the effective application of Internet technology from key network relationships, notably – although not exclusively – customers. Sawhney and Zabin (2002) point out that social capital 'is not limited to relationships with customers but also includes relationships with partners, suppliers, and employees'.

Implications and conclusions

The foregoing discussion has implications that are both theoretical and practical. From a theoretical perspective, the discussion provides direction for extending the internationalization literature through an eclectic approach combining knowledge-based and social capital theories. This is particularly useful in the multidisciplinary context in which contemporary internationalization research is being carried out. Future research utilizing this approach and developed further by the articulation of propositions, development of construct measures[6] and reliable survey instrument, and rigorous analysis of data from a range of empirical settings (e.g. from both developed and developing economies) is encouraged. Small knowledge-intensive firms constitute a particularly interesting subject for empirical research, owing to their inherent knowledge-intensity and propensity to leverage social capital, as seen in the literature (Prashantham and Berry 2004a).

Furthermore, in relation to future research, it has been emphasized that the role of the Internet must be actively considered. An objective of academic research dealing with the Internet has to be to separate the hyped claims of the past from the reality of the present – both potential and actual. Towards this end, the conceptual discussion presented in this chapter considers how, *potentially*, the Internet could influence the internationalization of firms. Empirical investigation which would entail similar attention to measures,[7] instrument and data analysis as mentioned above should aim at describing what, *in practice*, is the extent of the application of Internet technology for international business by firms and what impact, if any, it has on internationalization. Any theory–practice gap may well be an indication of the shortcoming of firms – due to ignorance or ineffectiveness in application. Whatever the case, rigorous and scholarly research alone will shed light on this important matter.

Managerial implications include the importance of managing knowledge, leveraging social capital and effectively applying Internet technology with a view to achieving successful internationalization outcomes. First, knowledge can be better managed when firms are aware of their extant knowledge stocks through gap analyses, which are often difficult to implement in reality. Nonetheless, a conscious effort to enhance, preserve and apply knowledge is vital. Firms will also do well to seek to acquire knowledge through inter-firm collaboration and interaction. Second, leveraging social capital can be managed effectively when firms consider their endowment of social capital. Furthermore, firms need to be aware of the extent to which they are leveraging extant social capital. Thus unexploited network relationships can be consciously strengthened and utilized; new network relationships can be sought when potentially useful. Third, the application of Internet technology to facilitate internationalization requires firms to utilize the whole spectrum of information applications, without confining themselves to information dissemination (Walczuch *et al.* 2000). Furthermore, they need to be systematic and consistent with their use of these technologies.

The foregoing managerial applications also lend themselves to policy implications in that policy-makers must facilitate the acquisition and development of skills for small firms to manage knowledge, social capital and technology. Policy-makers should foster inter-firm networks that lead to social capital. Further, knowledge-management and the management of learning within firms are vital for their international success; policy-makers would do well to educate (particularly smaller) firms on effective means of achieving this, including through the Internet. The key to successful internationalization, in the light of the discussion in this chapter, is a holistic approach of leveraging available and potential resources of the firm, with a particular emphasis on creating, acquiring and leveraging knowledge.

This chapter has sought to facilitate the continued progress of research in small firm internationalization, which is of considerable importance both in theoretical and in practical terms, given the significance of the internationalization phenomenon as noted at the outset. This chapter has presented an integrative knowledge-based conceptualization of internationalization that reconciles two dominant yet conflicting perspectives in the literature and incorporates the potential influence of Internet technology. In doing so it is acknowledged that the internationalization literature has not been exhaustively covered; this, however, was not the intent. Rather, the focus has been on demonstrating that more holistic (integrating apparently divergent views where possible and appropriate) and up-to-date (incorporating recent technological developments such as the Internet) approaches to studying this important subject are possible, and it is hoped that future research will continue to result in worthwhile contributions to internationalization theory and practice.

4 Technology and internationalization

Prashantham, S. and Berry, M.M.J. (2004) 'The Internet and the internationalization of small knowledge-intensive firms: a conceptual approach', in M.V. Jones and P. Dimitratos (eds) *Emerging Paradigms in International Entrepreneurship*, Northampton, MA: Edward Elgar, 192–213.

Introduction

There is growing interest in the internationalization of small knowledge-intensive firms (SKIFs), particularly with respect to their often rapid internationalization and the role played by network relationships. The research question that this chapter seeks to answer is: What is the potential impact of the Internet on the internationalization of SKIFs?

Berry *et al.* (2001) have drawn attention to the apparent tension between themes such as 'global strategy', 'multinational enterprise' and 'born globals' in the literature. It may be argued that this has arisen from the dominance of the study of large multinational firms in international business theory (Oviatt and McDougall 1994). However, it appears that more recently there has been growing interest in the internationalization of small firms. A specific subset of this interest has emerged in relation to those small firms that have exhibited accelerated internationalization (Shrader *et al.* 2000; Young 1987), in contradiction to prevalent notions of incremental and gradual internationalization. This phenomenon has been noticeable in SKIFs (Bell 1995; Crick and Jones 2000).

Given this propensity to internationalize at a rapid rate and early on in their lives, it seems fair to suggest that SKIFs lend themselves readily to enquiry in the realm of international entrepreneurship, going by McDougall and Oviatt's (2000) definition of international entrepreneurship as 'a combination of innovative, proactive, and risk-seeking behaviour that crosses national borders and is intended to create value in organizations'.

The focus of this chapter, as indicated, is small knowledge-intensive firms. A 'small' firm – based on the most common cut-off in the literature (Brock 2000) – is taken as a firm with less than 100 employees, and 'knowledge-intensity' as 'the extent to which a firm depends on the knowledge inherent in its activities and outputs as a source of competitive advantage' (Autio *et al.* 2000). Researchers such as McNaughton (2001) have accepted this definition of knowledge-intensity. It may be noted that some of the literature reviewed in subsequent sections makes reference to high technology or technology-based firms; using the above definition, such firms can be categorized as SKIFs.

The ensuing discussion begins with an overview of the literature on (a) the internationalization of SKIFs and (b) the Internet with respect to network relationships, followed by an attempt to synthesize these two bodies of literature with a view to inferring the potential impact of the Internet on the internationalization of SKIFs. In conclusion, implications for academics, managers and policy-makers are drawn; in relation to theory development, the virtual absence of published research on the impact of the Internet on the internationalization of small knowledge-intensive firms in a developing economy context is identified and highlighted.

The internationalization of SKIFs – the role of network relationships

Within the body of literature on internationalization theory it is seen that the so-called stage theories have acquired a dominant position. According to this school of thought there is an incremental process of internationalization among firms in terms of the commitment demonstrated through the selected entry mode (progressing from simple exporting to ultimately foreign direct investment to set up production facilities in international markets) and in terms of the psychic distance of the targeted markets. Key to this incremental process is the firm's progressively enhanced experiential market knowledge (Johansson and Vahlne 1977, 1990). Summaries and reviews of the key literature on internationalization of the firm are well documented (see for example Andersen 1993; Coviello and McAuley 1999; Leonidou and Katsikeas 1996), and therefore, rather than a repetitive account of internationalization theory in general, the specific focus of this section is on SKIFs.

The 'stage' theories have come under a fair amount of criticism (see e.g. Andersen 1993; Bell and Young 1998) particularly due to their failure to accurately predict the internationalization patterns of SKIFs. There is growing evidence that SKIFs have demonstrated acceleration in the internationalization process (Crick and Jones 2000) and are often examples of a 'born global' (Rennie 1993) or 'international new venture'. A 'international new venture' is defined as 'a business organization that, from inception, seeks to derive significant competitive advantage from the use of resources and sale of outputs in multiple countries.... In contrast to organizations that evolve gradually from domestic firms to MNEs, these new ventures begin with a proactive international strategy' (Oviatt and McDougall 1994).

Bell (1995) and Coviello and Munro (1995, 1997) have studied SKIFs – software firms – that demonstrated rapid internationalization. A significant factor that influenced the accelerated internationalization of these SKIFs was reported to be inter-firm relationships within a wider international network that might include customers, competitors, suppliers, support agencies – even family and friends. These network relationships influenced SKIFs' choice of markets and market entry mode. For example, Bell's (1995) study of software firms in Finland, Ireland and Norway suggests that three factors influenced the choice of market: client followership, sectoral targeting and computer industry trends – these in turn are influenced by relationships with other firms (such as clients).

Of course, there may be product and market characteristics that facilitate – and perhaps necessitate – such accelerated internationalization. For example, Coviello and Munro (1995) mention the high research costs, shorter product life cycle and competitive markets that SKIFs tend to operate in, while Jones (1999) and McNaughton (2001) make reference to SKIFs' greater uncertainty in terms of technology and strategy. However, in addition to these factors, it appears that network relationships accelerate SKIFs' internationalization process, resulting in what is often referred to as the 'network' approach. The interaction between firms is seen as the most important factor in the choices made by firms vis-à-vis targeted markets and entry mode. However, this does not mean that the 'stage' and 'network' schools of thought are mutually exclusive; they may be seen as complementary rather than contradictory (Bell and Young 1998; Coviello and McAuley 1999).

In the wider context of firm internationalization, Johanson and Mattsson (1988) drew attention to the impact of network relationships; this has been reiterated by other authors as well (see e.g. Johnsen and Johnsen 1999; Kornohen *et al.* 1996). Network scholars have identified three interdependent elements of networks: actors, activities and resources (Johnsen and Johnsen 1999). According to Johanson and Mattsson (1988), knowledge and social bonds between actors play a vital role in the emanation of international opportunities for members of a network. They made a useful distinction between the internationalization of firms and of their markets. Gulati *et al.* (2000) have proposed that networks can be 'strategic' for firms, that is, a source of competitive advantage albeit this may also be a constraining factor, given the low mobility across networks that many firms experience. A significant point they make is that firms could earn rents on network resources – those that are external to the firms but internal to their network.

Kogut (2000) points out that firms in a network will often compete and cooperate with each other simultaneously. Firms will often jostle for greater control within their networks, and their *relational position* – not unlike Johanson and Mattsson's (1988) *market position* – could be a source of competitive advantage (Gulati *et al.* 2000). This makes the issue of trust among members of a network a significant one, particularly among competing firms (Johnsen and Johnsen 1999). Distinction is made between a firm's cooperation with customers and suppliers on the one hand and competitors on the other (Chetty and Blankenburg Holm 2000). These challenges notwithstanding, the resources and markets that firms may have access to through their network relationships are clearly seen as potentially beneficial to them, and policy-makers have been urged to facilitate such relationship building (Demick and O'Reilly 2000; Welch *et al.* 1998).

In the context of network relationships it is worthwhile to touch upon the issue of clusters, given the interesting parallels between network theory and cluster theory. Clusters, according to Porter (1998a: 199), are 'geographic concentrations of interconnected companies, specialized suppliers, service providers, firms in related industries, and associated institutions (e.g. universities, standards agencies, and trade associations) in particular fields that compete but also cooperate'. Local rivalry tends to be of great intensity – partly since rival entrepreneurs compete not just commercially but also for a better position in the local social hierarchy (Enright 1998) – which pushes firms to achieve greater levels of innovation and success (Porter 1998b). A comparison of network and cluster, summarized in Table 4.1, suggests that – contrary to Enright's (1998; see his first footnote) distinction between clusters and business networks – it is reasonable to view a cluster as a type of network, albeit a geographically concentrated one. Indeed certain networks have been referred to as 'clusters' in the literature (Chetty and Blankenburg Holm 2000). In the words of Porter (1998a: 225), 'A cluster is a form of network that occurs within a geographic location, in which the proximity of firms and institutions ensures certain forms of commonality and increases the frequency and impact of interactions.'

Returning to the specific matter of the internationalization of SKIFs, network relationships within a cluster could lead to marketing externalities such as, for example, intra-cluster referrals (Brown and Bell 2000). Brown and McNaughton (2000) suggest that while the selection of the original location of a cluster may have been accidental rather than rational, younger firms often locate in such clusters to benefit from the ensuing externalities. While various so-called cluster strategies have been employed around the world by governments, a common element in these has been the facilitation of business networking and inter-firm collaboration; of vital importance in this connection is putting in place a coordination mechanism (Enright 1999). Thus network relationships that influence the internationalization of SKIFs may exist within clusters.

This section has reviewed a selection of the key literature on the internationalization of SKIFs and the main point made is the significance of influential network relationships – which may also be geographically concentrated within clusters – on this process. To gauge the potential impact of the Internet on the internationalization of SKIFs, it therefore seems worthwhile to review the literature on the Internet in relation to inter-firm relationships in a network,

Table 4.1 Parallels between network and cluster theory

Aspect of the collective entities (i.e. networks and clusters)	*Network scholars*	*Cluster scholars*
Simultaneous competition and cooperation exists	Kogut 2000	Porter 1998a
Main elements are interdependent firms, resources and activities	Johnsen and Johnsen 1999	Enright 1998
Resources that are external to firms but internal to the collective entity may be a source of competitive advantage	Gulati *et al.* 2000	Porter 1998a
The free flow of information and building of inter-firm bonds are vital to the success of thecollective entity	Johanson and Mattsson 1988	Saxenien 1990
Policy should facilitate strengthening of the collective entity	Demick and O'Reilly 2000; Welch *et al.*1998	Enright 1998; Porter 1998a

which is the subject of the following section. The subsequent section will then discuss how the Internet could influence the internationalization of SKIFs, in the light of the literature reviewed in this and the following section.

The Internet and network relationships

As evident from the wide coverage in the business press, the Internet was the object of much hype, which appears to have been the result of over-exaggerated faith in its ability to foster a new era in which old business or economic rules did not apply. The sentiment has dramatically changed since the heady days of 1999 and appears to be leading to a middle-of-the-road perspective that acknowledges the power of the Internet without abandoning business principles; it is the applications of the Internet that will create value, not the Internet itself (Porter 2001).

A key theme in the literature on the business applications of the Internet deals with the digital networking of companies, which is unsurprising given that the Internet is, by definition, a network of networks (Hamill 1997; Poon and Jevons 1997). A unique characteristic of this medium of communication, in comparison with traditional broadcast media, lies in its ability to support many-to-many communication, that is, interactivity (Hoffman and Novak 1996). Interactivity could greatly facilitate relationships with entities such as suppliers, customers and rivals as implied by the references made in the literature to: the 'e-business community' comprising networks of suppliers and distributors who communicate and transact via the Internet (Tapscott 1999); the 'virtual factory' (Upton and McAfee 1996) or 'virtual enterprise' (Schlegelmilch and Sinkovics 1998) that operate in 'marketspace' (Rayport and Sviokla 1995); 'microbusinesses' that tap into global networks that were previously the preserve of large MNEs (Malone and Laubacher 1998); and the 'b-web' which is 'a distinct system of suppliers, distributors, commerce services providers, infrastructure providers, and customers that use the Internet for their primary business communications and transactions' (Tapscott *et al.* 2000: 17).

While the literature tends to have a large-firm bias (see for e.g. Hacki and Lighton 2001; Hagel 1996), the opportunities for small firms are great (Cronin 1995). Poon and Jevons (1997) have addressed the issue of the Internet and network relationships from the perspective of small firms. Drawing on the work of Golden and Dollinger (1993), they argue that the Internet can enhance network relationships and discuss the potential impact of the Internet on four kinds of networks: confederations, conjugate collectives, agglomerate collectives and organic collectives, as shown in Table 4.2.

Three broad applications of the Internet in particular appear to contribute towards the building and/or enhancement of such relationships: Internet marketing, Internet-supported supply chain management and Internet-supported customer relationship management; these applications broadly correlate to Feeny's (2001) three dimensions of Internet application in companies: e-marketing, e-operations, and e-services respectively. These are briefly discussed below.

Table 4.2 The Internet and small firm network relationships

Inter-organizational relationship	*Definition*	*Internet marketing strategy*
Confederations	Firms which compete with one another but which maintain some contractual functional activities in common, co-ordinated by a central management (e.g. small business groups sharing resources through contractual agreements)	Central management provide resources for network members to market their products and services on the Internet (e.g. a virtual agency service). Include in the agreements to provide reciprocal homepage links between members included in the contract.
Conjugate collectives	Firms which have contractual arrangements for symbiotic purposes (e.g. closed group agreements between supplier and customer)	Allow reciprocal links on members' homepages. Make available market intelligence on the closed-group's intranet (if available) with login control. Share market intelligence in order to improve supplier–buyer relationship.
Agglomerate collectives	Firms which compete within the same industry but have no contractual 'business' arrangements (e.g. trade associations)	Trade association provide market intelligence data (local and international) on their homepage for members use. Mutual agreement between [international] trade associations to market the members' products and services.
Organic collectives (e.g. community service groups)	Firms (or the representative thereof) which engage in traditional networking, such as board memberships or other voluntary organization, in an indirect and non-contractual form.	Advertise products and provide low-cost/free services for charity members of community networks on the Internet (e.g. LinkNet; www.link.net.au) Link community calender of events to one's home page.

Source: Adapted from Poon and Jevons (1997: 36–37; based on Golden and Dollinger 1993).

Internet marketing

While firms now have access to Internet technology that facilitates inter-firm network relationships, the task of creating such relationships in the first place remains. One possible means of doing so is through Internet marketing, where firms seek to make themselves known to other entities in 'cyberspace' generally with a view to directing 'traffic' or visitors to a destination Web site (Kenny and Marshall 2000). In relation to destination Web sites, recommended procedures include registration on prominent search engines (Hamill and Ennis 1999) and partnership arrangements – another form of network relationships – such as obtaining reciprocal links on Web sites of interest (Hoffman and Novak 2000). Also of potential benefit in relation to creating inter-firm relationships is participation in business-to-business (B2B) Internet hubs, variously referred to as B2B marketplaces, exchanges or e-hubs (Kaplan and Sawney 2000).

Ramsdell (2000) defines a B2B marketplace as 'a World Wide Web site where goods and services can be bought from a wide range of suppliers'. He identifies three kinds of marketplaces based on their focus in terms of industry, product and function: vertical (based on industries), horizontal (based on products), and focusing on function (based on functional skills, e.g. human resources). According to Sculley and Woods (1999), 'the unique feature of a B2B Exchange is that it brings multiple buyers and sellers together (in a "virtual" sense) in one central market space and enables them to buy and sell from each other at a dynamic price which is determined in accordance with the rules of exchange' (Sculley and Woods 1999: 14). According to Kerrigen *et al.* (2001), B2B marketplaces offer 'four roads to value': expanded market reach, lower prices, reduced buying costs, and identification of industry best practices.

Internet-supported supply chain management

A second application pertains to digitizing and connecting business activities with those of other firms that may be operating in a value chain. While this has been practised through proprietary networks such as electronic data interchange (EDI) in the past, the advantage that the Internet provides is universal standards that broaden the scope of participation, particularly in favour of smaller firms (Evans and Wurster 1997, 2000). In the value chain, Internet-supported supply chain management primarily concerns three activities of the value chain: inbound logistics (e.g. real-time integrated scheduling), operations (integrated information exchange) and outbound logistics (e.g. real-time transaction of orders) (Porter 2001). The specific application of the Internet will depend on the nature of the supply chain that a firm operates in (Poon and Joseph 2000). Evans and Wurster (2000) highlight the implications for supply chain management of different kinds of companies and transactions as a consequence of the 'deconstruction' of businesses wrought by the Internet (Table 4.3).

Here again B2B hubs could play a useful role, especially those that are centred around the value chain of an industry or organization. Klein and Quelch

Table 4.3 The impact of the Internet on supply chains on businesses

Types of businesses and transactions	*Impact of the 'blowing up' of supply chains*
Large corporations doing business with each other	The richness and reach they want already exist (through VPNs). New technologies can provide operational (rather than strategic) benefit – lower costs, improved functionality.
Smaller companies (and larger companies e.g. Wal-Mart and mid-sized suppliers)	Reach is sacrificed at present for richness (through EDI which locks in suppliers). New technologies allow public networks to replace the private ones; reach is enhanced and 'vertical ties loosened'
Small, peripheral transactions	New technologies explode the possibilities for reach and comparing offerings at little extra cost.
Small companies doing business with each other	Market makers have great scope to reduce the difficulties and cost of search.

Source: Adapted from Evans and Wurster (2000: 171).

(1997) suggest that smaller firms can particularly gain from such entities, as they 'expand the market so that buyers and sellers, primarily smaller ones, who may have enjoyed only limited access to traditional distribution channels, can now participate on a more level playing field' (Klein and Quelch 1997: 346). According to Porter (2001: 70), the benefits to buyers of digital marketplaces include low transaction costs, easier access to price and product information, convenient purchase of related services and the pooling of volume of transactions; benefits to vendors include lower selling costs, access to wider markets and non-confrontation with powerful channels.

Internet-supported customer relationship management

There is a growing and prominent strand in the Internet-related business literature that highlights the role of the Internet in supporting customer relationships (Hamill and Prashantham 2001). The interactivity element of the Internet makes it particularly amenable to the creation and management of individual relationships or 'one-to-one marketing' (Peppers and Rogers 1997; Peppers *et al.* 1999) with other entities (Ellsworth and Ellsworth 1995; Wind and Mahajan 2001), especially customers. According to Siegel (1999), a customer-oriented web strategy should be based on principles such as discriminating and dealing appropriately with different types of 'e-customers' (e.g. on the basis of whether they are beginners, intermediates or experts).

Of vital importance in Internet-supported customer relationship management is the management of databases for the storage and subsequent utilization of knowledge about customers (or indeed, business partners) that may be captured through the firm's Web site or social interactions within a network (Brown and Duguid 2000; Davenport *et al.* 2001). Obtaining information as wide and deep as possible allows firms to obtain an in-depth understanding of customers (Seybold 2001), which in turn could result in collaborative new product development (Iansiti and McCormack 1997) and thereby greater personalization of service, something that may be especially important for SKIFs.

The Internet and the internationalization of SKIFs

Let us recall the research question that this chapter seeks to answer: What is the potential impact of the Internet on the internationalization of SKIFs? Answers are not easily forthcoming from the limited body of literature on the Internet and small firm internationalization, the main themes of which include the potential for leapfrogging conventional stages of internationalization and the diminished importance of psychic distance (see, e.g. Bennett 1997; Hamill 1997; Samiee 1998; Quelch and Klein 1996). However, the veracity of such claims, including those made by Yip (2000), that 'cyberspace' can substitute much of the learning that takes place in the traditional global marketplace, is difficult to judge as surprisingly little empirical work has been done in this area (Brock 2000). The answer must therefore, for the moment at least, be sought conceptually through a synthesis of the literature mentioned in the previous sections.

It should be evident from the preceding two sections that (a) network relationships have a strong influence on the internationalization of SKIFs and (b) the Internet offers applications that facilitate network relationships, enabling firms to interact more widely and intimately with other actors including customers, suppliers and fellow-competitors. It can thus be argued that the Internet offers SKIFs the potential for creating and enhancing network relationships, which in turn are likely to influence and shape their internationalization process. This section amplifies this argument, making reference to the three Internet applications discussed in the previous section and drawing out a key benefit of each that influences network relationships. Internet marketing is seen to contribute to greater visibility (Hoffman and Novak 2000) within a network; Internet-supported supply chain management can contribute to greater operational efficiency or performance (Fisher and Reibstein 2001); and Internet-supported customer relationship management could lead to greater intimacy (Seybold 2001; Siegel 1999) in network relationships.

Visibility

In relation to the first-mentioned application – Internet marketing – it is argued that this could potentially raise *visibility* for SKIFs in marketspace, as they seek to create network relationships. Visibility is important in view of the *competition* for network relationships that SKIFs will face from other SKIFs and actors in a network. It is argued that – although the literature does not seem to clearly deal with the strategic value of network relationships – in the internationalization of SKIFs, their network relationships are a potential source of competitive advantage and differentiation. Thus it is worthwhile for SKIFs to proactively seek network relationships that will potentially lead to useful internationalization opportunities. A starting point to this would be visibility within a network in the first place to provide the opportunity to interact with other players, which is clearly the chief benefit of Internet marketing.

Efficiency

In relation to the second-mentioned application – Internet-supported supply chain management – it is argued that this could potentially lead to *efficiency* in business activities conducted in the context of SKIFs' network relationships. Efficiency is important because of the issue of *control* in network relationships. Coviello and Munro (1995; 1997) have highlighted the jostling for power and control that typically accompanies those network relationships that influence the internationalization of SKIFs. The literature on the internationalization of SKIFs (e.g. Coviello and Munro 1997) and that on the Internet and network relationships (e.g. Hacki and Lighton 2001) mention the tendency for large firms to dominate networks. Such a scenario suggests that SKIFs could be at a relative disadvantage with greater need for inclusion in the network and consequently lower bargaining power. It is argued that efficient functioning of business activities could lead to better performance (say, in terms of meeting targets or deadlines, as well as cost-cutting) and thereby stronger financial position and reputation, which in turn could strengthen SKIFs' ability to control network relationships better, or at the very least be less buffeted by undesirable shaping of their internationalization by actors with greater power.

Intimacy

In relation to the third-mentioned application – Internet-supported customer relationship management – it is argued that this could potentially enhance the *intimacy* of SKIFs' network relationships in terms of helping them better understand the needs of their partners. Intimacy is important because of the *coherence* it can lead to in a SKIF's internationalization process. As has been alluded to, the literature that highlights the crucial role of network relationships in the internationalization of SKIFs does not appear to clearly grapple with the strategic issues involved; for example, can every opportunity that emanates from the network be acted upon irrespective of its fit with the firm's overall strategy (if it has one)? It is argued that a strategic approach is required on the part of SKIFs in relation to their internationalization process, and greater coherence in their strategy can be achieved by better understanding the strategic intents of their fellow-actors in the network as well as expressing their own. This can result when there is greater intimacy, that is, greater knowledge of the other actors. Further, intimate network relationships could lead to indirect positive consequences for SKIFs' internationalization process through a greater propensity to share business leads or do business in new foreign markets with them, rather than their rivals within a network. Table 4.4 summarizes the foregoing discussion.

Table 4.4 The Internet and the internationalization of SKIFs

Internet application	*Impact on network relationships*	*Impact on internationalization*
Internet marketing Involves the proactive marketing of a destination Web site, chiefly with a view to generating awareness and disseminate information	*Visibility* Makes the SKIF visible within a network and provides an opportunity to offer information about itself and credentials	*Competition* Visibility is important given that SKIFs and other actors within a network compete for network relationships that will positively influence their internationalization
Internet-supported supply chain management Involves the digitizing and connection of activities into a wider value chain network via the Internet and Web-enabled networks (such as Intranets)	*Efficiency* Provides savings of cost through greater efficiency of information transfer and the saving of time; also allows for the pooling of resources to achieve greater volumes and lower prices in B2B exchanges	*Control* Efficiency is important given that actors in a network jostle for control and greater efficiency could lead to a more competitive position and consequently greater bargaining power.
Internet supported customer relationship management Involves the building and maintenance of deep relationships with 'customers', a broad definition of which would include business partners	*Intimacy* Provides the opportunity for SKIFs to better understand the strategic intents and other aspects of fellow-actors in a network and to be better understood as well	*Coherence* Intimacy is important because it allows SKIFs to better ensure coherence and consistency in their internationalization strategies in relation to long-term objectives.

Implications

This chapter attempts to synthesize literature on the internationalization of SKIFs, and the Internet and network relationships. In doing so, the authors' aim is to develop a new conceptual approach to the potential impact of the Internet on the internationalization of SKIFs and to propose associated implications for theory development, management, and policy-making. This is now discussed below.

Theoretical implications

The development of the Internet and its growing ubiquity implies that Internet-related variables – such as access to the Internet, experience with Internet usage and so on – must inevitably be factored into macroenvironment- and firm-related variables while seeking to understand better the phenomenon of small firm internationalization. This, of course, is likely to be handled slightly differently depending upon the main thrust(s) of the theoretical base used in a piece of research. For example, a promising avenue of research is the impact of the Internet on international new ventures – there may well be a chicken-and-egg situation here, with the Internet encouraging firms to be international from inception, and internationally inclined firms finding it easier to be so, as a result of the Internet. It may be noted that studies of international new ventures in particular have used the resource-based view, which is characteristic of a substantial body of literature in strategy but not in internationalization (Bell and Young 1998). Viewing Internet technologies as resources and the ability to apply them as competencies will perhaps throw light on emerging means of managing the internationalization process more effectively.

As mentioned earlier, little empirical work in the area of the Internet and small firm internationalization has been done with notable exceptions being Bennett's (1997) study of British exporters with and without Web sites, Hamill and Gregory's (1997) study of Scottish exporters and non-exporters and Brock's (2000) study of German technology-based firms (possibly the only empirical work that deals specifically with SKIFs). Clearly there is need for further empirical study on the impact of the Internet on small firm internationalization in general, and SKIF internationalization in particular, given that the use of the Internet is no longer optional for firms.

It may also be noted that while the Internet's potential benefit for firms based in developing economies has been suggested (Quelch and Klein 1996), no empirical study appears to have been done in a developing economy context, as seen in Table 4.5. This applies to the area of the internationalization of SKIFs as well.

There is clearly a need to address the obvious gap in this area of the literature by conducting empirical research that examines the impact of the Internet, on the internationalization of SKIFs, in a developing economy context. Such work is critical if SKIFs in developing economies are to benefit from the Internet

Table 4.5 Examples of SKIF studies in developed economies

Author	*Nationality of sample studies*
Bell 1995, 1997	Finland, Ireland and Norway
Coviello and Munro 1995, 1997	New Zealand
Jones 1999	United Kingdom
Brock 2000	Germany
McNaughton 2001	Canada

since most of the small firm internationalization theory focuses on developed economy contexts and may not readily hold in a developing economy context (Ibeh 1999) that has peculiar market- and policy-related problems (Das 1994; Ibeh and Young 2001; Maddy 2000). A potentially interesting case would be the Bangalore software industry, which has been cited as an excellent example of a developing economy plugging into the wider global economy (Kobrin 1999).

Managerial implications

In the days after the Internet hype, it is perhaps easier – and certainly more useful – to assess realistically the benefits and applications of its technologies to firms in general, and SKIFs in particular. It has become more evident that the impact of the Internet is likely to be different on different industries (Evans and Wurster 2000) and on different parts of the value chain (Roehl *et al.* 2001). In the foregoing discussion it has been suggested that firms can improve their visibility, efficiency and intimacy with other actors in a network. This is a more broad-based view compared to the literature that has solely emphasized – sometimes unrealistically – the enhanced visibility that can come from a web site. Thus, an important implication for entrepreneurs and managers is the importance of viewing Internet technologies holistically and at the same time specifically, in terms of specific tools such as B2B exchanges. Managers can expect greater competition from rivals who will also seek cheaper suppliers and deeper customer relationships – to name just a couple of factors – through the Internet. Thus, the ability to exploit Internet technologies can be seen as a determinant of competitive advantage and success.

Another implication, in the context of internationalization, pertains to decisions of market selection and entry mode. Once again, a balanced approach would be prudent – caution is required when receiving the suggestion of certain authors (as discussed earlier) that the entire world is a potential market for a firm and that traditional entry modes are less relevant. Equally, it must be realized that certain barriers and the speed of market development may well be reduced. The network perspective that has been utilized in this chapter suggests that a useful approach is to examine the possibility of network relationships in markets of interest through the Internet, as discussed in this chapter, and the entry modes that are available through these relationships.

Managers responsible for the internationalization of SKIFs will need to actively take the applications of the Internet into account as part of their activities geared towards creating and enhancing network relationships through greater visibility, efficiency and intimacy in network relationships. Indeed in the case of SKIFs where rapid internationalization is virtually imperative owing to product and market characteristics, the use of the Internet to positively influence this by facilitating network relationships can be deemed to be obligatory. Of course other actors in the network will require access to the Internet as well; this, however, in the developed world at least, is likely to be the case more often than not. More importantly, managers must have the right mindset towards managing information technology such as the Internet and not be apathetic to its potential benefits (Bensaou and Earl 1998; Poon and Joseph 2000). Further, it is recommended that SKIFs adopt a strategic approach to their network relationships and internationalization process so that opportunism is tempered with long-term goals such as profitability.

There exists a strong need for managing knowledge and knowledge-building through collaboration with other firms for SKIFs (Tenkasi and Boland 1996). Such collaboration could constitute a part of a SKIF's internationalization activities. Irrespective of whether these firms are geographically concentrated or not, the application of the Internet as discussed in this chapter is especially relevant. The simple matter of using email has implications for how entrepreneurs and managers in SKIFs communicate, even in respect of the level of formality in their language – email correspondence can be very different from formal correspondence. The cross-cultural aspect of this – just as in other matters such as marketing – must be considered when the communication takes place across international borders. Email aside, more sophisticated components of knowledge management such as electronic repositories or databases of knowledge could use Internet-based interfaces to enhance access to it by network actors.

Policy implications

Policy-makers have a facilitative role to play to ensure that SKIFs have ready access to, and knowledge of, using the Internet. In the case of SKIFs this is expected to be less onerous a task as SKIFs are possibly technology-savvy with access to the Internet and related technologies; nevertheless, appropriate support must be extended to them to make the best use of the Internet in the context of their internationalization.

Indeed, inasmuch as a supportive environment of entrepreneurship is generally helpful, an 'Internet-friendly' environment should facilitate the adoption of Internet technology (Oxley and Yeung 2001). Such an environment could be created through greater access to the Internet. Further, initiatives should be taken to enable SKIFs – and indeed all small firms, in general – to become aware of the potential benefit of the Internet to their internationalization efforts. These firms could then be provided with access to technical expertise – including through consultants in the private sector – to help them apply Internet technologies in practice. These are particularly relevant to a developing economy and the efforts of multilateral funding bodies and aid agencies in this regard may be particularly helpful.

In relation to clustering policies for SKIFs – which are often based on the regional character of much of the innovation that occurs in an economy (Almeida 1999) – there is nothing to suggest that the Internet necessarily makes agglomeration less relevant or likely (Leamer and Storper 2001). There are therefore no grounds for reversing cluster-facilitating policies. Needless to say, however, firms within clusters can be expected to actively seek network partners beyond their geographic confines utilizing Internet technology, and this should be encouraged as mentioned above.

In the realm of export policy, governments now have to deal with the exports of digitized products, such as software, and this may be of particular concern in developing economies where imports and exports tend to be closely monitored with a view to ensuring that foreign exchange reserves are sufficient. Clearly, it is much more difficult and complicated to monitor the export of software code in comparison to tangible, manufactured goods. One potential approach for governments to take is to set up special export zones to take care of the needs of software firms and other such SKIFs, where the 'product' is exported digitally, which provide incentives to these firms by way of infrastructure but also allows easier monitoring of their activities.

Another aspect of policy that must be addressed pertains to international law (Kobrin 2001) governing Internet-related transactions across borders. This requires national governments both to come out with coherent and appropriate legislation pertaining to that nation and to cooperate with each other through forums and agreements that allow smooth transactions while taking into account national interests. For developing economies, the challenge is often to ensure that their legislation keeps pace with international developments in the more advanced economies. Achieving more cooperation in policy- and law-making may be a tall order both because of the degree of multilateral cooperation required and because of the rapidity with which technology changes vis-à-vis policy making, which could struggle to keep pace. Nonetheless, these policy efforts are vital, and imperfect solutions may be more useful than not having any.

Specifically in the context of a developing economy, the following recommendations made by The Boston Consulting Group (2001) to the Indian government are pertinent: legal and regulatory issues for e-commerce transactions should be resolved, development of communications infrastructure should be accelerated, computer and Internet education should be encouraged, the creation of technology standards should be facilitated and industry associations should be encouraged to benchmark Internet technology adoption across industries. Developing economies would do well to follow examples of good policy in advanced economies. For instance, in relation to the last mentioned point, useful examples that could be considered are Australia's tracking of Internet technology adoption by the Bureau of Statistics and the annual *Digital Economy* publication of the US Department of Commerce, which benchmarks e-commerce and IT adoption (The Boston Consulting Group 2001).

Concluding remarks

The ubiquity and importance of the Internet in the twenty-first century is beyond debate. As Porter (2001: 64) has said, 'The key question is not whether to deploy Internet technology – companies have no choice if they want to stay competitive – but how to deploy it.' In the context of small knowledge-intensive firms, whose very nature and operating environment present great challenge, utilizing the Internet to enhance their network relationships and thereby the internationalization process, is a strategic imperative, rather than a luxury. In the context of developing economies, where market- and policy-related factors intensify the challenge of internationalization for small firms, including SKIFs, the Internet offers application of great value. However, bridging the gap between theoretical promise and actual realization calls for considerably more effort on the part of entrepreneurs, managers, policy-makers and researchers.

Part II

Exploratory insights

5 The Indian software industry

Prashantham, S. (2004) 'Indian perspectives of International entrepreneurship', in L.P. Dana (ed.) *The Handbook on Research in International Entrepreneurship*, Northampton, MA: Edward Elgar, 481–498.

Introduction

Internationalization among small firms, and notably small knowledge-intensive firms (SKIFs), can be unusually rapid and is often influenced by three aspects of the international entrepreneur: knowledge, intent and networks. However, both internationalization-related and other entrepreneurial activities – and therefore international entrepreneurship – can be hampered by macroeconomic disincentives or a hostile environment. This often tends to be the case in developing economies such as India, given which, the success story of the Indian software industry acquires great significance as a notable exception to the rule. It has emerged as an exemplar for developing economy entrepreneurs seeking their fortune in the software and other industries. Drawing on the literature relevant to international entrepreneurship, as well as secondary and some primary data on the Indian software industry, this chapter points out that international entrepreneurs in a developing economy can be successful through their own entrepreneurial efforts, especially when encouraged and facilitated by favourable policy measures. There are, however, key challenges that they have to deal with.

Most studies of small firm internationalization have taken place in developed economy contexts (Bell and Young 1998), thus depriving aspiring business people in developing economies of rigorous research-based inputs on international entrepreneurship. Even as more empirical work in this area needs to be done, this chapter seeks to offer some insights into ways in which international entrepreneurs in developing contexts can achieve success, by drawing on literature relevant to internationalization and citing the example of the Indian software industry.

It is hoped that some of the issues dealt with in this discussion of the Indian software industry will be insightful and inspirational to international entrepreneurs in a developing economy context. The following sections deal with small firm internationalization, especially for knowledge-intensive firms, entrepreneurship and the role of entrepreneurs in small firm internationalization, incentives and disincentives for international entrepreneurs in developing economies, the Indian context in terms of fostering entrepreneurship, the development and growth of the Indian software industry, examples of four Indian software entrepreneurs who were drawn to found firms, implications of the preceding sections for theory, entrepreneurship and policy.

Small firm internationalization

Bell and Young (1998) point out that there is no unanimity in defining the term 'internationalization'. Welch and Luostarinen (1988) have defined it as 'the process of increasing involvement in international operations'. They suggest that internationalization can involve both inward and outward activities. A different perspective is provided by Naidu *et al.* (1997: 115): 'Internationalization is a gradual process whereby a firm develops a network of global trade relationships.'

Jones (1999) comments that surprisingly little is known about internationalization in relation to small firms and blames this on assumptions pertaining to the resource limitations of small firms and literature that is skewed towards the area of export, in part because of the relatively low risk and commitment involved. The focus on a single entry mode – exporting – has contributed to major shortcomings in internationalization theory (Leonidou and Katsikeas 1996). However, several other entry modes exist, which include exporting, licensing, franchising, management contracts, turnkey contracts, international subcontracting, industrial cooperation agreements, contractual joint ventures, equity joint ventures, wholly owned subsidiaries, mergers and acquisitions and strategic alliances – these various modes vary according to the commitment, cost efficiency, control and risk involved (Anderson and Gatignon 1986; Erramilli and Rao 1993; Young *et al.* 1989).

Some of the early thinking on internationalization emanated from work in the 1970s, such as that of Johanson and Wiedersheim-Paul (1975), Johanson and Vahlne (1977) and Bilkey and Tesar (1977), which have come to be known collectively as 'stage theories' or 'incremental frameworks'. These continue to be the dominant theories in the field (Coviello and McAuley 1999; Johanson and Vahlne 1990; Welch and Luostarinen 1988) although they have received much criticism (Andersen 1993; Bell 1995; O'Farrell *et al.* 1998; Turnbull 1987). Among the stage models, distinction has been made between the work of Nordic authors such as Johanson and Vahlne (1977) and American authors such as Bilkey and Tesar (1977); the former is referred to as the Uppsala Model and the latter as the Innovation Model (Andersen 1993). The overall thrust of both models is similar to the extent that they suggest that firms internationalize in incremental steps. They differ, however, in their emphasis: the Uppsala Model views the internationalization process as a result of firms' commitment and knowledge, while the Innovation Model views the internationalization process as the consequence of innovation, where firms respond to, for example, unsolicited orders.

Some authors take a resource-based view of the firm and suggest that small firm internationalization, at least initially, is largely a function of the firm's resources and competencies. The competencies of the management team, in particular, have been recognized (Aaby and Slater 1989; Chetty and Hamilton 1993). The resource issue also has a bearing on another theme mentioned in the internationalization literature: strategy, which follows, in part, from a firm's resource base. Young *et al.* (1989) rejected existing theories of internationalization and presented one of their own, based on the firm's objectives (short or long term) within the overall scope of the firm's corporate strategy.

An alternative perspective on internationalization has been the so-called networks approach, which can, however, be seen as complementary rather than contradictory to the stage theories (Coviello and McAuley 1999). Johanson and Mattsson (1988) argued that industrial networks involving other players such as customers and suppliers influence internationalization decisions of firms. Even Johanson and Vahlne (1990, 1992) have acknowledged the role of other actors in the internationalization process, while other scholars suggest that the network perspective is a contingency model to existing stage theories (Bell and Young 1998).

Network relationships are 'stable and changing' (Johanson and Mattsson 1988: 291) and may exist across borders or be spatially bound in 'clusters' (Enright 1999; Porter 1990). Clusters may influence the internationalization of SKIFs through *marketing externalities* such as, for example, intra-cluster referrals, credibility and reputation, informational spillovers and active joint marketing (Brown and Bell 2000). Brown and McNaughton (2000) suggest that, while the original location of a cluster may have been accidental rather than rational, younger firms often locate in such clusters to benefit from the ensuing externalities.

Network relationships have been found to accelerate the internationalization of small firms (Bell 1995; Coviello and Munro 1997), which is not altogether surprising given that small firms, in general, are renowned for their networking ability (Jones 1999). Indeed, some small firms have been deemed to be international from inception and variously referred to as 'born globals', 'new international ventures' and 'global start-ups' (Johnson 1999; Knight and Cavusgil 1996; McDougall *et al.* 1994; Madsen and Servais 1997; Oviatt and McDougall 1994, 1997; Rasmussen and Madsen 1999; Rennie 1993).

As with the literature on management strategy, individual theories of small firm internationalization at best proffer a partial view of the subject, and there is merit in taking an eclectic view (Dunning 1988; Mintzberg and Lampel 1999). The total incompatibility of the various views on internationalization is debatable. For instance, although sharp differences exist between an objective-led approach, where quantitative, fact-based methodology guides decision-making, and a process-based approach with incremental steps, it is quite conceivable that knowledge (as presented by Johanson and Vahlne 1977, 1990) can inform a firm's strategy process.

Entrepreneurship

While no particular personality trait is 'truly' entrepreneurial (Bhide 1994), the business-related characteristics of the entrepreneur have a strong bearing on the internationalization of small firms (Aaby and Slater 1989; Chetty and Hamilton 1993; Leonidou and Katsikeas 1996; Welch and Luostarinen 1988); this is particularly true in relation to firms that are international from inception (Madsen and Servais 1997; Rasmussen and Madsen 1999). A synthesis of the literature on entrepreneurship, small firms and knowledge-intensive firms (given this chapter's reference to software firms) suggests that three interdependent factors, which are mostly brought to the table by the entrepreneur himself or herself, play an important role in the development of small entrepreneurial firms, including their internationalization: knowledge, intent and networks.

Knowledge

Innovation is a key goal for small entrepreneurial firms (Acs *et al.* 1999; Almeida 1999; Audretsch 1999; Carlsson 1999; Hagel and Singer 1999; Hamel 1996; Lerner 1999) and knowledge is the chief preoccupation of knowledge-intensive firms (Alvesson 1993, 1995; Autio *et al.*2000; Elkjaer 2000; Nurmi 1998; Tenkasi and Boland 1996). Domains of specialized knowledge of the entrepreneur often determine the firm's main offerings and therefore the prior *experience* (including education) of the entrepreneur is crucial in the context of SKIFs and may have a bearing on his or her strategic and international orientation, innovativeness and network relationships (Berry 1998; Crick and Jones 2000; Ibeh and Young 2001; McDougall and Oviatt 2000; Madhok 1996; Young 1987). Related to knowledge is *innovativeness*, or innovative behaviour, of the entrepreneur (Baker 1979), which can have a positive impact on the firm's performance in international markets (Kundu and Katz 2000). Although some studies have failed to demonstrate this conclusively, the literature still maintains the importance of innovativeness alongside other characteristics such as autonomy, risk-taking and competitive aggressiveness (Lumpkin and Dess 1996). Innovation is crucial to SKIFs' coping with their competitive environments (Zahra and Neubaum 1998).

Intent

An entrepreneur's *strategic orientation* has a bearing on how well the technology strategy of the firm is integrated with the overall corporate strategy of the firm (Berry 1996; Kundu and Katz 2000) and also has a bearing on the type of planning style adopted. An important factor in the internationalization of SKIFs is the *international orientation* or vision of the entrepreneur (Aaby and Slater 1989). Reference has also been made to the importance of a 'global mindset' on the part of the technology entrepreneur, as a pre-state requirement for success in the global marketplace (Berry 1998). These notions refer to the entrepreneur's philosophy (Becherer and Maurer 1997) or attitude, which may have a bearing on decisions such as changes in entry mode (Calof and Beamish 1995). There is apparently a tension in the literature in terms of whether successful small entrepreneurial firms adopt – or ought to adopt – a formal or informal approach to *strategy formulation*, as captured in the debate between marketing orientation (MO) and entrepreneurial orientation (EO), respectively (Tzokas *et al.* 2001). The ideal situation for a small firm is when both an EO and MO coexist, notwithstanding the contradictory skill sets that they entail. Becherer and Maurer (1997) found support for their hypothesis that the EO of an entrepreneur-led firm is directly related to its MO, and concluded that EO and MO are part of the same underlying philosophy.

Networks

Network relationships with players such as suppliers, customers, universities and even competitors have a great influence on small firms' (and especially SKIFs') business activities. Small firms are resource-poor (Hadjimanolis 2000a; McNamee *et al.* 2000), and external network relationships can be vital to a small firm's viability, can compensate for resources it lacks (McNamee *et al.* 2000) and can facilitate knowledge building (Almeida 1999) and, therefore, innovation since resource-rich small firms innovate better than resource-poor ones (Hadjimanolis 2000b). These relationships may be available through regional networks (Saxenien 1990), and smaller firms have been seen to be more adept at integrating into local regional networks than larger firms (Almeida 1999); these subnational regions' climate may, however, be supportive, detrimental or neutral (Goetz and Freshwater 2001). The role of networks acquires significance when knowledge-intensive and high-technology firms (typically small ones) specialize (Carlsson 1999). As discussed earlier, network relationships are significant, both facilitating and constraining, for competitive advantage in general and internationalization in particular (Bell 1995; Coviello and Munro 1995). Strategic alliances may be entered into (Rao and Klein 1994) or the lead may be taken from key clients (Bell 1995; O'Farrell *et al.* 1998). Alvesson (1993) also mentions the importance of inter-firm networks in creating reputation for knowledge-intensive firms.

International entrepreneurship in a developing economy context

The macro-environment in which a firm operates may have certain disincentives with respect to international marketing. Das (1994) suggested that two distinct problems can be identified that face exporters from developing economies: (1) government policies and interventions and (2) market-related problems. She suggests that policy-makers need to focus promotion activities on key industries, motivate managers to export, encourage the diversification of exporters' product mix (i.e. shift to high-value offerings) and liberalize the economy. Policies generally reflect the politicoeconomic philosophy of a particular nation, which, for example, may have socialist leanings, as in the case of India (Vachani 1997). Calof and Vivier's (1995) study of South African small- and medium-sized enterprises (SMEs) found that problems that exporters faced pertained to, among other factors, domestic and international politics (including the dismantling of sanctions) and trade policy (including the implications of GATT).

Disincentives may take the form of institutional barriers or a lack of 'soft infrastructure' (Khanna and Palepu 1999: 126) such as efficient product, capital and labour markets as well as regulatory mechanisms. These often exist in developing economies and may be a disincentive both for host country firms and for international ones. Other disincentives include elaborate procedures (Jain and Kapoor 1996) and complex bureaucracy (Naidu *et al.* 1997). Ibeh and Young (2001) have identified the following disincentives among Nigerian firms: unstable political climate, low technology level, poor local infrastructure, unstable exchange rate and inconsistent implementation of government policy.

Given that internationalization – notably export development – is seen as a source of economic advancement (Naidu *et al.* 1997), incentives may also be available to firms as part of the local government policy. Government policy in terms of infrastructure provision and positive attitude to entrepreneurs can have a very beneficial impact, especially when concentrated in a geographic cluster, and is particularly beneficial where the national system of innovation is weak, such as in less advanced countries (Fontes and Coombs 1995).

Clearly, operating in a developing economy context can be challenging for an SKIF and requires tenacity, patience and capital resources. Maddy (2000), an African technology entrepreneur, distinguishes between two sources of capital for entrepreneurial firms in a developing economy: 'do-gooders' (e.g. quasi-government agencies) and 'do-wellers' (such as private investors). Disincentives in dealing with them are a lack of trust in the entrepreneur and highly demanding expectations of success, respectively. She warns prospective entrepreneurs that the going can be very very tough.

> The fact is, only 2% of the world's 6 billion people have access to the Internet. The revolution has hardly begun. Yes, change may come to emerging-market countries thanks to technology. But it will take time. Entrepreneurs can change the world as long as they don't try – as I did – to do it on a shoe string.
>
> (Maddy 2000: 62)

International entrepreneurship in India

It has been suggested that, owing to cultural factors such as the caste system, Indians have generally not been entrepreneurially minded (Dana 2000) although certain communities among Indians are noted for their business acumen both in India and in foreign lands where they have settled (Bhagwathi 1966). Furthermore, restrictive government policy has not been encouraging of international entrepreneurship. As Naidu *et al.* (1997: 119) say, '[H]igh levels of government interface [have] effectively inhibited international entrepreneurship.'

The underlying philosophy of the initial economic development activities after India gained independence from the British in 1947 was that the government knew best and therefore had to be the key driver of business activities. As a consequence, Indian entrepreneurs had to become adept at playing the game of obtaining requisite licenses, which involved a combination of lobbying strength and political connections, which often came at the cost of funding political parties or bribing officials. This, in turn, meant that it was mainly large business houses that had the financial and political clout to succeed over the long haul; small firms, despite the Gandhian sanction bestowed on them – Gandhi was a great believer in encouraging small firms through reserving certain products for their exclusive production – were often hampered by government control (Mahibala 1997; Ramu 1997; Sundarajan 1997). In relation to exports, the Indian government was not very encouraging, especially after an acute balance of payments (BoP) crisis in the 1970s. Public policy at the time tended to be inward-looking, with the emphasis being on import substitution, rather than exports. A key objective was to limit the use of valuable foreign exchange by Indian firms (Naidu *et al.* 1997; Vachani 1997).

The position today is a lot different, especially after the liberalization efforts initiated from 1991 onwards (Vachani 1997). Studies have demonstrated innovative abilities among Indian entrepreneurs (Manimala 1992a, 1992b, 1992c, 1992d). While competing in international markets is highly challenging for family-run businesses in India (Murthy 1999), Indian exporters seem to be upbeat, going by Jain and Kapoor's (1996) survey of the attitudes of Delhi-based entrepreneurs. According to them (Jain and Kapoor 1996: 80–81), 'On the whole, though the surveyed Indian firms viewed exporting as a more challenging and arduous task, they considered it as an activity worth the efforts as it enhances firm stability and entails greater growth and profit potential.' Most exporters had begun international marketing activity as a consequence of internal stimuli, which is different from American exporters discussed by Bilkey and Tesar (1977).

The optimism among Indian exporters detected by Jain and Kapoor is echoed by authors such as Naidu *et al.* (1997: 124), according to whom

> India has the potential of being a major player in world exports. It has the ingredients for success – entrepreneurial spirit of business people, ingenuity and motivation, and a wealth of resources. Nevertheless, the export sector has been stifled in the past through bureaucracy and disincentives. Recent liberalization of the Indian economy creates opportunities for Indian enterprises to successfully break into foreign markets. However, a proactive export assistance and promotion policy is required for achieving this objective.

While certain initiatives have been undertaken to foster entrepreneurship in India (as documented by Dana 2000), such as the National Institute for Entrepreneurship and Small Business Development and Entrepreneurship Development Institute of India, arguably the greatest impetus for international entrepreneurship has come from the much-publicized success of the Indian software industry, which has become an exemplar to budding Indian entrepreneurs, especially those dreaming of success in international markets.

The software industry in India: an exception and exemplar

The case of the Indian software industry is significant in that it has transcended difficulties associated with entrepreneurship in India such as unfavourable cultural biases (Dana 2000) and restrictive policy (Naidu *et al.* 1997; Vachani 1997). According to Correa (1996: 177), 'India is the most successful software exporter among developing economies.'

The origins of the Indian software industry, notable particularly because of its strong export focus, can be seen in the early 1970s when the government promoted software exports (Correa 1996). This was also a period when stringent regulations saw international IT majors such as IBM pulling out of the country, thus creating a void that domestic hardware vendors rushed in to fill. The early 1980s saw the personal computer (PC) revolution enhancing the international demand for software, as well as the beginnings of liberalization policies in the Indian economy. Software exports from India began to grow.

The game plan followed by most Indian software companies was remarkably simple and uniform. It entailed exploiting the low labour costs for software programming talent in India compared to the West and especially the United States through the provision of software developers for on-site work at client sites (often referred to as 'body-shopping'), supplemented by off-shore software development in India.

While the historical basis for the emergence of a pool of technical talent lies in the setting up of educational institutions and public sector undertakings (PSUs) in fields such as aeronautics, especially in the South Indian city of Bangalore (referred to as the Silicon Valley of India), a unique impetus to the Indian software industry came from multinational corporations (MNCs) that set up shop there after the liberalization initiatives of 1991 (Heitzman 1997). Notable in this regard are Motorola and Texas Instruments, who were instrumental in raising labour wages and offering professionals interesting (as opposed to low-end and tedious coding work) projects, with a view to attracting the best talent available locally. Today, several other IT majors such as Microsoft and Sun Microsystems have development centres, many of which deal with state-of-the-art design.

However, these developments have seen wages rise, and as a consequence, the cost advantage of Indian firms, especially reputable ones, is slipping in comparison to rivals in China and the Philippines. Therefore some of the better Indian firms are aggressively seeking to graduate to higher levels of the value chain. Some firms are seeking profitable forays into information technology-enabled services (ITES) such as call centres (Merchant 2001d). The vast majority of Indian software firms, however, remain focused on low-level coding work; their viability in the long term is in serious doubt (Daniel 2001; Merchant 2001a, 2001b; Sadagopan 1999).

It has been said that in recent times India has produced many successful software firms and beauty queens because the government was not involved! That may be somewhat unfair as government policy since the 1970s has justifiably encouraged software exports (Correa 1996). More recently, apart from the tax holiday that software firms enjoy, the government upgraded the Department of Electronics (DoE) into the Ministry of Information Technology (MIT), which has been entrusted to a prominent Cabinet minister. One of the key challenges of this ministry remains the creation of suitable infrastructure (Donald 2001b).

What are the factors that have led to the success of the Indian industry? Kundu and Katz (2000) have determined that managerial characteristics such as entrepreneurs' educational background, technological innovativeness and strategic orientation have played a vital role. According to Correa (1996), factors such as the widespread use of the English language, apart from programmers' skill and quick response to demand, have contributed to success; he warns other developing economies that some of these factors (such as the use of the English language) have a historical basis that other countries (such as, for example, Latin American countries) will find difficult to easily emulate. Although the widespread availability of technical education in India is often mentioned, Merchant (2001c) points out that supply of such education still falls well short of demand. The competencies of software professionals, stemming from their training and experience (Ram and Jagadish 1999), professional treatment of employees in the better software firms (Agarwal 1999) and network relationships with Indian software entrepreneurs in Silicon Valley, United States, (Luce 2001; Murdoch 2000) have been other success factors.

Indian software international entrepreneurs: four examples

As mentioned, the success of Indian software entrepreneurs has led to young entrepreneurs being encouraged to launch their own software start-ups. The following is a brief account of four such entrepreneurs, who were interviewed in Bangalore recently, in terms of their background, knowledge, intent, networks and view of policy. It gives an indication of diverse routes that entrepreneurs take to end up founding and leading a software firm in India.

Firm Vikas

Firm Vikas was started by an engineer upon his graduation in 1995 because of the 'fire in [his] belly' despite pressure from his parents to study further and become the first postgraduate in the family. He is neither from a prestigious Indian university nor foreign-trained; yet his passion to do something innovative led him to pursue aggressively his entrepreneurial dreams.

His knowledge base is constantly evolving, guided by market trends; having begun in software services he is leading the company into a diversification into ITES, such as call centres. His intent, in terms of internationalization, has been to avoid popular and highly competitive markets such as the United States.

Instead, he has focused on Australia, recently setting up a one-man marketing team there; his next targets are the 'virgin territories' of South Africa and Zimbabwe. His networks have mainly been domestic, with only recently proactive measures being taken to acquire and cultivate network relationships overseas.

The government, he says, has failed to make life easier for entrepreneurs and he has experienced many instances of running from pillar to post in order to get things done for the business. Policy measures are often half-baked according to him; for instance, the government may improve roads but 'forget that power also is essential'.

Firm New Creation

Firm New Creation was started by a computer professional trained at Rutgers University, after spending ten years in the United States. Although he harboured the occasional desire to become an entrepreneur at some point, his decision to start Firm New Creation was precipitated by a family crisis which forced him to return to his hometown of Bangalore in 2000. He was given a project to work on by a former American client.

His knowledge base is a function of his more recent work in the United States and deals primarily with e-commerce. His intent appears to be to remain fully focused on international business, as he feels he has a long way to go before establishing himself in India. Towards this end, he relies heavily on the Internet – through B2B portals such as that of *The Economist* magazine and NeoIT – for international business in non-American markets. His networks primarily stem from professional contacts in the United States, and he is trying to expand these by engaging business development contractors who, for a commission, canvass the wares of Indian firms in foreign markets.

In his experience, the government – specifically the Software Technology Parks of India (STPI) – can be very bureaucratic. While seeking to move premises, he found the paperwork and formalities to be cumbersome and unnecessarily multiple; a single-window mechanism would make things a lot easier, he feels.

Firm Ekomate

Firm Ekomate was started by a computer professional who studied at the University of Texas in Austin and stayed on in the United States for a brief professional stint. At Austin he had also attended entrepreneurship classes at the business school, clearly indicating an interest in starting up his own firm, which he did upon his return to India in 1996 after calculating that it could be more remunerative than a salaried job at an IT firm.

His knowledge was chiefly Internet-oriented due to his training and professional experience in the United States. Accordingly, his firm's chief mandate has been 'to help firms get on to the Net'. However, his knowledge base has evolved over time, expanding with client needs – especially those of loyal customers. To that extent, he feels that he has ceased to be a specialist and has become more of a generalist. His intent in terms of geographic focus has been flexible, and it took three years before he received his first international contract – an unsolicited order from a British firm who located him through Firm Ekomate's Web site and were impressed thereafter by his speed of response to requests for information and proposals. His networks today seem to primarily comprise of existing clients, although a few orders did come as a consequence of professional contacts in the United States.

In terms of government-related bodies, he has mainly dealt with the STPI and has found his association with them beneficial although he finds certain rules pertaining to customs bonding to be obsolete. Further, he feels that small firms in general do not have much of a voice in industry associations.

Firm Mitoken

Firm Mitoken has spun off from Motorola's Indian operations and is unique in terms of its focus on being a 'pure product player'; in other words, it offers packaged solutions rather than the customary software services offered by most Indian software firms (including the three discussed above). The directors of Firm Mitoken are graduates of prestigious business and engineering schools in India and abroad; the chief executive officer (CEO) is an alumnus of the Indian Institute of Managament in Bangalore, one of India's premier business schools. The timing of the directors' decision to successfully propose the spin-off coincides – rather significantly – with the craze for Internet start-ups. Not surprisingly, the company offers a software product for software companies that it describes as 'Web-native'. Nonetheless, the relevance of the offering has remained undiminished even after the collapse of most dot-coms.

The knowledge of the CEO and his core team follows from the work carried out initially at Motorola and from prior education. The intent has been to target software firms across the world in a cluster-by-cluster approach after initially operating in India, with a view to refining the product before launching overseas. It is envisaged, however, that in less than five years the vast majority of business will be from abroad. The networks, to which much attention is paid, emanate from Motorola and business school contacts, as well as venture capitalists and senior IT and business professionals who have been formally inducted as company 'advisors'.

While the CEO of Firm Mitoken did not voice any strong reservation about government policy, he felt that product-oriented firms did not receive quite the impetus or supportive industry forums that they needed – and even deserved.

Conclusion: implications for theory-building, entrepreneurship and policy

In terms of theory-building, the foregoing discussion has brought out the inadequacy of research in developing economy contexts and would suggest that greater collaborative research among scholars in developed and developing economies will bridge the knowledge gap that seeks to exist in terms of theory-building. A related issue is the need for forums and publications – such as this book – where insights about various economy contexts can be disseminated to wide audiences of international entrepreneurs. Such efforts, it is suggested, will be of mutual benefit, and international entrepreneurs based in developed economies may well find that they have useful lessons to learn – especially in relation to innovative behaviour – from their counterparts in developing economies who often have to make do with fewer resources and therefore are forced to devise ingenious ways of succeeding.

In terms of managerial practice, software entrepreneurs in India – and indeed, elsewhere in developing economies – would do well to address at least three issues that are emerging. First is the issue of *services versus products*; in other words, firms have to face competitive pressure to cease being mere low-level code-providers and upgrade their offerings to packaged solutions or products. Second is the issue of *software versus ITES*; in other words, software firms are faced with the question of whether or not to diversify in the light of emerging opportunities such as ITES, of which call centres constitute a prominent example. Long-term success will need to be balanced with short-term revenue goals. Third is the issue of *small versus large firms*; in other words, small firms are finding it increasingly hard to survive as large players strive to gain business in a considerably sluggish world economy, and achieving greater knowledge-intensity in specialized domains appears to be fast-becoming mandatory for SKIFs. This in turn will enhance – and make even more challenging – their scope for and efforts towards internationalization. Indeed, it is a matter of survival.

In terms of policy-making, governments in developing economies should seek to provide advanced training inputs to international entrepreneurs and enhance their network relationships through mentoring programmes; useful insight can be obtained from the Irish experience (Bell *et al.* 2004b). In the specific case of India, serious attention must be paid to various policy issues including defining small firms, financing, rules and procedures, technology applications, cluster formation and strategy formulation (Gulati 1997; Krishnan 1997; Mahibala 1997; Prabhu 1997; Ramu 1997; Sundarajan 1997; Thampy and Kulkarni 1997). From the interviews, it is evident that infrastructure in terms of power, communication facilities and transportation need to be improved and common interest groups facilitated for international entrepreneurs. In relation to exports, areas that require improvement include access to marketing information, international promotion, and procedures and documentation (Jain and Kapoor 1996).

6 Local networks and internationalization

Prashantham, S. (2004) 'Local network relationships and the internationalization of small knowledge-intensive firms', *Copenhagen Journal of Asian Studies*, 19: 5–26.

Abstract

This chapter discusses the role of network relationships in the internationalization of small knowledge-intensive firms (SKIFs) by highlighting their local, spatially concentrated network relationships, which can serve as a significant local resource. Little is known in this regard with respect to a developing economy context. Primarily on the basis of a study of four case-firms in Bangalore software industry and available secondary data, two issues are dealt with: (a) how local network relationships – such as those within clusters or industrial districts – are developed and (b) the impact that these relationships have on the internationalization of SKIFs, namely, reputation-related, quality-related and networking benefits. However, it also emerged from follow-up interviews with local academic experts that these benefits may be passively rather than actively accrued, suggesting that some local resources may be overlooked or wasted.

Introduction

Asian firms are renowned for their effective networking capacities (Chen 2003; Redding 1995). In the context of small firm internationalization, a case of special interest to scholars has been the small knowledge-intensive firm (SKIF),[1] which is similarly noted for its leveraging of network relationships, often leading to accelerated internationalization (Coviello and Munro 1997; Prashantham and Berry 2004a). Combining these two observations, it would seem likely that Asian SKIFs constitute a fascinating subject for study of networking dynamics, especially in the context of internationalization. That network relationships constitute a key driver of the internationalization of SKIFs seems consistent with the nature of such firms, their propensity for innovation and their resource-poverty lead to active leverage of network relationships. These relationships may be based locally (Porter 1998a) or overseas (Johanson and Mattsson 1988). Surprisingly little is known about the former, in the context of internationalization; the focus of most network-based studies is on the latter.

Recent work, however, suggests that local, spatially concentrated network relationships, such as those within a regional cluster, lead to positive externalities that facilitate SKIFs' internationalization (Brown and Bell 2001; Brown and McNaughton 2003) to a greater extent than in less geographically concentrated industries (Fernhaber *et al.* 2003). These studies, like much of the literature on SKIF internationalization, are based on developed economy contexts; little is known in this regard with respect to developing countries. Yet, improving extant understanding of the latter context seems a worthwhile endeavour, given that many developing countries are seeking to develop globally competitive firms, especially in Asia (Zeng and Williamson 2003). In such a setting, cultural and economic factors make external relationships a significant source of new information and know-how for local firms, and therefore a resource for enhancing international competitiveness (Zhou and Xin 2003). This chapter offers a preliminary step toward exploring a developing economy context in Asia, by shedding light on how small Indian software firms benefit from their local network relationships as they pursue international business.

Thus, the fundamental research question that this chapter seeks to address is: How do local network relationships influence the market-seeking[2] internationalization of SKIFs in a developing economy context? One difficulty in dealing with this topic stems from the relative dearth of dynamic, knowledge-intensive clusters in developing countries. Research was therefore undertaken in the Bangalore software industry, which proves to be a noted exception in this regard (Dunning 2000). Four case-firms were studied; this exercise was supplemented by expert interviews and available secondary data.

This chapter contributes to extant literature by providing a fresh perspective on the role of clusters in small firm internationalization, namely, access to local network relationships with foreign connections, such as with multinational subsidiaries situated within clusters (Birkinshaw and Hood 2000). It also lends its voice to prevailing warnings in the literature that clusters do not always have exclusively positive effects on constituent firms and that cluster-related benefits cannot be guaranteed nor can they be assumed to exist. Furthermore, drawing on the Asian character of the sample studied, the chapter makes the point that Western notions of proximity must be tempered with socio-cultural considerations such as the role of ethnic ties overseas, when examining the internationalization of specifically Asian entrepreneurial firms.

The chapter is structured as follows: the next section examines some of the literature on clusters, a concept closely related to local network relationships and resources. The subsequent section briefly discusses the Bangalore software industry, and provides a discussion of the views of entrepreneurs and experts in Bangalore about the impact of location on SKIF internationalization. The final section concludes with implications for academics, practitioners and policy makers.

The role of local network relationships in internationalization

A relevant strand of the literature in the context of local, geographically concentrated relationships is one that deals with clusters. One of the better-known definitions is that of Porter (1998a: 199): 'A cluster is a geographically proximate group of interconnected companies and associated institutions in a particular field, linked by commonalities and complementarities'. Enright (2000) has distinguished between two models of cluster-based development – one where clusters provide the opportunity for firms to develop locally and then compete internationally (see, for example, Porter 1990) and the other where peripheral regions seek to foster clusters and thereby develop the local economy (as discussed in, for example, Peters and Hood 2000). The cluster phenomenon has been generally ascribed to developed economy contexts; there appear to be few healthy clusters in developing economies (Porter 1998a).[3]

Geographic proximity among firms can reinforce trust, enhance inter-firm cooperation and facilitate the transfer of tacit knowledge (Malmberg *et al.* 1996). Clusters therefore yield potential network relationships[4] that are local and spatially concentrated to firms located within them, in the form of suppliers, customers, government agencies, multinational corporation (MNC) subsidiaries and even competitors (Birkinshaw and Hood 2000; Porter 1990). Related concepts in the literature include that of 'industrial district' and 'national innovative capacity'. A definition of the former is 'local clusters of numerous, mostly small enterprises which alternately compete and cooperate with one another and specialize in particular aspects and phases of production' (Staber 1998: 701); by virtue of this definition the discussion in this chapter pertains both to clusters and industrial districts interchangeably. National innovative capacity is clearly a different concept however, and encompasses a strong common innovation infrastructure, innovative industrial clusters and robust linkages between these two elements (Furman *et al.* 2002). The spatial concentration of firms does not automatically guarantee a strong innovative capacity.

Clusters emerge for a variety of reasons that span a continuum with serendipity at one end and purely deliberate action – of the public and/or private sectors – at the other. In other words, it is often a combination of serendipitous and deliberate actions and events that lead to the existence of clusters. Determinants of clusters include economies of scale, transport costs, search and transaction costs, innovation, cooperation, knowledge spillovers and uncertainty (Hoen 2001). Enright (1998) identifies the presence of unique natural resources, economies of scale, specialized labour, local suppliers and infrastructure as economic rationales for clusters. In this context, Balasubramanyam and Balasubramanyam (2000) emphasize educational institutions that produce trained technical labour, state support through tax incentives and subsidies, favourable living conditions, venture capital availability and linkages, both forward and backward. Based on the Porterian notion of clusters (Porter 1990, 1998b), the following factors are seen to foster the development of clusters: inherited factors, geography, climate, entrepreneurship, research and educational institutions, regional economy composition, public sector actions and private sector actions. This framework will underpin the discussion of the Bangalore software industry later in the chapter.

Extant literature on the role of clusters in firms' internationalization is at a nascent stage. A notable exception is a study by Brown and Bell (2001), which indicates that clusters may influence the internationalization of SKIFs through marketing externalities such as, for example, intra-cluster referrals, credibility and reputation, informational spillovers and active joint marketing. Brown and McNaughton (2003) suggest that while the original location of a cluster may have been accidental/fortuitous rather than rational/deliberate, younger firms often locate in such clusters to benefit from the ensuing externalities. Also, Fernhaber *et al.* (2003) have recently demonstrated that SKIFs based within clusters internationalize to a greater extent than their counterparts that are not based in geographically concentrated industrial areas. Clusters can be especially useful by providing external, regional relationships (Almeida 1999; Saxenien 1990) that can compensate for resources it lacks (McNamee *et al.* 2000), as well as facilitating knowledge-building and innovation (Almeida 1999; Audretsch and Feldman 1996; Shaver and Flyer 2000).

In fact, it is suggested that the very nature of innovation (Malmberg *et al.* 1996), which is facilitated by information flow (Enright 1998), causes technological activity to be locally confined. As a consequence, over time, sources of competitive advantage emerge, which are highly localized in nature (Berry and Taggart 1994; Enright 1999; Porter 1990, 1998b). Reiterating this fact, Cantwell and Iammarino (2001: 1007) state that 'innovative activity turns out to be spatially concentrated, and this can mainly be attributed to the benefits that stem from a specific case of agglomeration economies, i.e. knowledge externalities or spillovers'. Berry and Taggart (1994: 351) point out that 'technology development remains confined to local clusters of innovation in a variety of global locations'. Consequently, international networks often tap into the local milieu of clusters[5] (Todtling 1994), as evident when strategic asset-seeking MNC subsidiaries locate within clusters (Birkinshaw and Hood 2000).

Building upon the foregoing discussion, three potential benefits of being based within a cluster, for the internationalization of SKIFs, can be identified. First, a key benefit of location within a milieu of innovation is *reputation*. Reputation enhances the prospect of a firm within that region being perceived as being competent, and this resource resides outside a firm's boundaries within the collective network resources. When this reputation becomes international, it enhances the possibility of (a) unsolicited orders approaching the firms within the cluster and (b) a positive disposition towards a firm from the cluster that proactively seeks business from a prospective foreign customer (Karagozoglu and Lindell 1998). Second, another key benefit pertains to an *enhancement of quality*; this is distinguished from the perception of quality that comes from reputation, previously discussed. An important determinant of quality is the access to specialized resources, including manpower (Saxenien 1990), suppliers and support services (Lorenzoni and Ornati 1998; Pouder and St John 1996; Shaver and Flyer 2000), that a cluster typically affords its constituent firms. Third, SKIFs enjoy *access to local network relationships with useful international links*. Access to multinational subsidiaries that locate within a cluster (Birkinshaw and Hood 2000), for instance, provide an opportunity to SKIFs for collaboration (Enright 2000), which has the potential to lead to international business opportunities.

To elaborate on the third point, the paradoxical notion that local network relationships – such as with multinational subsidiaries or internationalized domestic firms – could provide useful access to foreign markets is perhaps the most interesting consideration and constitutes the essential focus of the chapter. Brown and Bell (2001) have already indicated that local network relationships can, when leveraged appropriately, lead to joint efforts that are synergistically efficient. This chapter offers an additional perspective, namely, access within clusters to international firms, both MNC subsidiaries (Birkinshaw and Hood 2000) and internationalized indigenous firms (Fernhaber *et al.* 2003), to facilitate small firm internationalization. Furthermore, dynamic clusters in Asia are likely to attract investment from ethnic entrepreneurial firms (e.g. based in the United States) who may wish to invest in their homeland (Saxenian 2002). Potentially, SKIFs could develop ties with such firms and benefit from their foreign links, through business opportunities (including links to their customer bases), trade leads/referrals and advice (Prashantham 2004a); this notion has certain normative and policy-related implications as discussed in the concluding section. The next section discusses the chapter's methodological approach.

Methodology

Two broad questions are addressed in this chapter.

1 How are systems of local network relationships built? This is addressed by highlighting the development of the Bangalore software cluster, largely based on ten in-depth interviews with experts and available secondary data.
2 How do these local network relationships influence SKIF internationalization? This question is addressed by synthesizing the views expressed by the chief executive officers (CEOs) of four case-firms, supplemented by the views of the experts. The findings are presented in the next section. This section provides further information on the selection of the four case-firms and research methodology employed.

In March 2002, four case studies of small software firms (Eisenhardt 1989; Yin 1994) were undertaken in Bangalore using in-depth interviewing technique, which was deemed as appropriate for this type of research (Easterby-Smith *et al.* 2001). In-depth interviews, ranging in duration from 60 to 120 minutes, were conducted with the four software entrepreneurs. An interview guide was followed to ensure consistency in the issues raised with each of the entrepreneurs. The main issues were

- the development and nature of local networks within the Bangalore software industry;
- the process of internationalization of SKIFs in Bangalore;
- the perceptions of the role played by location in Bangalore to local SKIFs' internationalization.

The selection of the four entrepreneurs was based on two variables: (a) the age of their firm and (b) the current extent of their firm's internationalization. Firms that were founded six or more years before the interview were deemed to be old[6] (Zahra *et al.* 2000) and firms with greater than 50 per cent of their revenues accruing from overseas were deemed highly international. Each of the entrepreneurs interviewed fall under different categories in relation to the two stated variables of firm's age and internationalization; in other words, a representative cross section was achieved by interviewing:

- an entrepreneur of an old, highly internationalized firm
- an entrepreneur of an old, less internationalized firm
- an entrepreneur of a young, highly internationalized firm
- an entrepreneur of a young, less internationalized firm.

The four case studies were then supplemented by in-depth interviews with ten experts who closely monitor the progress of the local software industry in their respective roles as academics (three experts), consultants (two experts) and managers (five experts).[7] A similar approach (interview guide; approximately 90 minutes' duration) as in the case of the CEOs was adopted. The purpose of these interviews was to elicit the experts' views on the development and trends in the Bangalore software industry; the main issue discussed was the role they perceived the Bangalore cluster to play in the internationalization of local SKIFs. The next section presents the findings of the study..

Role of Bangalore's local network relationships in SKIF internationalization

As noted, the literature is dominated with examples of dynamic clusters from developed (rather than developing) economy contexts. A significant exception is the Bangalore software industry (Balasubramanyam and Balasubramanyam 2000; Dunning 2000; Nadvi 1995), which could act as an exemplar for developing economies wishing to facilitate the emergence of competitive, knowledge-intensive industries and firms. The Bangalore software industry is discussed below based on the interviews conducted and available secondary data.

Table 6.1 Sample of four small Indian software firms

		Level of internationalisation	
		Low (*< 50% export intensity*)	*High* (*≥ = 50% export intensity*)
Firm age	*Young* (*< 6 years*)	Mitoken	New Creation
	Old (*≥= 6 years*)	Vikas	Ekomate

Inherited factors: One view that was expressed more than once by respondents is that Bangalore's software industry emerged quite by accident, facilitated by historical factors. At the time of national independence (August 1947), a strategic decision was taken to locate certain key entities away from the nation's capital of New Delhi owing to its proximity to two potentially hostile neighbours – China and Pakistan. Thus, Bangalore, a city located centrally within the South Indian peninsula and with an established military presence from the days of British rule, was chosen as the location of such vital public sector undertakings as Hindustan Aeronautics Limited and National Aeronautics Limited (Balasubramanyam and Balasubramanyam 2000). Additionally, the Indian Institute of Science was established in Bangalore and together these corporations and educational institutions attracted technical talent from across the country. This pool of talent was arguably the forerunner to the relatively abundant (yet not necessarily sufficient; see Merchant 2001) supply of software professionals now available in Bangalore, which was tapped into by global players such as Texas Instruments and Motorola when they set up offices in Bangalore during the early 1990s (Ramamurthi 2004).

Geography: As discussed above, the militarily 'safe' location of Bangalore induced the location of certain strategic defence-related organizations there.

Climate: Bangalore has a mild climate compared to other major cities in South India which is, at best, a minor incentive for software professionals to settle there as well as for international executives to base themselves there when required; climate, in general however, has little bearing on the software industry (Balasubramanyam and Balasubramanyam 2000).

Entrepreneurship: This, arguably, is of vital importance in relation to Bangalore. The greatest impact of the Indian software industry on the rest of the nation is arguably that of a model in terms of how entrepreneurship – and business management in general – can be a success. In a largely risk-averse part of the country, software entrepreneurs have demonstrated great enterprise and have won the respect of fellow practitioners, the media, the government and public at large (Arora *et al.* 2001). Doyens of the Indian software industry – who are mostly Bangalore based – such as N. R. Narayana Murthy of Infosys and Azim Premji of Wipro are popular speakers at top industry forums and business school convocations. Their esteem has indeed been hard-won, through innovatively attracting talent (such as through equity-sharing schemes, a novelty for India) and building processes of the highest quality (over half of the world's most stringently followed software quality management systems can be found in India-based companies, the majority of which are Bangalore based). These success stories have been an inspiration for others to follow suit and has helped somewhat in stemming the perennial problem of 'brain drain', whereby the best talent had a tendency to emigrate, especially to the United States (Saxenian 2000, 2002).

Research and educational institutions: As discussed, the early establishment of the prestigious and highly capable Indian Institute of Science gave an impetus to technical development in Bangalore. Although several hundreds of engineering colleges have also emerged, of vital significance are a couple of other centres of excellence which, though not purely technical, have fostered the availability of local talent. These are the Indian Institute of Management and the more recently established Indian Institute of Information Technology (Ramamurthi 2004; Saxenian 2000).

Regional economy composition: In terms of regional economy, there has really not been much else preceding the 'software boom' apart from the – almost accidental – location of aeronautical and related organizations in the region, as discussed. As such, the regional economy cannot be said to have greatly influenced the development of the software industry (Balasubramanyam and Balasubramanyam 2000).

Public sector actions: There are some who would argue that the Indian government's greatest contribution to the software industry lies in its benign neglect of it for so many years (Arora *et al.* 2001)! This apparently uncharitable view suggests that in India governmental intervention has not always been perceived to be conducive to private enterprise. Further, infrastructure shortcomings act as impediments for the software and other industries, and the benefits of technology have not percolated down to the masses of private citizens (Donald 2001a,b). It may be noted, however, that indirect effects of public policy – including an unmistakable element of protectionism and an emphasis on self-reliance – have resulted in the development of indigenous software firms. More recently, however, the government has sought to play a key role by transforming the Department of Electronics (DoE) into the Ministry of Information Technology (MIT), under an able member of the Cabinet, and by setting up Software Technology Parks. However, this is recent and as such it is private rather than public sector initiatives that account for the growth of the software industry in Bangalore (Ramamurthi 2004).

Private sector actions: Some of the most vital private sector actions that facilitated the growth of Bangalore came from foreign players: Texas Instruments and Motorola are often cited as pioneers in this area. Initially seeking low-end coding work to be handled out of their low-cost Indian bases, more and more multinational companies have set up development centres with an ever-growing mandate in terms of the quality of work required (Ramamurthi 2004). One company from Austin, Texas, is rumoured to be paying their Indian professionals in Bangalore the same salaries as their professionals in the United States. Such examples, however, are few and far between, and at this stage cost advantage continues to be a major attraction for foreign firms wishing to outsource labour-intensive parts of their businesses. In addition to the multinationals, Indian firms have also made a significant contribution to developing the software industry. As mentioned already, the most successful firms and their business leaders have emerged as national heroes. Many of them have gained from international networks – primarily involving Indian software professionals and entrepreneurs based in Silicon Valley (Luce 2001). In fact, it is said that one in every three Silicon Valley start-ups was founded or co-founded by an Indian (Murdoch 2000). A vital player in the Indian private sector initiative is the National Association for Software Service Companies (Nasscom), the key industry body that has taken a strong role both in terms of lobbying the government and representing the Indian software industry abroad in forums such as trade fairs (Arora *et al.* 2001).

The preceding discussion has sought to identify various factors that have led to the emergence of a system of local network relationships, that is, a dynamic cluster in Bangalore. As seen, these factors are a combination of fortuitous circumstances (some historically based) and deliberate public or private sector action. The discussion now turns to the role of local network relationships in the internationalization process, through a discussion of perceived benefits by the four case-firms that were studied in the Bangalore software industry.

The findings from the four case studies suggest a perception of certain benefits accruing from being Bangalore based, which in turn facilitates internationalization – this is a view supported by the received literature. The specific situations of the four firms varied greatly in terms of their origin, domain of expertise and endowment of local network relationships. The following is a brief account of the four firms with respect to their local network relationships.

Ekomate was started in 1996 by a software engineer returning to India following postgraduate study at the University of Texas. His father was also an entrepreneur, albeit in a traditional industry sector, but this has meant strong local business networks. A noticeable effect of this has been the appointment in 2002 of a senior executive of a large software firm as the company's chief mentor; this was a direct consequence of the entrepreneur's (and his father's) local social networks. This chief mentor has been influential in bolstering internationalization efforts and has provided useful foreign contacts of this own. Additionally, Ekomate has benefited from unsolicited business from the United Kingdom, which the entrepreneur perceives to be partially a consequence of the effects of Bangalore's reputation with respect to software development.

Mitoken is a unique company in that it was spun off from the Bangalore subsidiary of Motorola created to commercialize technology developed by the CEO and his team of three other directors while they were engineers at Motorola. Thus, in a sense, Mitoken was incubated by a multinational subsidiary. As all four managers hold qualifications from prestigious Indian and American engineering and business schools, there currently exist widespread networks both locally and overseas. Further, as a corporate sponsor, Motorola provides strong network ties in India and, potentially, abroad. Such a wealth of relationships has meant that Mitoken has adopted a global mindset from inception, although at the time of the interview all business was domestic. This was, however, a deliberate strategy to first perfect the technology with initial customers at home before venturing abroad. Thus, local network relationships with customers were clearly being utilized, albeit indirectly, in the context of internationalization.

New Creation, like Ekomate, was started by an Indian software engineer trained in the United States. However, this individual subsequently spent nearly a decade overseas as a software professional, and when he returned to India consequently, he found himself being far better endowed with foreign than local network relationships. To maximize this advantage, he has sought to focus primarily on international markets, specifically the United States.

Vikas Global Solutions presents the mirror image of New Creation in the sense that its entrepreneur was locally trained with strong local network relationships, but lacked – at least to start with – foreign ties. Consequently, this entrepreneur has always focused strongly on the domestic market; international business has come almost fortuitously and appears to be of relatively less importance in comparison with Ekomate or Mitoken. However, when he had the opportunity to serve foreign markets, he found that he was well placed to do so because of what he perceives as strong infrastructure in Bangalore, relative to other cities of India. Further, he believes that the likelihood of receiving unsolicited international business is higher in Bangalore than in other Indian cities.

The above-mentioned entrepreneurs clearly have different levels of network relationships and utilization of the same. Endowment of these network relationships seems to be largely entrepreneur driven; further, the entrepreneurs' education and prior work experience appear to determine their access to such connections. In terms of utilization or leverage, it appears to be the firms with a clear global mindset that leverage local network relationships, directly or indirectly, with a view to enhancing international competitiveness, thereby facilitating internationalization. Collectively, the four entrepreneurs' views regarding the benefits derived from local network relationships resonate with the literature as briefly discussed in the following text.

First, with respect to reputation, the equity of the 'Bangalore' brand was a recurring theme in the interviews. Especially with international customers, having Bangalore as their address 'makes the job of marketing much easier', in the words of one software entrepreneur. This was particularly the case when certain software 'booms' existed, such as the demand for software to help clients overseas deal with the Y2K (year 2000 problem) – apparently Bangalore was the first stop for many international customers. This is interesting because Bangalore does not boast a significantly larger number of firms than some other regions; in fact, some statistics (Arora *et al.* 2001) suggest that Bangalore had fewer software firms than the National Capital Region (Delhi and surrounding suburbs). Thus, Bangalore has clearly achieved an enviable reputation for its software industry vis-à-vis other Indian cities, and this – as has been discussed in the previous section – has emerged over time as the consequence of a combination of serendipity, entrepreneurial successes and policy efforts. One respondent's first international business contract was the result of a British businessman watching a television programme in the United Kingdom on the Bangalore software industry, which led him to seek out a Bangalore-based software firm through the Internet. Good reputation led to unsolicited orders for another SKIF as well, from Australia. The business this time from Australia was particularly significant for this firm because it did not otherwise have ready access to foreign network relationships, as the entrepreneur had neither worked nor studied overseas. These findings support Brown and Bell's (2001) thesis that clusters lead to externalities such as credibility and reputation.

Second, in relation to quality, a perceived effect of the Bangalore software industry on SKIFs' international competitiveness pertains to support services and infrastructure, which enabled firms to maintain a high level of quality in their offerings. The high standards of quality maintained by Bangalore-based software firms is evident from the fact that approximately half of the world's software companies with the highest international quality ratings[8] are based in Bangalore (Arora *et al.* 2001). One entrepreneur commented on the ease with which instructions can be given to architects, office equipment suppliers and plumbers as they are well acquainted with the requirements of a typical software office. Reputedly, this level of support service cannot be easily found in other upcoming software centres in India. Related to this locational advantage is the access to computing and communication facilities. The resultant remote electronic access to distant clients is critical to SKIFs' international business activities, especially when they provide real-time service to a customer in, for instance, North America or Europe. In terms of infrastructure, Bangalore city has made noticeable efforts in terms of drainage, cleanliness and garbage disposal and improvement of roads; furthermore, a new international airport is being built. Specifically in relation to internationalization, the presence of suitable infrastructure enhances the confidence of prospective international clients and also attracts foreign players to set up a presence in Bangalore, which could bring with it additional internationalization opportunities for local firms with whom network relationships are formed. One of the respondents was able to gain access in Bangalore to a new type of entity in the Indian software industry, namely, the business development contractor – who would canvass for international business for a set of non-competing clients. Once again, this finding is consistent with the literature (Saxenien 1990).

Third, with regard to cultivating foreign network relationships, it was mentioned during the interviews that networking – albeit primarily informal networking – within the software industry was a useful consequence of being located in Bangalore, and this supports the findings in the extant literature (e.g. Almeida 1999). The opportunities of meeting other entrepreneurs in similar situations are considerable in Bangalore. A few entrepreneurs listed the types of benefits that can accrue from such networking, include effective recruitment, lead generation and general sharing of insights and experiences. Two forums where software entrepreneurs meet were mentioned: one was The Indus Entrepreneurs (TiE) forum, spearheaded by Silicon Valley–based Indian entrepreneurs and the other was the Confederation of Indian Industry (CII) Information Technology panel. Caution must be applied here, however, because such networking can prove to be as much of a problem for entrepreneurs as an opportunity when, for instance, rivals 'poach' good employees from each other. Also, cooperation and sharing of insights may often be superficial and rather basic, given the obsession for confidentiality and secrecy among Bangalore-based software firms. This is consistent with concerns in the literature that the effects of social networks in general (Granovetter 1973) and clusters in particular (Porter 1998b) may not be entirely positive.

Table 6.2 Findings from the four case firms

	Ekomate	*Mitoken*	*New Creation*	*Vikas*	*Synthesis*
Endowment of local network relationships	Strong ties through family business	Strong local MNC ties through former employer, Motorola; also alumni network	No significant local ties owing to lengthy absence	Strong local ties through conducting business in that market for over six years	Entrepreneur responsible for most network relationships; prior education and work experience are a key source of ties
Leverage of local network relationships	Led to firm's chief mentor, a strong advocate of Ekomate's international business-seeking activities	Led to domestic customers; low-risk opportunity to improve technology before launching overseas	Negligible owing to dearth of relationships	Led to domestic customers, which is the primary focus for this company	Firms that leverage their local network relationships the best (provided they have them) are those with a clear global vision
Role of local network relationships in internationalization	Indirect access to valuable foreign ties through chief mentor; also reputation effects perceived	Indirect access to valuable foreign ties through Motorola	Bangalore's infrastructure is conducive to serving international customers	Bangalore provides good support services and human resources	Benefits that enhance international competitiveness: • Reputation • Infrastructure/ quality • Networks

Furthermore, the follow-up expert interviews indicated that the benefits accruing from being based within the Bangalore software cluster were often passive rather than active, with little evidence of collaborative marketing efforts or strong inter-linkages to the rest of the economy. This is a cause for concern as it could imply that key local resources are being overlooked and wasted. In the literature, proactive strategies are associated with successful or success-seeking firms (Liao *et al.* 2003) and regions (Beals *et al.* 1995). Asian managers have been found to adopt reactive rather than proactive strategies when faced with an environment that is perceived as hostile or non-conducive to their business (Tan and Litschert 1994). However, this does not generally seem to be the case either with Bangalore locally or the global technology markets that Bangalore-based software firms have traditionally served. Thus, there are clearly warning bells from the experts for the SKIFs in Bangalore that mere proximity to important local network relationships is not enough (Martin and Sunley 2003; Romijn and Albu 2002).

Finally, it must be borne in mind that the importance of proximity to other actors within a cluster or innovative milieu as emphasized in the (developed country) literature, must be 'balanced' by cultural factors in developing countries such as India, as manifested by the importance of family and ethnic networks.[9] For instance, there appear to be significant links between Bangalore-based software firms, both Indian and multinational, and the Silicon Valley cluster through technologists of Indian origin based in that region (Saxenian *et al.* 2002). An important link is provided by such Indian professionals returning to India, with 45 per cent of those based in Silicon Valley expressing an intention to do so eventually (Saxenian *et al.* 2002). A recent study has estimated that the preferred destination for these returning Indians is Bangalore (Leclerc 2004). Also, as already mentioned, the networking organization TiE provides useful connections between Indian professionals in the West and their counterparts in India. Ethnic ties can result in ethnic social capital, which has both bonding (in terms of ethnicity) and bridging (in terms of geography) properties, and is therefore of great potential value to resource-constrained firms in the home country (Prashantham 2006). Of course, this phenomenon is not surprising in light of Asian firms' acknowledged propensity to leverage network relationships, as noted at the outset. Thus, in the Asian context, Western models of clusters should be supplemented and moderated by cultural influences such as ethnic ties.

Conclusions and implications

This study has sought to contribute to an understanding of the phenomenon of SKIF internationalization in two ways. First, it has focused on local network relationships, which is a relatively neglected area in comparison with network relationships located overseas. Second, it has considered a developing economy context, on which there is generally a dearth of literature. Four case studies that were conducted in an Asian setting, namely, the Bangalore software industry, suggest that important benefits – particularly pertaining to reputation, quality and networks (including foreign ones) – do accrue to SKIFs in a developing economy. However, subsequent expert interviews highlighted the disturbing passiveness that generally characterizes the accrual of such benefits by these firms. This observation is a vital one and leads to several vital implications, considered in the following paragraphs.

In normative terms, a key implication for SKIFs is that there should be conscious leverage of spatially concentrated *local* network relationships; it may well be the case that SKIFs are overlooking significant resources that are 'right under their noses'. These local network relationships could lead to international business opportunities, thereby compensating for a firm's lack of foreign network relationships. There are several practical ways in which this can be achieved. There needs to be wider and more intensive utilization of valuable local forums such as industry bodies. In particular, efforts should be made to build ties with ethnic entrepreneurs in overseas markets, particularly in regions like Silicon Valley, which are at the cutting edge of technology; this of course is easier for certain countries (e.g. China, India and Israel) than others. As seen from (the somewhat extreme) case of Mitoken, potentially useful relationships can be fostered with local multinational subsidiaries (Enright 2000; Zhou and Xin 2003). Equally, ties can be usefully built with other local, domestic firms; SKIFs should seek to leverage economies of scale through efforts such as collaborative marketing (Brown and Bell 2001).

From a policy perspective, an intriguing challenge relates to how developing countries such as India can foster the development of more clusters like Bangalore. While historical factors, such as the linguistic benefits of colonial rule, cannot be reversed, the Bangalore experience does suggest that non-interference with entrepreneurial activities, a clear governmental commitment and the provision of infrastructure (such as the Software Technology Parks of India) can be great facilitators. Indeed, aspiring clusters should also be encouraged by the emerging success of other Indian cities like Hyderabad, which has received very strong governmental support in recent years (Leclerc 2004). Policy makers should make efforts to enhance the international reputation of clusters and, perhaps more importantly, to facilitate the accrual of active benefits for the internationalization of clusters' constituent firms. Additionally, of concern to policy makers in developing economies, such as India, should be the enhancement of the knowledge intensity of SKIFs so that they move up the value chain to compete for higher-value business from abroad and avoid becoming vulnerable to cost-based competition from other emerging economies, such as China.

In terms of theory development, clearly more scholarly work is required, involving larger samples and quantitative methodology, to provide generalizable findings on the role of clusters in the internationalization of SKIFs, particularly in a developing economy context. Issues of interest that could be explored are

- the differences in propensity to internationalization between SKIFs located within clusters and ones that are not;
- comparisons of developing economy clusters (e.g. Bangalore) with developed economy ones (e.g. Silicon Valley);

- the influence of MNC subsidiaries within a cluster and inter-cluster links on SKIF internationalization.

As for the last mentioned point, it could well be that there is an interesting phenomenon in terms of the link between the Bangalore software industry and Silicon Valley, with its strong Indian presence; this is an issue warranting further research. In summary, consistent with the managerial recommendations mentioned, the most valuable research will seek to unpack the conditions under which local network relationships are leveraged actively, effectively and creatively; herein may lie an important key that unlocks the potential for developing economy SKIFs to become world-class, globally competitive players.

7 Foreign networks and internationalization

Prashantham, S. (2006) 'Foreign network relationships and the internationalization of small knowledge-intensive firms', *International Journal of Entrepreneurship and Innovation Management*, 6(6): 542–553.

Abstract

This chapter discusses the role of network relationships in the internationalization of small knowledge-intensive firms (SKIFs) by specifically highlighting their foreign, spatially scattered network relationships, which can be a significant resource. The following two issues are dealt with: how foreign network relationships are developed and the impact they have on the internationalization of SKIFs. This chapter focuses on the Indian software industry and cites the example of four case-firms in Bangalore. Three effects of foreign network relationships on the internationalization of SKIFs, namely, opportunities, information and advice are noted. Managerial implications include the importance of leveraging network relationships proactively and with discernment.

Introduction

Over the past decade, the internationalization literature has reported cases of accelerated internationalization where the traditional stages of internationalization (Johanson and Vahlne 1977) were truncated or skipped (Bell *et al.* 2001; Wright and Etemad 2001). An important explanation that emerged for this pertained to the role of network relationships. For instance, network relationships could lead to client followership (Bell 1995), that is, a firm's client in a foreign market may open a subsidiary in a third market, leading the firm to follow suit with a view to servicing the client in that new market. Alternatively, an international client may provide useful trade leads in that foreign market.

The role of network relationships has been particularly associated with the internationalization of small knowledge-intensive firms (SKIFs)[1] (Coviello and Munro 1997; Dimitratos *et al.* 2003; Jones 2001), which seems entirely consistent with the characteristics of such firms (Prashantham and Berry 2004a) that are renowned for their networking abilities (Jones 1999). While their small size (resource poverty) warrants extensive networking with other firms possessing complementary resources (Gnyawali and Madhavan 2001), their knowledge intensity calls for a constant focus on innovation, which in turn is often greatly facilitated by collaborative network relationships (Baum *et al.* 2000). The internationalization of SKIFs is often distinctive as a consequence of its rapidity, the strategic imperative to be global from the outset and consequent technological learning; consequently, this phenomenon has attracted interest among managers, policy makers and academics (Acs *et al.* 2001). The network relationships influencing SKIF internationalization may be spatially concentrated or dispersed (Bell 1995; Coviello and Munro 1997). This chapter deals with the latter kind of network relationship, that is, *foreign, geographically scattered relationships*. Such relationships, it is argued here, are an important international resource that SKIFs often exploit in relation to their internationalization. Given the relative dearth of literature on internationalization in a developing economy context (Ibeh 2003), this chapter reports exploratory research conducted among SKIFs in Bangalore, India. A developing country context can be of interest to scholars because the resource poverty of SKIFs, a driver of the leverage of network relationships, is even more acute than that in developed economies; consequently, the insights that emerge from such a setting could be innovative and of interest to practitioners.

This chapter is structured as follows: the next section synthesizes relevant literature, the one following that discusses the research methodology used, the penultimate section reports the findings of four case studies of small Indian software firms and the final section concludes with some implications for further research, practice and policy.

The development of foreign, spatially scattered network relationships

A useful theoretical foundation for this study is social capital theory, the central tenet of which is that actors (including firms) exist in the context of, and draw resources from, their social relations (Adler and Kwon 2002; Burt 1997; Coleman 1988; Putnam 2000). In the context of small entrepreneurial firms, it is seen that social networks often provide owner-managers with access to critical resources, not available internally within the firm; the personal network of the owner-manager is perhaps the most important resource upon which he or she can draw, especially in the early stages of a firm's existence (Ostgaard and Birley 1994). Such networks are a source of advice, information and reassurance, and informal network relationships are much more predominantly used (Birley 1985). BarNir and Smith (2002) suggest that senior executives' social capital may account for as much as 20 per cent of the variance in the degree to which their (small) firms enter into alliances; as they state, '[E]xecutives' networks are particularly beneficial to small firms and to businesses with limited resources because the network constitutes a resource – a form of (social) capital – that may compensate for the lack of other resources' (221). Social capital is particularly useful in managing ambiguity arising from imperfect information about prospective business partners. According to Rangan (2000: 813), '... when actors need to but cannot, independently or via market mechanisms, cost-effectively ascertain the identity and reliability of potential exchange partners, then scope exists for social networks to appreciably and systematically influence efficiency'. Thus, social capital theory, which suggests that firms – and especially resource-constrained firms – 'should pursue strategies focusing on the development of valuable networks with external resource holders in order to succeed' (Lee *et al.* 2001: 616) is very relevant to the discussion in this chapter.

In the context of internationalization, valuable social capital emanates from foreign network relationships (Johanson and Vahlne 2003). How do foreign network relationships arise? The extant literature points broadly to two main sources: (a) the firm itself (Johanson and Mattson 1988) and (b) the firm's top management team or entrepreneur (McDougall *et al.* 1994). For a firm, foreign network relationships arise from its cross-border activities; for instance, the customer base has been identified as an important source of network relationships (Coviello and Munro 1997). For an entrepreneur, whose contact base is often a key influence on the firm's internationalization (Madsen and Servais 1997; Wiedersheim-Paul *et al.* 1978), two chief sources of foreign network relationships are (a) educational and (b) professional experience in a foreign country. Additionally, having been raised in or having visited a foreign land on holiday may also be sources of such relationships (Ibeh 2003). The significant role played by the entrepreneur implies that the burden on the entrepreneur of acquiring and nurturing spatially scattered network relationships for SKIFs is a heavy one.

The role of foreign network relationships in internationalization

According to the network approach to internationalization (Johanson and Mattson 1988; McNaughton and Bell 1999), international business opportunities and decisions are driven primarily from relationship considerations. Various studies have adopted or identified a similar approach to internationalization, especially in relation to SKIFs (Bell 1995; Coviello and Munro 1997; Lindell and Karagozoglu 1997; Madsen and Servais 1997; Oviatt and McDougall 1994). Drawing on this literature, three aspects of the facilitative role of foreign network relationships in SKIF internationalization can be identified: (a) the creation of *opportunities* for new international business through, for instance, client followership; (b) the provision of *information* such as trade leads and (c) the provision of *advice* on, for instance, the most appropriate timing of entry into a new market. Networks may sometimes expand as a consequence of serendipity (Meyer and Skak 2002); nonetheless, irrespective of their origin, network relationships have the potential to greatly facilitate internationalization (Lindell and Karagozoglu 1997). However, network relationships could be a double-edged sword (Mitsuhashi 2003); the small software firms that Coviello and Munro (1997) studied received, but were also denied, opportunities for internationalization, to the extent that mobility *across* networks (i.e. cliques) of firms was restricted or rendered difficult.

Methodology

Given the dearth of literature on SKIF internationalization in a developing economy context, the objective of this chapter is to provide insight into the role of foreign network relationships in the internationalization of small Indian software firms. India has a large economy with a well-known information technology industry, but is clearly a developing country marked by widespread poverty and great disparities in income. As such, an inductive case-based approach was deemed appropriate, given the exploratory nature of this study (Eisenhardt 1989; Yin 1994). During the summer of 2002, case-based research was conducted among four small Bangalore-based software firms – Ekomate, Mitoken, New Creation and Vikas Global Solutions. Purposive sampling was undertaken to provide four firms that varied across two variables: level of internationalization (where an export intensity of 50 per cent or above was taken as indicating a high level of internationalization) and age (where less than six years of existence was taken as indicating a young firm), as shown in the table below. All the four firms accepted to be interviewed and were willing to be identified. Their CEOs (also founding entrepreneurs) were interviewed for 90 minutes on average, and additional material about the firm (brochures, Web sites, etc.) were studied.

Development of foreign network relationships for the four firms

Ekomate was established in 1996, when Internet technology was still nascent, by a software engineer who had been trained in Austin, Texas, and had worked on this emerging medium at Intel in the United States. This entrepreneur has the advantage of prior education and work experience in the United States and, therefore, network relationships in that market. However, Ekomate's first international contract was fortuitous, and came from a British firm that found the firm's Web site on the Internet. The motivation to be international was nonetheless a conscious one and the vast majority (90 per cent) of the firm's revenues emanate from overseas. This interest in international business received further impetus when Ekomate appointed as chief mentor a retired senior manager with considerable experience within the Indian software industry and with whom the

Table 7.1 Sample of four small Indian software firms

		Level of internationalisation	
		Low (< 50% export intensity)	*High (≥= 50% export intensity)*
Firm age	*Young (< 6 years)*	Mitoken	New Creation
	Old (≥= 6 years)	Vikas	Ekomate

entrepreneur had a prior social relationship. The new chief mentor has exhorted Ekomate's owner-manager to further increase the firm's internationalization activities and has offered to make some of his own contacts in the United States available to the entrepreneur. The entrepreneur was also encouraged to proactively explore other non-US markets, such as the United Kingdom and New Zealand.

Mitoken is a rare example of a small Indian software firm that is a 'pure-product player' – it only develops and markets software products, rather than offering software services, as do the majority of Indian software firms. It was spun off from Motorola's Bangalore operations, and is now an independent entity. However, the firm's founders retain strong social and professional ties with senior managers at Motorola who act as mentors. Mitoken's motivation for internationalization lies in the global market potential for its offering (a software product targeted at software companies), and the small size of the domestic market. It is also an example of a SKIF that has considerable access to network relationships in the United States, given the educational background of the founders (trained in the United States or in prestigious Indian universities, many of whose alumni subsequently emigrate to the United States) and their close association with a large US multinational, from which Mitoken was spun off. However, at the time of the interview, the firm had no international business, owing to a conscious decision to first perfect their product in the domestic market. A strong intention to internationalize over the following year was expressed; the United States would be the first target market owing to its market potential as well as the extensive US-based contacts of the entrepreneurs.

New Creation is another firm with similarly strong American connections, given the fact that the founder entrepreneur lived in the United States for ten years prior to setting up the firm. The firm was started when he, a software engineer, decided to return to his hometown Bangalore for personal reasons. The firm is small, having fewer than ten employees. Due to his long absence from India, the entrepreneur has little desire to look for domestic business. Thus, this is an example of a firm that is entirely international from inception, and the motivation to be international stems from a lack of familiarity with the domestic market; as such, it appears to be an atypical case for an Indian SKIF with an Indian founder. The main projects to date for this firm are from the United States, and these directly emanated from former clients that the entrepreneur worked with at his former company. Clearly, therefore, network relationships have been utilized for international market entry and development. The entrepreneur is well aware that his connections in the United States are limited to his previous professional circle. At the time of the interview, he had therefore registered with an intermediary that matches Indian software firms with international, and especially American, clientele. This entrepreneur had, however, no business through this means and was considering the use of so-called new business agents who visit foreign markets on a business development mission, typically representing more than one non-competing Indian software firms. In other words, this entrepreneur has considered acquiring foreign network relationships contractually.

The strong American connection of the firms mentioned so far is in direct contrast to the situation of *Vikas Global Solutions*. This firm was started in the mid-1990s by an engineer who had no desire to work for anyone else and entered the software industry as it promised to be a growing one with the opportunity 'to be innovative'. However, he is locally trained and his business interests are primarily domestic; even today, the majority of his revenues come from within India. It was an unsolicited contract from Australia that brought in any motivation at all for international activities' as 'brought in some motivation for international activities. Having experienced the benefits of international business (such as higher margins and highly professional clients), the entrepreneur has subsequently made conscious efforts to obtain additional overseas contracts. He has deemed it best to avoid the American market given his lack of network relationships in that market, and is instead seeking to develop less popular or competitive markets such as South Africa. His biggest overseas market at present remains Australia, and it seems more than mere coincidence that this market was the source of his first international deal. This suggests that the firm's initial Australian contacts have been exploited, which presents a case of foreign, geographically scattered network relationships being leveraged for international market consolidation.

Role of foreign network relationships in the four firms' internationalization

The insights that emerged from the experiences of the four small Indian software firms, discussed above, mostly resonate with the received literature (Table 7.2). First, with respect to *opportunities*, one of the firm's (New Creation) internationalization was purely based on contracts received from the entrepreneur's former employer and clients in the United States. No instance of client followership was reported, but that is perhaps explained by the mostly offshore nature of the work done by the SKIFs that were interviewed; it seems plausible though that as clients' international operations expand, so will the amount of software development outsourced to these SKIFs. Second, in relation to *information*, it appears that at least two firms (Vikas and Ekomate), whose first contract from Australia and Britain, respectively, was unsolicited, made inroads into those two markets based on trade leads provided by their initial client in those markets. Another instance of information gleaned from foreign network relationships pertains to the lead received by one of the respondents from a former colleague that Korea had a high demand for that firm's offering. This entrepreneur is unlikely to have received this information from more conventional sources of information in India. Third, in terms of *advice*, Mitoken reported having received useful guidance from a former MBA classmate in the Bay Area, San Francisco, about when to approach (or not approach) venture capitalists. The foregoing discussion is summarized in the following text.

Further, in agreement with the literature, it was evident that entrepreneurs themselves are the most vital source of foreign network relationships, largely a

Table 7.2 Findings from the four case firms

	Ekomate	*Mitoken*	*New Creation*	*Vikas*	*Synthesis*
Endowment of foreign network relationships	Strong ties with former colleagues in the US	Strong ethnic ties through b-school network; also Motorola ties through former employer	Strong ties with former colleagues/ clients in the US	No significant foreign ties owing to lack of exposure/contacts	The entrepreneur is responsible for most network relationships; prior education/ work experience are key sources
Leverage of foreign network relationships	Some business gained (US); supplemented by ties arising from unsolicited business from the UK	No international business accrued, largely owing to a deliberate initial focus on the domestic market	*All* the business gained from the US through leveraging ties with former colleagues/clients	Initially not possible; unsolicited Australian customer subsequently leveraged however	Extent of leverage is not necessarily related to endowment; when leveraged, ties beget further ties
Role of foreign network relationships in internationalization	A direct source of business (opportunity); additionally, useful trade leads (information)	A source of information and advice (regarding potential opportunities and decisions	A direct source of business (opportunity)	Unsolicited new ties yielded useful trade leads (information)	Benefits that enhance international competitiveness: • Opportunity • Information • Advice

consequence of prior education and professional experience. Thus, for SKIFs, the network-generating burden on the entrepreneur is considerable. The *endowment* of such connections are, however, non-uniform, and entrepreneurs may have to adjust their ambitions to suit their stock of foreign network relationships; alternatively or additionally, they may have to innovatively *leverage* the contacts of their own contacts. For instance, a customer base, once developed, can further lead to network relationships being established with third parties (Lee *et al.* 2001); this behaviour is clearly seen in the case of Vikas and Ekomate. It thus seems reasonable to expect that network relationships beget network relationships – when leveraged skilfully – and that more internationalized firms have more varied and extensive network relationships. Building on the concepts of endowment and leverage of network relationships, the following typology of firms is suggested, the normative implication of which is that firms should seek to be proactive networkers or effective networkers; the former should progressively transform themselves into the latter category by expanding their contact bases.

In terms of the level of internationalization, there seems to be a clear difference with respect to the source of foreign network relationships – both the highly internationalized firms have entrepreneurs who have studied and worked in the United States, while the other two entrepreneurs were locally trained in India. Between the latter two as well, there is a clear difference between the Mitoken CEO who has an MBA from a reputed business school and work experience at an MNC, which suggests that it is only a matter of time before his networks are activated; in the case of Vikas, however, the CEO has a more commonplace education in India and, clearly, has little to draw on by way of foreign network relationships, except his extant customer base in Australia, the origin of which is serendipitous. In terms of the age of firm, no prominent difference was noted.

An interesting finding is the manner in which the entrepreneurs dealt with a lack of foreign network relationships where they had none. When the entrepreneur had no international contacts to start with (as in the case of Vikas), the main course of action was the avoidance of the more competitive markets of the United States and western Europe in favour of less-exploited (and less-lucrative) markets such as Australia. Of course, its situation was considerably facilitated by serendipity in the form of unsolicited custom from Australia, which he then leveraged to obtain other Australian contracts. When entrepreneurs sought

Table 7.3 Typology of small knowledge-intensive firms

		Endowment of network relationships	
Leverage of network relationships		*High*	*Low*
	High	Effective networker	Proactive networker
	Low	Passive networker	Non-networker

network relationships in specific new markets like Britain, at least two approaches were observed. The first, as in the case of Ekomate, was to leverage existing network relationships – both local and foreign – in an indirect fashion, that is, trying to establish contact with British contacts of their own network relationships. The second, as in the case of New Creation, was to hire business development agents; in effect, therefore, network relationships were sought at a monetary cost. This second approach appeared to be in its nascent stages, and its efficacy remains unclear at this juncture.

Finally, it has been pointed out in the discussion of the literature that network relationships can be a mixed blessing – both opportunity rich and yet potentially constraining. A comment made by one respondent highlights the need for vigilance and discrimination on the part of SKIFs while leveraging their network relationships. According to him, his firm had accepted every single opportunity that came its way from foreign network relationships – whether or not the required software development dealt with domains of expertise that the firm wanted to specialize in. As a consequence, although the firm is profitable, its image in the marketplace is diffuse in terms of its area of expertise. This firm's opportunism, while understandable in the context of a need for survival, is illustrative of the relatively negative consequences of international business opportunities gained from network relationships.

Implications and conclusions

From a managerial perspective, the foregoing discussion suggests that in relation to the facilitative role of foreign network relationships in the internationalization of SKIFs, a developing country like India is no different from any other. If anything, resource constraints make the leverage of networks even more imperative. Three implications for managers can be identified. First, network relationships should be *proactively* leveraged. A key insight from the study is the distinction between *endowment* and *leverage* of network relationships. Vikas provides a good example of a firm that transformed from being a non-networker to a proactive networker, with the advent of (serendipitous) business from overseas. In due course, it should seek to enhance its network and become an effective networker. Second, also related to the Vikas example and to that of Ekomate, *serendipity* should be exploited, when it occurs. While serendipity, by definition, cannot be planned for, opportunities arising from fortuitous developments should be speedily recognized and effectively exploited. Third, foreign network relationships can be sought for, indirectly, through *local* network relationships, as seen in Ekomate's access to the Bangalore-based chief mentor's overseas connections and Mitoken's access to American contacts through Motorola's Indian subsidiary. The point being made, overall, is that while a large endowment of network relationships per se is not a guarantee of success, a poor endowment can be no excuse. Furthermore, there should be greater attempts at leveraging economies of scope – in other words, SKIFs should enhance the returns, in terms of business itself or information such as trade leads, from extant network relationships. On a note of caution, *more* social capital is not necessarily *better*; thus, discernment in leveraging network relationships is required. This includes wisdom in judging which network relationships to leverage and to what extent.

From the perspective of advancing theory, further research on a larger scale utilizing quantitative analysis is encouraged. It is pointed out that the sample for this chapter was taken from Bangalore, the city most associated with the software industry in India. It may therefore be well worth comparing a sample of small software firms in Bangalore with one from another region – the National Capital Region (Delhi area) or Hyderabad – to see whether location has an impact on access to foreign network relationships. Alternatively, a sample of Indian software firms could be compared to one from a developed economy context (Ireland or the United States), and a comparison made of how foreign networks are leveraged; this could be related to differences in firm-level factors as well as macro-environmental factors such as infrastructure, policy, size of domestic market or culture (e.g. individualistic versus collectivist cultures). Other questions that remain to be explored include the following: Does the leverage of network relationships in international market entry and development vary with firms' size, knowledge intensity and market knowledge? What types of network relationships are particularly amenable to formalization through strategic alliances or joint ventures?

In terms of policy making, governments of developing economies such as India should follow the lead of developed economies (McNaughton and Bell 1999) to enhance opportunities for SKIFs – and indeed all exporting firms – to establish network relationships in overseas markets. Such efforts should be made increasingly outside the United States, particularly in key European markets, to mitigate the ill effects of a slowdown of the US economy. Initial meetings can and should be facilitated through trade bodies' market visits. In addition, policy-makers should provide training and mentoring programmes that will enhance SKIFs ability to successfully leverage their network relationships. A potential, but largely overlooked, bridge between Indian and Western (especially European) firms is ethnic Indian firms, that is, run by entrepreneurs of Indian origin in Western markets; policy measures to facilitate such linkages is worth considering and exploring further. Ultimately, what is most important for managers and policy makers alike is that networks on their own count for nothing; yet, when leveraged meaningfully, they can be a source of mutual benefit to the actors in the network. Achieving win–win outcomes should be the goal of SKIFs in India and, indeed, of firms anywhere in the world.

8 The Internet and internationalization

Prashantham, S. and Young, S. (2004) 'The Internet and the internationalization of small knowledge-intensive firms: promises, problems and prospects', *International Journal of Entrepreneurship and Small Business*, 1(1/2): 153–175.

Abstract

This chapter presents some exploratory insights; it is based on case studies, supplemented by a preliminary quantitative study from a developing economy context (i.e. the software industry in Bangalore), concerning the role of the Internet in the internationalization of small knowledge-intensive firms (SKIFs). Three main points are made in this chapter. First, the Internet holds great promise in facilitating the internationalization of small firms – especially those in peripheral regions like developing economies; the four Bangalore-based small case-firms shared this view. Second, Internet technology notwithstanding, traditional aspects of business such as the importance of face-to-face interaction and the building of trust remain vital; here a potential facilitator for small firms to overcome this barrier comes in the form of Internet-supported intermediaries. Third, ultimately the prospect that the Internet holds for internationalizing resource-poor firms is that of international growth; a preliminary study of 30 Bangalore-based small software firms suggests that this notion holds credence and is worthy of further study, on a larger scale. These findings have implications for future research, practice and policy making in terms of taking a holistic view of the use of Internet technology and the leveraging of social capital.

Introduction

According to Parasuraman and Zinkhan (2002: 287), 'Internet technology has the potential to alter almost every aspect of business operations'. Developments like the Internet compel business researchers to revisit the adequacy of existing conceptualizations to accommodate its role. The sub-field of small firm internationalization is no exception (Dana *et al.* 2004). Some light is sought to be shed through this chapter on the role of the Internet in the internationalization of small knowledge-intensive firms (SKIFs), an issue that is vital both for practitioners and policy makers seeking to understand how Internet technology can best be utilized to facilitate internationalization efforts. The chapter addresses the following research question: how can the Internet influence the internationalization of SKIFs? It does so by examining the relevant literature and four case-firms in the Bangalore software industry, which suggest the proposition that *small knowledge-intensive firms that apply the Internet intensively will achieve greater international growth than those that do not.* Preliminary support for this proposition based on data from 30 Bangalore-based software firms is presented. Part of the contribution that this chapter makes is the use of a developing economy context for the empirical setting, where there is generally a dearth of literature (Zafarulla *et al.* 1998).

As indicated, the specific type of firm behaviour of interest to this chapter is internationalization, the 'process of increasing involvement in international operations' (Welch and Luostarinen 1988), with special reference to SKIFs. More specifically, the focus is on outward, market-seeking internationalization. In the context of SKIFs, network relationships are known to influence, and often accelerate, their internationalization, resulting in a growing interest in this phenomenon among scholars (Coviello and Munro 1997). The Internet potentially lowers the cost of accessing and leveraging network relationships, by facilitating the enhancement of firms' visibility, efficiency and intimacy, with respect to their network relationships (Prashantham and Berry 2004b). The Internet's ease of use, universal standards and remote electronic access result in tools for communication and information sharing (Morgan-Thomas and Bridgewater 2004), enhancing visibility; in collaboration and commerce (Tiessen *et al.* 2001), enhancing efficiency and in communities and privileged-access networks (Tapscott 1999), enhancing intimacy. The Internet was expected to level the 'playing field' for resource-constrained firms, and some authors saw the Internet as a means through which small firms in a developing economy context could compete on a global basis with their developed-world counterparts (Quelch and Klein 1996). This argument is explored here through the synthesis of relevant literature and the findings of an exploratory study, comprising case studies that are supplemented by a preliminary quantitative study, conducted among small software firms in a developing economy context. The remainder of the chapter is structured as follows: the next section contains a review of relevant literature, followed by a brief discussion of the methodology employed in this study, after which findings are presented and finally some conclusions and implications are drawn out for academics, practitioners and policy makers.

Internationalization of small knowledge-intensive firms

The growth of the firm constitutes an area of interest for scholars in fields as diverse as economics, strategy, entrepreneurship and marketing. A key source of growth – particularly in an environment with strong globalization drivers – is market-seeking internationalization and subsequent international growth (Jones 2001; Luostarinen 1980; Young *et al.* 1989). Widespread criticism notwithstanding, a useful starting point in the conceptualization of internationalization is Johanson and Vahlne's (1977) Uppsala model of internationalization, which essentially posits that firms' internationalization increases as their *foreign market knowledge* does, which has been confirmed as being crucial (Eriksson *et al.* 1997). The role of market knowledge is that of a resource regulator; as this knowledge grows, so does the amount of resources allocated to a foreign market (Yli-Renko *et al.* 2002). Another source of knowledge that has been posited as being positively associated with a firm's internationalization is its *knowledge intensity* (Oviatt and McDougall 1994). Knowledge intensity leads to greater internationalization given that knowledge-intensive firms have a basis for introducing products and services to the market in the first place, and knowledge is globally mobile (Oviatt and McDougall 1994; Yli-Renko *et al.* 2002). The positive relationship between knowledge intensity and internationalization has been subsequently proved empirically by Autio *et al.* (2000). The role of network relationships in influencing – and often accelerating – internationalization is seen in the literature (Coviello and Munro 1997). As noted by Johanson and Mattsson (1988) – and several authors thereafter (e.g. Chetty and Holm 2000; Coviello and Munro 1997) – a firm may receive useful information and knowledge about foreign markets and opportunities therein from customers, suppliers or other network relationships. This strand of the literature is not necessarily at odds with the Uppsala model, as the importance of network relationships has been acknowledged by Johanson and Vahlne (1990, 2003). Indeed, there are growing calls for an integrative approach to the fragmentary internationalization where the role of market knowledge, knowledge intensity and social capital are incorporated (Bell *et al.* 2003; Yli-Renko *et al.* 2002); such an approach is adopted here.

SKIFs are of particular interest to scholars of small firms' internationalization owing to their often proactive and accelerated internationalization (Bell *et al.* 2004a; Coviello and Munro 1997; Young 1987). A synthesis of the literature on small firms and knowledge-intensive firms leads to the following definition of a SKIF: *A small knowledge-intensive firm is a small*[1] *firm, the majority of whose employees comprise a highly qualified workforce, which is its most important resource, and is engaged in knowledge work – meaning that knowledge is inherent in the firm's main activities – as its central preoccupation.* Drawing on this definition of a SKIF, four influences on the internationalization of SKIFs can be identified, explicitly or implicitly: size (smallness), knowledge intensity, the environment and the entrepreneur (McNaughton 1996; Oviatt and McDougall 1994). A common thread running through the literatures on all these aspects is the vital role of network relationships, that is, relationships with customers, suppliers, competitors, alliance partners, universities, government bodies, industry associations, and so on. The motivations for these include resource-poverty and competitive considerations arising from market pressure to innovate (Bell 1995; Jones 1999); indeed, a focus on innovation is especially important for internationalizing firms (Acs *et al.* 2001). Not surprisingly therefore, network relationships are found to be a key driver in the internationalization of SKIFs. A criticism of network-based approaches is that they are more descriptive than theory-based ones; in this regard, conceptualizing the role of network relationships in terms of *social capital*, a concept of growing interest and application for business scholars, promises to offer a fruitful approach for future research (Adler and Kwon 2002).

In the context of network relationships it is useful to consider the subject of clusters, given issues of common interest between network theory and cluster theory. Clusters, according to Porter (1998a: 199), are 'geographic concentrations of interconnected companies, specialized suppliers, service providers, firms in related industries, and associated institutions (for example, universities, standards agencies, and trade associations) in particular fields that compete but also cooperate.' Local rivalry pushes firms to greater innovation and success (Enright 1998; Porter 1998b). Themes common to network and cluster literatures include the coexistence of competition and cooperation (Kogut 2000; Porter 1998b); interdependence of firms, resources and activities (Enright 1998; Johanson and Mattsson 1988); the potential of network resources to contribute to competitive advantage (Gulati *et al.* 2000; Porter 1998b); the importance of free flow of information to build inter-firm bonds (Johanson and Mattsson 1988; Saxenien 1990) and the facilitative role that public policy can play (Enright 1998; Welch *et al.* 1998). The discussion on clusters indicates that internationalizing SKIFs are likely to leverage not only foreign network relationships (Coviello and Munro 1997) but also local ones (Brown and Bell 2001). Thus, it is seen that the network relationships influencing internationalization may be both spatially concentrated and local or spatially scattered and foreign. In general, it is noted that relatively little is known about the role of these networks in a developing economy context (Zafarulla *et al.* 1998); furthermore, the role of recent technological developments like the Internet has not been extensively considered, as seen in the following section.

The Internet and the internationalization of small knowledge-intensive firms

In the preceding section, the point was made that network relationships have a strong influence on the internationalization of SKIFs. In this section, extending the work of Prashantham and Berry (2004b), it is argued that the Internet offers applications that facilitate network relationships, enabling firms to interact more widely and intimately with other actors, including customers, suppliers and collaborators. The literature on the Internet has evolved substantially from the days when incumbent firms were seen as having failed to come to terms with the new technology.[2] The role of Internet technology has been recognized in the mainstream business literature; according to Porter (2001: 64), 'The key question is not whether to deploy Internet technology – companies have no choice if they want to stay competitive – but how to deploy it'. In the context of small firm internationalization it has been suggested that 'technological advances ... in telecommunications – especially the Internet – allow even the smallest firms access to customers, suppliers, and collaborators around the world' (Wright and Etemad 2001: 151). Yet, extant understanding of the role of the Internet in small firm internationalization is nascent (Brock 2001; Prasad *et al.* 2001). While this may in part be because small firms have only recently begun to embrace Internet technology (Tiessen *et al.* 2001), relatively few empirical studies of this phenomenon with strong theoretical underpinnings are available. A brief review of the Internet-related literature on internationalization is offered below.

Authors such as Quelch and Klein (1996) foresaw potential benefits for the internationalization efforts of small firms. They argued that the Internet was poised to revolutionize the way international marketing was taught and practised, including in developing economies. According to Quelch and Klein (1996: 62), 'Because distribution channels tend to be less developed, less direct, or less efficient in emerging markets than in the United States, the Internet may offer special opportunities in these markets.' Their work was closely followed by similar articles that made related points from researchers such as Bennett (1997), Hamill (1997), Hamill and Gregory (1997), Poon and Jevons (1997) and Samiee (1998). This was a period when these researchers seemed to be coming to terms with the fact that the Internet was being commercialized, and the primary thrust of their articles was the unprecedented opportunities for smaller firms that the Internet provided to overcome several of the barriers that may have hindered their internationalization potential and efforts in the past. Subsequent work indicates that the adoption of Internet technology is indicative of an entrepreneurial orientation (Knight 2001) and may constitute an 'episode' that leads to rapid internationalization thereafter (Bell *et al.* 2001). It may be noted, however, that this new literature is, surprisingly, not substantial at all; particularly little empirical study has been done (Brock 2001; Prashantham and Berry 2004b).

Of the relatively few empirical studies in this area, the work of Hamill and Gregory (1997) and Bennett (1997) are among the earliest and reveal that exporters and among them, younger firms were more inclined to adopt Web sites as an internationalization tool. Berthon *et al.*'s (1999) exploratory study of small international service firms indicated that the Internet was perceived as providing significant opportunities to target international markets while overcoming some of their traditional barriers to internationalization. Lituchy and Rail (2000) found similar optimism among small inns and bed and breakfasts in Canada and the United States who thought of the Internet as a relatively inexpensive form of marketing with global reach; however, using Web sites had also made them more aware of their own deficiencies, such as a lack of multilingual staff and competition from larger, better-known players. It further emerged that some of the respondents were afraid of the new technology and were in urgent need of training. Brock (2001) found in his study of German small technology-based firms that the Internet had a positive impact on attitudinal, resource-related, information-related and network-related aspects of internationalization, thereby facilitating the process; however, internationalization continued to follow an incremental path, the Internet notwithstanding. Prasad *et al.*'s (2001) study of American manufacturing firms involved in exporting suggests that firms' integration of Internet technology with their marketing activities has a positive impact on export performance when marketing orientation is leveraged. Tiessen *et al.*'s (2001) study of 12 case studies indicates that Internet adoption by smaller firms is driven by a host of factors including dramatic market changes, industry norms and firm characteristics. Kim (2003) found that internationalizing Internet firms in the United States sometimes did follow an incremental approach in entering foreign markets, while Morgan-Thomas and Bridgewater's

(2004) study of British exporters suggests that effective usage of even basic Web sites could lead to significantly higher international revenues.

For a subject that generated the excitement that it did a mere seven years ago (Quelch and Klein 1996), the extant academic literature on the Internet and small firm internationalization appears rather thin. Much of the Internet-related literature has emanated from *practitioners* rather than academics, and while this has certain merits in terms of application to the business world, it may have the failing of not being based on robust empirical inquiry. Further, there is the danger that some of the literature is essentially hype, buzz words or 'advertorials' for consultants – in other words, consultants may have a vested interest in gaining business by presenting concepts, which implies the potential for hyperbole in discussing the Internet's benefits. This chapter has sought to deal with this issue by being discriminatory in terms of the selection of literature that has just been reviewed.

Given the weaknesses of extant approaches to examining the role of the Internet in small firm internationalization, an approach is presented here that takes into consideration the information-related properties of the Internet and the determinants of internationalization, with special reference to SKIFs. The Internet has created an information-intensive environment (Glazer 1991) that offers possibilities that did not exist previously. These primarily pertain to information-related applications – such as the potentially global visibility that a firm can attain – that can influence the market-seeking internationalization of firms. Three possibilities of the application of Internet technology in the context of internationalization are noted. First, information dissemination could result in (theoretically) a foreign customer or client coming across a firm's Web site on the Internet, subsequently leading to an order being placed and, therefore, international growth for the firm. In other words, information dissemination could directly result in international growth (Morgan-Thomas and Bridgewater 2004; Quelch and Klein 1996). Second, information acquisition through the Internet – information on prospective markets, customers and business partners like suppliers, much of which is free – could lead to augmentation of extant stocks of the firm's market knowledge (Hamill 1997; Ward and Ostrom 2001). Third, information sharing through the Internet could lead to strengthening network relationships, leading to an increase in the firm's stock of social capital, which in turn could lead to both greater market knowledge and knowledge intensity, and ultimately to internationalization (Hoffman and Novak 1996; Tapscott 1999). Developing on Prashantham and Berry's (2004b) ideas, these information-related applications of the Internet could lead to an enhancement of SKIFs' visibility, efficiency and intimacy in the context of their network relationships, as discussed subsequently. However, it is also pointed out that the Internet per se does not guarantee success (Souitaris and Cohen 2003) or invalidate traditional notions of internationalization, such as the influence of knowledge (Kim 2003; Kotha *et al.* 2001) or location (Leamer and Storper 2001; Zaheer and Manrakhan 2001).

Visibility is the starting point in acquiring and leveraging network relationships (Coleman 1988). SKIFs, by their nature, are likely to target specific market niches, usually on a global scale (Berry *et al.* 2002). Thus, they are not likely to be well known outside their immediate circles of customers, suppliers and competitors, in contrast to very large knowledge-intensive firms such as IBM or Microsoft. Within their specific niche(s), however, SKIFs generally face stiff competition from other SKIFs to capture mindshare among those entities with which it has, or should have, ties (Jones 1999). It therefore becomes important for SKIFs to be generally visible within their networks, both with existing and potential network relationships. Enhanced visibility will ensure wider access to network relationships, and thereby more opportunities to acquire greater amounts of network resources such as information, influence and solidarity (Adler and Kwon 2002). The Internet provides SKIFs with the potential to achieve greater visibility, on a worldwide basis. According to Yip (2000), the Internet provides instant global reach, owing to its universal standards and easy reach, which has been reiterated by other authors such as Quelch and Klein (1996) and Hamill (1997). A specific Internet application that enhances visibility is Internet marketing through the registering of Web sites on search engines and business-to-business (B2B) hub sites (Hoffman and Novak 2000; Kaplan and Sawney 2000; Kenny and Marshall 2000)

Network relationships of SKIFs may involve a power struggle, with each actor seeking to achieve greater control; this is especially likely when the resource base of the actors involved is asymmetrical. When a SKIF's network relationship is with a larger entity, then the SKIF is often in a disadvantaged position; large firms generally appropriate the greater portion of value created in alliances with small firms (Alvarez and Barney 2001). Greater control is achieved (or the ill effects of a lack of control mitigated) when a SKIF exhibits superior operational efficiency in its network relationship transactions or operations. *Efficiency* is an important basis of reputation for SKIFs, which in turn can enhance the quality of network resources that flow to it owing to the positive disposition of network relationships towards it. The Internet provides SKIFs with the potential to achieve greater efficiency, as a consequence of the connection across value chain activities that it allows (Evans and Wurster 1997; Feeny 2001; Tapscott 1999). This is further accentuated in the case of the software industry where the 'product', that is, software code, is in digitized form. A specific application that is pertinent in this context is collaborative product development (or project management) between a SKIF and its client overseas, using Internet-supported groupware, a form of efficiency-enhancing Internet operation (Evans and Wurster 1997; Porter 2001).

Not every opportunity that emanates from a network relationship is consistent with a firm's strategic orientation (Coviello and Munro 1997). The perennial issue of how opportunistic a SKIF can afford to be does not have an easy answer. Often, strategic flexibility on the part of young firms is warranted and justified. Nonetheless, in the long run, a lack of strategic coherence will be unhelpful for a firm (Nohria *et al.* 2003). Therefore, SKIFs should seek to enhance intimacy among their network relationships. This in turn will result in superior quality of network resources in terms of relevance (Coleman 1988). In other words, leads and opportunities that arise out of network relationships are more likely to be aligned with a SKIF's own long-term agenda, the more intimately aware its network relationships are about it. The Internet provides SKIFs with the potential to achieve greater coherence as a consequence of the property of *intimacy*. A specific Internet application, relevant not merely to customers but also to business partners, is Internet-supported relationship management, in which regard Intranets and Extranets can be very useful (Davenport *et al.* 2001; Feeny 2001; Hoffman and Novak 1996; Peppers *et al.* 2001; Seybold 2001) (Table 8.1). The foregoing discussion is summarized in the following text.

While the Internet's potential benefit for firms based in developing economies has been suggested (Quelch and Klein 1996), few empirical studies appear to have been undertaken in a developing economy context. This applies to the area of the internationalization of SKIFs as well, where empirical work has chiefly been undertaken in developed economy settings. There is clearly a need to address the obvious gap in this area of the literature by conducting empirical research that examines the impact of the Internet, on the internationalization of SKIFs, in a developing economy context. Such work is critical if SKIFs in developing economies are to benefit from the Internet since most of the small firm internationalization theory focuses on developed economy contexts and may not readily hold in a developing economy context that has peculiar market- and policy-related problems (Maddy 2000). A potentially interesting case would be the Bangalore software industry, which has been cited as an excellent example of a developing economy plugging into the wider global economy (Kobrin 1999). In sum, the review of literature suggests that knowledge (market knowledge and knowledge intensity) and network relationships (more usefully, the social capital that emanates from network relationships) are important determinants of SKIFs' internationalization; furthermore, application of Internet technology in enhancing visibility, efficiency and intimacy with relation to their network relationships is likely to increase SKIFs' international growth.

Research methodology

There are three aspects of the research methodology employed in this study, which are briefly discussed below. The first – and main – aspect of the research methodology comprises the case studies (Eisenhardt 1989; Yin 1994) of four small Bangalore-based software firms during the summer of 2002, which were selected purposively using the researchers' contacts to ensure a spread in terms of age (young being taken as fewer than six years in existence, in keeping with authors like Oviatt and McDougall) and proportion of revenues accruing from international business (taken as 'high' when this was 50 per cent or more). Qualitative research is generally used to generate propositions, especially in the absence of an established body of literature and empirical findings, rather than to test propositions. The four case-firms that were studied are indicated below:

The second aspect of the research conducted was a supplementary case study

Table 8.1 The Internet and internationalization of SKIFs

Aspect of relationship	*Strategic issue*	*Impact on network relationships*	*Impact on network resources*	*Internet tool (example)*
Network relationship acquisition	Competition – other firms are competing for the same network relationships	Enhanced visibility – this will ensure wider access to network relationships, and thereby more opportunities to acquire network resources	Quantity – more visible firms are likely to attract more network resources	Internet marketing – such as through registering on B2B hub sites
Network relationship operations	Control – network relationships invariably involve a power struggle, especially in network relationships with larger or more focal firms	Enhanced efficiency – this will ensure satisfied network relationships; efficient operations will mitigate negative effects of a power struggle and will result in more positive associations with the firm	Quality (reputation) – more efficient firms are likely to attract positively-disposed referrals, as a consequence of their efficiency	Internet-supported collaborative product development – such as through the use of groupware
Network relationship development	Coherence – not every network resource that emanates from network is necessarily in sync with the overall strategy or welfare of a firm	Enhanced intimacy – this will result in more cohesive network relationships with entities that will have a greater understanding of the firm's strengths and overall strategic direction/goals	Quality (relevance) – more intimate firms are likely to attract more relevant network resources that are coherent with the firm's overall strategic direction and goals	Internet-supported relationship management – such as providing regular updates through access to the firm's Extranet/Intranet

Table 8.2 The four case-firms

	Young (< 6 years)	*Old (> 6 years)*
High internationalization (> = 50% of revenues accrue from international business)	New Creation Established: 2000 Employees: 8 International revenues: 100%	Ekomate Established: 1996 Employees: 30 International revenues: 90%
Low internationalization (< 50% of revenues accrue from international business)	Mitoken Established: 2000 Employees: 40 International revenues: 0%	Vikas Established: 1995 Employees: 70 International revenues: 20%

of a related firm, NeoIT, which was mentioned repeatedly by three of the four firms as being an important Internet-based intermediary that potentially had a vital role to play in the internationalization of SKIFs like the case-firms. As with the four software firms, the NeoIT case study was based on qualitative research through an in-depth interview with the firm's Bangalore representative, supplemented with secondary data through company reports and media articles.

The third and final aspect of the research was a modest attempt to strengthen the main proposition that this chapter presents, namely, that firms using the Internet intensively achieve greater international growth than those that do not; secondary data on international growth, Internet usage, social capital and knowledge were obtained from India's National Association of Software Service Companies (Nasscom) and company Web sites of 30 small software firms in Bangalore, and subsequently regressed. The focus of this chapter is on exploring and generating a valid proposition that can be tested rigorously in the future, especially in a developing economy contest. Nonetheless, a preliminary attempt is made to test the key proposition, and the findings are presented in this chapter.

Discussion: promises, problems and prospects

Promises

The study of the four case-firms focused on two aspects: (a) their process of internationalization, with special reference to the role of network relationships, both local and foreign, and (b) their perceptions of the role of the Internet in internationalization. In terms of internationalization, network relationships – local, foreign or both – were seen to play a vital role in the internationalization of the four case-firms as evident from the brief profiles given subsequently; thereafter, the collective views of the respondents on the role of the Internet are presented.

Ekomate: This firm was started in 1996 by an entrepreneur who returned from graduate studies and short-term employment in the US computer industry. The company received unsolicited business from a British firm and, shortly thereafter, business in the United States through former colleagues of the entrepreneur. Strong local links through the entrepreneur's father – also a businessman – led to the appointment of a senior Indian IT executive as the firm's chief mentor. Even though currently 90 per cent of Ekomate's sales revenues comes from international business, the chief mentor has been forcefully advocating the proactive pursuit of greater international growth, from the United States and from other markets including the United Kingdom, Australia and New Zealand. Consequently, the firm is seeking to strengthen its presence in overseas markets by utilizing network relationships based there.

Mitoken: While most Indian software firms focus on the software services segment, from its inception Mitoken elected to be a 'pure product player', with an offering targeted at software firms, which enables them to manage their work processes more effectively. The company was created in 2000 when four software engineers left Motorola's Indian subsidiary to commercialize technology developed there; Motorola is a corporate sponsor of Mitoken. Apart from these strong network relationships, by virtue of the prestigious Indian engineering and business schools attended by the four founders, they have access to an enviable network of former classmates now working overseas, chiefly in the United States. At the time of the interview, Mitoken had no revenue from international business, but this was clearly a deliberate strategy as they sought to perfect their technology in the domestic market first. Since then, a director of the company has relocated to the United States and the internationalization of the company is imminent.

New Creation: This firm was founded in 2000 when the entrepreneur returned home to Bangalore, having spent a decade in the United States. Family circumstances necessitated his return to Bangalore, where he was by now, rather unusually, bereft of local network relationships. Therefore, his focus has been on tapping prior network relationships among his former employer and former clients for business, and, consequently, 100 per cent of the firm's revenues accrue from the United States. He, however, wishes to diversify his portfolio of markets, through Internet-based efforts (such as through software service hub sites) and through business development contractors who represent non-competing firms on business trips to markets such as the United States and search for new business.

Vikas Global Solutions: This company was formed in 1995 by a graduate from a local engineering college. In the absence of foreign experience or elite local connections, he deemed it best to avoid active soliciting of business from large competitive markets like the United States and the United Kingdom. This strategy received further impetus when an unsolicited business order was obtained from Australia. Now, 20 per cent of the firm's sales revenues comes from overseas, predominantly from Australia, where a one-man sales office was opened in 2002. He is now seeking further international expansion through 'virgin territories' in South Africa and Zimbabwe.

In terms of the role of the Internet, it was evident that the Internet was a great source of hope and confidence for these firms, as evident from the following discussion. The Internet was essentially seen as a cost-effective means of reaching global market, especially where the entrepreneur had no personal contacts; thus, Hamill's (1997) notion of the Internet as a low-cost global gateway and Yip's (2000) suggestion that the Internet provides instant global reach were echoed by the respondents. Two of the four firms had received unsolicited business from overseas, and certainly in one case (business from Britain for Ekomate), the client had found the software firm's Web site by searching the Internet. Web sites apart, mention was made of hub sites, such as NeoIT in India, and *The Economist's* hub site for software services in the West. New Creation, for example, had registered on both of these hub sites and although no business had resulted from them at the time of the interview, it was hopeful, particularly about the latter. One entrepreneur saw the Internet as a useful means of keeping updated with technological trends around the world. Another emphasized the collaboration and interaction during the software creation process – with comments on work in progress being constantly posted and monitored on either side of the globe – as being greatly beneficial as a consequence of the Internet. Another use that seemed to hold great promise was for live or semi-live demonstrations of software to clients or prospective clients through the Internet. Mitoken, for example, reported having successfully conducted an extensive 'demo' for a prospective client in the United States, without having to physically leave their office in Bangalore, which was very cost-effective for them.

Thus, in terms of current usage of the Internet, there was evidence of visibility-oriented and, to a lesser extent efficiency-oriented, applications of the Internet. Apparently, firms were not yet exploiting relationship management applications of the Internet. Reasons for this included a base of network relationships that was too small to warrant such application and an acknowledgement that firms – even software firms in India – were yet to adopt the Internet in as sophisticated a manner as they could. As one respondent observed, 'Although the technology is revolutionary, its adoption is evolutionary'. One of the major problems in applying the Internet for internationalization that was perceived by respondents was the difficulty in building trust with prospective clients that they had never met and for whom their reputation was unknown; it was therefore felt that larger firms like Infosys, Tata Consultancy Services and Wipro with well-known brand names would increasingly squeeze out the smaller, less-known players. In this regard, virtually every respondent made mention of the potential benefits of an Internet-based intermediary that could bring small software firms like theirs in contact with Western clients, and in all cases an intermediary called NeoIT was mentioned. In terms of prospects for the future, respondents were confident that the Internet would foster international growth for resource-poor firms like their own; they remained hopeful that the current promise of the Internet as a facilitator of internationalization would hold and that the problem of trust building could be overcome. The problem and prospect mentioned by the respondents are explored in the following sections; a summary of the discussion hitherto of the case-firms is presented below.

Table 8.3 Summary of findings from the four case-firms

	Ekomate	*Mitoken*	*New Creation*	*Vikas*	*Synthesis*
Internationalization					
Process	Business both proactively obtained and from unsolicited business	Deliberate focus on domestic market first, but highly global ambition	Only international business through network relationships	Unsolicited international order sparked moderate interest in revenue from abroad	Entrepreneurial *vision* is crucial; the entrepreneur is responsible for most network relationships
Role of local network relationships	Strong ties through family business; led to firm's chief mentor	Strong MNC ties with former employer, Motorola	No significant local ties owing to lengthy absence	Bangalore provides good support services and human resources	Benefits: Reputation Infrastructure Networks
Role of foreign network relationships	Strong ties with former colleagues in the US.	Strong ethnic network relationships through b-school network	Strong ties with former colleagues/ clients in the US	No significant foreign ties owing to lack of exposure/contacts	Benefits: Opportunity Information Advice
The Internet					
Promises	New business received through the Internet; a more level playing field perceived	Live demos possible through the Internet	Cost-effective for seeking new business through B2B hubs	Allows rapid, cost-effective communication	Cost-effective global reach

Problems	More can be done through the Internet; for now, the role of NeoIT type intermediaries are important	The 'face' still counts; the Internet cannot replace traditional relationship building	Yet to apply the Internet for relationship management; contact base is too small at present	'Face' still counts; human relationships are important and difficult to build	Trust building (in the absence of name recognition or brand awareness)
Prospects	A great opportunity for resource-poor firms to access international markets	High international growth and rapid scaling up can be achieved if the vision is there	A potential source of cost-effective international growth	If there is a positive attitude to the Internet, it can lead to international growth	High international growth for resource-poor firms

.our case-firms acknowledged that there was scope to do more, mainly in terms of moving beyond achieving greater visibility and efficiency, towards achieving greater intimacy among network relationships. It appeared that there was an evolutionary pattern to the adoption of Internet technologies, their revolutionary capabilities notwithstanding. The more knowledge intensive the firm, the more it appeared to have adopted Internet technology more intensively, that is, to have demonstrated that Internet usage leads to greater efficiency and, ultimately, intimacy..

Greater visibility via the Internet, while an extremely useful starting point, did not in itself yield international business. A major issue that emerged from the preliminary expert interviews was the need for small software firms in India to develop trust among prospective clients, especially those based in the West, the Internet notwithstanding. Further, a major problem for them has been their inability to 'get a foot in the door' in the first place, as it were, to gain the attention of a company located halfway around the world. Having a Web site – even a database-driven one that is proactively registered on search engines – is of little use to a small software firm located in Bangalore when a prospective client in Berlin or Chicago looking to outsource software solutions is inundated by a large list of software firms that come up, should she or he search for one on an Internet search engine. In the absence of greater information, familiarity and trust, it becomes likely that many Western firms would be willing to pay a

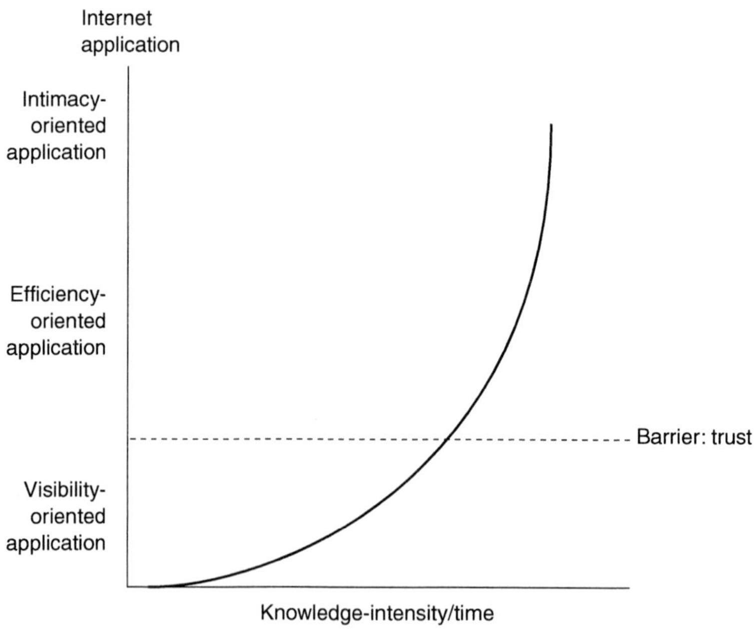

Figure 8.1 Evolution of adoption of Internet applications.

premium to obtain the services of a large, well-known Indian software company rather than run the risk of experimenting with a smaller, less-expensive one. It was suggested that a trusted – and ideally large or resource-rich – intermediary could play two useful roles in this regard: as an intermediary in matching prospective clients with software vendors, ensuring an optimal fit between the software requirement(s) and vendor's capabilities and pricing; and as a guarantor or auditor of smaller software firms' quality. It further emerged from these interviews that NeoIT is an outsourcing intermediary – possibly the best-known one in India – that seeks to fulfill these very roles, and it therefore seemed worthwhile to study it as a case-example.

Headquartered in San Ramon, California, with its Asian headquarters in Bangalore, NeoIT was set up in June 1999 by expatriate Indians with a view to helping buyers and vendors (primarily American and Indian respectively, going by the location of their main offices) of software services to come together. The rationale for this primarily relates to managing better or reducing search costs for buyers and marketing costs for vendors. The Internet is the medium through which software firms register themselves on NeoIT's pre-prepared templates, for a fee varying from $500 to $2,000 per year, depending on the firm's size. It is also through the Internet that prospective clients post their Requests for Information (RFIs) and Requests for Proposal (RFPs). The process that then ensues is one of short-listing *by NeoIT*, based on quality and cost parameters, and the short-listed firms are approached to make bids. At the final stage, two companies emerge as 'finalists', and they may have to further negotiate on the price; in fact, price might then become the deal maker or breaker.

NeoIT appears to have built a positive reputation for itself. In addition to the glowing customer testimonials posted on its Web site, it was regularly – and in some cases, exclusively – mentioned by the software industry experts interviewed in Bangalore. As for its outsourcing intermediary role, the key strength of NeoIT appears to be its template-driven database of software firms allowing in-depth knowledge of company *facts* and comparison across companies, to yield shortlists in a relatively short period of time. A report on one client's experience featured on NeoIT's Web site suggests that it took a mere three weeks from the RFP stage to selection of a software service company. While this, no doubt, represents an exceptionally speedy performance, it is indicative of how fast NeoIT may be obliged to react when prospective clients have urgent requirements. In addition, however, NeoIT engages in substantial face-to-face interaction with software companies to get a better sense of their *people* and, therefore, capabilities. This knowledge is factored into the short-listing process and, thus, a subjective element may, at times, be inevitable. While NeoIT is clearly addressing an important role as mentioned earlier – that of a trusted intermediary – there are, however, problems with its current approach. It emerged from the interviews with the four case-firms that transparency was not perceived as total in that often registered software vendors cannot view the RFIs or the RFPs. The imperfections of NeoIt notwithstanding, its case illustrates the Internet's potential in facilitating small firm internationalization.

Prospects

Extant problems notwithstanding, the chief prospect of the Internet for the internationalization of SKIFs that emerged from the interviews with the four case-firms is that firms that apply Internet technology intensively (i.e. progress to exploit the Internet to enhance not merely visibility but also efficiency and intimacy) will achieve higher international growth than firms that do not. The veracity of this proposition can only be known by a large-scale quantitative study, rather than the qualitative research exercise presented in this chapter – which is of course appropriate to help generate propositions in the absence of much previous empirical findings. In the interim, however, a modest exercise based on secondary data from India's apex software body the Nasscom and company Web sites was undertaken to test the aforementioned proposition. A total of 62 Bangalore-based firms adhering to this chapter's definition of a SKIF (i.e. where 'small' is defined as a firm with fewer than 100 employees) were identified from Nasscom's 2000 directory. Data on these firms' international revenue pertaining to 1997–1998 and 1998–1999 were available from that directory. Data for 1999–2000 was obtained from Nasscom's 2002 directory. There was a total of 30 firms, of the original 62, for which data could be found in the 2002 directory; the absence of the remaining is presumably owing to discontinuation of their membership of Nasscom or their business identity (owing to rebranding or acquisition, for example).

Table 8.4 Correlations

No.	*Variable*	*1*	*2*	*3*	*4*
1	Internet usage	1			
2	Social capital	0.492**	1		
3	Market knowledge	0.447*	–0.055	1	
4	Knowledge intensity	0.389*	0.292	0.223	1

Notes
* Correlation is significant at the 0.05 level (2-tailed).
** Correlation is significant at the 0.01 level (2-tailed.

Table 8.5 OLS regression estimates

Variable	*B*	*SE*
Constant	606.286	1004.181
Internet usage	521.884*	197.263
Social capital	59.958	177.694
Market knowledge	–546.020*	198.915
Knowledge intensity	110.233	198.525
Adj. R^2	0.307	

Notes
* Correlation is significant at the 0.05 level (2-tailed).
** Correlation is significant at the 0.01 level (2-tailed;

Using the data of these 30 firms, annualized international growth figures were calculated and regressed with crude measures for the following constructs, based on the earlier discussion of the internationalization literature: market knowledge (Johanson and Vahlne 1977), knowledge intensity (Autio *et al.* 2000; Oviatt and McDougall 1994) and social capital (Johanson and Mattsson 1988; Johanson and Vahlne 2003); to these are added Internet usage (Prashantham and Berry 2004b). Market knowledge was operationalized in terms of market diversity; it was assumed that the more diverse a firm's portfolio of markets (as reported in its profile in the Nasscom directory of 2000), the greater would be its market knowledge (Zahra *et al.* 2000). An independent exercise was undertaken with the assistance of an associate with intimate technical knowledge of the Bangalore software industry to calculate the knowledge intensity of each firm. Evidence of advisors, clients, customers and alliances – as indicated from a content analysis of Web sites – was used as a proxy of a firm's social capital, and firms were categorized as having low, medium or high stocks of social capital. Internet usage was measured using the company's current Web site as a proxy; the more sophisticated it was (i.e. the greater use of efficiency- and intimacy-related applications such as Extranets), the higher the score awarded to it. The operationalization of these constructs is discussed in more detail in the appendix. The results of the regression are indicated below.

The key findings can be summarized as follows:

- Internet usage is positively and significantly associated with international growth.
- Market knowledge is *negatively* and significantly associated with international growth.
- Market knowledge, knowledge intensity and social capital are positively and significantly correlated with Internet usage.

The results of this small effort must be interpreted with caution owing to severe limitations such as the small size of the sample and the crudeness of the measures used. Nonetheless, there appears to be reason to believe that the proposition that Internet application and international growth will be strongly related is one that is well worth testing in future research. The surprising direction of relationship between 'market knowledge' and international growth is perhaps understood in the context of the measure used – which was one of market diversity. A closer inspection of the data revealed that 28 of the 30 firms listed North America (and specifically the United States) as a market. Thus, high scores for this construct reveal that the firm had diversified its portfolio of markets to include others too. It thus appears that the firms with the highest international growth rates were those that focused more or less exclusively on the US market between 1997 and 2000, which should not come as a surprise given the unprecedented growth of IT spending in the American economy during that period. It appears that other markets simply did not yield comparable returns to Indian software firms, which may have well had to also contend with lower familiarity with these non-US markets. This may well change over time, given the subsequent slowing down of the US economy and, indeed, the more successful Indian software firms of the future may well be those with interests in non-US markets as well, ensuring that all their 'eggs' were not in 'one basket'. The positive correlation between market diversity and Internet application is interesting because it suggests that a wider international experience is accompanied by growing sophistication in Internet technology deployment. Similarly, it can be conjectured that firms possessing stronger technological skills (greater knowledge intensity) and extensive network relationships (greater social capital) have a stronger incentive, and capability, to apply the Internet more intensively – using the Internet not merely to enhance visibility but also to improve efficiency and intimacy in their networks. In sum, tenuous support for the proposition that the Internet facilitates international growth for resource-constrained knowledge-intensive firms is found.

Conclusions and implications

Three main points have been made in this chapter. The first is that the Internet holds great promise in facilitating the internationalization of small firms – especially those in peripheral regions like developing economies; clearly, the four small software firms in Bangalore that were studied shared this hope. The second is that Internet technology notwithstanding, traditional aspects of business such as the importance of face-to-face interaction and the building of trust remain vital; here a potential facilitator for small firms to overcome this barrier comes in the form of Internet-supported intermediaries that attract prospective clients and match them to small firms, whose quality they guarantee. The third is that ultimately the prospect that the Internet holds for internationalizing resource-poor firms is that of international growth; a rudimentary study of 30 Bangalore-based small software firms suggests that this notion holds credence and is worthy of further study, on a larger scale.

The implications of this chapter for academics, managers and policy makers are several. Academics will enhance extant understanding of the role of the Internet in small firm internationalization only through further empirical work. A promising avenue of research is the impact of the Internet on international new ventures. An issue of concern here is establishing causality; Does the Internet encourage firms to be international from inception or are globally minded start-ups able to internationalize more readily as a consequence of the Internet? Longitudinal studies, in particular, will be helpful in unravelling these issues. Entrepreneurs and managers would do well to think holistically about the application of Internet technology to transcend mere visibility-oriented applications and implement efficiency- and intimacy-enhancing applications as well. A related point is that practitioners must think about the portfolio of their network relationships and engage them on an ongoing basis such that greater intimacy results in a greater proclivity for social capital to emanate from these relationships and be leveraged. Furthermore, the value of local network relationships should not be overlooked. In terms of policy making, while efforts to broker network relationships for internationalizing small firms are underway in many parts of the world, policy makers will do well to facilitate a more sophisticated understanding of types of social capital (e.g. bonding *and* bridging; foreign *and* local) and their potential role in internationalization; further, efforts must be made to educate small firms on how the Internet can be productively used to foster not merely visibility but also efficiency and intimacy among network relationships. The onus is on the users of Internet technology to maximally utilize its potential.

Appendix

Source of secondary data: The National Association of Software and Service Companies (Nasscom) is the leading software industry body in India. Nasscom's directories constitute the most reliable source of secondary information about member-companies, which includes:

- Number of employees
- Year of founding
- Total revenue
- International revenue
- Profile – technological capabilities
- Indian and overseas contact details

Measure for market knowledge: Based on the fact that the global market for knowledge-intensive industries like software tend to be concentrated in the Triad markets of North America, Western Europe and Japan (Berry *et al.* 2002), a score from 1 to 7 was calculated for each firm based on its list of foreign markets by assigning 2 points each for the three Triad regions and 1 point for the rest of the world.

Measure for knowledge intensity: Based on the profile of technological capability from the Nasscom directory, a judgemental score from 1 to 7 was computed for the knowledge intensity of each firm. Evidence of strong technical expertise was awarded 2 points; platform availability, 1 point; services offered, 1 point; software products, 2 points and software quality, 1 point.

Measure for social capital: The firm's current Web site was content analyzed for evidence of advisors, customers, partners and alliances; where the evidence was high, a judgemental score of 7 was assigned, where moderate, a score of 4 was assigned and where small or non-existent, a score of 1 was assigned.

Measure for Internet usage: The firm's current Web site was used as a proxy for the firm's Internet usage. A score from 1 to 7 was assigned such that lower scores were given to brochure-ware-type Web sites and higher scores were given for evidence of interactivity and the potential to leverage network relationships (through Intra-/Extranets). A score of 1 was awarded in the absence of a Web site, 2 for a brochure Web site of limited design appeal, 3 for a brochure Web site that was well designed, 5 for a Web site with rudimentary evidence of being database driven, 6 for a well-designed, database-driven site and 7 for a Web site with access to an Intra- or Extranet.

Part III

Future research directions

9 MNC social capital

Prashantham, S. and McNaughton, R.B. (2006) 'Facilitating links between MNC Subsidiaries and SMEs: The Scottish Technology and Collaboration (STAC) Initiative', *International Business Review*, 15: 447–462.

Abstract

Multinational subsidiaries constitute a potential source of social capital for small- and medium-sized enterprises (SMEs) that can help in the internationalization process. Such social capital is particularly valuable because it is a form of bridging (socially heterogeneous), rather than bonding (socially homogenous), social capital, and could therefore potentially lead to new information, ideas and opportunities. However, even in the best situations, limits on information exchange and trust hamper collaboration between SMEs and multinational corporation (MNC) subsidiaries. Facilitation by a neutral agency may help in overcoming these barriers. This chapter presents the case of the Scottish Technology and Collaboration (STAC) initiative as an illustration of the facilitation process – comprising architecting, brokering and coaching – and its outcomes, chiefly the formation of social capital, which in turn has the potential to lead to knowledge outcomes and, ultimately, internationalization for the SME. This case reveals important implications for both policy and theories of SME internationalization, especially the need to recognize and lever underutilized sources of social capital.

Introduction

The phenomenon of 'born globals' and more generally the pace and pattern of internationalization by small- and medium-sized enterprises (SMEs) is an important topic at the intersection of research in entrepreneurship (Zahra and George 2002a), international business (Dimitratos and Jones 2005) and strategy (Hitt *et al.* 2001). Of importance in the international entrepreneurship literature is the notion of accessing resources through social capital in networks of relationships (e.g. Johanson and Mattsson 1988; McNaughton and Bell 1999). Indeed, social capital is frequently cited as playing a role in both knowledge creation (Eriksson and Chetty 2003) and accessing international markets (Yli-Renko *et al.* 2002), especially in the context of knowledge-intensive sectors (Sharma and Blomstermo 2003).

A limitation of the extant literature is that *sources* of social capital have received little attention. Different sources may yield different types of social capital – for instance, bonding (from socially homogeneous ties) or bridging (from socially heterogeneous ties) social capital (Davidsson and Honig 2003; O'Brien *et al.* 2005). Putnam (2000: 22) asserts that 'of all the dimensions along which forms of social capital vary, perhaps the most important is the distinction between *bridging* (or inclusive) and *bonding* (or exclusive)'. Bridging ties may foster novel ideas, knowledge and opportunities that are valuable to internationalizing SMEs; yet, they tend to be geographically distant and difficult to access (McEvily and Zaheer 1999). However, certain ties may be *local yet bridging* in nature for SMEs – such as ties with local multinational corporation (MNC) subsidiaries – that appear to be overlooked by researchers (and perhaps practitioners) who focus on network relationships between SMEs rather than between SMEs and large MNCs (Etemad *et al.* 2001).

Research from the perspective of MNC subsidiaries finds that subsidiaries tap into rich local networks such as those that locate within industrial clusters (Birkinshaw and Hood 2000) and disseminate locally assimilated knowledge within the wider enterprise (Moore and Birkinshaw 1998). These characteristics are especially associated with 'metanationals' that actively leverage local resources to global advantage (Doz *et al.* 2001).

The thesis of this chapter is that relationships between SMEs and the local subsidiaries of MNCs are bridging (yet local) ties that have considerable potential to yield social capital benefits for knowledge-intensive SMEs. However, bridging social capital is, by definition, more difficult to develop in comparison to bonding social capital. Moreover, limitations of time and resource may result in SMEs under-investing in social capital. Therefore, public intervention is often desirable to promote relationships that can contribute to the growth and internationalization of local firms (McNaughton and Bell 2001).

A case study of the Scottish Technology and Collaboration (STAC) illustrates this argument. STAC facilitates relationships between local SMEs and subsidiaries of MNCs, *creating social capital* that SMEs can lever as part of their internationalization process. The chapter proceeds by reviewing literature pertaining to SME internationalization, MNC subsidiaries and formation of social capital between firms. Subsequent sections describe the method employed and the findings of the case study. The final section presents conclusions and their implications for future research, practice and policy.

Literature

SME internationalization: a social capital perspective

The dominant view in SME internationalization points to the importance of knowledge; SMEs leverage their technological and market knowledge to expand into international markets (Autio 2005; Johanson and Vahlne 1977; Oviatt and McDougall 1994; Prashantham 2005; Zahra 2005). Firm resources and the role of the entrepreneur are vital influences on the accumulation of knowledge. But, consistent with the view that knowledge creation is a social process (Nahapiet and Ghoshal 1998) are external networks. Unsurprisingly, there is a strong tradition of network-oriented perspectives on internationalization (Coviello and Munro 1997; Johanson and Mattsson 1988; Johanson and Vahlne 1992, 2003; McNaughton and Bell 1999, 2001).

Indeed, inter-organizational relationships (IORs) are the focus of management research in a variety of contexts. Barringer and Harrison (2000) provide an instructive overview of a range of theoretical lenses through which IORs have been studied: transaction cost economics, resource dependence, strategic choice, stakeholder theory, organizational learning and institutional theory. They, however, encourage 'blending the theoretical paradigm' in future IOR research to combine some of the above approaches (Barringer and Harrison 2000: 382). More recently, social capital theory has emerged as a useful perspective from which to examine IORs (Adler and Kwon 2002), including in the context of internationalization (e.g. Yli-Renko *et al.* 2002; see also McNaughton and Bell 1999). By social capital, we mean, 'the sum of the actual and potential resources embedded within, available through, and derived from the network of relationships possessed by an individual or a social unit' (Nahapiet and Ghoshal 1998: 243). This perspective combines ideas from at least three of the lenses reviewed by Barringer and Harrison (2000), namely, resource dependence theory, strategic choice and organizational learning, but particularly the latter.

Social capital facilitates the creation and acquisition of knowledge (Nahapiet and Ghoshal 1998). While networks or IORs can be a source of international opportunity (e.g. trade leads or repeat business in a new market) (Bell 1997; Coviello and Munro 1997), they are often a conduit of vital new information and resources that lead to enhanced knowledge, and thereby internationalization (McNaughton and Bell 1999; Yli-Renko *et al.* 2002). Thus, social capital facilitates learning that results in internationalization (Autio *et al.* 2000). In this regard, a useful concept to consider is absorptive capacity – a dynamic capability to acquire, assimilate, adapt and apply knowledge (Zahra and George 2002b). Lane and Lubatkin (1998) suggest that absorptive capacity within a dyad is relative in nature. Firms' knowledge exchanges – interactive learning – are more effective when there is commonality in their basic knowledge bases, compensation practices and research communities. O'Dwyer and O'Flynn (2005: 402) note, 'firms tend to establish alliances with other firms where they have overlapping technological capabilities'. Interactions in dyadic relationships influence both parties (Lane and Lubatkin 1998), although learning is not necessarily symmetrical between them as their strategic intents and learning capabilities may not be matched (Inkpen 2000; O'Dwyer and O'Flynn 2005). Thus, SMEs and MNCs would not necessarily have reason to interact given the disparities in their capabilities, implying that bridging social capital, in general, does not form easily and, yet, can be very useful to firm learning and growth (McEvily and Zaheer 1999).

Bridging social capital and SME internationalization: the role of MNC subsidiaries

While there is a tradition of interpreting SME internationalization from a network perspective (which has recently drawn on social capital theory), the extant literature pays little attention to the source of social capital (Brown and McNaughton 2003). Much of the literature on this topic focuses on networks of relationships between SMEs (Barclay and Porter 2005; Coviello and Munro 1997; Cubillo and Cerviño 2004; Lin and Zhang 2005; McNaughton and Bell 1999, 2001; Narula 2004). However, ties with large firms are important in terms of both practice and theory, as they are a potential source of bridging (as opposed to bonding) social capital (Putnam 2000).

Bonding social capital, 'brings together people who are like one another in important aspects (ethnicity, age, gender, social class, etc.)' (Putnam and Goss 2002: 11). From the perspective of SMEs, firm size is an important bonding dimension and as noted above, SME networks are not uncommon. Forming bonding social capital is relatively easy. It is likely that smaller firms share similar aspirations and challenges, which enhance cognitive simpatico (Lane and Lubatkin 1998). Bridging social capital arises from ties that link otherwise disparate networks and broker non-redundant information, while bonding ties link similar firms and networks, thus sharing considerable redundant information (McEvily and Zaheer 1999). Bridging social capital thus holds considerable value to firms.

In making the conceptual distinction between bonding and bridging social capital, we recognize that firms may possess combinations of both types. We would expect social capital types to have differential effects on internationalization outcomes since 'bridging and bonding social capital are good for different things' (Putnam 2000: 363). Also, in reality since most forms of social capital are a blend of bridging and bonding social capital, it is possible to identify relevant dimensions (e.g. firm size) and establish whether social capital is predominantly bonding or bridging (Davidsson and Honig 2003). Thus, on the dimension of firm size, large firms constitute a potential (though overlooked) source of bridging social capital (Etemad *et al.* 2001).

Moreover, Coviello and Munro (1997) observed a tendency among SMEs to look overseas for relationships to further their internationalization objectives, rather than thinking about first leveraging relationships with other local firms. Given the utility of bridging social capital, it is interesting to note that bridging ties are associated with spatial dispersion, not proximity (McEvily and Zaheer 1999). We make the counterintuitive suggestion here that some local ties can also be a source of bridging social capital.

The local multinational subsidiary is a potential source of local, yet bridging, social capital (Etemad *et al.* 2001; O'Dwyer and O'Flynn 2005). Birkinshaw *et al.* (2005: 228) note:

> as subsidiaries develop resources and capabilities of their own, they take on additional responsibilities – tapping into new ideas and opportunities in the

> local market, interacting with other actors in the local environment, and building unique capabilities on which the rest of the MNC can draw.

This is more likely to occur when subsidiaries are cluster based, entrepreneurial and knowledge oriented. Cluster-based subsidiaries make greater strategic contributions to the parent company and are a useful conduit for the transfer of skills and capabilities (Birkinshaw and Hood 2000). In addition, cluster development may be a tool to attract foreign direct investment (FDI) (Young *et al.* 1994), and clusters and subsidiaries can benefit from each other (Enright 2000). Entrepreneurial subsidiaries similarly have the potential to enhance worldwide learning capabilities of MNCs and achieve 'glocalization' (Birkinshaw 1997). Finally, knowledge-oriented subsidiaries are often concerned with assimilating and transferring valuable knowledge to other parts of the MNC (Doz *et al.* 2001; Moore and Birkinshaw 1998). These three characteristics – cluster based, entrepreneurial and knowledge oriented – are by no means mutually exclusive, and the probability of overlap is high.

Relatively little attention is paid by established streams of literature to collaboration between SMEs and MNC subsidiaries. There are a few relevant studies in the context of Asian countries that are both important destinations for FDI and where social capital is a defining characteristic of business culture (e.g. Hitt *et al.* 2002). For example, Zhou and Xin (2003: 133) studied the Zhongguancun IT cluster in Beijing. They found that the 'relationship between MNCs and local firms can also be interdependent even though it is hierarchical', and cite the example of China's largest accounting software firm, Ulsoft, being able to target an untapped niche (namely, the SME market for enterprise-wide resource planning (ERP) software) in collaboration with Oracle's local subsidiary. In another example, Prashantham (2004b) studied the Bangalore software cluster. He found little evidence of collaboration between MNC subsidiaries and local SMEs, but reports the case of Mitoken, a spin-off company from Motorola's local software operations, which actively collaborates with and leverages social capital from the 'parent', that is, Motorola India. Chew and Yeung (2001) in a Singaporean study found that MNC subsidiaries and SMEs enjoy mutual benefits from collaboration, with the latter's main contribution being their local knowledge. These relationships required proactive effort on the part of SMEs and facilitation by 'local institutions' that 'create an atmosphere for inter-firm cooperation' (Chew and Yeung 2001: 445). Such collaboration, it would then appear, will likely require the lowering of the substantial barriers to the development of bridging social capital that seem to exist between these sets of firms, as seen below.

Generating bridging social capital: the need for intervention

There are a variety of barriers that prevent the formation of bridging social capital. These include a lack of visibility, efficiency and intimacy within networks (Prashantham and Young 2004). *Visibility* refers to awareness of the firm and is important because of the competition in networks for actors' scarce attention and resources (Johanson and Mattsson 1988). When there is a lack of information about actors in a (potential) network, there is low visibility. *Efficiency* refers to transactional competence in carrying out business activities, which may be helpful in mitigating the control exerted by larger and resource-rich actors in inter-firm networks (Chew and Yeung 2001). There is limited efficiency when there is a lack of processes to facilitate interaction and transactions. *Intimacy* refers to a deeper understanding of a firm's goals and resources by other actors, and is of potential utility in allowing greater coherence in the firm's activities and progress (McNaughton and Bell 1999; Spence 2004). A lack of intimacy often follows from a lack of trust. Thus, without high levels of visibility, efficiency and intimacy in local networks, SMEs struggle to engage with larger actors, including MNC subsidiaries. In other words, there are significant barriers because of lack of information, processes and trust. These barriers are particularly problematic in relation to asymmetrical ties, that is, IORs between dissimilar actors (e.g. small and large firms), which although potentially mutually beneficial (Narula 2004), are often faced with problems of ambiguity and inter-cultural differences at the interface (Doz 1988).

There is a substantial literature in sociology showing how small firms cooperate within trusting networks (e.g. Uzzi's (1997) study of textile companies in New York). However, these often tend to be in closely knit geographic communities, with family or other ties. These studies illustrate some of the advantages that can come from networking, but also a tendency for SMEs to focus on bonding – rather than bridging – social capital. Thus, a further problem, notwithstanding examples to the contrary, is that SMEs are known to under-invest in social capital, especially bridging social capital. A number of studies confirm this assumption. For example, Curran *et al.* (1993) found that small firms shunned 'voluntary relationships', and made little use of networking even to overcome problems that threatened the survival of the firm. Curran *et al.* suggest that this is because of the independent attitude of entrepreneurs, coupled with the time constraints created by having to deal with many day-to-day management problems. In addition, the entrepreneurs studied were sometimes fearful of outside interference, loss of control and the potential for local competitors to gain inside knowledge. In another example, Human and Provan (1997) compared firms in two relatively large networks with a control sample of 'market firms' and found that market firms made only minimal use of inter-firm relationships. Managers explained this to be due to limited time, no perceived need and fear of losing proprietary information.

The same considerations that inhibit network formation also mitigate the development of mechanisms for co-ordination within networks. Namely, the benefits of co-ordination are difficult for an individual firm to appropriate, and to achieve collective benefits, firms must give up some autonomy and call on uncommon managerial skills (i.e. managing between firms rather than within them). This is particularly difficult for small firms with few slack resources and for entrepreneurs who have limited experience outside their own firm. The presence of economic development policies aimed at brokering hard networks of small firms is evidence that they under-invest in social capital (McNaughton and Bell 1999).

Thus, public policy intervention is often required to compensate for SMEs' own under-investment in social capital. Moreover, in the case of asymmetric inter-firm ties – such as between SMEs and MNC subsidiaries – there are significant barriers to be overcome, as discussed previously. Little is known, however, about measures that effectively deal with these barriers and their theoretical implications. Public programmes have long sought to enhance the export success of SMEs through direct intervention, and these have been widely studied (Alvarez 2004; Brown and McNaughton 2003; McNaughton and Bell 1999, 2001). Other policy measures by local government agencies that may indirectly facilitate internationalization include increased access to venture capital, science parks and new venture incubators (Collinson 2000). However, little is known about policy measures that could facilitate the formation of asymmetrical inter-firm ties and, thereby, the generation of bridging social capital. Bridging social capital, in turn, facilitates knowledge creation, which may eventually lead to internationalization. The research reported in this chapter addresses this gap.

Method

Our starting point was secondary data on established information and communication technology (ICT) clusters in both developed and developing countries such as in Bangalore, Beijing, Scotland, Silicon Valley, Singapore and Stockholm. We contacted ten academics and/or policy makers associated with internationalization activities in Australia, Canada, China, India, Ireland, Sweden, the United Kingdom and the United States. Enquiries with these experts identified only one major initiative – the STAC initiative – that explicitly targets relationships between SMEs and MNC subsidiaries. The discovery of STAC was the consequence of a conversation with the then Deputy Chairman of Scottish Enterprise, which is Scotland's main economic development agency. Birkinshaw (2000) notes that Scottish Enterprise, while welcoming foreign investment to set up assembly units in Scotland, is keener to attract R&D-related investment.

Despite the drawback of a single case study (Yin 1994), taking such an approach is appropriate in this instance given the uniqueness and rareness of the phenomenon. Apart from the fact that most policy initiatives focus on fostering relationships between SMEs, the uniqueness of STAC in large measure stems from the strong mutual learning orientation of *both* the SMEs and multinational subsidiaries that are involved. This is quite different from other instances of MNC–SME engagement that are purely transactional, that is, merely a supplier–customer relationship (O'Dwyer and O'Flynn 2005). A single-case approach has precedents in the literature both in terms of clusters (e.g. Birkinshaw's (2000) study of the Stockholm IT cluster and Enright's (2000) study of the Hong Kong financial services cluster, and of interventionist efforts (e.g. McNaughton and Bell's (1999) study of a networking scheme in New Zealand and Prashantham and Young's (2004) study of an international business intermediary in the Indian software industry. The Scottish IT industry provides a suitable setting for the present study. It contains subsidiaries where all three conditions (entrepreneurial, cluster based and knowledge oriented) overlap in several cases (Birkinshaw *et al.* 2005). One such example is Sun Microsystems Scotland, which was instrumental in the creation of STAC. Scottish public policy has long been concerned with increasing knowledge transfer from what are perceived to be 'lightly embedded' subsidiaries (Collinson 2000), and hence the STAC initiative is relevant to the overall business environment in which it exists.

An overview of the STAC initiative is presented based upon ten interviews with managers involved in the programme conducted between February and November 2004. A daylong participant-observation exercise at the STAC offices in mid-November permitted detailed interaction with the staff members. This approach is similar to Spradley's (1979) ethnographic interviewing technique, which is not ethnography in the strictest sense, but seeks to combine interviews and observation to obtain insight into the phenomenon under study. In addition to interviews with the STAC staff, five interviews were conducted with relevant non-STAC informants in Scotland (e.g. software entrepreneurs not involved in STAC and economic developmental professionals) to corroborate the views expressed by the STAC-related informants. We were also given access to consultancy reports from two different and independent sources on STAC's progress and prospects. Confidentiality agreements preclude referring to those reports in any detail. There was substantial consistency between these reports and the data we collected about STAC. In addition, secondary data were analysed including presentations, reports and case studies of current collaborations.

Findings

The origin of STAC

The origin of the STAC initiative can be traced to a suggestion made in 2002 by Gordon Cameron, then an executive with Sun Microsystems Scotland and a director on the board of the software trade body, ScotlandIS. Cameron, himself a Scot, voiced a desire to engage meaningfully with local innovative SMEs (also represented on the ScotlandIS board) with a view to combining complementary capabilities and achieving mutually beneficial outcomes such as new product development and innovation.

This suggestion was well received, and a feasibility study was conducted during the first half of 2003. This study indicated widespread support for a collaboration-facilitating initiative, but also highlighted the existence of barriers, in terms of limitations of information, processes and trust. Scottish Enterprise and ScotlandIS granted funding for a pilot project in June 2003, and Minister for Enterprise Jim Wallace formally launched STAC in November 2003. Wallace summarized the intended benefits:

> Smaller companies at the cutting edge of ideas will benefit by working with larger companies and being able to access new markets. Previously they might have had difficulty attracting the attention of the global players. The larger companies can benefit by knowing which companies in Scotland have the ideas they need, where previously they might have had to shop further afield. All benefit from a greater awareness of what is happening elsewhere in the Scottish software sector and from sharing ideas
>
> (Scottish Executive 2003)

Within the first year, 270 members (of which 25 per cent are ScotlandIS members) signed up as STAC members – though a much smaller number have actually engaged in building 'stacs' (i.e. actual collaborative programs).

STAC's approach

STAC's approach is based on the notion of 'virtual enterprise' where firms collaborate to exploit a business opportunity by focusing on different aspects of the value chain (Katzy and Schuh 1998). In the specific case of the STAC initiative, the approach involves the compilation of so-called 'stacs'. A 'stac' is a group of companies that jointly work towards an innovative outcome, usually a new product offering. A 'stac' typically involves a 'pillar' MNC subsidiary and two SMEs. These actors pool complementary resources and capabilities to develop, typically, new product offerings. An early learning outcome for STAC was the utility of identifying and involving a potential customer in the collaborative effort.

STAC's intervention entails three key activities – 'architecting', brokering and coaching. *Architecting* is the first stage and typically begins when an initial approach is made by a company (be it an SME or an MNC) with a new product idea. STAC's 'architects' (two full-time staff members) identify the complementary skills needed from other actors and specific potential candidates from its database of organizations. *Brokering* is the next step and is undertaken by the architects (although previously this was outsourced to a networking organization). Brokering involves introducing potential collaborators and facilitating a process of determining a mutually satisfactory work arrangement (e.g. pertaining to intellectual property), often with the help of external legal experts. *Coaching* is included in the mix of activities based on the notion that technological compatibility is no guarantee for interpersonal harmony. A specialist coach (also a former software entrepreneur) is therefore part of the team.

STAC's outcomes

In its first year (November 2003–November 2004), the initiative identified eight 'stacs'. These had made different rates of progress. Two were designated as 'fast-track' stacs given their rapid and substantial progress. In both cases, the MNC subsidiary involved is Sun Microsystems' Scottish unit, from which the idea for STAC had originated in the first place. However, it is also clear that Sun's involvement is not explained by the idiosyncratic behaviour of an individual, since both of these stacs developed after Cameron had left the organization. Thus, Sun's participation in the stacs seems to reflect organizational characteristics – such as its embeddedness within the cluster, entrepreneurial orientation and knowledge intensity.

One of these fast-track stacs is briefly described to illustrate the potential outcomes of the programme. This stac involved two Scottish SMEs, one with expertise in oceanic research and the other, in wireless software. These two firms decided (without external facilitation) to work together on a solution to enhance accuracy in product tracking for the Scottish seafood industry. However, they lacked a technology that could enhance the solution, namely, radio frequency identification (RFID). Sun Microsystems Scotland possessed RFID technology. Through STAC, a stac was 'architected' and brokered involving the two SMEs and Sun. The architect of the stac describes their efforts:

> The STAC team highlighted the project as being both extremely innovative and having strong international potential and offered support. STAC brokered the introduction of the two SMEs to a major technology company [i.e., Sun Microsystems] with an internationally renowned RFID capability. STAC team members worked closely with the three companies to build trust and develop a strong collaborative relationship. STAC subsequently facilitated a working session with one of Scotland's top legal firms who, as STAC partners, contributed time and expertise on potential business, IPR and partnership models to the project.

This stac illustrates a common situation – the SMEs found it relatively easy to engage with each other, but struggled to gain the attention of larger multinational entities. Equally, it is evident that Sun Microsystems in Scotland were actively seeking local innovative companies to work with, but failed to identify the local SMEs on their own.

It is worth highlighting the activities that STAC carried out to facilitate joint product development. Sun's input was manifested in the form of meetings arranged at various points in time in the process, initially bringing together the three companies and subsequently other stakeholders as well, such as a prospective client from the Scottish seafood industry. Additionally, the STAC coach had individual meetings with the three companies in order to understand their respective mindsets and aspirations, which he believed was important if he was to foster trust and collaboration among them. In addition, a session with external input was arranged on possibilities and pitfalls concerning legal arrangements of collaboration, covering issues like ownership of intellectual property. Our non-STAC respondents gave us the impression that STAC generally exhibited proactiveness in arranging such inputs and the meetings referred to above.

In this case, the STAC worked to increase the visibility of the two SMEs. A

Sun Microsystems executive commented: 'STAC … enabl[ed] Sun to gain *visibility* of, and access to, innovative Scottish SMEs' [emphasis added]. There was a similar enhancement of efficiency, brought about by legal advice on working arrangements. The managing director of one of the SMEs commented: 'STAC provided our companies with a top class legal session that helped us cut through the complexities and multiple options involved to suggest workable strategies'. The specific intended outcome of the collaboration was a new product offering, with the clear intent of taking it to international markets. Sun Microsystems Scotland, in turn, benefited from an opportunity to demonstrate and improve its technological capability as it sought an enhanced mandate for RFID research from its parent company. As of November 2004 when this study was concluded, it was unclear whether either of these outcomes would be achieved. The strategic intent and potential for these outcomes – through the formation of social capital – could, however, be clearly seen.

Discussion

Our synthesis of the extant literature suggests that barriers exist that impede the formation of asymmetric ties such as those between MNC subsidiaries and SMEs. Such barriers relate to a lack of information (low visibility), processes (limited efficiency) and trust (absence of intimacy). STAC's interventionist activities of architecting, brokering and coaching address these gaps. They reflect differences from the creation of hard networks of SMEs (McNaughton and Bell 1999) where the issue primarily addressed is under-investment in social capital rather than the aforementioned barriers per se, which hamper the formation of asymmetrical inter-firm ties, such as those between SMEs and MNC subsidiaries.

Overcoming a lack of information

The architecting process addresses a macro-level information gap – regarding what other capabilities are *available* in the region in the first place. Professional in-groups often create bonding social capital that 'blinkers' actors who, as a consequence, have limited awareness of other fields of expertise (Putnam 2000). This is particularly so if these fields comprise dissimilar organizational entities. Thus, in the Scottish IT industry, STAC's architecting educates actors about other capabilities that can be found in the region. In a similar vein, the architecting function overcomes related informational gaps by identifying specific organizations with relevant and complementary capabilities. The brokering function overcomes somewhat more specific barriers through the provision of technical information of what needs to be done in operational or legal terms in order to establish a collaborative arrangement. Finally, coaching may overcome intra-team information barriers – once a stac is formed – that allows greater visibility for the specific individuals involved in the product development project.

Overcoming a lack of processes

Architecting addresses an extant process-related barrier, namely, that of *assembly* of a set of actors that are prospective collaborators. In the case study, this is achieved through entry into STAC's membership fold. Brokering addresses more specific process issues such as the precise nature of the collaborative arrangement as well as management of the consequences of collaboration – in the case of STAC, mainly intellectual property. Thus, skilful brokering can be useful in facilitating more efficient interfaces between MNC subsidiaries and SMEs (Doz 1988). Coaching also addresses important process issues since merely bringing together actors with complementary goals and capabilities will not by itself result in successful alliances (Inkpen 2000). Coaching helps to develop soft skills such as teamwork. This could facilitate effective processes of teamwork for the product team *and* cross-functional working with the personnel subsequently involved in internationalization.

Overcoming a lack of trust

Architecting brings together, at a more macro-level, 'trustworthy' actors, given STAC's non-partisan image. Perhaps more pertinently, brokering ensures this to a greater extent, at a more specific level, through the quality assurance involved in this process; STAC 'brokers' alliances only after ensuring actors' bona fides. The coaching process facilitates direct and honest communication and empathy, thereby fostering reciprocity and trust. Trust is an important hallmark of social capital, which in turn facilitates the creation and acquisition of knowledge (Nahapiet and Ghoshal 1998; Yli-Renko *et al.* 2001). Of course, while social capital is often treated at the inter-organizational level, in reality social capital arises from the interactions of *individuals*. The coaching process – which is perhaps the most unique and innovative aspect of STAC's intervention – helps to improve this very aspect through improved communication and empathy, as noted earlier. This discussion is summarized in Table 9.1.

It would seem that STAC's three-fold approach has a dual impact on the relationship between social capital (generated among the stac collaborators) and knowledge outcomes (in this case, product development). These outcomes, in turn, have the potential to lead to internationalization. The first impact pertains to the development of social capital. All the three processes of architecting, brokering and coaching seem relevant through the lowering of barriers that impede the formation of network ties, as just noted. The second impact, we argue, pertains to the development of relative absorptive capacity (Lane and Lubatkin 1998). Absorptive capacity, as seen earlier, is the dynamic capability to acquire, assimilate, adapt and apply knowledge (Zahra and George 2002b). It is a key factor in the occurrence of organizational learning in the context of IORs (Barringer and Harrison 2000) where there is the intention, willingness and compatibility to learn (O'Dwyer and O'Flynn 2005). In particular, the activities along the 'diagonal' (top left to bottom right) in Table 9.1 are likely to be particularly

Table 9.1 STAC's activities – overcoming barriers to social capital formation

STAC activity	*Lack of information (visibility)*	*Lack of processes (efficiency)*	*Lack of trust (intimacy)*	*Synthesis*
Architecting	Overcomes broader information gaps of capabilities available within the region	Overcomes broader processual voids through a set of potential collaborators (via STAC's membership)	Overcomes broader trust issues through STAC's non-partisan, credible image	In general deals with barriers at a more macro (i.e. regional) level
Brokering	Overcomes more specific firm-related information gaps in terms of operational aspects of collaboration	Overcomes more specific firm-related processual voids through legal expertise/arrangements	Overcomes more specific firm-related trust issues through quality assurance	In general deals with barriers at a more meso (i.e. inter-organizational) level
Coaching	Overcomes information gaps at a more micro level (e.g. within an inter-firm project team)	Overcomes processual voids amongst collaborators through 'soft' skills (e.g. teamwork)	Overcomes trust issues within 'stacs' by facilitating honest and direct communication	In general deals with barriers at a more micro (i.e. intra-'stac' or collaborative team) level

relevant in fostering absorptive capacity. In other words, absorptive capacity is enhanced by (a) the role of architecting in overcoming informational barriers, (b) the role of brokering in overcoming process-related barriers and (c) the role of coaching in overcoming trust-related barriers. Of course, the ultimate outcome expected from the process is SME internationalization, through leverage of the ensuing knowledge creation (particularly in the tangible form of a new product). As noted, as of November 2004, it was too early to gauge the realization of these potential outcomes. We recognize this as a limitation of the study. Nevertheless, here we have an insightful illustration of a public policy initiative that recognized a source of (MNC subsidiaries), and sought to develop, local bridging social capital with the clear intent of facilitating international entrepreneurship among local SMEs.

Conclusions

In seeking to shed some light on an underutilized (and under-researched) source of social capital for knowledge-intensive SMEs, this article highlights three points. First, MNC subsidiaries are potentially a source of social capital that may lead to desirable internationalization outcomes. Second, barriers (in terms of a lack of information, processes and trust) to the creation and advantage of such social capital exist. Third, credible facilitative intervention – characterized by 'architecting', brokering and coaching – can lower these barriers, as seen from the example of Sun Microsystems and the two SMEs.

Despite the exploratory nature of this study, some useful implications for theory and practice can be drawn. The study suggests a number of research propositions that future research could fruitfully test. These include the notion that multinational subsidiaries can be a source of social capital to SMEs and that intervention in terms of architecting, brokering and coaching lead to social capital and strengthen the likelihood of knowledge outcomes through greater absorptive capacity, which in turn potentially leads to internationalization. It would also be useful for further exploratory research to be carried out to shed more light on SME–MNC subsidiary relationships. This would include further exploring evidence of the incidence of such ties (including unearthing more examples of successful and less-successful case studies), the barriers to establishing these linkages and measures – by both practitioners and policy makers – that seem to overcome these barriers. Our study is a modest effort to highlight some of the basic insights but we anticipate that much more exploratory and theory-testing work can be undertaken quite fruitfully in this overlooked aspect of international entrepreneurship.

International entrepreneurship scholars have called for the broadening and nuancing of the research agenda (Dimitratos and Jones 2005; Oviatt and McDougall 2005b; Zahra 2005) as it moves beyond its first decade (1994–2004). In keeping with its eclectic nature, international entrepreneurship research could fruitfully draw upon ideas from international business and economic geography on locational effects (Buckley and Ghauri 2004), and from research at the intersection of strategy and entrepreneurship on the role of social capital in small/new ventures' growth (Florin *et al.* 2003). Combining these ideas, the effects of a small/new firm's *local* social capital on early internationalization and performance merit closer attention. This is particularly true when such social capital is bridging in nature, as recognized by entities such as STAC. Thus, cluster-related initiatives and efforts to bridge small/new firms with valuable sources of social capital, such as MNC subsidiaries, could give rise to born globals. Understanding such phenomena better can enhance extant understanding of born globals and help broaden the international entrepreneurship agenda.

The recognition that MNC subsidiaries constitute a source of social capital to local knowledge-intensive SMEs is of considerable theoretical significance to international business research, but also has useful practical implications. Normatively, entrepreneurs and managers should be encouraged to proactively recognize and leverage sources of social capital that may be underutilized. Such efforts, and policy measures to facilitate this, may be most effective when undertaken within knowledge-intensive clusters. Even in such settings, however, concerted efforts by all actors are necessary. Interventionist efforts need to establish themselves as neutral and honest brokers. Also, a longer time horizon may be necessary before the impact of these interventions can be properly gauged, given that knowledge outcomes (e.g. new product development) are likely to mediate international entrepreneurship. This calls for persistence and patience on the part of practitioners and policy makers. However, there is little doubt that ties between SMEs and MNC subsidiaries hold importance, not just in already thriving business settings but also, potentially, for wider economic development. A recent UN report urges policy makers in developing countries to 'develop linkages with multinational and large domestic companies to nurture smaller companies' (UNDP 2004: 3). Initiatives such as STAC can be vitally important in this regard.

10 Future research directions

This volume's introductory chapter highlighted the significance of small-firm internationalization as a natural domain of strategic entrepreneurship, the core idea of which is that 'firms need to be simultaneously entrepreneurial and strategic' (Hitt *et al.* 2001: 488). The subsequent eight chapters have sought to make a modest collective contribution to extant understanding of how small firms internationalize resourcefully. As noted, network relationships (the study of which is also an important domain of strategic entrepreneurship) can greatly facilitate small-firm internationalization. This idea has been the focus of the volume, comprising both conceptual pieces and the empirical papers based on case study research in the Bangalore software industry. Despite the efforts that this volume represents and the scholarly contributions of many (e.g. Coviello 2006; McNaughton and Bell 1999; Yli-Renko *et al.* 2002), there is still scope for more research in the future that would enhance understanding of this subject and, in particular, deepen linkages to other domains of strategic entrepreneurship. This concluding chapter offers some thoughts on two interrelated future research directions: (1) the utility of integrating internationalization and innovation research with respect to small firms and (2) the potential role of MNCs as a source of social capital. These are discussed in relation to three key themes of this volume:

1 the development of social capital;
2 the leverage of social capital;
3 the management of portfolios of social capital.

Research Direction 1: integrating innovation and internationalization research

As noted earlier in this volume, there is an important interplay between resources (especially knowledge) and networks (social capital). There continues to be great scope to study the role of resources, learning and networks in innovation (e.g. Yli-Renko *et al.* 2001) and internationalization (e.g. Yli-Renko *et al.* 2002). A key thrust in this call for future research concerns the potentially reciprocal relationships between innovation and internationalization. The broad inter-

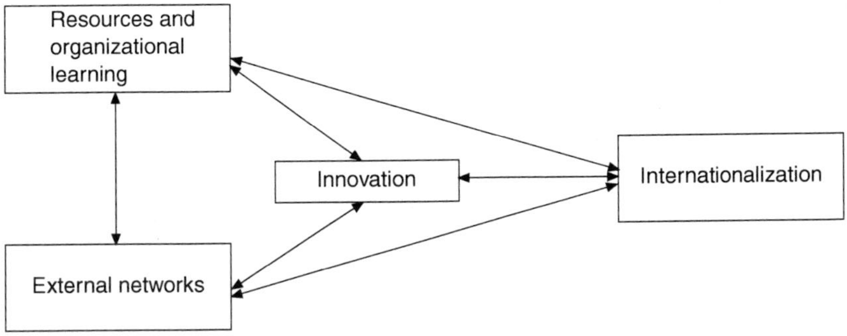

Figure 10.1 An integrated perspective of internationalization research.

relationships between various domains of strategic entrepreneurship are depicted in Figure 10.1.

Developing social capital

While useful insights on the development of social capital have emerged from research on networks and internationalization (including the studies in this volume), clearly more needs to be done to understand *how* internationalizing small firms develop social capital. For instance, little is known about which networking *behaviours* are most strongly associated with achieving greater visibility. Another issue that merits attention is whether social capital types and networking strategies have substitution effects. Also, it would be of interest to understand the nature of knowledge that lies at the core of firms' capability to replenish social capital stocks. Johanson and Vahlne (2006) suggest that social capital and knowledge co-evolve, which implies that inasmuch as social capital leads to knowledge (Nahapiet and Ghoshal 1998; Yli-Renko *et al.* 2002), knowledge may lead to social capital. If so, then surely more research is required to extend our understanding of how, over time, 'firms learn how to work effectively with partners and build trusting relationships' (Hitt *et al.* 2001: 482).

A related aspect of research concerns the distribution of entrepreneurs and top management teams' attention across different network relationships. Indeed, one of their most scarce resources is their attention (Ocasio 1997). The cultivation of network relationships and social capital calls for the allocation of attention across ties (Granovetter 1973). Little is presently known about how international entrepreneurs prioritize their attention across network relationships. Another issue warranting deeper insight is the role of programmes that seek to foster the development of social capital. Private and public sector efforts (e.g. the initiative discussed in Chapter 9) represent the expenditure of considerable time, money and effort to enable small firms to build social capital. However, little is known about their efficiency, and as such this phenomenon seems undertheorized in the internationalization literature.

Furthermore, in relation to the development of social capital, it could be useful to draw upon economic geography to understand better the links between spatial concentration of industries – which have an impact on innovation (Porter 1998b) – and social capital formation. This could relate both to small firms' local milieu as well as to their sub-national location within international markets. Dimitratos *et al.* (2003) have highlighted the fact that internationalizing small firms increasingly establish a presence in international markets, often via alliances and network governance mechanisms (Oviatt and McDougall 1994), which can lead to improved firm performance (Lu and Beamish 2001). Less appears to be known about *sub-national* location choices within international markets. Location within dynamic clusters in international markets could facilitate the formation of social capital (Birkinshaw and Hood 2000; Inkpen and Tsang 2005). It is also likely, however, that such milieus are characterized by greater competition for other actors' scarce attention, thereby increasing the challenge of gaining visibility within social networks. As such, the role of regional agglomeration in social capital formation for internationalizing small firms merits more scholarly attention in the future.

Leveraging social capital

While the preceding chapters shed light on the useful effects of leveraging social capital actively (rather than passively), a more holistic perspective can be obtained by focusing not merely on internationalization outcomes but also on innovation outcomes. As noted in the introductory chapter, like internationalization, innovation is a naturally occurring domain at the strategy/ entrepreneurship interface (Hitt *et al.* 2001). However, research in these areas has tended to be undertaken in parallel. To illustrate, Yli-Renko *et al.* (2001) found inter-organizational social capital to facilitate innovation outcomes (e.g. new product development) for a sample of 180 British small/new knowledge-intensive firms. Focusing on key customer relationships, they argue: 'By intensifying knowledge-sharing activities, social interaction serves to increase the relative capacity and effectiveness of a young technology-based firm in recognizing and absorbing external knowledge from the key customer' (Yli-Renko *et al.* 2001: 591). Yli-Renko *et al.*'s (2001) study fails to consider how innovation outcomes from social capital in the *domestic* market could lead to *internationalization*. Separately, Yli-Renko *et al.* (2002) studied small/new Finnish knowledge-intensive firms that grew internationally through leveraging inter-firm social capital. Once again, explicit links between innovation and internationalization are not made.

Such parallel studies suggest that it is plausible that social capital could have mutually reinforcing benefits on innovation *and* on internationalization. Social capital in the local milieu could lead to product innovation (Yli-Renko *et al.* 2001), which in turn could allow smaller firms to make globally mobile offerings, leading thereby to rapid and accelerated internationalization (Autio *et al.* 2000). Furthermore, social capital may not only help smaller firms to internationalize, but also new stocks of social capital may arise in international markets as a consequence of internationalization. Social capital gained in international markets could lead to technological learning (Zahra *et al.* 2000), which in turn may strengthen or create product innovation. Prior research appears to have overlooked an *integrative* perspective of innovation and internationalization in the context of smaller firms. Future work could go further to shed light on smaller firms' innovation *and* internationalization activities, especially as innovation and internationalization would seem to be strongly intertwined for internationalizing small knowledge-intensive firms (consider the mini-case in the previous chapter, for example).

Managing social capital portfolios

It was noted in the introductory chapter that the spatial concentration (local/domestic versus foreign/overseas) of network relationships is an important means of categorizing social capital within a small firm's portfolio. Research presented in this volume indicated differential effects of local and foreign network relationships on internationalization (Chapters 6 and 7). Future research should take into account the idea that local networks *do* matter in the context of small-firm internationalization. Another potential area of enquiry relates to the nature of learning associated with different network relationships. For instance, it may be that exploratory learning is more strongly associated with weak ties and exploitative learning with strong ties (Hite and Hesterly 2001). The rationale for this suggestion is that weak ties are associated with greater novelty of information (McEvily and Zaheer 1999) that would be conducive for knowledge exploration. Strong ties, on the other hand, are associated with greater trust, a requisite for the inter-firm collaboration that is often entailed in knowledge exploitation (Yli-Renko *et al.* 2001). As a variant of this idea, it may be that certain types of alliances tend to be formed with strong ties rather than weak ties, and vice versa. Lavie and Rosenkopf (2006), for instance, associate new product development (NPD) alliances with exploration while alliances that are focused on sales, which may be referred to as new business development (NBD) are concerned with exploitation. Linking this to the point made previously, strong ties may be associated with NPD alliances (Yli-Renko *et al.* 2001) and weak ties with NBD alliances (Coviello 2006). Of potential interest would also be research into the behaviour and cognition associated with internationalizing small firms being able to leverage network relationships to simultaneously achieve exploration and exploitation. In other words, future research could fruitfully examine strategic ambidexterity in internationalizing small firms (Lubatkin *et al.* 2006).

The innovation–internationalization relationship

A key point made in advocating a more integrated strategic entrepreneurship perspective in small-firm internationalization research is that more attention ought to be paid to the (potentially reciprocal) relationship between innovation and internationalization. Although it is suggested that 'companies that have internationalized experience economies of scale and have a larger market from which to obtain returns on their innovation' (Hitt *et al.* 2001: 485), relatively little is known about the interplay between innovation and internationalization in the context of the smaller firm.

Innovation may be an antecedent or consequence of internationalization. As an antecedent, there is some ambiguity about the extent to which innovation is associated with internationalization; for example, Bloodgood *et al.* (1996) failed to find a positive relationship between ventures' R&D intensity and extent of internationalization, but Zahra (1996) suggests that internationally oriented smaller firms are inclined to pursue radical innovations aggressively. As an outcome, internationalization is associated with innovation in established MNCs as they have 'incentives to invest in innovation, resources to invest in innovation, and greater returns from innovation' (Hitt *et al.* 1997: 775). The small-firm internationalization literature also indicates that international expansion could lead to useful technological learning outcomes (Zahra *et al.* 2000). More needs to be understood about the causal mechanisms of precisely how technological learning arises through exposure to international markets (Zahra *et al.* 2000) as well as when and how such learning would translate into innovation outcomes. It is also worth highlighting the distinction between incremental and radical innovation and considering the circumstances under which each type constitutes an antecedent or consequence of entrepreneurial internationalization.

As such, paying greater attention to the relationships between innovation and internationalization is pertinent given that other domains in strategic entrepreneurship – notably resources/organizational learning and external networks – are potentially of great relevance to *both* innovation and internationalization (Yli-Renko *et al.* 2001, 2002).

Research Direction 2: the potential role of MNC social capital

Additionally, an interesting notion is that of network relationships that can *span* geographies. An example from the chapter on local network relationships (Chapter 6) relates to the MNC as a source of social capital. This notion was further expanded upon in the previous chapter where a public policy initiative to link small firms with MNC subsidiaries was discussed. Other authors too allude to the possible beneficial outcomes of such links. Acs and Terjesen (2005) describe a mediated route to internationalization for innovative small firms wherein their innovations are absorbed into large MNCs' value chain and, indirectly, deployed on a global scale. It may also be possible for more direct involvement of the smaller firm in its own internationalization while engaging with large MNCs. The appeal of MNCs as a source of social capital[1] lies in the potential for ties to be formed in the small firms' *local* milieu and yet for benefits to accrue in *international* markets as well. The interest in MNCs as a source of social capital lies, at least partially, in the scope it may provide small firms to deal with various tensions and tradeoffs that they must deal with. Three such tensions are discussed below, each relating to the three key themes of developing social capital, leveraging social capital and managing social capital portfolios.

Developing social capital: the overembeddedness trap

As firms develop social capital, they forge an identity for themselves within a network of relationships. It is argued that as these firms' network range, density and centrality increase, and so does their social capital (Coviello 2006). In many ways, the consequences of being embedded within a network are positive; firms' influence, solidarity and information benefits can increase (Adler and Kwon 2002). However, network relationships also have a 'dark side'. One of the key problems is the constraining effects that network relationships may have. Firms that are overly embedded in their social networks may get caught up in a mode of groupthink, a potential problem of which is that they cease to be sufficiently critical in their thinking (Uzzi 1997). Furthermore, overembedded firms are less inclined to behave in a manner that adversely affects the status quo and therefore prefer to engage in incremental rather than radical, entrepreneurial behaviour (Simsek *et al.* 2003). Radical entrepreneurial behaviour, which is more likely to be associated with radical innovation outcomes (Zahra 1996), could lead to competition and friction and may therefore be shunned by the overembedded firm.

Thus, a tension that confronts innovative small firms is a dilemma between getting deeply embedded in a social network – which can result in greater solidarity and support (Adler and Kwon 2002; Granovetter 1973) – and remaining only lightly embedded. Put differently, a tension pertains to how innovative small firms can participate in their social networks without diminishing their propensity for radical entrepreneurial behaviour. Admittedly, not all firms may be conscious of this dilemma or strongly focused on radical entrepreneurial behaviour; indeed, some firms may be content to engage in incremental entrepreneurial behaviour. However, for those small firms and new ventures that are serious about developing technological innovations, they face a dilemma in terms of the extent of the breadth and depth of their network relationships – in other words, about the extent of their embeddedness within inter-firm networks (Simsek *et al.* 2003).

Leveraging social capital: the ambidexterity challenge

It has been argued that effective smaller firms do not passively engage within their inter-firm networks, but rather leverage their social capital actively. In order to leverage their social capital, firms must recognize social capital to be a resource and be able to build trust with other actors (Hitt *et al.* 2001). However, an issue that small firms must consider is to what end they utilize their social capital. As seen, an important benefit of social capital is the creation and acquisition of knowledge – in other words, learning outcomes (Johanson and Vahlne 2006; Nahapiet and Ghoshal 1998; Yli-Renko *et al.* 2002). The learning outcomes may, however, vary in terms of their orientation towards exploitation or exploration (March 1991). Differing learning outcomes (exploitation vs. exploration) may result from the nature of *activities* pursued through inter-firm efforts. Lavie and Rosenkopf (2006) attribute exploitation outcomes to activities concerned with new business development and exploration to new product development efforts. Exploratory innovation (e.g. new product development) is certainly an important dimension for many small knowledge-intensive firms. Such innovation may have been required for international expansion to have been feasible in the first place. Local network relationships may be utilized in the new product development process (Yli-Renko *et al.* 2001). Subsequent activities may be more exploitative in terms of achieving international sales; strategic alliances with actors possessing valuable local knowledge in international markets may be helpful in this regard (Dimitratos *et al.* 2003).

Even after internationalization commences, the imperative for technological innovation does not cease. Ever shortening product life cycles, competitor moves and client feedback – all can put pressure on small firms to continue generating innovations. Thus, internationalization and innovation are ongoing and often concurrent processes, where learning outcomes – both exploitative and exploratory – are constantly required. The tension between exploitation and exploration is well documented in the literature. Both represent important learning outcomes and both are required. As March (2006: 205) asserts, 'Exploitation without exploration leads to stagnation and failure to discover new, useful directions. Exploration without exploitation leads to a cascade of experiments without the development of competence in any of them or discrimination among them'. It is difficult to achieve both simultaneously because these knowledge processes are contradictory (Smith and Tushman 2005). However, firms that are able to achieve ambidexterity consequently achieve superior performance (Lubatkin *et al.* 2006). While firm-specific factors such as top managers' cognition and behaviour (Lubatkin *et al.* 2006; Smith and Tushman 2005) influence firms' ability to balance exploitation and exploration, clearly an additional issue comes into the picture – learning outcomes as a consequence of social capital, as seen.

Managing social capital portfolios: the attention deficiency

It has been noted that firms possess portfolios of network relationships that differ variously – for instance, in terms of intimacy (strong vs. weak ties) or social homogeneity (bonding vs. bridging social capital). It has been argued that geographic proximity (local vs. foreign network relationships) is another relevant dimension in the context of small-firm internationalization. As noted, social capital in both the local milieu and in international markets can lead to innovation outcomes. However, the spatial distribution of network relationships across national borders (local vs. foreign) can be a source of tension, given the limited amount of attention (Cyert and March 1963; Ocasio 1997) that small firms have to devote to the cultivation of network relationships. Despite advances in communication technology that facilitate the nurturing of relationships (see Chapters 4 and 8), choices have to be made in terms of prioritizing attention across network relationships. International travel and face-to-face communication remain important. Entrepreneurs, who bear a great burden in terms of managing social capital as seen in this volume, have finite resources of attention and travel budgets that they must judiciously utilize. From the perspective of innovation, the acquisition of technological knowledge from international markets may require large amounts of attention to be allocated to key relationships (Yli-Renko *et al.* 2001; Zahra *et al.* 2000). The challenge of managing cross-border social capital portfolios is also exacerbated by cross-cultural differences – greater attention may be required when dealing with network relationships where these differences are considerable.

The role of MNC social capital

While scholars tend to focus on internationalization or innovation when studying small and new firms, in reality the firms have to deal with both challenges simultaneously, which leads to certain tensions. Those firms that adopt a strategic entrepreneurship perspective would seek to deal with these issues using 'entrepreneurial action with a strategic perspective' (Hitt *et al.* 2001: 480). With respect to each, the potential role of MNC social capital in alleviating these tensions is briefly considered, with a view to stimulating future research.

In terms of the overembeddedness trap, relationships with local MNC subsidiaries could be a useful antidote. MNC subsidiaries are known to be fleet-footed and lightly embedded (Birkinshaw and Hood 2000) – often to the regret of local policy makers who would prefer their closer involvement with local actors. However, this very attribute of MNC subsidiaries could be a 'blessing in disguise' for small firms; in other words, ties with MNC subsidiaries are likely to be devoid of the intense reciprocity that may characterize other local network relationships (e.g. with other local, small firms). Consequently, smaller firms may be less inhibited from engaging in radical entrepreneurial behaviour (Simsek *et al.* 2003). Indeed, it is likely that MNC partners would encourage such behaviour without feeling threatened by smaller firms that are unlikely to pose direct competition.

In terms of the ambidexterity challenge, MNC social capital provides scope for both exploration (e.g. new product development) and exploitation (e.g. new business development) activities. Subsidiaries of MNCs like IBM and Microsoft offer partnering programmes that cover both of these activities as long as firms use their technology platforms. Initial activities tend to comprise exploratory innovation, that is, new product development; resources that small firms could tap into include free software and free advice from the MNCs' in-house competency centres. Subsequently, MNCs are often willing to promote the technological offering worldwide, that is, to engage in exploitation (new business development), especially if there are derivative sales for its own technology platform (e.g. an operating system). In reality, this of course means that a small firm would compete with several other firms that sign up for the same partnership programme. Moreover, not every subsidiary or sub-unit of the MNC may be equally cooperative or interested in assisting small firms. Nonetheless, at least in principle, frameworks are in place for partnering activities that cover both exploration and exploitation. In other words, MNC social capital can be a vehicle for ambidexterity.

In terms of small firms' attention deficiency, the MNC provides the scope for both local and international relationships by virtue of itself being a globally dispersed multi-unit network. The small firm may have to take the initiative to become well known within the local subsidiary in the first instance and, in due course, gain visibility at the MNC's headquarters and/or other subsidiaries. Nonetheless, the *possibility* exists that the MNC can provide an efficient focus for small firms' attention, thereby offsetting the burden of allocating scarce attention across milieus owing to its inherent spatial dispersion.

Thus internationalizing small firms have to cope with various tensions – which may interact and overlap with each other, as evident from the above discussion – as they develop and leverage their social capital portfolios. It is conceivable that ties developed with MNCs via their local subsidiaries could help small firms deal effectively with these tensions. An important theoretical consideration is that these *geography-spanning* relationships could provide an efficient means for small firms to channel their attention into *both* local and international markets through MNC links. Given the ever-growing pressure to identify and absorb external innovation across the world (Doz *et al.* 2001), many technology-intensive MNCs are making exactly such an offer to innovative small firms through partnership programmes. Provided the small firm uses the MNC's technology, the offered links could potentially facilitate NPD in the local market and subsequently NBD efforts in international markets. In short, MNCs can be a source of social capital that spans geographies (local vs. international milieus) and functions (exploratory innovation via NPD and exploitative learning via NBD). Attractive though the proposition may be to some small firms, the challenge of building visibility, efficiency and intimacy would be, if anything, even greater when engaging with giants such as IBM or Microsoft. MNCs are complex organizations where the development and leverage of social capital calls for boundary-spanning activities across various sub-units (Inkpen and Tsang 2005; Kostova and Roth 2003).

It is worth pointing out, in passing, that MNCs are likely to pursue not only conventional innovation such as technological breakthroughs or improvement (Doz *et al.* 2001). They are also poised to increasingly seek out non-conventional innovation that allows them to benefit from opportunities at the 'bottom of the pyramid' comprising millions of people of the lowest means (Prahalad 2004). The argument is that the bottom of the pyramid represents a largely untapped market for those innovative MNCs that can adopt a novel mindset and formulate relevant offerings at appropriate price points (see Prahalad 2004 for examples such as rural microfinance and shared telephony services in the Indian subcontinent). In doing so, MNCs will almost certainly have to engage with local actors, including small knowledge-intensive firms which possess valuable, local knowledge. It is conceivable that these smaller firms, especially those based in developing countries, could achieve unprecedented innovative outcomes in concert with MNCs at the bottom of the pyramid. Given the widespread dispersion of bottom of the pyramid markets across the world, the opportunity is inherently international.

* * *

And so in conclusion, it is suggested that a wonderful opportunity exists for small-firm internationalization researchers to extend the field through explicitly integrating innovation into their work and by considering the role of MNC social capital. Of course, it is not implied that either achieving innovation outcomes or building social capital with MNCs is that easy. These endeavours are certainly not for the faint-hearted; yet for those innovative small firms that do engage in these activities, potentially great rewards will accrue. Even as innovative and internationally minded small firms have unprecedented opportunities before them, small-firm internationalization researchers should be pleased that the research agenda in this area promises to remain as exciting as ever.

Notes

Preface

1 My subsequent work has used survey data in hypothesis-testing mode.

3 Knowledge and internationalization

1 The contributions, along similar lines, of other scholars such as Bilkey and Tesar (1978) and Luostarinen (1980) are acknowledged; however, on the basis of its widespread citation, Johanson and Vahlne's (1977) thesis has clearly been the most dominant perspective in the literature and informs this chapter's discussion as the standard treatment of traditional internationalization theory.
2 The contribution, along similar lines, of Knight and Cavusgil (1996) is acknowledged; however, based on citation count, the Oviatt and McDougall thesis is taken as the standard treatment of more recent perspectives of internationalization that have challenged traditional approaches, as typified by Johanson and Vahlne (1977).
3 Market knowledge encompasses three dimensions, identified by Eriksson *et al.* (1997) as business knowledge, institutional knowledge and internationalization knowledge:
- Business knowledge pertains to knowledge about the micro external environment of foreign market(s), that is, knowledge about such aspects as market's customers, competitors and distributors.
- Institutional knowledge pertains to knowledge about such aspects as business laws, cultural norms, regulatory standards and language skills; in other words, those facets of a market that typically lead to psychic distance (Johanson and Vahlne, 2003).
- Internationalization knowledge refers to knowledge that leads to an ability to develop and implement an internationalization strategy; one anonymous reviewer refers to this as international business 'how-to'.

4 The author thanks an anonymous reviewer for this helpful suggestion.
5 This chapter is *not* concerned with proposing a social capital theory of internationalization. Rather, the focus is on knowledge, in which context social capital can be fruitfully integrated as discussed in this section.
6 For knowledge construct measures, see Autio *et al.* (2000) and Eriksson *et al.* (1997); for social capital construct measures see Yli-Renko *et al.*(2001, 2002).
7 New construct measures pertaining to the application of Internet technology may have to be developed, but see Brock and Berry (2004) for an example of how this could be done.

6 Local networks and internationalization

1 This study adopts Prashantham and Berry's (2004a: 152) definition of a small knowledge-intensive firm: a firm:

that has fewer than 100 employees, the majority of whom comprise a highly qualified workforce which is its most important resource and is engaged in knowledge work – meaning that knowledge is inherent in the firm's main activities – as its central preoccupation.

2 While it is recognized that internationalization may be both inward and outward (market seeking), the latter remains a vital component of the firm's growth and continues to attract widespread policy interest. Moreover, the work that this chapter builds upon (e.g. Brown and Bell 2001) explicitly focuses on market-seeking internationalization, and as such, that is where this chapter's interests lies.

3 Harvard's meta-study of clusters worldwide (Van der Linde, 2002, 2003) identified no fewer than 106 clusters in India; however, only one appears to be a truly knowledge-intensive one, namely, the software cluster in Bangalore. Another software cluster identified in the study is based in Dublin, Eire. It thus appears that although other regions in India, such as the National Capital Region surrounding and including Delhi, have a comparable number of software firms, they are not densely concentrated or perceived to be a cluster. Of course, other authors such as Ramamurthi (2004) take the view that India's software industry comprises a 'cluster of clusters' but even he acknowledges the leading role played by Bangalore as evident from the fact that eight of the top 20 MNC subsidiaries, in terms of software exports, are located in Bangalore, more than in any other Indian city.

4 The study adopts Prashantham and Berry's (2004a: 153) definition of network relationships, which are 'relationships with customers, suppliers, competitors, alliance partners, universities, government bodies, industry associations and so on'. Thus, a distinction is made between the concept of a cluster and of network relationships; the latter form a constituent of a cluster and cannot be deemed to be a given; indeed, they must be created and cultivated (Dyer and Singh, 1998; Gulati, 1999). Local network relationships can be a valuable resource to firms (Westlund and Bolton, 2003).

5 Paradoxically, the emergence of information technology and digitization has been argued as reinforcing, rather than dampening, agglomerative tendencies of firms including those in the information technology sector, owing to their propensity for innovation-seeking behaviour, as noted earlier. Leamer and Storper (2001) point out that the Internet facilitates 'conversations' but not 'handshakes', and therefore the clustering of knowledge-intensive firms can be expected to continue.

6 This proved to be quite appropriate and useful in the case of the sample given that firms with at least six years of existence were likely to be quite different from younger ones, given the impetus – particularly around 1998/1999 – for new venture creation to leverage software-related business opportunities arising from requirements in developed countries relating to Y2K and Euro conversion.

7 The experts were a professor from the Indian Institute of Management, two professors from the Indian Institute of Information Technology, a consultant each from McKinsey and Boston Consulting Group, two executives each from Sun Microsystems and MindTree and a manager from VisualWeb.

8 Bangalore is home to 19 of the world's 40 companies with the highest international quality ratings based on the system developed by Carnegie Mellon University's Software Engineering Institute (i.e. Capability Maturity Model or SEI CMM level 5 companies).

9 The author thanks an anonymous reviewer for the thoughtful suggestion of including this facet of SKIFs in Bangalore in the present discussion.

7 Foreign networks and internationalization

1 Integrating the literatures on small firms and knowledge-intensive firms, Prashantham and Berry (2004a: 152) define a SKIF as a firm:

> *that has fewer than 100 employees, the majority of whom comprise a highly qualified workforce which is its most important resource and is engaged in knowledge work – meaning that knowledge is inherent in the firm's main activities – as its central preoccupation.*

This chapter adopts their definitions.

8 The Internet and internationalization

1 While there is no universally accepted definition of a 'small firm', a review of the literature suggests that the most common operationalization of firm size is in terms of number of employees, and firms with fewer than 100 employees are generally seen to be 'small firms'. This is the understanding adopted in the fieldwork reported in this chapter.

2 A typical sentiment of the dot-com era is: 'History will pity the managers of the 1990s. The Internet touched down in their midst like a tornado, tearing up the old game book, disrupting every aspect of business, and compelling them to manage for a new economy' (Brown and Duguid 2000: 74).

10 Future research directions

1 See also Hitt *et al.* (2006) for a discussion of MNC social capital in the context of internationalizing professional service firms.

References

Aaby, N.-E. and Slater, S.F. (1989) 'Management influences on export performance: a review of the empirical literature 1978–88', *International Marketing Review*, 6(4): 7–26.

Acs, Z.J. and Terjesen, S. (2005) 'Born global: two views on global startups', Paper presented at the JIBS Frontier Conference, September.

Acs, Z.J., Morck, R. and Yeung, B. (1999) 'Evolution, community, and the global economy', in Z.J. Acs (ed.) *Are Small Firms Important?: Their Role and Impact*, Norwell, MA: Kluwer.

Acs, Z.J., Morck, R.K. and Yeung, B. (2001) 'Entrepreneurship, globalization and public policy', *Journal of International Management*, 7: 235–251.

Adler, P.S. and Kwon, S.-W. (2002) 'Social capital: prospects for a new concept', *Academy of Management Journal*, 27: 17–40.

Afuah, A. (2003) 'Redefining firm boundaries in the face of the Internet: are firms really shrinking', *Academy of Management Review*, 28: 34–53.

Agarwal, N.M. (1999) 'Managing knowledge workers: benchmarking Indian it organisations', *Management Review*, June: 81–92.

Almeida, P. (1999) 'Semiconductor startups and the exploration of new technological territory', in Z.J. Acs (ed.) *Are Small Firms Important?: Their Role and Impact*, Norwell, MA: Kluwer.

Alvarez, E.R. (2004) 'Sources of export success in small- and medium-sized enterprises: the impact of public programs', *International Business Review*, 13: 383–400.

Alvarez, S.A. and Barney, J.B. (2001) 'How entrepreneurial firms can benefit from alliances with large partners', *Academy of Management Executive*, 15: 139–148.

Alvesson, M. (1993) 'Organizations as rhetoric: knowledge-intensive firms and the struggle with ambiguity', *Journal of Management Studies*, 30: 997–1015.

Alvesson, M. (1995) *Management of Knowledge-Intensive Firms*, Berlin: De Grutyer.

Andersen, O. (1993) 'On the internationalisation process of firms: a critical analysis', *Journal of International Business Studies*, 24: 209–231.

Anderson, E. and Gatignon, H. (1986) 'Modes of foreign entry', *Journal of International Business Studies*, 17: 1–26.

Arenius, P.M. (2002) 'Creation of firm-level social capital, its exploitation, and the process of early internationalization', Unpublished doctoral dissertation, Helsinki University of Technology.

Arora, A., Arunachalam, V.S., Asundi, J. and Fernandes, R. (2001) 'The Indian software services industry', *Research Policy*, 30: 1267–1287.

Athreye, S.A. (2001) 'Competition, rivalry and innovative behaviour', *Economic Innovation & New Technology*, 10: 1–21.

Audretsch, D.B. (1999) 'Small firms and efficiency', in Z.J. Acs (ed.) *Are Small Firms Important?: Their Role and Impact*, Norwell, MA: Kluwer.

Audretsch, D.B. and Feldman, M.P. (1996) 'R&D Spillovers and the Geography of Innovation and Production', *American Economic Review*, 86: 630–639.

Autio, E. (2005) 'Creative tension: the significance of Ben Oviatt's and Patricia McDougall's article "Toward a Theory of International New Ventures"', *Journal of International Business Studies*, 36: 9–19.

Autio, E., Sapienza, H.J. and Almeida, J.G. (2000) 'Effects of age at entry, knowledge intensity, and imitability on international growth', *Academy of Management Journal*, 43: 909–924.

Baker, M.J. (1979) 'Export Myopia', *The Quarterly Review of Marketing*, Spring: 1–10.

Balasubramanyam, V.N. and Balasubramanyam, A. (2000) 'The software cluster in Bangalore', in J.H. Dunning (ed.) *Regions, Globalization and the Knowledge-based Economy*, London: Routledge.

Barclay, I. and Porter, K. (2005) 'Facilitating innovation across SME networks', *International Journal of Entrepreneurship and Innovation Management*, 5: 20–38.

Barney, J.B. (1991) 'Firm resources and sustained competitive advantage', *Journal of Management*, 17: 155–171.

BarNir, A. and Smith, K.A. (2002) 'Interfirm alliances in the small business: the role of social networks', *Journal of Small Business Management*, 40: 219–232.

Barringer, B.R. and Harrison, J.S. (2000) 'Walking a tightrope: creating value through interorganizational relationships', *Journal of Management*, 26: 367–403.

Bartlett, C.A. and Ghoshal, S. (2000) 'Going global: lessons from late movers', *Harvard Business Review*, 78(2): 132–142.

Baum, J.A.C., Calabrese, T. and Silverman, B.S. (2000) 'Don't go it alone: alliance network composition and startups' performance in Canadian biotechnology', *Strategic Management Journal*, 21: 267–294.

Beals, C., Ehrig, S. and Pelz, M. (1995) 'Iowa's proactive strategy for commercial development', *Economic Development Review*, 13(2): 26–28.

Becherer, R.C. and Maurer, J.G. (1997) 'The moderating effect of environmental variables on the entrepreneurial and marketing orientation of entrepreneur-led firms', *Entrepreneurship Theory and Practice*, 22: 47–58.

Bell, J. (1995) 'The internationalization of small computer software firms', *European Journal of Marketing*, 29: 60–75.

Bell, J. (1997) 'A comparative study of export problems of small computer software exporters in Finland, Ireland and Norway', *International Business Review*, 6: 1–20.

Bell, J. and Young, S. (1998) 'Towards an integrative framework of the internationalization of the firm', in G. Hooley, R. Loveridge and D. Wilson (eds) *Internationalization: Process, Context and Markets*, London: Macmillan.

Bell, J., Crick, D. and Young, S. (2004a) 'Small firm internationalization and business strategy: an exploratory study of "knowledge-intensive" and "traditional" manufacturing firms in the UK', *International Small Business Journal*, 22: 21–52.

Bell, J., Demick, D., Callaghan, I. and O'Reilly, A. (2004b) 'Irish perspectives on developing international entrepreneurs', in L.P. Dana (ed.) *Handbook of Research on International Entrepreneurship*, Northampton, MA: Edward Elgar.

Bell, J., McNaughton, R. and Young, S. (2001) ' "Born-again global" firms: an extension to the "born global" phenomenon', *Journal of International Management*, 7: 73–189.

Bell, J., McNaughton, R., Young, S. and Crick, D. (2003) 'Towards an integrative model of small firm internationalisation', *Journal of International Entrepreneurship*, 1: 339–362.

Bennett, R. (1997) 'Export marketing and the Internet: experiences of Web site users and perceptions of export barriers among UK businesses', *International Marketing Review*, 14: 324–344.

Bensaou, M. and M. Earl (1998) 'The right mind-set for managing information technology', *Harvard Business Review*, 76(5): 118–128.

Berry, M.M.J. (1996) 'Technical entrepreneurship, strategic awareness and corporate transformation in small high-tech firms', *Technovation*, 16: 487–498.

Berry, M.M.J. (1998) 'Strategic planning in small high tech firms', *Long Range Planning*, 31: 455–466.

Berry, M.M.J. and Brock, J.K.-U. (2004) 'Marketspace and the internationalisation process of the small firm', *Journal of International Entrepreneurship*, 2: 187–216.

Berry, M.M.J. and Taggart, J.H. (1994) 'Managing technology and innovation: a review', *R&D Management*, 24: 341–353.

Berry, M.M.J. and Taggart, J.H. (1998) 'Combining technology and corporate strategy in small high tech firms', *Research Policy*, 26: 883–895.

Berry, M.M.J., Dimitratos, P. and McDermott, M. (2001) 'Globalisation and the smaller firm: reconcilable notions?' Paper presented at the AIB (UK Chapter) Conference, Cardiff, April.

Berry, M., Dimitratos, P. and McDermott, M. (2002) 'Globalisation and the smaller firm: reconcilable notions?' in F. McDonald, H. Tuselmann and C. Wheeler (eds) *International Business: Adjusting to New Challenges and Opportunities*, New York: Palgrave.

Berthon, P., Pitt, L., Katsikeas, C.S. and Berthon, J.P. (1999) 'Virtual services go international: international services in the marketspace', *Journal of International Marketing*, 7: 84–105.

Bhagwathi, J. (1966) *The Economics of Underdeveloped Countries*, New York: McGraw Hill.

Bhide, A. (1994) 'How entrepreneurs craft strategies that work', *Harvard Business Review*, 72(2): 150–161.

Bilkey, W.J. and Tesar, G. (1977) 'The export behaviour of smaller sized Wisconsin manufacturing firms', *Journal of International Business Studies*, 8: 93–98.

Birkinshaw, J. (1997) 'Entrepreneurship in multinational corporations: the characteristics of subsidiary initiatives', *Strategic Management Journal*, 18: 207–229.

Birkinshaw, J. (2000) 'Upgrading of industry clusters and foreign investment', *International Studies of Management and Organization*, 30: 93–113.

Birkinshaw, J. and Hood, N. (2000) 'Characteristics of foreign subsidiaries in industry clusters', *Journal of International Business Studies*, 31: 141–154.

Birkinshaw, J., Hood, N. and Young, S. (2005) 'Subsidiary entrepreneurship, internal and external competitive forces, and subsidiary performance', *International Business Review*, 14: 227–248.

Birley, S. (1985) 'The role of networks in the entrepreneurial process', *Journal of Business Venturing*, 1: 107–117.

Blomstermo, A., Eriksson, K. and Sharma, D.D. (2004) 'Domestic activity and knowledge development in the internationalization process of firms', *Journal of International Entrepreneurship*, 2: 239–258.

Bloodgood, J., Sapienza, H.J. and Almeida, J.G. (1996) 'The internationalization of new high-potential US ventures: antecedents and outcomes', *Entrepreneurship Theory and Practice*, 20: 61–76.

Bourdieu, P. (1986) 'The forms of capital', in J.E. Richardson (ed.) *Handbook of Theory of Research for the Sociology of Education*, New York: Greenwood.

Brock, J.K.-U. (2000) 'Virtual globals – marketspace and the internationalisation of small technology-based firms', Unpublished PhD Thesis, University of Strathclyde, Glasgow

Brock, J.K.-U. (2001) 'Market space and the new mechanism of internationalisation: some preliminary insights', in J.H. Taggart, M. Berry and M. McDermott (eds) *Multinationals in a New Era: International Strategy and Management*, New York: Palgrave.

Brouthers, K.D., Brouthers, L.D. and Werner, S. (1996) 'Dunning's eclectic theory and the smaller firm: the impact of ownership and locational advantages on the choice of entry-modes in the computer software industry', *International Business Review*, 5: 377–394.

Brown, J.S. and Duguid, P (2000) 'Balancing act: how to capture knowledge without killing it', *Harvard Business Review*, 78(3): 73–80.

Brown, P. and Bell, J.D. (2000) 'Industrial clusters and small firm internationalisation', Paper presented at the AIB (UK Chapter) Conference, Glasgow, April.

Brown, P. and Bell, J.D. (2001) 'Industrial clusters and small firm internationalisation', in J.H. Taggart, M. Berry and M. McDermott (eds) *Multinationals in a New Era: International Strategy and Management*, New York: Palgrave.

Brown, P. and McNaughton, R.B. (2000) 'Cluster development programmes: panacea or placebo for promoting SME growth and internationalisation?', paper presented at the McGill Conference on International Entrepreneurship, Montreal, September.

Brown, P. and McNaughton, R.B. (2003) 'Cluster development programmes: panacea or placebo for promoting SME growth and internationalisation?' in H. Etemad and R.W. Wright (eds) *Globalization and Entrepreneurship: Policy and Strategy Perspective*, Northampton, MA: Edward Elgar.

Buckley, P.J. and Ghauri, P.N. (2004) 'Globalisation, economic geography and the strategy of multinational enterprises', *Journal of International Business Studies*, 35: 81–98.

Burt, R.S. (1992) *Structural Holes*, Cambridge, MA: Harvard University Press.

Burt, R.S. (1997) 'The contingent value of social capital', *Administrative Science Quarterly*, 42: 339–365.

Calof, J.L. and Beamish, P.W. (1995) 'Adapting to foreign markets: explaining internationalization', *International Business Review*, 4: 115–131.

Calof, J.L and Viviers, W. (1995) 'Internationalization behavior of small- and medium-sized South African enterprises', *Journal of Small Business Management*, 33(4): 71–79.

Cantwell, J. and Iammarino, S. (2001) 'EU regions and multinational corporations: change, stability and strengthening of technological comparative advantages', *Industrial and Corporate Change*, 10: 1007–1037.

Carlsson, B. (1999) 'Small business, entrepreneurship, and industrial dynamics', in Z.J. Acs (ed.) *Are Small Firms Important?: Their Role and Impact*, Norwell, MA: Kluwer.

Chen, T.-J. (2003) 'Network resources for internationalization: the case of Taiwan's electronics firms', *Journal of Management Studies*, 40: 1107–1130.

Chetty, S. and Blankenburg Holm, D. (2000) 'Internationalisation of small to medium-sized manufacturing firms: a network approach', *International Business Review*, 9: 77–93.

Chetty, S.K. and Hamilton, R.T. (1993) 'Firm-level determinants of export performance: a meta-analysis', *International Marketing Review*, 10: 26–34.

Chew, Y.-T. and Yeung, H.W.-C. (2001) 'The SME advantage: adding local touch to foreign transnational corporations in Singapore', *Regional Studies*, 35: 431–448.

Cohen, W. and Levinthal, D. (1990) 'Absorptive capacity: a new perspective on learning and innovation', *Administrative Science Quarterly*, 35: 128–152.

Coleman, J.S. (1988) 'Social capital in the creation of human capital', *American Journal of Sociology*, 94: S95–S120.

Collinson, S. (2000) 'Knowledge networks for innovation in small Scottish software firms', *Entrepreneurship and Regional Development*, 12: 217–244.

Correa, C.M. (1996) 'Strategies for software exports from developing countries', *World Development*, 24: 171–182.

Coviello, N.E. (2006) 'Network dynamics of international new ventures', *Journal of International Business Studies*, 37: 713–731.

Coviello, N.E. and Jones, M.V. (2004) 'Methodological issues in international entrepreneurship research', *Journal of Business Venturing*, 19: 485–508.

Coviello, N.E. and McAuley, A. (1999) 'Internationalisation and the smaller firm: a review of the contemporary empirical research', *Management International Review*, 39: 223–256

Coviello, N.E. and Munro, H. (1995) 'Growing the entrepreneurial firm: networking for international market development', *European Journal of Marketing*, 29(7): 49–61.

Coviello, N.E. and Munro, H. (1997) 'Network relationships and the internationalization process of small software firms', *International Business Review*, 6: 361–386.

Crick, D. and Jones, M.V. (2000) 'Small high-technology firms and international high-technology markets', *Journal of International Marketing*, 8(2): 63–85.

Cronin, M.J. (1995) *Global Advantage on the Internet: From Corporate Connectivity to International Connectedness*, New York: John Wiley.

Cubillo, J.M. and Cerviño, J. (2004) 'International entrepreneurship in local SME supplier networks', *International Journal of Entrepreneurship and Innovation*, 5: 231–239.

Curran, J., Jarvis, R., Blackburn, R. and Black, S. (1993) 'Networks and small firms: constructs methodological strategies and some findings', *International Journal of Small Business*, 11(2): 13–25.

Cyert, R.M. and March, J.G. (1963) *A Behavioral Theory of the Firm*, Englewood Cliffs, NJ: Prentice-Hall.

Dana, L.P. (2000) 'Creating entrepreneurs in India', *Journal of Small Business Management*, 38(1), 86–91.

Dana, L.P., Etemad, H. and Wright, R.W. (2000) 'The global reach of symbiotic networks', *Journal of Euro-Marketing*, 9(2): 1–16.

Dana, L.P., Etemad, H. and Wright, R.W. (2001) 'Multi-polarity and relationships in the new economy', Paper presented at the McGill Conference on International Entrepreneurship, Glasgow, September.

Dana, L.P., Wright, R.W. and Hamid, E. (2004) 'Back to the future: international entrepreneurship in the new economy', in M.V. Jones and P. Dimitratos (eds) *Emerging Paradigms in International Entrepreneurship*, Northampton, MA: Edward Elgar.

Daniel, C. (2001) 'Confident mood persists as challenge gathers pace', *FT-IT Review (with Financial Times)*, February 21, XV.

Das, M. (1994) 'Successful and unsuccessful exporters from developing countries: some preliminary findings', *European Journal of Marketing*, 28(12): 19–33.

Davenport, T.H., Harris, J.G. and Kohli, A.K. (2001) 'How do they know their customers so well?', *MIT Sloan Management Review*, 42(2): 63–73.

Davidsson, P. and Honig, B. (2003) 'The role of social and human capital among nascent entrepreneurs', *Journal of Business Venturing*, 18: 301–331.

Demick, D.H. and O'Reilly, A.J. (2000) 'Supporting SME internationalisation: a collaborative project for accelerated export development', *Irish Marketing Review*, 13(1): 34–45.

Demsetz, H. (1991) 'The theory of the firm revisited', in O.E. Williamson and S.G. Winter (eds) *The Nature of the Firm*, New York: Oxford University Press.

Dimitratos, P. and Jones, M.V. (2005) 'Future directions for international entrepreneurial research', *International Business Review*, 14: 119–128.

Dimitratos, P., Johnson, J., Slow, J. and Young, S. (2003) 'Micromultinationals: new types of firms for the global competitive landscape', *European Management Journal*, 21: 164–174.

Donald, A. (2001a) '"Village India" has a long way to go', *FT-IT Review (with Financial Times)*, February 21: XV–XVI.

Donald, A. (2001b) 'Infrastructure bottlenecks hinder IT expansion', *FT-IT Review (with Financial Times)*, February 21: XVI.

Doz, Y.L. (1988) 'Technology partnerships between larger and smaller firms: some critical issues', *International Studies of Management and Organization*, 17(4): 31–57.

Doz, Y.L., Santos, J. and Williamson, P. (2001) *From Global to Metanational: How Companies Win in the Knowledge Economy*, Cambridge, MA: HBS Press.

Dunning, J.H. (1988) 'The eclectic paradigm of international production: a restatement and some possible extensions', *Journal of International Business Studies*, 18: 1–30.

Dunning, J.H. (2000) 'Regions, globalization, and the knowledge economy: the issues stated', in J.H. Dunning (ed.) *Regions, Globalization and the Knowledge-based Economy*, London: Routledge.

Dyer, J.H. and Singh, H. (1998) 'The relational view: cooperative strategy and sources of interorganizational competitive advantage', *Academy of Management Review*, 23: 660–679.

Easterby-Smith, M., Thorpe, R and Lowe, A. (2001) *Management Research: An Introduction*, 2nd edn, London: Sage.

Eisenhardt, K.M. (1989) 'Building theories from case study research', *Academy of Management Review*, 14: 532–550.

Eisenhardt, K.M. and Martin, J.A. (2000) 'Dynamic capabilities: what are they?' *Strategic Management Journal*, 21: 1105–1121.

Elkjaer, B. (2000) 'Learning and getting to know: the case of knowledge workers', *Human Resource Development International*, 3: 343–359.

Ellsworth, J.H. and Ellsworth, M.V. (1995) *Marketing on the Internet*, New York: John Wiley.

Enright, M.J. (1998) 'Regional clusters and firm strategy', in A.D. Chandler Jr, Ö. Sölvell and P. Hagström (eds) *The Dynamic Firm: The Role of Technology, Strategy, Organization and Regions*, Oxford: Oxford University Press.

Enright, M.J. (1999) 'The globalization of competition and the localization of competitive advantage: policies towards regional clustering', in N. Hood and S. Young (eds) *The Globalization of Multinational Enterprise Activity and Economic Development*, London: Macmillan.

Enright, M.J. (2000) 'Regional clusters and multinational enterprises: independence, dependence, or interdependence?' *International Studies of Management and Organization*, 30: 114–138.

Eriksson, K. and Chetty, S. (2003) 'The effect of experience and absorptive capacity on foreign market knowledge', *International Business Review*, 12: 673–695.

Eriksson, K., Johanson, J., Majkgård, A. and Sharma, D. (1997) 'Experiential knowledge and cost in the internationalization process', *Journal of International Business Studies*, 28: 337–360.

Erramilli, M.K. and Rao, C.P. (1993) 'Service firms' international entry mode choice: a modified transaction cost analysis approach', *Journal of Marketing*, 57(3): 19–38.

Etemad, H. and Wright, R.W. (2003) 'Internationalization of SMEs: toward a new paradigm', *Small Business Economics*, 20: 1–4.
Etemad, H., Wright, R.W. and Dana, L.P. (2001) 'Symbiotic international business networks: collaboration between small and large firms', *Thunderbird International Business Review*, 43: 481–499.
Evans, P.B. and Wurster, T.S. (1997) 'Strategy and the new economics of information', *Harvard Business Review*, 75: 70–82.
Evans, P.B. and Wurster, T.S. (2000) *Blown to Bits: How the New Economics of Information Transforms Strategy*, Boston: Harvard Business School Press.
Feeny, D. (2001) 'Making business sense of the e-opportunity', *MIT Sloan Management Review*, 42(2): 41–51.
Fernhaber, S.A., Gilbert, B.A. and McDougall, P.P. (2003) 'The impact of geographic location on the internationalization of new ventures', paper presented at the Babson Kauffman Entrepreneurship Research Conference, Boston, June.
Fiol, C.K. and Lyles, M.A. (1985) 'Organizational learning', *Academy of Management Review*, 10: 803–813.
Fisher, M. and D.J. Reibstein (2001) 'Technology-driven demand: implications for the supply chain', in J. Wind and V. Mahajan (eds) *Digital Marketing: Global Strategies from the World's Leading Experts*, New York: John Wiley.
Florin, J., Lubatkin, M. and Schulze, W. (2003) 'A social capital model of high-growth ventures', *Academy of Management Journal*, 46: 374–384.
Fontes, M. and Coombs, R. (1995) 'New technology-based firms and technology acquisition in Portugal: firms' adaptive responses to a less favourable environment', *Technovation*, 15: 497–510.
Fontes, M. and Coombs, R. (1997) 'The coincidence of technology and market objectives in the internationalisation of new technology-based firms', *International Small Business Journal*, 15(4): 14–35.
Furman, J., Porter, M.E. and Stern, S. (2002) 'The determinants of national innovative capacity', *Research Policy*, 31: 899–933.
Glazer, R. (1991) 'Marketing in an information-intensive environment: strategic implications of knowledge as an asset', *Journal of Marketing*, 55(4): 1–19.
Gnyawali, D.R. and Madhavan, R. (2001) 'Cooperative networks and competitive dynamics: a structural embeddedness perspective', *Academy of Management Review*, 26: 431–445.
Goetz, S.J. and Freshwater, D. (2001) 'State-level determinants of entrepreneurship and a preliminary measure of entrepreneurial climate', *Economic Development Quarterly*, 15(1): 58–70.
Golden, P.A. and Dollinger, M. (1993) 'Cooperative alliances and competitive strategies in small manufacturing firms', *Entrepreneurship Theory and Practice*, 17(4): 43–56.
Granovetter, M. (1973) 'The strength of weak ties', *American Journal of Sociology*, 78: 1360–1380.
Grant, R.M. (1996) 'Prospering in dynamically-competitive environments: organizational capability as knowledge integration', *Organization Science*, 7: 375–387.
Grant, R.M. (2002) 'The knowledge-based view of the firm', in C.W. Choo and N. Bontis (eds) *The Strategic Management of Intellectual Capital and Organizational Knowledge*, Oxford: Oxford University Press.
Gulati, M. (1997) 'Industrial clusters and SSI development', *IIMB Management Review*, October–December: 97–103.

Gulati, R. (1995) 'Does familiarity breed trust? The implications of repeated ties for contractual choices', *Academy of Management Journal*, 35: 85–112.

Gulati, R. (1999) 'Network location and learning: the influence of network resources and firm capabilities on alliance formation', *Strategic Management Journal*, 20: 397–420.

Gulati, R., Nohria, N. and Zaheer, A. (2000) 'Strategic networks', *Strategic Management Journal*, 21: 203–215.

Hacki, R. and Lighton, J. (2001) 'The future of the networked company', *The McKinsey Quarterly Review*, 3: 26–39.

Hadjimanolis, A. (2000a) 'A resource-based view of innovativeness in small firms', *Technology Analysis & Strategic Management*, 12(2), 262–281.

Hadjimanolis, A. (2000b) 'An investigation of innovation antecedents in small firms in the context of a small developing country', *R&D Management*, 30(3), 235–245.

Hagel, J. (1996) 'Spider versus spider', *The McKinsey Quarterly*, 1: 4–19.

Hagel, J. and Singer, M. (1999) 'Unbundling the corporation', *Harvard Business Review*, 77(2): 133–141.

Hamel, G. (1996) 'Strategy as revolution', *Harvard Business Review*, 74(4): 69–82.

Hamill, J. (1997) 'The Internet and international marketing', *International Marketing Review*, 14(5): 300–323.

Hamill, J. and Ennis, S. (1999) 'The Internet: the direct route to growth and development', in M.J. Baker (ed.) *The Marketing Book*, 4th edn, Oxford: Butterworth-Heinemann.

Hamill, J. and Gregory, K. (1997) 'Internet marketing in the internationalisation of UK SMEs', *Journal of Marketing Management*, 13: 9–21.

Hamill, J. and Prashantham, S. (2001) 'Internet supported customer relationship management: a key opportunity for the twenty-first century', *International Marketing Review*, 18: 102–104.

Heitzman, J. (1997) 'High technology entrepreneurship and development in Bangalore', *IIMB Management Review*, October–December: 85–96.

Hite, J.M. and Hesterly, W.S. (2001) 'The evolution of firm networks: from emergence to early growth of the firm', *Strategic Management Journal*, 22: 275–286.

Hitt, M.A., Bierman, L., Uhlenbruck, K. and Shimizu, K. (2006) 'The importance of resources in the internationalization of professional service firms: the good, the bad, and the ugly', *Academy of Management Journal*, 49: 1137–1157.

Hitt, M.A., Hoskisson, R.E. amd Kim, H. (1997) 'International diversification: effects on innovation and firm performance in product diversified firms', *Academy of Management Journal*, 40: 767-798.

Hitt, M.A., Ireland, R.D., Camp, S.M. and Sexton, D.L. (2001) 'Strategic entrepreneurship: entrepreneurial strategies for wealth creation', *Strategic Management Journal*, 22: 479–491.

Hitt, M.A., Lee, H.-U. and Yucel, E. (2002) 'The importance of social capital to the management of multinational enterprises: relational networks among Asian and Western firms', *Asia Pacific Journal of Management*, 19: 353–372.

Hoen, A. (2001) *Clusters: Determinants and Effects*, Amsterdam: CPB Netherlands Bureau for Economic Policy Analysis.

Hoffman, D.L. and Novak, T.P. (1996) 'Marketing in hypermedia computer-mediated environments: conceptual foundations', *Journal of Marketing*, 60(3): 50–68.

Hoffman, D.L. and Novak, T.P. (2000) 'How to acquire customers on the Web', *Harvard Business Review*, 78: 179–188.

Holm, D.B., Eriksson, K. and Johanson, J. (1996) 'Business networks and cooperation in international business relationships', *Journal of International Business Studies*, 27: 1033–1053.

Hult, G.T.M and Ketchen, D.J. (2001) 'Does market orientation matter?: a test of the relationship between positional advantage and performance', *Strategic Management Journal*, 22: 899–906.

Human, S.E. and Provan, K.G. (1997) 'An emergent theory of structure and outcomes in small-firm strategic manufacturing networks', *Academy of Management Journal*, 40: 368–403.

Iansiti, M. and MacCormack, A. (1997) 'Developing products on Internet time', *Harvard Business Review*, 75(5): 108–117.

Ibeh, K.I.N. (1999) 'Initial export stimulation: any difference between developed and developing country factors?' working paper, University of Strathclyde.

Ibeh, K.I.N. (2003) 'Toward a contingency framework of export entrepreneurship: conceptualisations and empirical evidence', *Small Business Economics*, 15: 49–68.

Ibeh, K.I.N. and Young, S. (2001) 'Exporting as an entrepreneurial act: an empirical study of Nigerian firms', *European Journal of Marketing*, 35: 566–586.

Inkpen, A.C. and Tsang, E.W.K. (2005) 'Social capital, networks, and knowledge transfer', *Academy of Management Review*, 30: 146–165.

Inkpen, A.C. (2000) Learning through joint ventures: a framework of knowledge acquisition. *Journal of Management Studies*, 37: 1019–1044.

Jain, S.K. and Kapoor, M.C. (1996) 'Export attitudes and behaviour in India: a pilot study', *Journal of Global Marketing*, 10(2): 75–95.

Johanson, J. and Mattsson, L.-G. (1988) 'Internationalization in industrial systems – a network approach', in N. Hood and J.-E. Vahlne (eds) *Strategies in Global Competition*, London: Croon Helm.

Johanson, J. and Vahlne, J.-E. (1977) 'The internationalization process of the firm – a model of knowledge development and increasing foreign market commitment', *Journal of International Business Studies*, 8: 23–32.

Johanson, J. and Vahlne, J.-E. (1990) 'The mechanism of internationalization', *International Marketing Review*, 7(4): 11–24.

Johanson, J. and Vahlne, J.-E. (1992) 'Management of foreign market entry', *Scandinavian International Business Review*, 1(3): 9–27.

Johanson, J. and Vahlne, J.-E. (2003) 'Business relationship learning and commitment in the internationalization process', *Journal of International Entrepreneurship*, 1: 83–102.

Johanson, J. and Vahlne, J.-E. (2006) 'Commitment and opportunity development in the internationalization process: a note on the Uppsala internationalization process model', *Management International Review*, 46: 165–178.

Johanson, J. and Wiedersheim-Paul, F. (1975) 'The internationalization of the firm – four Swedish cases', *Journal of Management Studies*, 12: 305–322.

Johnsen, R.E. and Johnsen, T.E. (1999) 'International market development through networks: the case of the Ayrshire knitwear sector', *International Journal of Entrepreneurial Behaviour and Research*, 5: 297–312.

Jones, M.V. (1999) 'The internationalization of small high-technology firms', *Journal of International Marketing*, 7(4): 15–41.

Jones, M.V. (2001) 'First steps in internationalisation: concepts and evidence from a sample of small high-technology firms', *Journal of International Management*, 7: 191–210.

Jones, M.V. (2003) 'Doctoral thesis: creation of firm-level social capital, its exploitation, and the process of early internationalization (P.M. Arenius. Helsinki University of Technology)', *Journal of International Entrepreneurship*, 1: 415–417.

Jones, M.V. and Coviello, N.E. (2005) 'Internationalisation: conceptualising an entrepreneurial process of behaviour in time', *Journal of International Business Studies*, 36: 282–303.

Kaplan, S. and Sawney, M. (2000) 'E-hubs: the new B2B marketplaces', *Harvard Business Review*, 78(3): 97–103.

Karagozoglu, N. and Lindell, M. (1998) 'Internationalization of small and medium-sized technology-based firms: an exploratory study', *Journal of Small Business Management*, 36(1): 44–59.

Katzy, B.R. and Schuh, G. (1998) 'The virtual enterprise', in A. Molina, J.M. Sanchez and A. Kusiak (eds) *Handbook of Life Cycle Engineering: Concepts, Methods and Tools*, Norwell, MA: Kluwer.

Kenny, D. and Marshall, J.F. (2000) 'Contextual marketing: the real business of the Internet', *Harvard Business Review*, 78(6): 119–125.

Kerrigen, R., Roegner, E.V., Swinford, D.D. and Zawada, C.C. (2001) 'B2Basics', *The McKinsey Quarterly*, 1: 45–53.

Khanna, T. and Palepu, K. (1999) 'The right way to restructure conglomerates in emerging markets', *Harvard Business Review*, 77(4): 125–134.

Kim, D. (2003) 'The internationalization of US Internet portals: does it fit the process model of internationalization?' *Marketing Intelligence & Planning*, 21(1): 23–36.

Klein, L.R. and Quelch, J.A. (1997) 'Business-to-business market making on the Internet', *International Marketing Review*, 14(5): 345–361.

Knight, G.A. (2001) 'Entrepreneurship and strategy in the international SME', *Journal of International Management*, 7: 155–171.

Knight, G.A. and Cavusgil, S.T. (1996) 'The born global firm: a challenge to traditional internationalisation theory', *Advances in International Marketing*, 8: 11–26.

Knight, G.A. and Cavusgil, S.T. (2004) 'Innovation, organizational capabilities, and the born-global firm', *Journal of International Business Studies*, 35: 124–141.

Kobrin, S.J. (1999) 'Development after industrialization: poor countries in an electronically integrated global economy', in N. Hood and S. Young (eds) *The Globalization of Multinational Enterprise Activity and Economic Development*, London: Macmillan.

Kobrin, S.J. (2001) 'Territoriality and the governance of cyberspace', *Journal of International Business Studies*, 32: 687–704.

Kogut, B., (2000) 'The network as knowledge: generative rules and the emergence of structure', *Strategic Management Journal*, 21: 405–425.

Kogut, B. and Zander, U. (1993) 'Knowledge of the firm and the evolutionary theory of the multinational corporation', *Journal of International Business Studies*, 24: 625–645.

Kohli, A.K. and Jaworski, B.J. (1990) 'Market orientation: the construct, research propositions, and managerial implications', *Journal of Marketing*, 54: 1–18.

Kohli, A.K., Jaworski, B.J. and Kumar, A. (1993) 'MARKOR: a measure of market orientation', *Journal of Marketing Research*, 30: 467–477.

Koka, B.R. and Prescott, J.E. (2002) 'Strategic alliances and social capital: a multidimensional view', *Strategic Management Journal*, 23: 795–816.

Kornohen, H., Luostarinen, R. and Welch, L. (1996) 'Internationalization of SMEs: inward-outward patterns and government policy', *Management International Review*, 36: 315–329.

Kostova, T. and Roth, K. (2003) 'Social capital in multinational corporations and a micro-macro model of its formation', *Academy of Management Review*, 28: 297–317.

Kotha, S., Rindova, V.P. and Rothaermel, F.T. (2001) 'Assets and actions: firm-specific factors in the internationalization of US Internet firms', *Journal of International Business Studies*, 32: 769–791.

Krackhardt, D. (1992) 'The strength of strong ties: the importance of philos in organizations', in N. Nohria and R.G. Eccles (eds) *Networks and Organizations: Structure, Form and Action*, Boston: Harvard Business School Press.

Krishnan, R.T. (1997) 'Is strategy important for small companies', *IIMB Management Review*, October–December: 105–111.

Kundu, S.K. and Katz, J.A. (2000) 'The internationalization of small firms: an empirical study of the Indian software industry', paper presented at the McGill Conference on International Entrepreneurship, Montreal, September.

Kundu, S.K. and Katz, J. (2003) 'Born-international SMEs: BI-level impacts of resources and intentions', *Small Business Economics*, 20: 25–47.

Lane, P.J. and Lubatkin, M. (1998) 'Relative absorptive capacity and interorganizational learning', *Strategic Management Journal*, 19: 461–477.

Lavie, D. and Rosenkopf, L. (2006) 'Balancing exploration and exploitation in alliance formation', *Academy of Management Journal*, 49: 797–818.

Leamer, E.E. and Storper, M. (2001) 'The economic geography of the Internet age', *Journal of International Business Studies*, 32: 641–665.

Leclerc, E. (2004) 'Circulation of Indian IT professionals to Hyderabad and beyond: integrating India in a global work force', working paper, New Delhi: Centre de Sciences Humaines.

Lee, C., Lee, K. and Pennings, J.M. (2001) 'Internal capabilities, external networks, and performance: a study on technology-based ventures', *Strategic Management Journal*, 22: 615–640.

Leonidou, L. and Katsikeas, C.S. (1996) 'The export development process: an integrative review of empirical models', *Journal of International Business Studies*, 27: 517–551.

Lerner, J. (1999) 'Small business, innovation, and public policy', in Z.J. Acs (ed.) *Are Small Firms Important?: Their Role and Impact*, Norwell, MA: Kluwer.

Liao, J.L., Welsch, H. and Stoica, M. (2003) 'Organizational absorptive capacity and responsiveness: an empirical investigation of growth-oriented SMEs', *Entrepreneurship Theory and Practice*, 28: 63–85.

Liebeskind, J.P. (1996) 'Knowledge, strategy, and the theory of the firm', *Strategic Management Journal*, 17(Winter Special Issue): 93–107.

Liesch, P.W. and Knight, G.A. (1999) 'Information internalization and hurdle rates in small and medium enterprise internationalization', *Journal of International Business Studies*, 30: 383–394.

Lin, C.Y.-Y. and Zhang, J. (2005) 'Changing structures of SME networks: lessons from the publishing industry in Taiwan', *Long Range Planning*, 38: 145–162.

Lindell, M. and Karagozoglu, N. (1997) 'Global strategies of US and Scandinavian R&-D-intensive small- and medium-sized companies', *European Management Journal*, 15: 92–100.

Lituchy, T.R. and Rail, A. (2000) 'Bed and breakfasts, small inns, and the Internet: the impact of technology on the globalization of small businesses', *Journal of International Marketing*, 8(2): 86–97.

Lorenzoni, G. and Lipparini, A. (1999) 'The leveraging of interfirm relationships as a distinctive capability: a longitudinal study', *Strategic Management Journal*, 20: 317–338.

Lorenzoni, G. and Ornati, O.A. (1998) 'Constellations of firms and new ventures', *Journal of Business Venturing*, 3: 41–57.

Lu, J.W. and Beamish, P.W. (2001) 'The internationalization and performance of SMEs', *Strategic Management Journal*, 22: 565–586.

Lubatkin, M.F., Simsek, Z., Ling, Y. and Veiga, J.F. (2006) 'Ambidexterity and performance in small-to medium-sized firms: the pivotal role of top management team behavioral integration', *Journal of Management*, 32: 646–672.

Luce, E. (2001) 'India lures the expat dollar', *Financial Times*, February 28: 17.

Lumpkin, G.T. and Dess, G.G. (1996) 'Clarifying the entrepreneurial orientation construct and linking it to performance', *The Academy of Management Review*, 21: 135–172.

Luostarinen, R. (1980) *Internationalization of the Firm*, Helsinki: Helsinki School of Economics.

Maddy, M. (2000) 'Dream deferred: the story of a high-tech entrepreneur in a low-tech world', *Harvard Business Review*, 78(3): 56–69.

Madhok, A. (1996) 'Know-how-, experience-, and competition-related considerations in foreign market entry: an exploratory investigation', *International Business Review*, 5: 339–360.

Madsen, T.K. and Servais, P. (1997) 'The internationalization of born globals: an evolutionary process?' *International Business Review*, 6: 561–583.

Mahibala, M. (1997) 'SSIs: simplifying rules and procedures', *IIMB Management Review*, October–December: 69–70.

Malmberg, A., Solvell, O. and Zander, I. (1996) 'Spatial clustering, local accumulation of knowledge and firm competitiveness', *Geografiska Annaler*, 78B(2): 85–97.

Malone, T.W. and Laubacher, R.J. (1998) 'The dawn of the e-lance economy', *Harvard Business Review*, 76(5): 144–152.

Manimala, M.J. (1992a) 'Entrepreneurial heuristics: a comparison between high PI (pioneering-innovative) and low PI ventures', *Journal of Business Venturing*, 7: 477–504.

Manimala, M.J. (1992b) 'Innovative entrepreneurship: testing the theory of environmental determinism', in B.L. Maheshwari (ed.) *Innovations in Management for Development*, New Delhi: Tata McGraw Hill.

Manimala, M.J. (1992c) 'Entrepreneurial innovation: beyond Schumpeter', *Creativity and Innovation Management*, 1(1): 46–55.

Manimala, M.J. (1992d) 'New venture strategies: the innovators' choice', *The Journal of Social and Economic Studies*, 3–21.

Manolova, T.S. and Manev, I.M. (2004) 'Internationalization and the performance of the small firm: a review of the empirical literature between 1996 and 2001', in M.V. Jones and P. Dimitratos (eds) *Emerging Paradigms in International Entrepreneurship*, Northampton, MA: Edward Elgar.

March, J.G. (1991) 'Exploration and exploitation in organizational learning', *Organization Science*, 2: 71–87.

March, J.G. (2006) 'Rationality, foolishness and adaptive intelligence', *Strategic Management Journal*, 27: 201–214.

Martin, R. and Sunley, P. (2003) 'Deconstructing clusters: chaotic concept or policy panacea?' *Journal of Economic Geography*, 3: 5–35.

McDougall, P.P. and Oviatt, B.M. (2000) 'International entrepreneurship: the intersection of two research paths', *Academy of Management Journal*, 43: 902–906.

McDougall, P.P. and Oviatt, B.M. (2003) 'Some fundamental issues in international entrepreneurship', *United States Association for Small Business and Entrepreneurship White Paper* (Available online at: www.usasbe.org/knowledge/whitepapers/mcdougal l2003.pdf)

McDougall, P.P., Shane, S. and Oviatt, B.M. (1994) 'Explaining the formation of international new ventures: the limits of theories from international business research', *Journal of Business Venturing*, 9: 469–487.

McEvily, B. and Zaheer, A. (1999) 'Bridging ties: a source of firm heterogeneity in competitive capabilities', *Strategic Management Journal*, 20: 1133–1156.

McGrath, R.G. and MacMillan, I. (2000) *The Entrepreneurial Mindset*, Boston: Harvard Business School Press.

McNamee, P., Greenan, K. and McFerran, B. (2000) 'Shifting the predominant cultural paradigm in small businesses through active competitive benchmarking', *Journal of Strategic Marketing*, 8: 241–255.

McNaughton, R.B. (1996) 'Foreign market channel integration decisions of Canadian computer software firms', *International Business Review*, 5: 23–52.

McNaughton, R.B. (2001) 'The export mode decision-making process in small knowledge-intensive firms', *Marketing Intelligence and Planning*, 19(1): 12–20.

McNaughton, R.B. and Bell, J.D. (1999) 'Brokering networks of small firms to generate social capital for growth and internationalization', in A.M. Rugman and R.W. Wright, (eds) *Research in Global Strategic Management. International Entrepreneurship: Globalization of Emerging Businesses*, Stamford, CT: JAI Press.

McNaughton, R.B. and Bell, J.D. (2001) 'Channel switching between domestic and foreign markets', *Journal of International Marketing*, 9: 32–47.

Melin, L. (1992) 'Internationalization as a strategy process', *Strategic Management Journal*, 13: 99–118.

Merchant, K. (2001) 'Supply fails to meet demand', *FT-IT Review (with Financial Times)*, February 21: XVI.

Merchant, K. (2001a) 'Sector hopes it can turn problems into solutions/India's software exporters serve an increasingly global market', *FT-IT Review (with Financial Times)*, February 21: XIII–XIV.

Merchant, K. (2001b) 'Defining the Indian software brand in a competitive world', *FT-IT Review (with Financial Times)*, February 21: XIV.

Merchant, K. (2001c) 'Supply fails to meet demand', *FT-IT Review (with Financial Times)*, February 21: XVI.

Merchant, K. (2001d) 'India learns language of customer service', *Financial Times*, April 4: 14.

Meyer, K. and Skak, A. (2002) 'Networks, serendipity and SME entry into Eastern Europe', *European Management Journal*, 20: 179–188.

Mintzberg, H. and Lampel, J. (1999) 'Reflecting on the strategy process', *Sloan Management Review*, 40(3): 21–30.

Mitsuhashi, H. (2003) 'Effects of the social origins of alliances on alliance performance', *Organization Studies*, 24: 321–339.

Moore, K. and Birkinshaw, J. (1998) 'Managing knowledge in global service firms: centres of excellence', *Academy of Management Executive*, 12(4): 81–92.

Morgan-Thomas, A. and Bridgewater, S. (2004) 'Winner and losers in the internet game: a study of British exporters', in F. Donald, M. Mayer and T. Buck (eds) *The Process of Internationalization: Strategic, Cultural, and Policy Perspectives*, Houndmills: Palgrave.

Murdoch, A. (2000) 'India: a software giant awakens', *Scotland on Sunday*, December 5: 5.

Murthy, K.R.S. (1999) 'The challenge of globalisation for Indian family business', *IIMB Management Review*, March: 95–102.

Nadvi, K. (1995) *Industrial Clusters and Networks: Case Studies of SME Growth And Innovation*, Vienna: UNIDO Small and Medium Enterprises Programme.

Nahapiet, J. and Ghoshal, S. (1998) 'Social capital, intellectual capital, and the organizational advantage', *Academy of Management Review*, 23: 242–266.

Naidu, G.M., Cavusgil, S.T., Murthy, B.K. and Sarkar, M. (1997) 'An export promotion model for India: implications for public policy', *International Business Review*, 6: 113–125.

Narula, R. (2004) 'R&D collaboration by SMEs: new opportunities and limitations in the face of globalisation', *Technovation*, 24: 153–161.

Nebus, J. (2006) 'Building collegial information networks: a theory of advice network generation', *Academy of Management Journal*, 31: 615–637.

Nelson, R. and Winter, S. (1982) *An Evolutionary Theory of Economic Change*, Cambridge, MA: Belknap Press.

Nohria, N., Joyce, W. and Robertson, B. (2003) 'What really works', *Harvard Business Review*, 81(7), 42–52.

Nurmi, R. (1998) 'Knowledge-intensive firms', *Business Horizons*, May–June, 26–32.

O'Brien, D.J., Philips, J.L. and Patsiorvokovsky, V.V. (2005) 'Linking indigenous bridging and bonding social capital', *Regional Studies*, 39: 1041–1051.

O'Dwyer, M. and O'Flynn, E. (2005) 'MNC-SME strategic alliances – a model framing knowledge value as the primary predictor of governance modal choice', *Journal of International Management*, 11: 397–416.

O'Farrell, P.N., Wood, P.A. and Zheng, J. (1998) 'Regional influences on foreign market development by business service companies: elements of a strategic context explanation', *Regional Studies*, 32: 31–48.

Ocasio, W. (1997) 'Towards an attention-based view of the firm', *Strategic Management Journal*, 18: 187–206.

Ostgaard, T.A. and Birley, S. (1994) 'Personal networks and firm competitive strategy – a strategic or coincidental match?' *Journal of Business Venturing*, 9: 281–305.

Oviatt, B.M. and McDougall, P.P. (1994) 'Toward a theory of new international ventures', *Journal of International Business Studies*, 25: 45–64.

Oviatt, B.M. and McDougall, P.P. (1997) 'Challenges for internationalization process theory', *Management International Review*, 37: 85–99.

Oviatt, B.M. and McDougall, P.P. (2005a) 'Defining international entrepreneurship and modeling the speed of internationalization', *Entrepreneurship Theory and Practice*, 29: 537–554.

Oviatt, B.M. and McDougall, P.P. (2005b) 'The internationalization of entrepreneurship', *Journal of International Business Studies*, 36: 2–8.

Oxley, J.E. and Yeung, B. (2001) 'E-commerce readiness: institutional environment and international competitiveness', *Journal of International Business Studies*, 32: 705–723.

Parasuraman, A. and Zinkhan, G.M. (2002) 'Marketing to and serving customers through the Internet: an overview and research agenda', *Journal of the Academy of Marketing Science*, 30: 286–295.

Peng, M.W. (2001) 'The resource-based view and international business', *Journal of Management*, 27: 803–829.

Peng, M.W. (2004) 'Identifying the big question in international business research', *Journal of International Business Studies*, 35: 99–108.

Penrose, E. (1959) *The Theory of the Growth of the Firm*, New York: Wiley.

Peppers, D., Rogers, M. and Dorf, B. (1999) 'Is your company ready for one-to-one marketing', *Harvard Business Review*, 77(1): 151–160.

Peppers, R. and Rogers, M. (1997) *Enterprise One to One: Tools for Competing in the Interactive Age*, London: Piatkus.

Peters, E. and Hood, N. (2000) 'Implementing the cluster approach: some lessons from the Scottish experience', *International Studies of Management & Organization*, 30(2): 68–92.

Poon, S. and Jevons, C. (1997) 'Internet-enabled international marketing: a small business network perspective', *Journal of Marketing Management*, 13(1): 29–41.

Poon, S. and Joseph, M. (2000) 'Product characteristics and Internet commerce benefit among small business', *Journal of Product and Brand Management*, 9: 21–34.

Porter, M.E. (1990) 'The competitive advantage of nations', *Harvard Business Review*, 68(2): 73–93.

Porter, M.E. (1998a) *On Competition*, Boston: Harvard Business School Press.

Porter, M.E. (1998b) 'Clusters and the new economics of competition', *Harvard Business Review*, 76(6): 77–90.

Porter, M.E. (2001) 'Strategy and the Internet', *Harvard Business Review*, 79(3): 62–78.

Pouder, R. and St John, C.H. (1996) 'Hot spots and blind spots: geographical clusters of firms and innovation', *Academy of Management Review*, 21(4): 1192–1225.

Prabhu, G.N. (1997) 'SSIs and technology management', *IIMB Management Review*, October–December: 75–78.

Prahalad, C.K. (2004) *The Fortune at the Bottom of the Pyramid: Eradicating Poverty Through Profits*, Philadelphia, PA: Wharton School Publishing.

Prahalad, C.K. and Hamel, G. (1990) 'The core competence of the corporation', *Harvard Business Review*, 68(3): 79–91.

Prasad, V.K., Ramamurthy, K. and Naidu, G.M. (2001) 'The influence of Internet-marketing integration on marketing competencies and export performance', *Journal of International Marketing*, 9(4): 82–110.

Prashantham, S. (2004a) 'Indian perspectives of international entrepreneurship', in L.P. Dana (ed.) *Handbook of Research on International Entrepreneurship*, Northampton, MA: Edward Elgar.

Prashantham, S. (2004b) 'Local network relationships and the internationalization of small knowledge-intensive firms', *Copenhagen Journal of Asian Studies*, 19: 5–26.

Prashantham, S. (2005) 'Toward a knowledge-based conceptualization of internationalization', *Journal of International Entrepreneurship*, 3: 37–52.

Prashantham, S. (2006) 'Foreign network relationships and the internationalisation of small knowledge-intensive firms', *International Journal of Entrepreneurship and Innovation Management*, 6: 542–553.

Prashantham, S. and Berry, M.M.J. (2004a) 'The small knowledge-intensive firm: a conceptual discussion of its characteristics and internationalisation', *International Journal of Entrepreneurship and Innovation Management*, 4: 150–158.

Prashantham, S. and Berry, M.M.J. (2004b) 'The Internet and the internationalization of small knowledge-intensive firms: a conceptual approach', in M.V. Jones and P. Dimitratos (eds) *Emerging Paradigms in International Entrepreneurship*, Northampton, MA: Edward Elgar.

Prashantham, S. and Young, S. (2004) 'The Internet and the internationalization of small knowledge-intensive firms: promises, problems and prospects', *International Journal of Entrepreneurship and Small Business*, 1: 153–175.

Putnam, R. (2000) *Bowling Alone: The Collapse and Revival of American Community*, New York: Simon and Schuster.

Putnam, R.D. and Goss, K. (2002) 'Introduction', in R.D. Putnam (ed.) *Democracies in*

Flux: The Evolution of Social Capital in Contemporary Society, Oxford: Oxford University Press.

Quelch, J.A. and Klein, L.R. (1996) 'The Internet and international marketing', *Sloan Management Review*, 37(3): 60–75.

Ram, V.A. and Jagadish, S. (1999) 'Project managers in the software industry – a competency profile', *IIMB Management Review*, June: 67–74.

Ramamurti, R. (2004) 'Internationally competitive clusters in developing countries: India's IT Industry', Paper presented at the Academy of International Business Conference, Stockholm, July.

Ramsdell, G. (2000) 'The real business of B2B', *The McKinsey Quarterly*, 3: 174–184.

Ramu, S.S. (1997) 'Small industries policy', *IIMB Management Review*, October–December: 51–56.

Rangan, S. (2000) 'The problem of search and deliberation in economic action: when social networks really matter', *Academy of Management Review*, 25: 813–828.

Rao, P.M. and Klein, J.A. (1994) 'Growing importance of marketing strategies for the software industry', *Industrial Marketing Management*, 23: 29–37.

Rasmussen, E.S. and Madsen, T.K. (1999) 'The founding of the born global company in Denmark and Australia', Paper presented at the Cross Cultural Consumer and Business Studies Research Conference, Cancun, December.

Rayport, J.F. and Sviokla, J.J. (1995) 'Exploiting the virtual value chain', *Harvard Business Review*, 73(6): 75–85.

Redding, G. (1995) 'Overseas Chinese networks: understanding the enigma', *Long Range Planning*, 28: 61–69.

Rennie, M.W. (1993) 'Global competitiveness: born global', *The McKinsey Quarterly*, 4: 45–54.

Reuber, A.R. and Fischer, E. (1997) 'The influence of the management team's international experience on the internationalization behaviors of SMEs', *Journal of International Business Studies*, 28: 807–825.

Robertson, M. and Hammersley, G.O. (2000) 'Knowledge management practices within a knowledge-intensive firm: the significance of the people management dimension', *Journal of European Industrial Training*, 24: 241–253.

Roehl, T.W., Standifird, S. and Globerman, S. (2001) 'Globalization and electronic commerce: inferences from retail brokering', *Journal of International Business Studies*, 32: 749–768.

Romijn, H. and Albu, M. (2002) 'Innovation, networking and proximity: lessons from small high technology firms in the UK', *Regional Studies*, 36: 81–86.

Sadagopan, S. (1999) 'Information technology: redefining boundaries', *IIMB Management Review*, June: 49–66.

Samiee, S. (1998) 'Exporting and the Internet: a conceptual perspective', *International Marketing Review*, 15: 413–426.

Sampler, J.L. (1998) 'Redefining industry structure for the information age', *Strategic Management Journal*, 19(4), 343–355.

Sapienza, H.J., Autio, E., George, G. and Zahra, S.A. (2006) 'A capabilities perspective on the effects of new venture internationalization on survival and growth', *Academy of Management Review*, 31: 914–933.

Sapienza, H.J., Autio, E. and Zahra, S. (2003) 'Effects of internationalization on young firms' prospects for survival and growth', *Academy of Management Best Paper Proceedings*.

Sawhney, M. and Zabin, J. (2002) 'Managing and measuring relational equity in the network economy', *Journal of Academy of Marketing Science*, 30(4), 313–332.

Sawhney, M. Prandelli, E. and Verona, G. (2003) 'The power of infomediation', *MIT Sloan Management Review*, 44(2): 77–82.

Saxenien, A. (1990) 'Regional networks and the resurgence of Silicon Valley', *California Management Review*, Fall: 89–112

Saxenian, A.L. (2000) 'The Bangalore boom: from brain drain to brain circulation?' in *Bridging the Digital Divide: Lessons from India*, (eds) K. Keniston and D. Kumar, Bangalore: National Institute of Advanced Study.

Saxenian, A.L. (2002) 'Transnational communities and the evolution of global production networks: the cases of Taiwan, China and India', *Industry and Innovation*, 9(3), 183–202.

Saxenian, A.L., Motoyama, Y. and Quan, X. (2002) Local and global networks of immigrant professionals in Silicon Valley, San Francisco, CA: Public Policy Institute of California.

Schlegelmilch, B.B. and Sinkovics R. (1998) 'Marketing in the information age – can we plan for an unpredictable future?' *International Marketing Review*, 15(3), 162–170.

Scottish Executive (2003) Press release on the Scottish Technology and Collaboration initiative [Available on the Scottish Executive Web site].

Sculley, A.B. and Woods, W.W.A. (1999) *B2B Exchanges: The Killer Application in the Business-to-Business Internet Revolution*, Bermuda: ISI.

Seybold, P.B. (2001) 'Get inside the lives of your customers', *Harvard Business Review*, 79(5): 81–89.

Shane, S. (2003) *A General Theory of Entrepreneurship: The Individual-Opportunity Nexus*, Northampton, MA: Edward Elgar.

Sharma, D.D. and Blomstermo, A. (2003) 'The internationalization process of born globals: a network view', *International Business Review*, 12: 739–753.

Shaver, J.M. and Flyer, F. (2000) 'Agglomeration economies, firm heterogeneity, and foreign direct investment in the United States', *Strategic Management Journal*, 21: 1175–1193.

Shrader, R.C., Oviatt, B.M. and McDougall, P.P. (2000) 'How new ventures exploit trade-offs among international risk factors: lessons for the accelerated internationalization of the 21st century', *Academy of Management Journal*, 43: 1227–1247.

Siegel, D. (1999) *Futurize Your Enterprise: Business Strategy in the Age of the E-Customer*, New York: John Wiley.

Simmonds, K. and Smith, H. (1968) 'The first export order: a marketing innovation', *British Journal of Marketing*, 2: 93–100.

Simsek, Z., Lubatkin, M.H. and Floyd, S.W. (2003) 'How networks influence entrepreneurial behavior: a structural embeddedness perspective', *Journal of Management*, 29: 427–442.

Singh, N. and Kundu, S. (2002) 'Explaining the growth of e-commerce corporations (ECCs): an extension and application of the eclectic paradigm', *Journal of International Business Studies*, 33: 679–697.

Smith, W.K. and Tushman, M.L. (2005) 'Managing strategic contradictions: a top management model for managing innovation streams', *Organization Science*, 16: 522–536.

Souitaris, V. and Cohen, M. (2003) 'Internet-business or just business? impact of "-Internet-specific" strategies on venture performance', *European Management Journal*, 21: 421–437.

Spence, M. (2004) 'Efficiency and personalization as value creation in internationalizing high-technology SMEs', *Canadian Journal of Administrative Sciences*, 21(1): 65-78.

Spender, J.-C. (1994) 'Organizational knowledge, collective practice and Penrose rents', *International Business Review*, 3: 353–367.

Spradley, J. (1979) *The Ethnographic Interview*, New York: Holt, Rinehart and Winston.

Staber, U. (1998) 'Inter-firm co-operation and competition in industrial districts', *Organization Studies*, 19: 701–724.

Sundarajan, S. (1997) 'Promoting entrepreneurship: future policy directions', *IIMB Management Review*, October–December: 49–50.

Tallman, S. and Fladmoe-Lindquist, K. (2002) 'Internationalization, globalization, and capability-based strategy', *California Management Review*, 45: 116–135.

Tan, J.J. and Litschert, R.J. (1994) 'Environment strategy relationship and its performance implications: an empirical study of the Chinese electronics industry', *Strategic Management Journal*, 15: 1–20.

Tapscott, D. (ed.) (1999) *Creating Value in the Network Economy*, Boston: Harvard Business School Press.

Tapscott, D., Ticoll, D. and Lowy, A. (2000) *Digital Capital: Harnessing the Power of Business Webs*, London: Nicholas Brearley.

Teece, D.J., Pisano, G. and Shuen, A. (1997) 'Dynamic capabilities and strategic management', *Strategic Management Journal*, 18: 509–533.

Tenkasi, R.V. and Boland, R.J. (1996) 'Exploring knowledge diversity in knowledge intensive firms: a new role for information systems', *Journal of Organizational Change*, 9: 79–91.

Thampy, A. and Kulkarni, P.S. (1997) 'Financing SSIs: two perspectives', *IIMB Management Review*, October–December: 57–64.

The Boston Consulting Group (2001) *E-Commerce Opportunities for India Inc.*, New Delhi, India: National Association of Software and Service Companies.

Tiessen, J.H., Wright, R.W. and Turner, I. (2001) 'A model of e-commerce use by internationalizing SMEs', *Journal of International Management*, 7: 211–233.

Todtling, F. (1994) 'The uneven landscape of innovation poles: local embeddedness and global networks', in A. Amin and N. Thrift (eds) *Globalization, Institutions, and Regional Development in Europe*, Oxford: Oxford University Press.

Tsai, W. and Ghoshal, G. (1998) 'Social capital and value creation: the role of intrafirm networks', *Academy of Management Journal*, 41: 464–476.

Turnbull, P.W. (1987) 'A challenge to the stages theory of the internationalization process', in S. Reid and P. Rosson (eds) *Managing Export Entry and Expansion*, New York: Praeger.

Tzokas, N., Carter, S. and Kyriazopoulos, P. (2001) 'Marketing and entrepreneurial orientation in small firms', *Enterprise and Innovation Management Studies*, 2(1): 19–33.

UNDP (2004) *Unleashing Entrepreneurship: Making Business Work for the Poor*, New York: UNO.

Upton, D.M. and McAfee, A. (1996) 'The real virtual factory', *Harvard Business Review*, 74(4): 123–133.

Uzzi, B. (1997) 'Social structure and competition in interfirm networks: the paradox of embeddedness', *Administrative Science Quarterly*, 42: 36–67.

Vachani, S. (1997) 'Economic liberalization's effect on sources of competitive advantage of different groups of companies: the case of India', *International Business Review*, 6: 165–184.

Van der Linde, C. (2002) *The Cluster Meta-Study: List of Clusters and Bibliography*, Boston: Harvard Business School.

Van der Linde, C. (2003) 'The cluster bibliography', in J. Bröcker, D. Dohse and R.

Soltwedel (eds) *Innovation Clusters and Interregional Competition*, Berlin: Heidelberg.

Venkataraman, S. and Sarasvathy, S.D. (2001), 'Strategy and entrepreneurship: outlines of an untold story', in M.A. Hitt, E. Freeman and J.S. Harrison (eds) *Handbook of Strategic Management*, Oxford: Blackwell.

von Krogh, G. (2003) 'Open-source software development', *MIT Sloan Management Review*, 44(3): 14–18.

Walczuch, R.M., van Braven, G. and Lundgren, H. (2000) 'Internet adoption barriers for small firms in the Netherlands', *European Management Journal*, 18: 561–572.

Ward, J.C. and Ostrom, A.L. (2001) 'The Internet as information minefield: an analysis of the source and content of brand information yielded by net searches', *Journal of Business Research*, 56: 907–914.

Welch, D.E. and Welch, L.S. (1996) 'The internationalization process and networks: a strategic management perspective', *Journal of International Marketing*, 4(3): 11–28.

Welch, D.E., Welch, L.S., Young, L.C. and Wilkinson, I.F. (1998) 'The importance of networks in export promotion: policy issues', *Journal of International Marketing*, 6(4): 66–82.

Welch, L.S. and Luostarinen, R. (1988) 'Internationalization: evolution of a concept', *Journal of General Management*, 14(2): 36–64.

Westlund, H. and Bolton, R. (2003) 'Local social capital and entrepreneurship', *Small Business Economics*, 21: 77–113.

Wiedersheim-Paul, F., Olson, H.C. and Welch, L. (1978) 'Pre-export activity: the first step in internationalization', *Journal of International Business Studies*, 9: 93–98.

Wiklund, J. and Shepherd, D.A. (2001) 'Intentions and growth: the moderating role of resources and opportunities', *Academy of Management Proceedings*, ENT: F1–6.

Wiklund, J. and Shepherd, S. (2003) 'Knowledge-based resources, entrepreneurial orientation, and the performance of small and medium-sized businesses', *Strategic Management Journal*, 24: 1307–1314.

Wind, J. and Mahajan, V. (2001) 'The challenge of digital marketing', in J. Wind and V. Mahajan (eds) *Digital Marketing: Global Strategies from the World's Leading Experts*, New York: John Wiley.

Wright, R.W. and Dana, L.P. (2003) 'Changing paradigms of international entrepreneurship Strategy', *Journal of International Entrepreneurship*, 1: 137–154.

Wright, R.W. and Etemad, H. (2001) 'SMEs and the global economy', *Journal of International Management*, 7: 151–154.

Wright, R.W. and Ricks, D.A. (1994) 'Trends in international business research: twenty-five years later', *Journal of International Business Studies*, 25: 687–701.

Yin, R.K. (1994) *Case Study Research: Design and Methods*, London: Sage.

Yip, G.S. (2000) 'Global strategy in the Internet era', *Business Strategy Review*, 11(4): 1–14.

Yli-Renko, H., Autio, E. and Sapienza, H.J. (2001) 'Social capital, knowledge acquisition, and knowledge exploitation in young technology-based firms', *Strategic Management Journal*, 22: 587–613.

Yli-Renko, H., Autio, E. and Tontti, V. (2002) 'Social capital, knowledge and the international growth of technology-based new firms', *International Business Review*, 11: 279–304.

Young, S. (1987) 'Business strategy and the internationalization of business: recent approaches', *Managerial and Decision Economics*, 8: 31–40.

Young, S., Hamill., J., Wheeler, C. and Davies, J.R. (1989) *International Market Entry and Development*, Hemel Hempstead: Harvester Wheatsheaf.

Young, S., Hood, N. and Peters, E. (1994) 'Multinational enterprise and regional development', *Regional Studies*, 28: 657–677.
Zafarulla, M., Ali, M. and Young, S. (1998) 'The internationalisation of the small firm in developing countries – exploratory research from Pakistan', *Journal of Global Marketing*, 11: 21–40.
Zaheer, S. (1995) 'Overcoming the liability of foreignness', *Academic Management Journal*, 38: 341–363.
Zaheer, S. and Manrakhan, S. (2001) 'Concentration and dispersion in global industries: remote electronic access and the location of economic activities', *Journal of International Business Studies*, 32: 667–686.
Zahra, S.A. (1996) 'Technology strategy and new venture performance: a study of corporate-sponsored and independent biotechnology ventures', *Journal of Business Venturing*, 11: 289–321.
Zahra, S.A. (2005) 'A theory of international new ventures: a decade of research', *Journal of International Business Studies*, 36: 20–28.
Zahra, S.A. and Dess, G. (2001) 'Defining entrepreneurship as a scholarly field', *Academy of Management Review*, 26: 8–10.
Zahra, S.A. and George, G. (2002a) 'International entrepreneurship: the current status of the field and future research agenda', in M.A. Hitt, D. Ireland, D. Sexton and M. Camp (eds) *Strategic Entrepreneurship: Creating an Integrated Mindset*, Oxford: Blackwell.
Zahra, S.A. and George, G. (2002b) 'Absorptive capacity: a review, reconceptualization, and extension', *Academy of Management Review*, 27: 185–203.
Zahra, S.A. and Neubaum, D.O. (1998) 'Environmental adversity and the entrepreneurial activities of new ventures', *Journal of Developmental Entrepreneurship*, 3: 123–140.
Zahra, S.A., Ireland, R.D. and Hitt, M.A. (2000) 'International expansion by new venture firms: international diversity, mode of market entry, technological learning, and performance', *Academy of Management Journal*, 43: 925–950.
Zeng, M. and Williamson, P.J. (2003) 'The hidden dragons', *Harvard Business Review*, 81(10): 92–99.
Zhou, Y. and Xin, T. (2003) 'An innovative region in China: interaction between multinational corporations and local firms in a high-tech cluster in Beijing', *Economic Geography*, 79: 129–152.

Index